*Edward Stafford,*
*Third Duke of Buckingham, 1478-1521*

*Barbara J. Harris*

# EDWARD STAFFORD

## *Third Duke of Buckingham, 1478-1521*

STANFORD UNIVERSITY PRESS   1986

Stanford, California

Stanford University Press
Stanford, California

© 1986 by the Board of Trustees of the
Leland Stanford Junior University

Printed in the United States of America

CIP data appear at the end of the book

Published with the assistance of
the Andrew W. Mellon Foundation
and Pace University

To my son, Clifford S. Harris

# *Acknowledgments*

It is a great pleasure to have the opportunity to express my gratitude to all the people who have contributed to the completion and publication of this book. First and foremost, thanks go to Dr. Joseph E. Houle, Dean of the Dyson School of Arts and Sciences, Pace University, whose support and generosity made publication of this work possible. I am also grateful to the Scholarly Research Committee, Pace University, which has granted me financial support and reduced teaching loads over many years. I also wish to thank Dr. Joseph M. Pastore, now Provost of Pace University, for a 1983 summer research grant from the office of the executive vice president, which allowed me to complete the penultimate version of this book.

Gerald L. Harriss, Clive Holmes, JoAnn McNamara, David Starkey, Joel T. Rosenthal, A. J. Slavin, and Eugenie D. Trott all generously contributed their time and energy to this book by reading the complete manuscript and suggesting both substantive and editorial changes. There is no way to express adequately my gratitude for the help they gave me. I hope they think the result justifies their efforts.

Thanks also go to the members of the family history study group of the Institute for Research in History, who read very early versions of chapters 2 and 3 and contributed to the first crucial process of revising them.

I wish to thank the Master and Fellows of Magdalene College, Cambridge, who generously gave me permission to reproduce the portrait of Edward Stafford that hangs in the college hall, and Dr. Richard Luckett, Keeper of the Pictures, who supplied the photograph suitable for reproduction. I am also grateful to the

Society of Antiquaries of London, which has allowed me to reproduce a diagram of Thornbury that appeared in W. D. Simpson, "'Bastard Feudalism' and Later Castles," *Antiquaries Journal*, 26 (1946), 166.

Thanks are due *The Journal of Social History*, for permission to include material that originally appeared in my article "Marriage Sixteenth-Century Style: Elizabeth Stafford and the Third Duke of Norfolk," 15, no. 3 (Spring 1982), 373–82 (in Chapter 3 of this book); the Past and Present Society, for the right to use material I initially published in "Landlords and Tenants in the Later Middle Ages: The Buckingham Estates," *Past and Present*, no. 43 (May 1969), 146–50 (in Chapter 5); and the *American Journal of Legal History*, for permission to include my article "The Trial of the Third Duke of Buckingham—A Revisionist View," 20, no. 1 (Jan. 1976), 15–26 (in Chapter 8).

Finally, I want to express my appreciation to Norris Pope, of Stanford University Press, for the support he has given this project and for his efforts to make publication possible.

B.J.H.

# Contents

## Appendixes

## Reference Matter

*Edward Stafford,*
*Third Duke of Buckingham, 1478-1521*

# Introduction

Edward Stafford was the only duke in England when Henry VII ascended the throne in 1485. He was also undoubtedly the largest private landowner in the country, with estates stretching through 24 English counties and the marches of Wales. The extravagance and ostentation of both his private and his public lives fascinated his admiring and envious contemporaries: he employed scores of servants and retainers in the great household at Thornbury, entertained hundreds of guests during the twelve days of Christmas, and appeared in incredibly rich clothing at the pageants and ceremonies that marked life at the Tudor court. Then, in 1521, with little warning, Buckingham was arrested and executed for high treason. To shocked observers his sudden and unexpected downfall rapidly took on the proportions of dramatic tragedy, illustrating the dreadful capriciousness of fate and the awful malice of Cardinal Wolsey. Decades later it furnished the material for the opening scenes of Shakespeare's play *Henry the Eighth*.

To twentieth-century historians, Buckingham is less significant as a tragic figure than as a magnate whose life reveals the precarious position of the upper nobility during the reigns of both Henry VII and Henry VIII. Although the duke's dramatic execution has inevitably attracted the attention of scholars, his political experience as a whole seems not to have influenced recent interpretations of the early Tudor state. In fact, the evidence from Stafford's life and death raises serious questions about current views of the relationship between crown and nobility that emphasize the common interests and the interdependence of king and peerage. The duke's story suggests to the contrary that

both Henry VII and Henry VIII persistently regarded the nobility with suspicion, and that a fundamental conflict did exist
between the goals of royal policy and the interests of the greater
peers. The purpose of this book, therefore, is to examine Buckingham's political experience in order to revise our understanding
of the early Tudor monarchy.

The unusually large amount of archival material about Buckingham has made this study feasible. At the time of the duke's
arrest and trial, the government seized, and therefore preserved,
many of the duke's personal and estate papers, which are now in
the Public Record Office in London. In addition, the duke's son
and grandson, Lords Henry and Edward Stafford, continued the
family tradition of collecting and saving information about the
Staffords' history and property. They compiled and preserved
cartularies, registers, letter books, and other materials now on
deposit at the Stafford County Record Office as part of the Bagot
collection. The Stafford Record Office also possesses scores of
manorial records and court rolls from the fifteenth and sixteenth
centuries, mostly from properties restored to the Stafford family
after the third duke's attainder. Various collections at the British
Library contain important materials on Buckingham and his
family, as do smaller archives, such as those at Westminster Abbey.[1] Taken together, these manuscripts probably reveal as much
about the third duke of Buckingham and his family as we can
know about any members of the nobility during the early years
of the Tudor dynasty.

Despite the richness of these archives, no one has yet written
a book on the third duke of Buckingham that combines biography and political history. Carole Rawcliffe's monograph, *The
Staffords, Earls of Stafford and Dukes of Buckingham, 1394–1521,*
covers three generations of the Stafford family and concentrates
almost exclusively on the growth and management of their estates.[2] Although the extant material does not include the personal information or first-person sources that would make a full-
scale biography possible, it does allow the historian to draw
convincing portraits of the duke and his family and to recon-
struct his public career.

Furthermore, the Stafford archives are a treasure chest of information on topics of great interest to social historians, such as child rearing, education, the arrangement of marriages, and relations within the family, that have received surprisingly little attention in previous works on the early Tudor period. This brings us to a secondary goal of this study: to paint as complete and detailed a picture as possible of the daily life of the duke, his family, and his household. The book will shed light on some relatively unfamiliar areas of early sixteenth-century life, as well as on the values and world view of the English nobility.

Schematically, this book is organized as a series of concentric circles, moving outward from Edward Stafford and his family through his household, where the public and private worlds intersected, to his vast estates, which constituted the economic basis for his high rank, conspicuous consumption, and local political power. From his property, I turn to his patronage network and the methods he used to try to control an outlying region of England on the borders of Wales. Finally, I follow the duke from his "country" to London and the court, where he encountered and interacted with other peers, with government officials, and, above all, with the king.

Although it is possible to separate these circles for analytical and descriptive purposes, they were not, in fact, separate in real life. The duke's household was the center of his patronage network and his regional power; it was also the place where his family lived and where his leading estate administrators and councillors worked. The patronage network did not—and could not—exist at all apart from the household and vast estates, which provided the offices and rewards on which the clientage system depended. Therefore, throughout this study I have underscored these connections in order to avoid presenting an overly schematic view of Buckingham's life. Wherever possible, I have also tried to explain the significance of my findings by bringing in comparable facts about other noblemen or by relating the material to current debates about the early Tudor period.

The opening chapter of this book discusses the Stafford family in the century and a half before the third duke of Buckingham's birth. It was during this period that the Staffords accumulated the estates and titles that made Duke Edward the highest-ranking and wealthiest lord in early Tudor England. Both his ambitions and the methods he used to pursue them grew out of his desire to maintain the power and prestige of his proud lineage. To understand the life of the third duke of Buckingham, therefore, it is necessary to know something about the history of his family.

## CHAPTER ONE

# The Stafford Heritage

The late medieval English peerage was not a caste of ancient blood made up of a fixed group of noble families, but a class whose membership fluctuated throughout the fourteenth and fifteenth centuries. The most conspicuous mark of nobility was a personal summons from the king to attend parliament, but a summons on one occasion was not necessarily a precedent for the future. Recruits from below regularly replaced families that had died out in the male line as a result of infertility (by far the most common cause), disease, war, or political violence, or that had fallen into political disgrace or economic decline. The ranks of the upper nobility—the dukes and earls—were particularly unstable.[1] Men who gained new titles or rose within the peerage generally owed their good fortune to being related to the king, having performed military or administrative service to the crown, having married a wealthy heiress, or some combination of these factors.[2] Profits from land alone were never sufficient to account for this kind of social and political ascent. On the other hand, once a family had accumulated large landholdings and had achieved a place in the upper ranks of the nobility, the income from its property was crucial in maintaining the military retinues and patronage networks required to serve the crown and to sustain the family's regional power. The greatest threat to this income came not from economic factors—poor estate management or even the unfavorable demographic conditions of the late medieval period—as important as these were, but from the premature death of a peer who left minor heirs and a long-lived widow entitled to large tracts of the land as her dower.

The rise of the Stafford family from a simple barony to a dukedom in the fourteenth and fifteenth centuries provides an excellent illustration of these generalizations. Although the Staffords traced their ancestry back to Robert de Toeni, a Norman baron who followed William the Conqueror to England, they did not reach the first rank of the nobility until the reign of Edward III.[3] Their remarkable fertility for almost two centuries certainly facilitated, if it did not account for, their rise. In the 170 years that separated the creation of the Stafford earldom in 1351 from the extinction of their dukedom in 1521, five holders of the title or their heirs died violently, and three others died prematurely from natural causes.[4] Yet the Staffords never lacked a male heir in the direct line. On the other hand, because of these early deaths, they experienced a number of long minorities and several periods when widows held large portions of the family estates.

Ralph, the first earl of Stafford, owed his title to a long life of civil and military service to Edward III. Stafford apparently first earned the king's affection and gratitude by helping him to overthrow the Mortimers; subsequently, he was made steward of the royal household.[5] He fought in both Scotland and France, and was one of the noblemen who found the Hundred Years' War a profitable adventure. Stafford's greatest military exploit took place in 1342, when he undertook to reinforce the king's troops in Brittany. He was joint commander of the expedition that relieved Brest, burned the French galleys, and overran the country.[6] Four years later, he fought at the great victory of Crécy under Edward III's eldest son, the Black Prince.[7] In 1348 he was a founding member of the Order of the Garter[8] and also became the king's retainer. In return for a fee of 600 marks (one mark was equal to two-thirds of a pound, or 13s 4d), he promised not to join anyone else's retinue and to serve Edward with 60 men-at-arms when required. Five years later, Edward raised the fee to 1,000 marks and the required number of men-at-arms to 100.[9] Stafford's profits from the war were particularly high during this period. The king paid him £6,100 for his service as lieutenant in Gascony between April and December of 1352 alone. The next year, Ralph sold the ransom of Jean Boucicaut to the exchequer for £1,000.[10]

Ralph's most profitable exploit, however, did not take place in the field of battle but in the marriage bed. In 1336 he abducted and married Margaret, daughter and heiress of Hugh de Audley, earl of Gloucester. The king apparently protected him from the consequences of his deed and may even have brought about a reconciliation between him and Audley.[11] Margaret brought him a vast array of estates in England, including Tonbridge, in Kent, and Thornbury, in Gloucester, and his first lordship in Wales, Newport. They were valued at the princely sum of £2,314 per annum.[12] Soon thereafter, he inherited the castle and lordship of Caus, Shropshire, from his grandmother, Alice Corbet.[13] In 1351 came the climax of his career: the king created him earl of Stafford, with an annuity of 1,000 marks.[14]

Ralph's second son and heir, Hugh, succeeded to the earldom in 1372. Like his father, he gained distinction on the battlefields of France and became a member of the Order of the Garter.[15] He had a distinguished political career during the 1370's. The Good Parliament chose him as a member of the enlarged council in 1376, and later he served as councillor to Richard II.[16]

Again like his father, Hugh turned marriage into a profitable venture: his wife, Philippa Beauchamp, daughter of Thomas, earl of Warwick, brought him the huge dowry of £2,000.[17] The couple's five sons barely sufficed to carry on the family line, owing to premature deaths. Indeed, the experience of this generation of Staffords illustrates the wide variety of accidents that made it difficult for a noble lineage to survive in the male line over a long period. Hugh's eldest son, Ralph, was murdered in 1385 by John Holland. Holland, the king's half brother, was avenging the death of his favorite esquire, who had been killed by one of Ralph's archers.[18] Ralph had not yet married or produced an heir. Embittered when Richard II broke his promise not to pardon Holland,[19] Hugh departed on a pilgrimage to the Holy Land. He died at Rhodes on the return trip in 1386.[20]

After Hugh's death, the Stafford earldom passed in rapid succession to his second, third, and fourth sons, all minors in 1387. The wardship of the boys belonged to Richard II. Luckily, Earl Hugh had had the foresight to assign most of his property to feoffees before he left England, so that the better part of his sons' inheritance escaped the burdens and risks of wardship.[21]

In 1389, while Thomas, the third earl, was still a minor, Richard II retained him for life, reduced his marriage fine from 3,000 to 2,000 marks, and granted him custody of his inheritance.[22] Soon thereafter the young nobleman married the king's nine-year-old cousin, Anne, daughter of Thomas of Woodstock and Eleanor de Bohun.[23] When Thomas died in 1392, the earldom passed in rapid succession to his brothers William (d. 1395) and Edmund.[24] Since both boys were still minors, the king assigned custody of their property to Woodstock, the third earl's father-in-law.[25] In 1398 Edmund, the fourth of Hugh's sons, married his brother's widow, Anne.[26] The next year he took possession of his estates.[27]

Unfortunately, Edmund, the fifth earl, did not live to enjoy either his wife or his property for long. Richard II was deposed in 1399, and his cousin, Henry Bolingbroke, eldest son of John of Gaunt, ascended the throne as Henry IV. When the Percies, who controlled the North, joined the Welsh rebellion led by Owain Glyn Dŵr against the new king, Edmund rallied to Henry's side. He died fighting at Shrewsbury in 1403, when he was only 26 years old. An infant son, Humphrey, survived him.[28]

The real importance of this period in the history of the Stafford family is that Edmund's wife, Anne, unexpectedly became sole heir of her mother, Eleanor de Bohun, who had been, in turn, heir to half the vast Bohun estates. Her inheritance included extensive property in the Southeast and the Midlands, and the lordships of Brecon, Hay, and Huntingdon in Wales. In addition, Anne inherited from her father, Thomas of Woodstock, claims to the earldom of Buckingham and the lordships of Oakham, in Rutland, and Holderness, in Yorkshire. The Staffords did not, of course, gain control of these lands for decades. Anne, twice the widow of an earl of Stafford, received one-third of the family property as her dower on each occasion. Until her death in 1438, she therefore held more than half the Stafford inheritance, as well as the lands she had received from her parents. For much of her life she was the wealthiest woman in England.[29]

When Countess Anne died, her vast estates came at last into the Staffords' hands. By that time her son and heir, Humphrey, was already 36 years old and well embarked on his military career. Almost overnight his income soared from £1,300 to £5,000 per annum. This sum made him one of the wealthiest, and therefore potentially one of the most powerful, men in England.[30] His lands enabled him to live magnificently and to bring vast numbers of retainers onto the field of battle. With these assets, he played an increasingly important role in the complicated and treacherous politics of the 1440's and 1450's. His huge inheritance was also an important factor in his elevation to the rank of duke of Buckingham in 1444.[31] With good reason, a manorial record referred to him as being "as myghty [a] prince as any in this reaume."[32]

Buckingham's enormous landed estate was the product of lucrative marriages in three successive generations. Duke Humphrey was much richer than either his father or his grandfather had been—a fact that K. B. McFarlane found to be characteristic of the mid-fifteenth-century peerage.[33] Indeed, the Staffords were a perfect example of his generalization that "any family that continued to produce male heirs could scarcely fail to increase its inheritance by marriage with an heiress—or a series of heiresses."[34] Nonetheless, this comparative wealth did not, as McFarlane apparently concluded, enable Buckingham and his fellow magnates to avoid serious financial problems.[35] Buckingham's situation is a good case in point. Although the net annual value of his estates was £5,000, this figure represented potential rather than real income. In the late 1440's, the duke actually received only £3,700 per annum from the land.[36] His routine annual expenditure at that time was at least £4,000, a figure that rose to £4,400 by the end of the next decade.[37] In this context, the losses he incurred in the service of the crown were catastrophic: his eight years as captain of Calais cost him £11,000, his decade as constable of Dover and warden of the Cinque Ports £1,262.[38] Not surprisingly, he had difficulty meeting the costs of arranging suitable marriages for his daughters Joan and Katherine in the 1450's.[39]

Duke Humphrey's career clearly illustrated the conditions in which service to the crown threatened the financial stability of the peerage. In contrast to the victorious Edward III, who rewarded his followers from the spoils of battle, Henry VI waged a long-drawn-out war that drained his treasury and yielded few if any profits. The king was unable not only to enrich the noblemen who served him, but often even to pay their wages and the expenses of their retinues. Nobles who, like the duke of Buckingham, were not members of the inner circle at court found themselves expending vast sums from their own pockets with little hope of repayment by the crown. In contrast to the situation under Edward III, therefore, peers who fought for Henry VI often experienced serious financial difficulties.

Buckingham's long service in France undermined his financial position in still another way, by turning him into an absentee landlord. Because of his military and political duties, he was rarely personally involved in supervising his estates.[40] This situation had particularly serious consequences in Wales, where profits fell to alarmingly low levels. When William Herbert of Raglan held the same properties in the 1460's, income rose noticeably, an improvement T. B. Pugh attributed to Herbert's closer personal attention to the estates.[41] Absenteeism was also a major problem among the duke's stewards throughout the Welsh marches and on the larger English manors, because the duke used stewardships to recruit influential gentry into his service and to provide his friends and servants with annuities and fees. Like most magnates, he viewed the appointment of estate officials as an opportunity to build up the retinues that maintained his local power and enabled him to serve the crown on a scale befitting his rank. He thus routinely sacrificed profits to political considerations and the requirements of royal service, a pattern evident in the administrative practices of many of the great peers.[42] Still another problem lay in his persistent laxity in exploiting casual sources of revenue, an obvious mark of inefficient management and one very frequently connected with absentee landlords.[43]

These conditions on the Stafford estates raise questions about Carole Rawcliffe's description of the management of Duke Humphrey's property as relatively efficient and as yielding a reasonable profit.[44] Her interpretation accords well with K. B. McFarlane's more comprehensive work on the late medieval nobility. McFarlane characterized the magnates as capable estate managers who created effective, centralized financial and administrative organizations staffed by loyal and competent officials.[45] It is salutary to discard the old stereotype of this class as feckless and incompetent in the management of its property; however, revisionism should not be carried so far in the other direction as once again to distort the truth.[46]

The actual income drawn from Buckingham's estates hardly warrants an overly enthusiastic view of his success in exploiting them. In the late 1440's and 1450's, significant arrears accumulated in all the English receiverships except that of Kent and Surrey, and the evidence from this one is very meager. In Wales, where the lordships of Brecon and Newport were supposed to provide one-third of the duke's income, profits declined drastically while arrears skyrocketed. According to A. C. Reeves, these lordships never recovered from the devastation of Glyn Dŵr's rebellion, which had led to widespread burning of mills and barns between 1402 and 1409. The net profits of the lordship of Newport, for example, were £199 10s in 1447–48, compared with £526 17s in 1401–2. Arrears rose from £35 19s in 1447–48 to £466 2s in 1451–52 and £723 3s in 1456–57. An additional £500 a year was required to compensate for losses in Wales. Overall, Duke Humphrey's income regularly fell £1,300 short of the net figure in the valors of his estates.[47]

Despite this decline, he routinely—and imprudently—based his expenditure on the figures in the valors rather than on the revenues he actually received. Rawcliffe's comment that Buckingham had little control over his huge expenses since he incurred them in the service of the crown is only partly true. The fact is that the duke's regular household and wardrobe expenses exceeded his actual income by £300 or more a year.[48]

Financial pressure stemming from the gap between his income and his expenses often made Buckingham a harsh and exacting landlord, particularly when dealing with his Welsh tenants. The Breconshire antiquarian Hugh Thomas (d. 1714) described him as "a most miserable grinding man that mighty oppressed the contry."[49] Theophilus Jones, a historian of that county, reported that Duke Humphrey forced the freeholders within his lordships to exhibit the deeds to their lands or submit to his judgment of their rights.[50] At a period when men rarely possessed written proof of title and depended instead on the testimony of their neighbors to defend their interests, this procedure was certainly a harsh one. When one of the tenants involved, Evan ap Philip Howel of Llanfrynach, refused to pay homage or custom for his land, or to acknowledge any lord other than the king of England, the duke had him imprisoned in Gloucester, where he remained for three years before his case was heard.[51]

Throughout the marches, the duke used the Great Sessions to extort a substantial fine from the inhabitants, rather than to do justice. The Great Sessions were an institution peculiar to the Welsh marches, dependent on the supreme criminal and civil jurisdiction of the marcher lord. At periodic intervals, the lord suspended the ordinary courts and sent his justices on a progress throughout the lordship to inquire into law enforcement and to decide outstanding cases. The institution was very similar to the English eyre of the twelfth and thirteenth centuries and should have offered the same advantages; it should, in other words, have provided some sort of control over the lord's own officials, expedited the legal process, and encouraged obedience to the law. During Owain Glyn Dŵr's rebellion in the first decade of the fifteenth century, however, the duke's Welsh tenants avoided the dire consequences of rebellion by paying him a collective fine in return for a general pardon. Unfortunately, this expedient, designed to deal with an emergency, developed into the regular practice of "redeeming the sessions," that is, paying the duke not to hold his court and not to enforce the law.

From then on, the Great Sessions became a source of money, rather than an opportunity to render justice. The marcher lord gained thereby a substantial increment to his revenues: it was far easier to levy a fine for group redemption than to collect individual fines and penalties imposed during the sessions. The tenants secured a blanket remission of the lord's claim to judicial penalties and profits and, in addition, were relieved of the burden of attending the sessions. Of the inhabitants, the criminals clearly benefited most from this arrangement; the law-abiding majority in effect paid a tax to save wrongdoers from punishment.[52] The Great Sessions of Newport were redeemed in 1427, 1432, 1445, 1449, and 1456.[53] As an example of the huge sums of money involved, the fine levied in Newport was 1,000 marks.[54]

Buckingham's dealings with his Welsh tenants were obviously a response to his desperate need for cash, not part of an efficient system of estate management. McFarlane was wrong when he cited the "harsh efficiency" of Duke Humphrey and his peers to defend their skills as landlords.[55] Arbitrary behavior increased tenants' resistance to paying their dues and made it more difficult to secure a regular flow of cash from them. In Brecon, for example, Buckingham had to forgo completely the fines for redeeming the sessions in 1453 and 1454.[56]

This interpretation of the evidence about the management of the Stafford estates and the income derived from them throws light on some of the general concerns of historians studying the mid-fifteenth century. Considerable debate has developed about whether the income of the great lay lords was rising or falling, particularly the portion of their income that came from their lands. Conclusions about these issues are then used as evidence in evaluating the competence and ability of the peerage as a class. McFarlane, the most influential recent historian concerned with these questions, estimated their abilities and success as estate managers quite highly. He also specifically denied that they suffered from a general collapse of agricultural profits in the fifteenth century, although he admitted that one rarely found a manor yielding higher profits at the end of any 50-year period than at the beginning.[57] On the other hand, A. R. Bridbury, M. M. Postan, and R. R. Davies all have seen fifteenth-century economic conditions as fundamentally unfavorable to profits from landed estates, which tended to stagnate or decline. To quote Bridbury:

> Some members of the nobility undoubtedly did manage to increase their means sufficiently to compensate themselves for the loss of purchasing power. It may be that the entire nobility managed to ride out its somewhat unusual cost of living problems in this way. The small sample of noble families from whose inadequate records McFarlane got the impression that the nobility was outstandingly successful in this respect may very well prove to have justified his faith in it. But the whole class . . . could not possibly have compensated itself at the expense of labour. . . . That was out of the question because the transformation of relative scarcities, which was the determining factor in so much of later medieval economic life, had raised the exchange value of labour as decisively as the land famine of previous centuries had lowered it. This is the problem that estate management could not possibly have hoped to tackle successfully in the fifteenth century, and the reason why even the most efficient management could have done no more than minimize the losses that were bound to occur.[58]

Magnates did not, of course, depend solely on their lands for income. As the history of the Stafford family itself showed, the nobility accrued its greatest wealth through marriage, the profits of war, and the fruits of office and royal favor.[59] Duke Humphrey's problem was an inability to compensate himself from these sources for his inadequate income from land. English reverses in France reduced the income he received from conquered territory, while his military offices cost him thousands of pounds instead of enriching him. He was never a member of the inner court party and did not grow rich on royal largesse as did the earl of Suffolk, Cardinal Beaufort, and others. In Buckingham's case, at least, Postan's skepticism about the peers' ability to compensate themselves for declining income from land seems completely justified.[60]

Most of the time, of course, the first duke of Buckingham was much more concerned with his military and political career than with his estates and finances. He began fighting across the Channel in 1421, when he was only nineteen years old.[61] He served both Henry V and Henry VI abroad and became constable of France when he was 28 years old.[62] From 1442 to 1450 he was captain of the town and marches of Calais and of the tower of Risbanke, "being retained by Indenture, for that service, by the space of ten years . . . having with him two hundred and sixty Men at Arms, himself accounted."[63] Throughout the 1450's, he served as constable of Dover and warden of the Cinque Ports.[64]

Until the late 1430's, Buckingham remained relatively neutral in the struggle for control of the government that raged between Humphrey, duke of Gloucester, on one side, and the Beauforts and William de la Pole, earl of Suffolk, on the other. At that time, he joined the latter faction, which had gained ascendancy at court and favored ending the disastrous war in France.[65] How much he was influenced by conviction, how much by his marriage connection to the Beaufort family, and how much by a desire to be on the side that appeared to be winning is impossible to say.[66] Whatever his motive, he served with Cardinal Beaufort on unsuccessful commissions to treat for peace in 1439 and 1444.[67]

As the feud between the two factions became increasingly bitter, Buckingham played a leading role in the campaign to destroy Gloucester. In 1441, Suffolk and the Beauforts struck at the duke through his wife Eleanor Cobham, who was accused of witchcraft. Buckingham was on the committee of investigation that convicted the duchess and sentenced her to life imprisonment and the humiliating penance of walking barefoot through London with a taper.[68] Five years later, when the court party felt strong enough to strike at Gloucester directly, Buckingham was one of the lords who arrested him on a charge of treason.[69] As a reward for his part in this ugly episode, he received Gloucester's manor of Penshurst.[70]

By the 1450's, the kind of bitter factionalism seen in the struggle between Gloucester and Suffolk was becoming endemic to English political life.[71] The responsibility for this development lay with Henry VI, who was completely unfit to perform even the most minimal duties of kingship. He habitually allowed a group of favorites to capture control of the council, court, and government. The domination of one party prevented the crown from performing one of its major functions—settling quarrels between the magnates. The ascendant faction controlled access to the king and monopolized royal offices, grants, and favors. Unless peers outside the charmed circle were prepared to surrender all their claims to political power and royal patronage, they had no choice but to try to oust the court party and its supporters. This was the origin of the quarrel between the duke of York and the faction eventually dominated by the queen, Margaret of Anjou.

The struggle for control of the government at the center took place in an environment of increasing disorder and violence. Law enforcement had always been a tenuous matter in medieval England. But the mid-fifteenth century saw an unusual degree of corruption, perversion of established legal procedures, and ability to flout the law, even to commit violent crimes, with impunity. Throughout the kingdom, members of the nobility and the gentry pursued quarrels against each other. The farther a region was from London, the more likely it was to suffer from their violence and small-scale warfare. Thomas Courtenay, earl of Devon, and William Lord Bonville, carried on their hideous feud for years without any effective interference from the crown. The quarrel over the Berkeley inheritance led to an interminable cycle of lawsuits, riots, murders, and petty warfare that involved the Berkeleys, the Talbots, and Richard Beauchamp, earl of Warwick, to mention only the leading participants. Things were not much better in Derbyshire, though it was the gentry and not the nobility that bore responsibility for the trouble there. The dukes of Suffolk and Norfolk, with their henchmen, kept East Anglia in turmoil. In Herefordshire, Sir Walter Devereux and his son-in-law, Sir William Herbert of Raglan, both partisans of the duke of York, contributed to a rising tide of crime and violence. Worst of all was the gradual escalation of the quarrel between the Percies and the Nevilles in the North. Their clashes eventually assumed the proportions of small battles. The coalescence of their rivalry with the struggle of York (whose mother was a Neville) to gain control at the center was a major cause of the outbreak of the Wars of the Roses.[72]

Although the duke of Buckingham is conventionally labeled a Lancastrian and died fighting for Henry VI, he adopted a moderate position throughout the 1450's. He never committed himself completely to the court faction or to Margaret of Anjou's policy of totally defeating York and his supporters, nor did he display personal animosity toward York or the Nevilles. Duke Humphrey's persistent and laudable goal was to restore peace among the lords. By 1458 he and his half-brother, Thomas Bourchier, archbishop of Canterbury, were the only persons trusted by both sides.[73] His ruling principle was apparently personal loyalty to Henry VI.[74]

Buckingham's position was an important factor in the balance of power between Yorkists and Lancastrians because he could bring an enormous number of men into the field. Rawcliffe thinks his decision to support the queen hastened the outbreak of hostilities at one point during the wars by giving her an overwhelming numerical superiority.[75] In 1442 Duke Humphrey spent £565 14s on annuities for 83 knights, esquires, lawyers, yeomen, and domestic servants. He paid £585 9s 1d on 84 annuities in 1447–48. In the interim he granted at least eleven additional fees.[76] However, the actual size of his military force swelled to many times this number because he could also call on his vast array of estate officials and tenants. Furthermore, when the duke summoned his followers, many of his retainers, household servants, tenants, and estate officials brought their own tenants and dependents with them.

Buckingham's payments to his estate officials raised his annual expenditure on wages and fees to more than £900.[77] This represented about a quarter of his *net* annual income.[78] His expenditure may be compared with that of his contemporary, the third earl of Northumberland, who spent one-third to one-half of his *gross* landed income on fees and wages. Percy of course received an annual salary of £2,500 as Warden of the East March, which went a long way toward offsetting his costs.[79] Since Buckingham had no such compensatory income, Rawcliffe has incorrectly minimized the strain imposed by maintenance of his retinue.[80] When Henry VI's madness triggered the crisis of 1454, the rumor spread that Buckingham had 2,000 badges made in preparation for attending parliament.[81] The next year, after the first battle of St. Albans, he rewarded ninety men from Kent and Sussex alone.[82]

When London was threatened by the rebel Jack Cade and his Kentish followers in 1450, Duke Humphrey and Sir Richard Woodville entered "with greet power of people in lyvereis arraied for werr."[83] Cade's insurrection was a protest against the corruption of court officials, the breakdown of law and order, and the defeats abroad. The rebels demanded that certain persons around the king be removed and executed, and that the dukes of York, Exeter, Buckingham, and Norfolk be added to the privy council. In typical medieval fashion, they attributed injustices to the king's evil advisers and had faith in his "natural councillors," the great magnates.[84] On June 16, Buckingham and the archbishop of Canterbury actually met with Cade and promised a redress of grievances.[85] Their promise was not kept, however, for the king balked at "such mean personys" taking on his authority.[86] The rebels responded to this rebuff by invading London and were finally defeated not by the forces of the king but by the angry citizens, who would not tolerate the disorder Cade's forces brought in their train.

Duke Humphrey was back in London in 1456 on a commission of oyer and terminer to suppress antiforeign riots among the apprentices.[87]

But the Comons of the Cyte Did Arme theym secretly in theyr howsis, and were in purpoos to have Rungyn the Comon Belle callid Bowe belle, but they were lette by sadde and welavisyd men, which when it Cam to the knowlage of the duke of Bokyngham and othir lordis there beyng with hym, they Incontynently arose, feryng longer to abyde, for it was shewid to theym that alle the Cyte wolde Aryse upon theym.[88]

Buckingham's final service to Henry VI was fighting with his large forces in the battles of the Wars of the Roses. Duke Humphrey was on the Lancastrian side at the first battle of St. Albans (1455), where he was wounded and, according to *Bale's Chronicle*, taken prisoner by the duke of York and his allies.[89] During the amnesty that followed, he tried in vain to mediate between Queen Margaret and the duke of York.[90] He again fought for Henry VI when the two sides clashed at Northampton in 1460. In Robert Fabyan's words, "bothe hostys there mette and fought there a cruell batayll."[91] The duke of Buckingham was one of the casualties that day, dying less than a year before Henry VI was driven from the English throne and the duke of York's son Edward was crowned king of England.[92]

The duke of Buckingham's property and title descended to his grandson Henry, the heir of his eldest son, who had died of the plague in 1458, and Margaret Beaufort, daughter of Edmund, duke of Somerset (d. 1455).[93] This Margaret Beaufort must not be confused with Henry VII's mother, the countess of Richmond, who was her first cousin. Henry VII's mother was the daughter of John, duke of Somerset, elder brother of the aforementioned Edmund.

When Edward IV ascended the throne in 1461, Henry, the young duke of Buckingham, was only six years old.[94] His prospects at that point were rather grim: the new king might well take advantage of his position and Henry's youth to retaliate for the fact that his grandfather had fought for Henry VI. In any case, a long minority was inevitable. Actually, in line with his inclination to clemency, Edward treated the young Stafford heir with a great deal of restraint. Indeed, he made obvious efforts to bind him to the new regime.[95] In 1464 he purchased Henry's wardship from the first duke's executors, Anne, the widowed duchess of Buckingham, and Archbishop Bourchier.[96] Duchess Anne retained control of both her jointure lands and her late husband's other English properties; only the two Welsh receiverships changed hands.[97] Custody of Henry and his younger brother Humphrey went first to the king's sister Anne, duchess of Exeter, and later to his wife, Elizabeth Woodville, whose household the two boys joined in August 1465.[98] At about this time, the king married Henry to the queen's sister, Katherine Woodville, as a way of tying him to the new dynasty and of providing for his large number of sisters-in-law.[99] This match infuriated both the young duke, who considered the Woodvilles upstarts, and the earl of Warwick, who saw the Woodville sisters marrying all the men who would have been suitable matches for his two daughters.[100] Stafford received no dowry with his bride, but his close relationship to the king may have been responsible for his receiving special livery of his lands three years before he came of age.[101]

Contrary to the usual experience, the minority, which lasted from 1460 to 1473, was a relatively prosperous period for the Stafford estates.[102] Under Duchess Anne's competent supervision, the English properties were administered much more efficiently than they had been with her husband in charge. She was especially successful in controlling costs at the local level. Rawcliffe thinks that the profits from all six English receiverships increased during this period. The duchess's dower lands alone increased in value from £884 6s in about 1460 to £1,245 in 1473.[103] In Wales, the earl of Warwick held the lordship of Brecon, which remained as unprofitable to him as it had been to the first duke. The income barely covered the £433 6s 8d assigned for the living expenses of Duke Henry and his younger brother. On the other hand, William Herbert, first earl of Pembroke, extracted large profits from the lordship of Newport. As a Welshman with his own estates in the area, he implemented and benefited from a policy of close personal supervision over judicial profits. He solved the problem of arrears by imprisoning recalcitrant officials in Newport Castle.[104]

The second duke of Buckingham reaped few if any political benefits from his marriage to Katherine Woodville. The king bestowed power and enormous rewards for service to the crown on a new Yorkist nobility dominated by the Woodvilles; William Lord Hastings; William Herbert, earl of Pembroke; and Humphrey Stafford, earl of Devon.[105] Whether he particularly distrusted Henry because of his family's Lancastrian background or was generally wary of the established nobility,[106] Edward excluded Stafford from power and the business of government, employing him only for ceremonial purposes.[107] Furthermore, the establishment of a royal council in Wales gave effective regional authority to the Woodvilles and their associates, consigning the young duke to political limbo.[108] Whatever the wisdom of the king's policy, Buckingham's later behavior suggests that he resented it bitterly.

Buckingham faced serious financial problems as well as political frustrations during Edward IV's reign. The scattered extant documents suggest that his income was inadequate. Until 1480, his grandmother held a large portion of his inheritance as her jointure, and in 1474, eleven English manors were set aside to pay the dowry of his Aunt Joan, Viscountess Beaumont.[109] Problems stemming from absentee landlordism in Wales continued. Given this situation, the duke was deeply disappointed when the king rejected his claim to half the Bohun inheritance. Half had already passed into the hands of the Staffords as a result of the marriage of Eleanor de Bohun's daughter Anne to Edmund Stafford.[110] The other half had gone to the crown through the marriage of Eleanor's sister, Mary de Bohun, to the future Henry IV. Buckingham claimed that since Henry VI had died without heirs in 1471, he was next heir to the property. The issue was a sensitive one, aside from the huge amount of land involved, because recognition of Buckingham's claim might suggest, particularly to erstwhile Lancastrians, that he had also inherited Henry VI's claim to the throne. The duke certainly did not help matters by assuming Thomas of Woodstock's arms to emphasize his descent from the Bohuns, and therefore from royalty.[111]

Whether or not he lived in retirement at Brecon during most of Edward IV's reign, as Howell Evans suggested,[112] Buckingham certainly appeared at court from time to time. In 1475, he accompanied the king on an expedition to France in support of the duke of Burgundy.[113] Three years later he attended the marriage of Edward's second son, Richard, duke of York, to Anne de Mowbray.[114] That same year he acted as lord high steward at the trial of the king's brother, George, duke of Clarence.[115] On the very day that Clarence was executed, the king granted Buckingham the royal manor and lordship of Cantref Selyf in Wales, which the Staffords had claimed as part of the lordship of Brecon ever since the partition of the Bohun inheritance between Henry IV and Countess Anne Stafford in 1421.[116]

The king's death on April 9, 1483, unleashed a ruthless struggle between the Woodvilles and Richard, duke of Gloucester, for control of the new king, Edward V, then only twelve years old. In that conflict the second duke of Buckingham threw his power decisively behind Gloucester. His anger at the way Edward IV had treated him and the clear intention of the Woodvilles to continue his exclusion from power made his decision inevitable. Buckingham particularly resented the Woodvilles' determination to predominate in Wales, which he considered his rightful bailiwick. Duke Richard promised him a key role in the government, virtually regal authority in Wales, and the disputed half of the Bohun inheritance.[117]

The conspirators made their first move during Edward's progress from Wales to London for his coronation. They arrested the queen's brother, Earl Rivers, and her son, Lord Richard Grey, in order to wrest physical control of the king from the Woodvilles.[118] When they arrived in London with Edward, Buckingham suggested that he be lodged in the Tower; the young monarch was never seen outside it again.[119] Richard rewarded the duke for these services by appointing him chief justice and chamberlain in North and South Wales, custodian of virtually all the Welsh royal castles and lands, and supreme military commander in Shropshire, Herefordshire, Somerset, Dorset, and Wiltshire.[120]

The culmination of Gloucester's conspiracy during June saw Buckingham in the forefront of events. Gloucester and his ally began a military buildup in London on the pretext that "the Quiene, hir blode adherentts and affinitie . . . have entended, and daly doith intend, to murder and utterly distroy us and or cousyn the duc of Bukkyngham, and the old royall blode of this realm."[121] On June 13, Richard ordered the summary execution of Lord Hastings on the ground that he "had conspired the same day, to have slaine the lord protector and the duke of Buckingham sitting in the counsel."[122] The Croyland chronicle reported that Gloucester and Buckingham summoned armed men "in fearful and unheard of numbers, from the north, Wales, and all other parts then subject to them."[123] On June 21, Simon Stallworth wrote to Sir William Stonor, "yt is thought ther schalbe XX thousand of my lord protectour and my lord of Bukyngham men in London this weeke: to what intent I knowe note but to kepe the peas."[124] Stallworth also noted that after Hastings' execution, his men had joined Buckingham's retinue.[125] Dominus Mancini, a contemporary observer, reported that Duke Richard had summoned 6,000 men from his and Buckingham's estates because he feared disturbances during his upcoming coronation;[126] Polydore Vergil subsequently explained Richard's order to Robert Radcliffe to bring 5,000 soldiers from Yorkshire in the same way.[127] Most of the men did not actually reach London until the last week in June, and their number never exceeded 4,000 or 5,000.[128]

During this period, Buckingham played a leading role in the maneuvers to get the king's younger brother, Richard, duke of York, out of sanctuary at Westminster Abbey.[129] The archbishop of Canterbury responded to a threat of force on June 16, prevailing upon Elizabeth Woodville to surrender her second son to Buckingham at Westminster Hall.[130]

On Tuesday, June 24, Buckingham asserted in a speech at the Guildhall that Edward IV's children were illegitimate and not true heirs to the throne of England. He even insinuated that Edward himself was a bastard and concluded that the genuine right to the crown belonged to Richard, duke of Gloucester.[131] The assembled citizens responded unenthusiastically to the duke's harangue and remained silent when he asked them whether they favored the protector. After the recorder of London repeated the substance of Buckingham's speech, "a bushment of the dukes servantes, and Nashefeldes and others longing to the protectour, with some prentises and laddes . . . began sodainelye . . .

to crye owte as lowdes as their throtes would guve: King Rycharde King Rycharde, and threwe up their cappes in token of joye." [132] Duke Henry chose to regard this feeble demonstration as an expression of assent. He appeared at Baynard Castle the next morning with the lord mayor of London and many lords, gentlemen, and principal citizens to "humble desire, pray, and require [Richard] that accordyng to this eleccion of us the Thre Estates of this Lande, as by youre true Enherritaunce, ye will accepte and take upon You the said Crown and Roayll Dignities . . . as to You of right bilongyng, as wele by Enherritaunce as by lawfull Eleccion." [133]

Buckingham also played a leading role in the coronation festivities that followed Gloucester's success. On July 5, he rode in state with the new king from the Tower to Westminster. [134] The next day he bore Richard's train in the solemn procession from Westminster Hall to the abbey for the coronation service, carrying the white staff that signified the office of lord high steward of England. [135]

Immediately after his coronation, Richard III set out on a royal progress through the west of England. Buckingham accompanied him as far as Gloucester and then retired to Brecon Castle. This was his last appearance on the national scene until October, when he suddenly burst forth at the head of a movement to depose his former ally.

Neither Henry Stafford's contemporaries nor modern historians have been able to explain the rapidity with which he switched his political allegiance. The commonest explanation is that Richard alienated Buckingham by rejecting his claim to the half of the Bohun inheritance still in the possession of the crown. [136] A signed bill granting the duke the coveted lands has survived, [137] but James Gairdner raised the question of whether it constituted complete restitution. A signed bill was

usually no more than a means of obtaining letters patent under the Great Seal . . . The bill itself, as granted by the King, has been printed by Dugdale from the family archives at Stafford. It is also formally registered in the journals of King Richard's grants. But it is not enrolled on the Patent Rolls, and there seems good reason for believing that it never passed the Great Seal. For, if it had, the signed bill would have been delivered up to the Lord Chancellor, and therefore would not have been found among the family archives.[138]

He and a number of other historians have therefore maintained that Buckingham never received the Bohun lands and have attributed his subsequent rebellion to disappointment on this score. Recently, however, Charles Ross has argued that Gairdner was incorrect—that during Richard's reign, grants had full force when they passed the signet and did not need to be issued subsequently under the Great Seal.[139]

Closely related to the question of the Bohun inheritance was Henry's claim to be hereditary constable of England, a right that also depended on his being recognized as closest living heir of Humphrey de Bohun, seventh earl of Hereford. Once again, historians disagree on whether Richard actually granted him what he desired. Those who hold the negative view give this as a further reason for his revolt.[140]

Pride and ambition may have been even more important than the denial of his claims to the Bohun inheritance in turning Buckingham against his former ally. "Very trouth it is," Thomas More wrote, "the duke was an high minded man, and evyll could beare the glory of an other, so that I have heard of som that said thei saw it, that the duke at such time as the crown was first set upon the protectors hed, his eye could not abide the sight thereof."[141]

Buckingham might even have begun to reflect on his own claim to the throne.[142] He was, after all, a descendant of Edward III through both John of Gaunt (in the Beaufort line) and Thomas of Woodstock. On the maternal side, his claim to the throne depended on recognition of the legitimacy of the Beauforts, who were born before Gaunt married their mother, Catherine Swynford. Gaunt had tried to protect them by securing letters patent from Richard II declaring them legitimate. In 1407, Henry IV, Gaunt's son by his first wife, Blanche of Lancaster, confirmed this legitimization by an act of parliament, but only with the express reservation that the rights created did not extend to a claim to the throne. It was, however, debatable whether the reservation could legally negate the rights created by the original grant.[143] Buckingham possessed the letters patent containing the unqualified conferral of legitimacy.[144] With this document in hand and Richard III increasingly unpopular, he may well have felt that the way to the throne was open to him.

Robert Fabyan and Edward Hall suggested still another reason for Buckingham's betrayal of Richard: remorse for the murder of Edward IV's two young sons.[145] This explanation is fraught with difficulty because of the innumerable questions surrounding that event, and because it does not fit most of what we know about the duke's character. Contemporary and near-contemporary sources indicate that the two princes were probably murdered between Hastings' execution and the duke's rebellion.[146] Whoever carried out the deed, Richard III was ultimately responsible, as even his recent defender, Paul Kendall, admits.[147] Kendall's attempt to prove that Buckingham committed the crime is completely unconvincing.[148] None of the reliable evidence supports that view. However, the duke probably knew about the murders by the time he reached Brecon, and that knowledge may well have influenced his decision by dramatically altering the prospects of his new candidate for the throne: Henry Tudor, earl of Richmond.[149]

In their accounts of the origins of Buckingham's conspiracy, both More and Vergil attached considerable importance to the conversations between the duke and his prisoner at Brecon, John Morton, bishop of Ely, but they handled the material very differently. More showed the bishop manipulating the duke until he agreed to rebel in favor of Richmond.[150] Vergil, however, indicated that the duke had made the decision before he reached Brecon, where *he* took the initiative in revealing himself to Morton and drawing the bishop into treason.[151]

The reasons for Buckingham's agreeing to forgo his own claim to the crown and support Richmond are almost as obscure as his reasons for turning against Richard in the first place. Apparently, he recognized, either independently or at Morton's prompting, that an attempt in his own behalf was doomed to failure. The political facts were simple: the two groups most opposed to Richard were the supporters of Edward IV's children, headed by their mother, Elizabeth Woodville, and the supporters of Henry Tudor, headed by his mother, Margaret Beaufort. A successful rebellion against Richard depended on their active assistance. If the two groups were to make common cause against Buckingham, he would be isolated and doomed to failure. Such an alliance was in the air, since Margaret Beaufort had already proposed the marriage of her son to Edward IV's eldest daughter, Elizabeth of York.[152]

Meanwhile, an independent movement to liberate the princes from the Tower was growing in the southern counties from Kent to Devonshire.[153] When the rumor that the princes had been murdered grew to almost irresistible proportions in the late summer of 1483, the rebels had no one to turn to but Duke Henry and his candidate for the throne.[154] Thus the second duke of Buckingham became head of a much more widely based revolt than the one he originally contemplated.

The rebellion was set for October. There were to be independent risings at Maidstone, Newbury, Salisbury, and Exeter; Buckingham was to cross the Severn from Wales into Gloucestershire and join the Courtenays in Cornwall; and Henry Tudor was to land in England with support from Brittany. Unfortunately for Buckingham, such a large-scale conspiracy could not be kept secret, and Richard learned about the plot well in advance.[155] His bitterness at Buckingham's betrayal is evident in the hasty note he wrote to his chancellor. "Here, loved by God, ys all well and trewly determined, and for to resyst the malysse of hym that hadde best cawse to be true, thi Duc of Bokyngham, the most untrewe creatur living."[156] As usual, Richard reacted to the emergency "in no drowsy manner, but with the greatest activity and vigilence"[157] and assured his chancellor that "there was never false traytor better purvayde for."[158]

Outbreaks occurred in early October,[159] beginning in Kent and spreading to Berkshire, Wiltshire, Devonshire, and Cornwall.

Buckingham set out from Brecon Castle by the 18th at the latest.[160] According to tradition, the weather defeated Buckingham and his fellows: an extraordinary flood prevented him from crossing the Severn, while a storm drove Richmond's fleet back to Brittany and Normandy.[161] The earliest account, however, attributes Buckingham's failure to the effectiveness of Richard's preparations in mobilizing Sir Humphrey Stafford of Grafton and the Vaughans, Welsh gentry who had been the Staffords' retainers for a half century, against him.[162] When it became clear that the duke was trapped in Wales, his army of Welshmen, "brought to the feild agaynst ther wills, and withowt any lust to fight for him, rather by rigorus commandment than for money," began to melt away.[163] The duke, "foresaken suddaynly of the more part of his soldiers," had no choice but to flee for his life.[164] He sought refuge with one Ralph or Humphrey Bannaster, a retainer in Shropshire, who was then persuaded by the temptation of a reward of one thousand pounds and betrayed his master.[165] Buckingham was taken to Salisbury, which the king had reached two days earlier with a large army. The duke was summarily executed in the public marketplace, "notwithstanding the fact that it was the Lord's Day."[166]

When Duke Henry died, his son and heir Edward was six years old. The family history outlined in this chapter proved to be a determining influence in Edward's life, for it shaped his personality, his ambitions, and the early Tudors' attitude toward him. Edward never forgot that his ancestors had been powerful political figures and companions of kings for generations. Throughout his life, he sought comparable power and prestige. On the other hand, his sovereigns, Henry VII and Henry VIII, never forgot the example of his father, who had shown how dangerous an overly ambitious duke of Buckingham could be. These different responses to the past contained the making of still another Stafford tragedy.

## CHAPTER TWO

# The Young Duke

Edward Stafford, third duke of Buckingham, was born at Brecon Castle in 1478.[1] That nothing is known about the first six years of his life reflects a lack of interest, characteristic of the period, in recording the lives of young children. He probably lived at Brecon, his father's main residence during those early years. Edward, who was known as Lord Stafford, first appeared in the historical record in October 1483 when his father, the second duke of Buckingham, rebelled against Richard III. The rebellion nearly proved fatal to the young nobleman.[2]

Before the second duke embarked on his insurrection, he had sent his wife and two sons to Weobley, Herefordshire, the home of Walter Devereux, Lord Ferrers.[3] There he entrusted his heir to Sir Richard Delabeare, who came from a leading Herefordshire family long connected to the Staffords.[4] For greater safety Sir Richard decided to take Edward to his own home at Kinnersley. Sir William Knevet, a relative of the Staffords, and twenty other people accompanied the young nobleman.[5] Like other children of his class, Edward was always surrounded by large numbers of retainers and personal attendants, both as a sign of his status and as a means of protection.[6] At Kinnersley, Sir Richard placed Lord Stafford in the care of Dame Elizabeth Delabeare and William ap Symon. Dame Elizabeth proved to be both courageous and resourceful in the dangerous situation now confronting her.[7]

As soon as Richard III received word of the second duke's rebellion, he put a reward of £1,000 on Edward's head and £500 on his younger brother Henry's. The Vaughans, longtime Stafford retainers, turned against them at this crisis. They probably resented Duke Henry's overwhelming predominance in the marches. Furthermore, the king had promised them a generous reward from the Staffords' property in return for their assistance. The Vaughans sacked Brecon Castle and led the search for the duke's sons. They also took some young gentlewomen, who may have included the duke's daughters Elizabeth and Anne, from Brecon to Tretower, the home of the head of the Vaughan family, Sir Thomas.

In the face of this danger, Dame Elizabeth shaved Edward's head and dressed him like a girl.[8] Twice search parties arrived at Kinnersley; twice Dame Elizabeth and William ap Symon told them defiantly that the duke's son was not there. Luckily, they had been warned long enough in advance both times to smuggle Edward to safety. But they did not fool Richard's men, who knew very well that Edward was somewhere in the neighborhood and that Dame Elizabeth could tell them where. The king arrested Sir Richard Delabeare in the vain hope that this arrest would pressure her into revealing the boy's whereabouts. The king also discovered Katherine, the duchess of Buckingham, at Weobley and sent her to London as a prisoner. Some months later, Richard assigned her a modest annuity of 200 marks (£133 6s 8d) from her late husband's forfeited estates.[9]

About a fortnight after Katherine had been taken prisoner, warning came that Kinnersley would be searched a third time. Elizabeth took Edward and sat with him on her lap in the park of Kinnersley until William ap Symon brought word four hours later that the danger was past. This incident convinced them that it was too dangerous to keep the young Stafford heir at Kinnersley any longer. They disguised him as a young gentlewoman and took him in broad daylight to a friend of Dame Elizabeth in Hereford. He rode seated sideways on a pillow behind William ap Symon in the style of a proper young lady.

Following this adventurous escape, Edward Stafford disappeared from the historical record again, only to reappear after Henry VII's accession in August 1485. Young Edward had a number of claims on the new king. First, he was Henry VII's distant cousin through the Beaufort line. Second, he was the heir of the first nobleman to rise against Richard III in the Tudor cause. Third, in 1485 his mother married Jasper Tudor, the king's uncle and newly created duke of Bedford, further strengthening Edward's ties to the new regime.[10] The boy attended Henry's coronation in October 1485 and was created knight of the bath.[11] Henry VII's first parliament reversed the attainder passed against the second duke of Buckingham under Richard III and restored Edward to his titles and inheritance.[12]

Since the third duke of Buckingham was only eight years old and his younger brother only six in 1485, Henry VII assumed the right of wardship over them. Wardship, an incident of feudal land tenure to which the English nobility and gentry were subject because they held their land as tenants-in-chief of the crown, was the most profitable of the king's feudal rights and the most costly to the landowning classes. The king assumed responsibility for rearing and educating the minor children of his deceased feudal tenants. In return, he received the income from their property during the children's minority. He also had the right to arrange the marriage of each ward, a right easily turned to profit because heirs and heiresses were valuable commodities on the marriage market. Generally, the king sold the wardship and right of marriage to the highest bidder. The purchaser received the income from his ward's property and either married him or her to one of his own children or resold the right for further profit. Obviously, the value of a particular wardship depended on the size of the minor's inheritance. In the case of Edward Stafford, heir to the largest block of land held by any English nobleman, the potential profits were enormous.

In the case of a boy, wardship ended at age 21; in the case of a girl, at sixteen or upon her marriage.[13] Before the male heir could take possession of his inheritance, however, he had to complete a complicated legal process called "suing general livery." Suing one's lands out of livery could be a difficult matter, because one was required to name and locate each piece of property. If any mistake, however trivial, was made, the process failed and had

to be begun again.[14] A great landowner such as the duke of
Buckingham, who had property scattered over 24 counties and
the Welsh marches, was bound to make some errors. Therefore,
heirs to large inheritances sued the king for "special livery,"
which allowed them to enter their lands without going through
this complicated legal procedure. Special livery was a favor
granted at the discretion of the king, usually in return for a substantial payment or for services rendered during the minority.[15]

On a political level, wardship served a number of functions
that were rarely articulated. By its very existence it asserted the
crown's lordship over the aristocracy. In addition, during periods
of dynastic insecurity, such as the late fifteenth and early sixteenth centuries, the king often tried to use his custody rights to
encourage ties of loyalty between the royal family and key members of the peerage. The circulation of children among noble
households also undoubtedly promoted class solidarity within
the peerage and reinforced ties among kin.

Henry VII assigned custody of both Edward and Henry to his
mother, Margaret Beaufort, countess of Richmond, along with
500 marks from the Stafford estates toward their support.[16] Lands
valued at 1,000 marks went to the duke's mother, now the duchess of Bedford, as her jointure; the rest of Buckingham's inheritance went to the countess of Richmond, with the proviso that
she pay £1,000 of the annual income into the royal household.[17]

It may seem strange to the modern-day reader that the king
did not assign custody of Edward and Henry Stafford to their
mother. Her marriage to Jasper Tudor certainly made her politically reliable, and the choice appears a natural one to us. At that
time, however, the English assumed that the young were better
raised by someone other than their parents. Children of all
classes were sent away from home between the ages of eight and
fifteen. Boys from the noble and knightly classes were frequently
placed as servants in the household of magnates. Their position,
which usually involved serving the lord personally, was considered an honorable one and the best way of completing their
training in the manners and mores of the class. A male heir, par-

ticularly among the major feudatories, was therefore rarely left in the care of his widowed mother.[18] John Howard, who was to become the first duke of Norfolk, spent his childhood in the household of his uncle, one of the Mowbray dukes of Norfolk. His son Thomas divided his time between his father's home and that of his cousin, another Mowbray duke of Norfolk; his grandson, also named Thomas, spent his youth as a page at court.[19] Margaret and John Paston placed their second son in the household of one of the dukes of Norfolk to learn about the world and to make connections.[20]

The custom shocked at least one foreigner, a Venetian who visited England around 1500. He particularly disapproved of parents who "put out" their offspring when economic necessity did not force them to do so. In these cases, he attributed the practice to selfishness and a national lack of affection. He felt that the well-to-do did not want to share their comforts—especially their elaborate meals—with their offspring, and furthermore, that they thought other people's children served them better than their own. He totally discounted the English claim that they sent their young away to learn better manners.[21] A rare insight into the way the English themselves explained the custom comes from a letter written in the 1570's by Sir Robert Sidney to his wife about his daughters: it would be "more to their Good, and less to my charges. . . . Heer they cannot learne, what they may do in other Places; and yet, perhaps, take such Humors, which may be hurtful for them heerafter."[22]

Henry VII's choice of Margaret Beaufort as guardian for the duke of Buckingham and his brother was, of course, an indication of their high status and importance. The countess was undoubtedly one of the most influential people at the Tudor court,[23] and a great deal of evidence attests to the deep affection between her and her normally reserved son.[24] Her relationship by marriage to the Staffords made her a particularly appropriate guardian for the boys in a period when the English often looked to kin to raise their children. Lady Margaret's second marriage, to Henry Stafford, a younger son of the first duke of Buckingham and the boys' great-uncle, took place in 1459, before her eighteenth birthday.[25] The duke settled some property in Suffolk on the couple and left them 400 marks. The legacy may have been in the form of an income from land, since Margaret held most of the Stafford property in Wiltshire and Hampshire from 1460/61.[26] Anne, the dowager duchess of Buckingham, bequeathed four books to her daughter-in-law when she died in 1480, which suggests that the two women shared intellectual interests. When Sir Henry died, the countess was his executrix and residual legatee, and she continued to hold their estates until her own death in 1509.[27]

Because of her well-deserved reputation for piety and learning, the countess of Richmond's household functioned as a school for children of high birth.[28] Lady Margaret employed tutors to assist her in educating her wards. In 1494, for example, she wrote to the chancellor of Oxford University, asking him to excuse Maurice Westbury, M.A., from residence "as we have ordeined the saide Master Maurice to applie hym to the erudition and doctrine of certayn young gentilmen at our findying for a season."[29] The Stafford boys were only two of the noblemen who spent part of their youth under her tutelage. At various times, she also had charge of her grandson, the future Henry VIII;[30] Edward IV's unmarried daughters;[31] two of the fourth earl of Northumberland's children;[32] the earl of Westmorland;[33] possibly Henry Clifford, first earl of Cumberland;[34] her nephew Sir John St. John;[35] and three future bishops, Hugh Oldham, William Smyth, and James Stanley, her stepson.[36]

Children and adolescents who live together away from home often develop strong friendships that continue into adulthood. Henry VIII's lifelong affection for the first earl of Cumberland, with whom he was reared, is a good example.[37] There is no evidence, however, of relationships of this sort in the case of the third duke of Buckingham. None of the people raised in Lady Margaret's household played a significant role in his later life with the exception of Henry VIII, who was not born until 1491 and therefore did not live with the countess at the same time as the young duke.

Being raised by Henry VII's mother does not seem to have made Buckingham particularly loyal to the Tudors or willing to acquiesce in their policies. It is interesting that the tactic of using wardship to bind the nobility to a new dynasty had also failed with Buckingham's father. The second duke of Buckingham had been Edward IV's ward and lived successively in the king's sister's household and in his queen's. At a very young age, he married the king's sister-in-law. Nonetheless, within a few days of Edward IV's death, the second duke had joined Gloucester's conspiracy against the late king's sons.[38]

Very little specific information exists about the third duke of Buckingham's education, although enough is known to discount completely J. S. Brewer's suggestion that he was illiterate.[39] Extant manuscripts written in Buckingham's own hand prove that he could take an active part in administering his own affairs when he wanted to, although his script was sometimes an illegible scrawl, rather than the controlled aesthetic hand of the professional scribe. These documents include a household account for 1519, numerous memoranda about his debts, and two letters to Reginald Bray.[40] Most of the time, of course, men and women of the duke's class depended on secretaries to do their writing for them.[41]

There is a legend, repeated in Charles Henry Cooper's *Athenae Cantabrigienses*, that Buckingham attended Cambridge, but this appears to have been incorrectly deduced from his gifts to the university, and from the presence to this day of his portrait in the hall of Magdalene College.[42] In 1505, for example, he bestowed 31 acres of meadow in Essex on Queens' College, Cambridge, at the suggestion of Lady Margaret, his former guardian.[43] The next year he either gave or sold land in Huntingdonshire to St. Michael's College, Cambridge.[44] He also gave gifts to Christ's College, Cambridge, and St. Paul's School in London, and confirmed an earlier donation by his family to Merton College, Oxford.[45]

Buckingham showed an interest in education and books throughout his life. As an adult he followed his guardian's example and employed a "late scholar of Oxford" as "schoolmaster" to his own henchmen and wards.[46] From time to time he purchased books for these children, as well as for himself and his son.[47] On at least one occasion the duke acted as patron to the infant book trade. In 1512 Wynkyn de Worde published an edition of a chivalric tale, *The History of Helyas, Knight of the Swan*, "at thynstygacyon of the puyssant and illustrious Prynce Lorde Edwarde Duke of Buckyngham."[48] When he died in 1521, three persons described as scholars were receiving annuities from him.[49]

However praiseworthy Buckingham's activities in this area, the evidence hardly justifies Rawcliffe's assertion that Duke Edward "was clearly among the first English noblemen to whom the term 'renaissance aristocrat' can properly be applied."[50] At a very minimum, that label implies that the nobleman concerned knew and appreciated the classics and understood and supported the humanist conception that the revival of ancient learning provided one of the keys to a better life on earth. A more fitting evaluation places Buckingham in the mainstream of late medieval aristocratic culture. After all, *The History of Helyas* was a popular medieval romance; and his gift to Queens' College was made "for his safe state while living, and for the good of the souls of his ancestors and of his own soul after his death," thus emphasizing the college's function as a chantry rather than as an educational institution.[51]

Furthermore, we now know that in the late middle ages neither the magnates nor their wives were as illiterate or as indifferent to learning as Brewer suggested.[52] To give some examples, John Howard, the first duke of Norfolk, kept accounts in his own hand and owned a library containing chivalric and romantic tales. He sent his son and heir to Thetford Grammar School.[53] The tenth Lord Clifford eventually learned to read and write, despite the fact that he was disguised as a shepherd for many years during his childhood. After assuming his title, he immersed himself in the study of astronomy, astrology, and alchemy.[54] The fifth earl of Northumberland was a patron to Lydgate and Skelton, and founded preceptorships in philosophy and grammar at the monastery of Alnwick.[55] The printed collection of Clifford letters contains signed letters from members of the Clifford, Conyers, Dacre, Percy, Scrope, and Stanley families, as well as holograph letters by Henry Percy, the sixth earl of Northumberland; Anne Clifford, the first earl of Cumberland's sister; and Lady Katherine Scrope, Cumberland's daughter.[56] A letter from Lord William Hastings to Sir John Paston contains a postscript in Hastings' own hand.[57] And Edward Stafford's grandmother, Anne, first duchess of Buckingham, has already been mentioned as owning a number of books.

Such examples suggest that besides members of the fifteenth-century nobility renowned for their learning (such as Humphrey, duke of Gloucester; John Tiptoft, earl of Worcester; and Margaret, countess of Richmond), literacy and some degree of education were fairly widespread within the class. This does not mean, of course, that standards were as high as they would become in the sixteenth century, when an educational revolution occurred in the ruling classes, nor that most magnates were among the intelligentsia.[58] But it does mean that historians must cease to repeat the old clichés that ignore the vitality of education and learning in the later middle ages and insist that any signs of intellectual life must be associated with the onset of the Renaissance.

Although wardship carried certain responsibilities for the care and education of the young heir, it functioned primarily as a source of profit for his guardian. Henry VII was particularly notorious for squeezing the last penny from all his feudal rights, and wardship was no exception.[59] As the young duke of Buckingham discovered, the king had no scruples about taking advantage of the fact that his wards were virtually at his mercy.

Buckingham's lands were obviously a source of great potential profit for the king. However, since they were spread over 24 counties and the marches of Wales, they presented complicated problems of management. To exploit them efficiently required the constant supervision of an elaborate administrative hierarchy whose members were prone to laxity, dishonesty, and collusion with recalcitrant tenants. With his usual shrewdness, Henry VII arranged matters so that he received a substantial income from the lands without assuming any administrative responsibility for them, dividing Buckingham's properties between the duke's mother and his own. They, therefore, assumed the expense and trouble of managing them. By the simple expedient of assigning £1,000 of the income from his mother's portion to the royal household, the king appropriated a considerable part of the countess's potential profit at no cost to himself. Henry VII also reserved the feudal rights—knights' fees, profits from wardships and marriages, and reliefs—from her share of Buckingham's property.[60] Finally, he retained the rights of arranging Edward's marriage and assessing the fine for suing his lands out of livery.

Edward Stafford's financial future depended in large measure on how the custodians of his property managed it during his long minority. If they administered it carefully, he would receive his inheritance intact when he came of age. If, on the other hand, they "wasted" his lands by selling off capital resources and by failing to make repairs, or allowed estate officials to become lax and corrupt, or permitted arrears of rent and other dues to grow, his property would lose value steadily and be worth much less when he came of age. Because incompetent administration or downright neglect was the likely state of affairs during a minority, the landowning classes particularly detested this aspect of feudal tenure.

No evidence suggests that either the duke of Bedford, who managed his wife's jointure, or the countess of Richmond wasted Buckingham's inheritance to maximize their own profits.[61] Both proved to be careful and conscientious administrators. Nonetheless, there was probably a regular shortfall in the income from Buckingham's property. Contemporary surveys, or valors, set the total net annual value of his estates at about £5,000.[62] Yet an examination of the accounts of officials who actually collected the income indicates that profits rarely reached that level.

In Gloucestershire, administered by Jasper Tudor, the borough of Newnham showed no profits at all during the minority. The total income from estates in that county rarely came close to the estimated £363 19s.[63] In the four years beginning in 1488, the profits were £132 15s, £206 5s, £339 3s, and £237 8s.[64] In 1494 they were £271 13s.[65] In 1496 and 1497 the income fell to the unbelievably low figures of £42 6s and £28, probably due to confusion following Jasper Tudor's death in 1495.[66] Lady Margaret's collections in Stafford, Cheshire, and Shropshire were hardly more encouraging. The receiver was able to pay £256 3s of the £300 9s expected of him in 1498,[67] but earlier in the minority he had usually fallen short by about £100.[68]

As usual, things were worst in Wales. The lordship of Brecon suffered from the cumulative effects of the turmoil and sporadic warfare endemic in the 1480's. The Vaughans had raided and looted Brecon Castle in 1483. Even after 1485 and the ostensible return of peace, 140 soldiers were employed there against rebels.[69] In 1485/86, the reeve of Brecon Manor reported that "a great multitude of horsemen, diverse rebels against the king" had plowed up a pasture. Formerly let at 40s, it could not be disposed of now even at the reduced rent of 6s 8d.[70] The Great Forest of Brecon, leased for £93 8s as recently as 1482, now brought only £61 17s.[71] There was no income at all in 1486 from the manor of Brecon or from the lordships of Hay and Huntingdon. Three years later, there were still no receipts from Hay and Huntingdon.[72] Annual profits from four receivers' accounts for the lordships of Brecon, assigned to Lady Margaret, in the period of Edward's minority failed to reach the expected £903 16s. No money at all was turned over to the receiver general from the lordship in 1486 or 1489. In 1494 revenue was just under £300, and in 1496 it rose to £436 19s.[73] In 1488 the fine for redeeming the Great Sessions in Brecon had to be reduced from the usual 2,060 marks to 760.[74]

In the neighboring lordship of Newport, administered by Jasper Tudor, profits of the court fell from £87 3s in 1466 to £4 5s in 1498.[75] Newport produced only £164 1s of the expected £281 6s in the last year of the minority.[76] At the same time, the Welsh lordship of Caus, managed by Lady Margaret, yielded only two-thirds of its expected return.[77]

The clearest overview of the situation on Buckingham's properties appears in the receiver's accounts for the estates held by Lady Margaret. They show that the estates yielded only £1,206 6s in 1486, £1,529 16s in 1487, and £1,496 4s in 1488, a total of £4,153 6s. In this three-year period, ordinary expenses plus payments owed to the king and the allowance for the two young Staffords came to £4,380 7s.[78] Matters improved only slightly in the following years. In 1496 the countess received £1,694 2s, barely enough to pay the annual charges.[79]

The gap between the actual income from Stafford's estates and the net figures in the valors resulted from deep-rooted problems of estate management and a persistent tendency to overvalue Buckingham's property. It is worth remembering that a similar situation existed during the lifetime of the first duke (1402–60).[80] Conditions were worst in Wales in both the 1450's and the late 1490's. Long-term, wholesale negligence had taken its toll.[81] The circumstances did not bode well for the third duke of Buckingham when he came of age. Unless he could raise the profits from his estates to levels that had not been attained for decades, he would have to hold his expenditures to a figure considerably below the income estimated in the valors or else face a continual accumulation of debts. In the face of a similar situation, his great-grandfather, the first duke, had chosen the latter course.

During the third duke's minority, the person who bore the brunt of the shortfall in profits from his estates was the king's mother, Lady Margaret. Buckingham's own mother was protected because the net value of the property specifically assigned to Buckingham's mother by act of parliament was £1,500 rather than the 1,000 marks (£666 13s 4d) specified as her rightful jointure.[82] Income from these estates could therefore fall considerably below their estimated value and still yield the jointure to which she was entitled. We have seen that Henry VII had insulated himself by taking a large fixed income from his mother's share of the estates. Theoretically, the countess of Richmond's portion of the property was worth £3,500.[83] That left over £2,000 after she paid £1,000 to the royal household and spent 500 marks (£333 6s 2d) to support Edward and Henry Stafford. But, in fact, the income from the lands she held only covered these expenses plus ordinary costs in one of the four years for which we have records. As one of the wealthiest women in England, the countess could well absorb the loss. She undoubtedly agreed to the arrangement because of her sense of duty to the king and because of the prestige involved in rearing children of such high birth. In any case, enormous grants from the crown more than offset her losses on this particular transaction.[84]

As the heir to the largest block of land held by any English peer, Duke Edward was a valuable commodity on the marriage market. Henry VII was clearly determined to exploit this fact for his own political and financial advantage. In the first years of his reign, he proposed to marry Buckingham to Anne, eldest daughter of the duke of Brittany, to prevent France from absorbing the duchy. The young duke was evidently important enough to whet Brittany's appetite, but the project fell through because Ferdinand of Aragon convinced the king that the match would alienate Anne's guardian, Alan d'Albret, a powerful Gascon noble who wanted to marry Anne himself.[85]

In 1489, Henry arranged to have Duke Edward, then twelve years old, marry Alianore Percy. Since Alianore, eldest daughter of the fourth earl of Northumberland, who had been murdered in a tax riot earlier that year, was also a royal ward, the king was able to help himself to a sizable portion of the Percy inheritance. The executors of the earl's estate promised to pay Henry £4,000 "in consideration" of the marriage.[86] This was an exorbitant sum in a period when the average marriage portion of peers' daughters was £1,150.[87] Although Henry VII in effect received Alianore's dowry, her husband was responsible for providing her jointure. In his last will, the duke promised her the generous sum of 2,000 marks.[88]

In the years following his marriage, while he was still in his teens, Buckingham began to appear at court and to play a minor role in public affairs. He spent a good deal of the fall and winter of 1494–95 in London; during that time, he attended the ceremony creating Prince Henry duke of York.[89] He was appointed to commissions of oyer and terminer in Middlesex and Kent but probably did not play an active role on them.[90] He was at court again in 1496 and 1497. On the latter occasion, he assisted the king in greeting the new Venetian ambassador, Andrea Trevisano.[91] His most exciting public activity was to lead a group of West Country gentlemen against Perkin Warbeck at the siege of Exeter in 1497, the kind of service to the crown that most appealed to great nobles.[92]

During these years, Buckingham had his first direct financial dealings with Henry VII. Like most of his peers, he found the experience a costly one. In 1496, Buckingham's mother, once again a widow, took Sir Richard Wingfield as her third husband without the king's license and incurred a fine of £2,000.[93] Henry demanded payment from her son rather than from her new husband, although, according to Edward, "yt was against right and good conscience that I should paie yt forasmoche as I hade none of his goods."[94]

Two years later, perhaps in recognition of the fact that Buckingham had begun to assume the responsibilities of an adult of his class, Henry VII granted him special livery of his lands.[95] Edward's claim to be of age when he entered into his lands in March 1498 was supported by a certificate of the priory of St. John's in Brecon that registered his birth on February 3, 1478.[96] Nevertheless, the patent granting him special livery expressly stated that he was receiving the favor "notwithstanding his minority."[97] The duke later claimed that the king had agreed to grant him his lands for a fine of £1,000 but then received false information that Buckingham was still under age and tripled the charge. From the evidence it is impossible to tell whether the confusion about the duke's age was genuine or simply a device to extort as much money from him as possible. In either case, Buckingham deeply resented the enormous extra expense. During the first year of Henry VIII's reign, he petitioned the king for restitution.[98] When the new king failed to act on his suit, he grew impatient and, in 1515, sued Henry VII's executors for recovery of his £3,000. The case was heard before the king's council and a majority of the royal judges. The court ruled against Buckingham on the ground that special livery was a favor and the recipient thus had to pay whatever price the king demanded for it. Nevertheless, Henry VIII graciously restored £1,000 to the duke in an effort to obtain his goodwill.[99]

As a further condition of gaining possession of his inheritance, Buckingham had to promise to pay Henry VII all the arrears in his Welsh lordships. These arrears amounted to more than £600 in Brecon alone.[100] Even then, the king withheld the lordships of Cantref Selyf, Penkelly, and Alexanderstone, although these were undoubtedly part of the duke's rightful inheritance.[101] He did not recover them until January 1509, after he had surrendered his rights to these lordships to the king, paid £1,000, and received them back as a new grant.[102] Buckingham claimed that the suit to the king for restitution of this property cost him 2,000 marks.[103]

Thus, between 1496 and 1498 Henry VII levied fines of £5,600 on the young duke. He then had to pay an additional £1,000 to recover the three Welsh lordships that had been withheld. In addition, Henry VII had appropriated Alianore Percy's dowry in a period when members of the nobility counted on their wives' dowries to ease their financial situation. Since Buckingham was almost always short of cash, the king probably had to satisfy himself with recognizances for the greater part of the money owed him. The duke later complained to Henry VIII that he had had to take a loan from a Lombard on extremely unfavorable terms so that he could meet "such great and importunate chardge as I was dryven to paie our said late soveraign lord at certayn daies."[104] In 1504, for example, he paid 500 marks;[105] in 1508 the king canceled four recognizances for £160 each.[106]

The duke of Buckingham's long minority established a pattern in his relations with the Tudors that persisted in various forms for the rest of his life. During these years, Henry VII recognized the duke's importance as a leading member of the peerage while simultaneously behaving in ways certain to alienate him. The king acknowledged the young duke's position by placing him in his mother's household, but destroyed any possibility that Buckingham would develop strong ties to the Tudor dynasty by exploiting him financially. To maintain a standard of living commensurate with his rank, Buckingham would have to wrest more money from his property than it had yielded in at least half a century. On top of this, thanks to Henry VII he would have to pay off enormous debts to the crown. His anger at this situation would come to outweigh any loyalty or affection he might have developed for the Tudors during the years he lived in Lady Margaret's household.

## CHAPTER THREE

# The Third Duke and the Stafford Family

From the moment he gained control of his inheritance in 1498, the third duke of Buckingham assumed the responsibilities and prerogatives of the head of the Stafford family. Contemporary sources make clear that the duke defined his family as the group that eventually included his wife, his children and their spouses, his siblings and their spouses, his grandchildren, his wife's brother (Henry Percy, fifth earl of Northumberland), and the immediate relatives of his many in-laws. Throughout his life he maintained meaningful economic and emotional ties with the members of this large group.

At the center of the duke's family were those who actually lived in his household: his wife, his only son and heir, and his unmarried daughters and siblings. The shifting membership of this central group reflected the patrilineal and primogenitural bias of English inheritance customs and conceptions of lineage. When the duke's son married, his wife joined the household and subsequently gave birth to her first child there.[1] On the other hand, his daughters all left home on marrying. Buckingham's brother and sisters also lived elsewhere after they married, although Anne returned to the duke's home for a short period after the death of her first husband.[2] Significantly, the departure of the duke's daughters and siblings did not seem to weaken his ties to them. As we shall see, a number of sources underscore Buckingham's continued paternalistic interest in his sisters. In the case of the duke of Buckingham's family, therefore, it is incorrect to equate family with residence in the household, and of only limited usefulness to speak of his family as either nuclear or extended.

Although the duke of Buckingham's marriage to Alianore Percy lasted more than thirty years, ending only with his death in 1521, little evidence exists in the extensive source material about the duchess's relationship to her husband or about her position in his household. A memorandum to the duke's chancellor, Robert Gilbert, in November 1520 furnishes the single glimpse into their life together. Buckingham instructed him to explain "the demeanour of my Lady our wife" to Lady and Lord Fitzwalter, his sister and brother-in-law, and to ask his sister to find the duchess a new lady-in-waiting, "for we thynke the demeanour of my lady ys suche that Margaret Geddynge wol be loth to be about her." He asked Gilbert in the same instruction to find out "who told her [Alianore] of the thyngs that we shuld doo at Southamptone." An earlier item in the memorandum indicates that Margaret had recently been discharged from service. The duke wanted his sister's advice about whether to re-employ her.[3]

The wording of the memorandum indicates that some connection existed between Geddynge, the events planned for Southampton, and the duchess's anger, a connection that raises the possibility that Geddynge was involved sexually with Buckingham. If so, the relationship may have been a long-standing one. Margaret, described in the accounts as a gentlewoman, was a member of the duke's household as early as 1499–1500.[4] By 1502–3 she was receiving an annuity of £6 13s 4d from him;[5] a wardrobe account recorded a gift to her in 1516–17.[6] During this period, Geddynge was one of the duchess's ladies-in-waiting and mistress of the nursery at Thornbury.[7] In 1519, the duke gave her the substantial sum of £13 6s 8d on New Year's.[8] Whatever the reason for her being discharged, she was rehired by March 1521[9] and at the time of Buckingham's death held the farm of demesne lands in Eastington and Alkerton, Gloucestershire.[10]

Duke Edward certainly took advantage of the freedom of men of his class to engage in extramarital sex. He had three illegitimate children—two sons and a daughter. He provided for the daughter by purchasing a royal ward from Henry VIII and contracting the two in marriage.[11] Long after his death, the duke's son Henry granted the presentation of a church to his deceased father's two bastard sons Henry and George.[12] The matter-of-fact provision for these children illustrates the open acceptance of the double standard among the aristocracy in the early sixteenth century.

In fulfilling her role as a wife, one of the duchess of Buckingham's most important functions was providing her husband with a male heir. She gave birth to her only son, Henry, at Penshurst, Kent, on September 18, 1501.[13] She also had three surviving daughters. The eldest, Elizabeth, was born in 1497.[14] The birth dates of the other two, Catherine and Mary, are unknown, but probably at least one of them was also older than Henry, since an indenture of June 1502 refers to Buckingham's daughters.[15] Margaret Geddynge was in charge of the children's nursery; four other women, including two gentlewomen, worked under her.[16] Although Buckingham probably followed the custom of his class and used a wet nurse for his infants, no positive evidence on that point exists.

We do know that in June 1502 he arranged to board his children with a gentlewoman named Margaret Hexstall at Bletchingley, one of his manors in Surrey. He specifically charged her to "daylie and nightlie, during the tyme of absence of my Lord and my Ladye, geve good and dewe attendance unto my Lord Stafford, sonne and heire unto my said Lord's grace, and unto my yonge Ladyes, daughters unto the same." While the children were in Hexstall's care, seventeen people attended them. The duke agreed to pay a weekly allowance of 28s 4d for the servants' food, to provide their bedding and fuel, and to pay the wages of all their servants except Margaret Hexstall herself. She was responsible for providing all the other "stuffe and implements" necessary to serve her charges and their attendants. Considering that Henry was only nine months old at the time and the duke's eldest daughter but five, their father's directions for their diet were extraordinary by modern standards: they were to receive four or five dishes of meat or fish daily.[17]

The 1502 indenture does not make clear whether the arrangement with Margaret Hexstall was a long-term one. The wording, particularly the specific reference to the "tyme of the absence of my Lorde and my Ladye," suggests that it was not,[18] and that the Stafford children usually lived with their parents in the ducal household. The household book of 1508 lists a daily food allowance for Buckingham's son Henry. In 1516, when Henry was fifteen years old, Cardinal Wolsey suggested that Buckingham send him to court "to be acquainted." The duke demurred, saying, "I had but one son, wherefore I would be loth he should come . . . [a]browd, specially for dread of contageous [disease] . . . if he had once a wife and a child he would not [mind parting with] . . . him." His remark strongly suggests that Henry still lived at home. It also suggests that the duke was more concerned about the survival of his lineage than about his son as an individual, since he was apparently willing to expose Henry to the dangers of the court once he had a wife and child.[19] As for his daughters, the cofferer's accounts show that Elizabeth lived at home at least as late as 1508,[20] and Mary was living at home shortly before her marriage in 1519.[21]

Wherever they resided, Buckingham saw that all his children received some education. Their mother, Alianore, wrote a prayer to the Virgin in verse, which suggests some level of cultivation. Positive evidence exists for the literacy of two of his three surviving daughters.[22] John Skelton called Duke Edward's eldest daughter, Elizabeth, an admirer and friend of the muses and his particular patron.[23] His son grew up to be one of the best-educated members of the early Tudor peerage and developed decidedly scholarly interests. By the time Henry was fifteen, his father was purchasing books for him, mostly of a religious nature.[24] Henry mastered Latin and French, attended both universities, and was admitted to Gray's Inn in 1521.[25] He encouraged the continuation of the *Mirror for Magistrates*, a collection of moral tales in the form of biography, and secured a license for its publication; he also translated a work on forests from the French.[26] After the break with Rome, he became involved in the religious controversies of the day. About 1548 Henry translated a Lutheran tract by Edward Fox, bishop of Hereford, from the Latin.[27] On Mary's accession, he reverted to Roman Catholicism and translated two of Erasmus's letters against Luther.[28] In 1556 his library contained more than 350 books and manuscripts.[29]

During the years that he was raising his own children, Buckingham also had definite responsibilities for his brother and two sisters. All were still unmarried when he assumed the position of head of the Stafford family in 1498. The duke's siblings expected his help in arranging their marriages, protecting their property, and carrying on their lawsuits. They also expected his financial help, in the form of grants of land or annuities. In return, the duke expected his brother and sisters to recognize his authority and to defer to his opinion.

Over and above these practical and economic bonds between Buckingham and his siblings were other, less tangible, ties. Contemporary sources reflect a degree of warmth and trust in Buckingham's attitude toward his sisters that rarely appears in his other relationships.[30] Behind this evident emotional attachment may well have been the years they had spent together at Brecon Castle in their early childhood. Their father's abortive rebellion in 1483 had broken up this household, and nothing is known about where or how the Stafford children lived for the next two years, except for the short period covered in the contemporary account of Edward's escape from Richard III (see Chapter 2). After Henry VII's accession, the boys were reunited in Lady Margaret's household, but the whereabouts of the girls at that time cannot be ascertained.

Buckingham found husbands for his two sisters, Elizabeth and Anne, within a few years of attaining his majority. The responsibility was probably at least partially a welcome one, since it gave him the opportunity to form useful ties to other noble families while his own children were still young. On February 15, 1500, Anne married Sir Walter Herbert.[31] Herbert was the illegitimate son of William, earl of Pembroke, but had gained control of Raglan Castle in Wales after the death of his legitimate brother, the earl of Huntingdon, in 1491. Until his own death more than fifteen years later, he held Raglan de facto;[32] his marriage to Anne therefore strengthened her brother's position in the Welsh marches. Sir Walter promised his wife a jointure of 300 marks and conveyed land to trustees for that purpose.[33] When he died in September 1507, he and Lady Anne had no children.[34]

The widowed Lady Anne returned to her brother's household at Thornbury, where she was attended by a dozen or more people. She remained there until her remarriage two years later. During this period, the duke paid her regular sums from her jointure.[35] He also worked to ensure that he would not lose the political fruits of her first marriage: control of Raglan Castle. In January 1509, he secured a grant of Raglan to trustees for his sister's use. The duke's purpose in securing the grant was revealed in the names of the eight trustees, six of whom were his councillors and servants. Henry VII made the grant "out of affection to his kinswoman Anne Herbert, widow," although he acknowledged the superior right of her niece Elizabeth.[36]

That same year, Anne remarried, this time to George Lord Hastings, who would become earl of Huntingdon in 1529.[37] Again, the purpose of the marriage was to strengthen Buckingham's position in the Welsh marches. Hastings made the duke steward of all his Welsh properties in 1511.[38]

A charming letter that Hastings wrote to his wife from London in 1528 while recovering from a serious illness indicates that their marriage was a happy and affectionate one. The letter opens, "Myne owne good Anne, with all my hoole hart I recommend me unto you as he that is most glad to here that you be mery and in good helthe, which I pray God long to continuew, for that shalbe my moost comforte of anny othur erthely thing." In response to his wife's offer to come to him, he wrote, "And, myne owne good trull, I moose hartely thancke you for your kind and loving offer to cum to me . . . but rather than I wold will you to take such a jornay apon you considering your febulness and also the foule way I ensure you I wold be glad to cum hoome a foot." After telling her the latest news, he closed with the following lines: "I have send you by this berar a box of the best cordiall lozenges that ever Mastur Chambur devised for comforting of the hart, and anny thing els ye will have send me worde and ye shal nott faute therof. And yett oones againe fare well, good Anne. Your trew loving bedfellow, George Hastynges."[39] Lady Anne and her husband had eight children, five boys and three girls.[40]

Much less is known about the advantage to Buckingham of his sister Elizabeth's marriage to Robert Radcliffe, Lord Fitzwalter, in 1505.[41] Fitzwalter had serious political and financial problems. In the year of his marriage, he agreed to pay Henry VII £5,000 to secure the reversal of his father's attainder. Although he actually paid £2,000, he did not regain all the family estates.[42] Elizabeth, the first of Radcliffe's three wives, had at least three sons and a daughter.[43]

Buckingham retained a paternal interest in his sisters even after their marriages. He continued to administer the jointure from Anne's first marriage.[44] The best example of his paternalism occurred in 1510, when both women were at court and became involved in a minor scandal. Sir William Compton, a favorite of Henry VIII's, was courting the younger of the sisters; according to court gossip he was really trying to win her for the king. When the elder sister, a member of Catherine of Aragon's household, passed the rumor on to her brother, he burst into the younger's chamber in a temper, only to find Compton there. "Women of the Stafford family," he shouted, "are no game for Comptons, no, nor for Tudors either." He handed his younger sister over to her husband, who took her from court and deposited her in a convent some sixty miles away. Meanwhile, Compton went straight to the king. Henry, whose temper quite equaled Buckingham's, gave the duke such a dressing down that he rushed out of the royal presence, exclaiming he would not pass another night under the palace roof. The next morning, after a furious quarrel, Henry forced the queen to dismiss Buckingham's talkative sister from her suite.[45]

Warm social relations existed between Buckingham, his sisters, and their husbands. As we have seen, when the difficulties involving Margaret Geddynge developed, the duke turned to the Fitzwalters for advice.[46] Throughout the years, he exchanged visits and letters with his sister Anne and her husband.[47] In January 1508 the duke met Lord Fitzwalter for dinner on his way to London.[48] He invited Hastings to dinner while he was in the capital in 1516.[49] Evidently, Buckingham and Fitzwalter gambled together on occasion, for there is a note that the duke lost 6s 8d to him at dice in 1519.[50]

Buckingham's relations with his brother Henry seem to have been more difficult than his relations with his sisters. As a younger son, Henry spent his life in the awkward position of being dependent on and subordinate to his older brother, who headed the family and controlled most of its property. The will of the fourth earl of Northumberland (d. 1487) clearly expresses contemporary views about the appropriate relationship between younger sons and their older brothers. Northumberland left his youngest son Josselyn lands worth 300 marks per annum in Sussex "to the extent that the said Gosslyne shall be of loving and lowly dispocion toward the said Henry his broder and to give him his allegiance, and that I charge him to do and to be."[51] In the case of the Staffords, Henry required Duke Edward's assistance to maintain a standard of living appropriate to his birth and to make an advantageous marriage. In these circumstances Henry was obviously willing—and perhaps even eager—to help his brother manage the vast Stafford estates. Buckingham regularly employed him to try to impose order in the turbulent Welsh lordships and to extract money from the recalcitrant tenants. In 1500 Henry headed the commission appointed to survey his brother's properties in Wales, Thornbury, and Bedminster.[52] In 1502 he was present at an audit of the Gloucestershire estates to check the accounts.[53] He returned to Wales the next year on the commission appointed to hold the Great Sessions in Newport and Brecon.[54] From 1500 to 1521 he served as steward of the Welsh lordships of Brecon, Hay, Huntingdon, Newport, and Caus.[55] Throughout most of this period he was also sheriff of

Newport, Wentloog, and Machen.[56] His payment for these services came to £40 a year.[57]

In 1504 or 1505, Henry married Cicely, widow of Thomas Grey, marquess of Dorset, who was nineteen years older than he and the mother of fifteen children by her first husband. Duke Edward, though only a couple of years older than Henry, had already been married for fourteen years. This kind of disparity between the ages of an heir and his younger brother at marriage was a common one in that period. Heirs were the most desirable objects on the marriage market, younger sons quite the opposite. The financial difficulties younger sons faced often led them to choose widows, who received jointures from their previous husbands. By marrying a woman well over forty, Henry reduced the possibility of his having any children and therefore of having to worry about providing for them.[58]

Henry obviously expected his match to be a profitable one, since he paid the king £2,000 for permission to marry Cicely. Half the sum was to be paid in biannual installments of £100 over a period of five years. The other half took the form of an obligation to be canceled if, for the rest of his life, Henry did "demeane and behave hymself truely to oure said souverain lord and to his heires and not to be reteigned or towards any other persoune."[59] Lady Cicely granted her husband Henry a life estate in lands worth £1,000 a year from properties she had inherited. She also promised him the rest of her inheritance if her son and heir, Thomas, marquess of Dorset, died.[60] Despite her generosity, Henry's marriage did not solve his financial problems. In 1521 he owed the king the hefty sum of £4,407 4s.[61] In 1524, a year after Henry's death, his widow disposed of her property. She gave £1,000 to each of her four surviving daughters and small annuities to her younger sons, kept 300 marks a year for herself, and set aside the rest to pay her second husband's debts.[62]

At the time of Henry's marriage, Buckingham settled an estate on his brother's wife and their male heirs. He later regretted his generosity and instituted a lawsuit to establish that Henry and his wife had only a life interest in the property. Henry paid the king £400 for his favor in the matter, but since no decision in the case survives, it is impossible to tell whether the money was well spent.[63] Despite Buckingham's unwillingness to endow a cadet branch of the Stafford family permanently, he tried to exploit the ties to the Greys that his brother's marriage had created. He granted one of Henry's stepsons, Lord John Grey, an annuity of £6 6s 8d; another, Lord Edward Grey, appears to have been a member of his household in 1508.[64] By 1516 or 1517, still another of Henry's many stepsons, George, had joined the household at Thornbury.[65]

Within a few years of arranging his sister Anne's second marriage, Buckingham began to think about arranging marriages for his own children to ensure the continuance of his direct line and to strengthen his ties to other leading members of the peerage.[66] He expected his children to acquiesce in his decisions in this area and paid little attention to their feelings about them. Many years after her marriage to Thomas Howard,* Elizabeth wrote that her father had originally betrothed her to his ward Ralph Neville, earl of Westmorland. "He and I had loved together two years, and if my Lord my husband had not sent immediate word after my lady, and my Lord's first wife was dead, and made suit to my father . . . I had been married before Christmas to my Lord of Westmorland."[67] Howard, widowed in 1511, apparently pressed his suit with vigor, undoubtedly influenced by the fact that at the time Buckingham was the only duke in England. Elizabeth's dowry of 2,000 marks also was an important factor in his enthusiasm.[68] As she noted many years later, "He had but little when he married me first but his lands, and he was always a great player [gambler]."[69] At first Buckingham tried to get Howard to agree to take one of his other daughters, since Elizabeth preferred her match to Westmorland. But Howard remained firm: "he would have none of my sisters, but only me."[70] He may

* When Thomas Howard married Buckingham's daughter Elizabeth in 1512, he was known by the courtesy title of Lord Howard, and his father was the earl of Surrey. In 1513, when Surrey became the second duke of Norfolk, the younger Howard acquired the title earl of Surrey. He was known by that title until 1524, when his father died and he became the third duke of Norfolk.

have found Elizabeth the most appealing of the three girls. Or age may have been the crucial factor. Howard, already 35, may well have felt that fifteen-year-old Elizabeth was quite young enough.[71] Indeed, she was more than four years younger than the average bride from English ducal families in the early Tudor period.[72] Buckingham eventually yielded, despite Elizabeth's reluctance, and the marriage took place in 1512.[73] Since the earl of Westmorland was Buckingham's ward, the duke simply married him to another one of his daughters, Catherine. Their wedding took place sometime before March 31, 1517.[74] In this way, without much difficulty, Buckingham succeeded in securing husbands from distinguished old families for two of his daughters.[75]

In 1516, with Cardinal Wolsey's assurances that King Henry VIII would approve, Buckingham proposed a double marriage between his son and the earl of Shrewsbury's daughter, and the earl's son and his daughter.[76] Buckingham apparently had told Shrewsbury years before that he could have his son "better cheap by 1,000 marks than any other man." Nonetheless, Shrewsbury refused the match on the ground that it was too expensive. He wrote to Richard Sacheverell, who was serving as an intermediary, "I trust with a little help to marry all my daughters with the sum he asked with one of them." He claimed to be too much in debt to the king and others to raise the money required.[77]

Duke Edward continued to look for a wife for his heir and, following another suggestion of Wolsey's, eventually settled on Ursula Pole, daughter of Margaret, countess of Salisbury.[78] Ursula's dowry was 3,000 marks and was to be increased by another 1,000 "if the Countess get back certain lands from the king."[79] Her mother also settled lands in Somerset and Devon worth 700 marks on the couple and their children.[80] In return, Buckingham was to set aside lands worth £500 as Ursula's jointure. He also paid all the expenses of the wedding except for Ursula's clothes, which were provided by her mother.[81] The wedding took place on February 16, 1519, when Henry was not yet eighteen years old.[82] Because of his father's fear that he would die before he produced an heir, he was considerably younger than most grooms of his class; their average age between 1480 and 1679 was 24.3.[83] Since he was so young, Buckingham did not feel that marriage entitled Henry to assume the responsibilities of adulthood. Not only did he live in his father's household, but the duke continued to hire guardians for him. In November 1520, for example, he instructed his chancellor to "speke wyth my lord of Burgaveny and to desyre hym that he woll have communicacione with Thomas Lewkener to serve us, and to take charge of our sonne the lord Stafford, and suche payments as shal be made for hym . . . and hys wyfe to be in our howse at mete and drynke, and wageys yf he and she shall be so contented."[84]

Buckingham's third daughter, Mary, married George Neville, Lord Bergavenny, also in 1519. She was his third wife.[85] Although Mary could not have been more than 21 at the time, her husband was 40, about the same age as her father.[86] The wedding apparently took place before June, although the duke's accounts show a payment of £6 14s 9d to the Pope for a dispensation in November.[87] The duke gave Mary a dowry of £1,660 13s 4d, somewhat more than Elizabeth had received on her marriage to Thomas Howard.[88]

All Buckingham's children's marriages were a great success from the viewpoint of continuing the Stafford line. Most important, of course, was Henry's marriage to Ursula Pole. Within ten years of their wedding, the couple had seven children.[89] By 1537 they had twelve, with one more on the way.[90] The first was born in the duke's household in November 1520, less than two years after the wedding. Buckingham paid a midwife from Bristol 10s for attending his daughter-in-law. Some months later, he employed a nurse for his grandchild.[91] Henry Stafford's children eventually included seven boys and seven girls.[92] Of these, at least one boy died young, but little is known about whether the others survived. Two of his sons, Henry and Edward, certainly grew to maturity, since they inherited their father's title in 1563 and 1566, respectively.[93] At least three of his daughters, Dorothy, Anne, and Susan, survived into the late 1540's.[94]

Duke Edward was obviously not as concerned about his daughters' children as he was about his son's. If the male line had failed, however, he need not have worried about the extinction of the family. Catherine, countess of Westmorland, had seven sons and nine daughters by her husband, Ralph, the fourth earl.[95] Giving birth to a large family and managing an extensive household apparently did not exhaust Lady Catherine's energies. According to a report at the time of the Pilgrimage of Grace, she responded vigorously when disturbances broke out in the absence of her husband and the bishop of Durham: "My lady of Westmorland, with such counsel as she taketh to her, stayeth the country for a time; I assure your lordship she rather playeth the part of a knight than of a lady."[96]

Her elder sister, Elizabeth, duchess of Norfolk, had five children, of whom three grew to adulthood: Henry, who would become earl of Surrey; Thomas, who would become Viscount Bindon; and Mary, who married Henry VIII's illegitimate son, the duke of Richmond. Buckingham's third daughter, Mary, Lady Bergavenny, gave birth to a child by November 1520, a little over a year after her wedding. Her father sent "certain pots" for the christening, but clearly did not attend or know much about what was happening, since he considered writing to ask his sister, Lady Fitzwalter, who the child's godparents were.[97] Mary's family grew to six children—a son and five daughters. The son, Henry, eventually inherited his father's title and property.[98]

In addition to ensuring the continuance of the Stafford line, Buckingham hoped that his children's marriages would strengthen his political position. The matches he arranged for his offspring linked him to the Howards, the Poles, the Neville earls of Westmorland, and the Neville lords Bergavenny. His own marriage had connected him to the Percies; his siblings', to the Hastingses, Radcliffes, and Greys. What is notable about these families is that in addition to being distinguished members of the pre-Tudor nobility, each of them had been in serious trouble with Henry VII, with the notable exception of the

Hastingses; and even Lord Hastings was summoned to the Star Chamber early in Henry VIII's reign for keeping too many liveried retainers.[99] None had a completely secure position under either of the first two Tudors. From a political point of view, therefore, these alliances were probably less advantageous than Duke Edward might have wished. Whether the duke was blind to political reality or whether more secure families feared alliance with peers who seemed to be under a cloud is a difficult question to answer. However, it may be significant that the earl of Shrewsbury rejected Buckingham's overtures for a marriage alliance, since the Talbots were an old family that managed to avoid serious trouble with the Tudors and become successful servants of the new dynasty.[100]

Marriage ties did not, of course, automatically create warm relationships, common interests, or political alliances between Buckingham and his in-laws. The increasing concentration of patronage at the court, where there were never enough offices, pensions, grants of land, and other favors to satisfy everyone, encouraged rivalry and factionalism among the nobility and interfered with the networks created by marriage. Personality traits also affected the duke's relations with individual members of the large kin group created by his own marriage and the marriages of his siblings and children. It is therefore incorrect for historians to assume that a group of relatives constituted a unified political faction or interest group.

Apparently Buckingham did have warm relationships with his three brothers-in-law, Lord Hastings, Lord Fitzwalter, and the earl of Northumberland. The extant evidence shows purely social contacts with Hastings and Fitzwalter. The friendship between Stafford and Percy, however, seems to have been both personal and political in nature. The two men exchanged estate offices, each carrying an annual salary of £20. Northumberland was steward of Buckingham's estates in Holderness, Yorkshire; Buckingham of Northumberland's in Somerset.[101] Since the center of Percy's influence was in the North and Buckingham's in the

West, this exchange may have increased their control over out-lying parts of their estates.

The state papers contain a great deal of evidence of their political alliance. In August 1509, Lord Darcy reported that since Bishop Fox was unable to oust his rivals, who included the earl of Surrey, from the council, "he will prove another way, which is to bring and bolster himself to rule all with the Duke of Bukyng-ham and the Earl of Northumbr." He also wrote that Northumberland's servants claimed that "my lord of Buckyngham should be protector of England and that their master should rule all from the Trent North and have Berwick and the marches." [102] Whether or not Darcy's report was accurate, it shows that the two brothers-in-law were members of the same faction at court. In 1519, Buckingham and Northumberland both fell under suspicion, and Henry ordered Wolsey to put them under "good watche." [103] The story that the cardinal instigated Percy's imprisonment in 1521 so that he could deal more easily with Buckingham is false, but it is a testimony to their cooperation in the endless maneuvering for influence and power. [104]

Evidence exists about Buckingham's relations with two of his three sons-in-law: George Neville, Lord Bergavenny, and Thomas Howard. In both cases, there were definite signs of strain and ill will. Many years after the duke's death, Howard recalled that "the duke of Bukyngham confessed . . . that of all men living he hated me most." [105] Both Buckingham and Howard were of a proud and somewhat violent nature, which probably made it difficult for them to get along. [106] Since they were the same age, Buckingham could not easily use his superior position as father-in-law to impose his will on Howard. [107]

The rivalry at court between Buckingham and the Howards undoubtedly exacerbated what might have been a difficult situation in any case. In the early years of Henry VIII's reign, when the earl of Surrey, the future second duke of Norfolk (that is, the father of Buckingham's son-in-law), was struggling with Bishop Fox for control of the council, Buckingham sided with Fox.[108]

Buckingham must have been intensely jealous when Surrey's victory at Flodden Field in 1513 brought the Howards the glory and favor he himself craved. Henry VIII rewarded Surrey with the dukedom of Norfolk and made his son and heir, Buckingham's son-in-law, earl of Surrey. Substantial grants of land accompanied these titles: Norfolk received thirty manors and an annuity of £50, Surrey sixteen manors, two castles, and an annuity of £20.[109] Norfolk's elevation deprived Buckingham of his position as the only peer of ducal rank, an eminence he surely did not enjoy sharing. Even after 1514, when Wolsey clearly overshadowed Norfolk at court, he retained a more important position than Buckingham would ever achieve. In the years that followed, the two dukes remained members of different factions. In the spring of 1516, for example, when Buckingham was in high favor and "hath all his desires, with great thanks from the King," the earl of Surrey, his son-in-law, was "put out of the Council Chamber."[110] Whatever lay behind the mysterious undated letter in which Henry VIII instructed Wolsey to keep an eye on a small group of nobles, it is noteworthy that the group included Buckingham; his brother, the earl of Wiltshire; and his brother-in-law and ally Henry Percy, but neither Norfolk nor Surrey.[111] When Buckingham fell into disgrace in 1520 for illegally retaining a royal servant named Sir William Bulmer, he openly acknowledged Norfolk's influence at court by writing to him and his wife for help and advice.[112] The evidence does not indicate whether Norfolk actually tried to do anything for Buckingham at this juncture. We do know that when Buckingham was accused of treason less than a year later, Norfolk accepted appointment as lord high steward at his trial.[113]

The relatively scant evidence suggests that marriage ties also failed to produce a political alliance between Buckingham and another son-in-law, Lord Bergavenny. Apparently, he too belonged to a different faction. In 1516, when Buckingham was in such high favor, Bergavenny was put out of the council along with the duke's son-in-law, the earl of Surrey.[114] The indictment against Buckingham in 1521 charged that two years earlier he had told Bergavenny that if the king died, he intended to rule England. Buckingham did not trust Bergavenny to keep sensitive information to himself and on one occasion threatened that if Bergavenny repeated something he had said, he "would fight him in that quarrel, and strike him on the head with his sword." [115] Buckingham even tried to turn Bergavenny's brother, Sir Edward Neville, against him. He appointed Sir Edward steward of his lands in Kent and Surrey with an annual fee of £10, the customary payment being only £5, and gave him an additional pension of 100s. [116] The duke's chancellor stated that he had given Sir Edward a doublet of silver cloth and then bragged to Bergavenny that "he had gotton the good will of his brother . . . [and] was sure that my lord Bergavenny could not get the good will . . . from him." [117]

Buckingham did maintain cordial relations with his daughter-in-law Ursula's family, the Poles. The fact that a woman, Margaret, countess of Salisbury, was head of the Pole family probably facilitated this friendship since she was not Stafford's rival at court. Also, Ursula was married to the duke's heir and lived in his household, a situation that undoubtedly encouraged intimacy between the two families. The duke's accounts for 1519 reveal a great deal of social contact between them. In particular, he gambled frequently with Ursula's older brother, Henry Lord Montague. [118] The families became so close that the Venetian ambassador mistook the Pole brothers for Buckingham's nephews. [119] When the duke was arrested in 1521, no family came in for a greater share of the king's displeasure than the Poles.

Getting beyond a sketchy sense of personal relations between the Staffords is difficult because of the nature of the extant evidence: most of the information about the family appears incidentally in public documents or household and estate accounts. In the early Tudor period, there were no diaries and few letters written by members of the aristocracy themselves rather than by their secretaries. Most letters functioned to communicate information and to carry on business, not to express intimate feelings. Furthermore, in a period when society unequivocally defined the family in political and economic terms, and aristocratic families performed key functions in these areas, social convention encouraged close relatives to use the language of economic advantage and favor in their dealings with one another. This language may well have masked a great deal of emotion that is consequently invisible to historians, just as in our society, which emphasizes emotional relationships within the family, the language of emotion often masks economic calculation and the exercise of power.

The great exception to these generalizations regarding the lack of evidence about personal relations between the Staffords is the set of letters generated by the collapse of Elizabeth Stafford's marriage to Thomas Howard, by then third duke of Norfolk, in the 1530's. The duke of Buckingham, Elizabeth's father, had died years before, in 1521, but almost everyone else in the family was drawn into the public scandal accompanying her separation from her husband. In the correspondence generated by that unhappy event, the duchess of Norfolk and her relatives openly expressed their feelings about one another and explicitly discussed some of their attitudes toward family life. The letters are, therefore, a rare and valuable historical source.[120]

Trouble between the duke and duchess of Norfolk began in 1526 when Norfolk fell in love with a woman named Bess Holland, who became his mistress.[121] Infidelity was common, and at least tacitly acceptable, among men of the duke's class. Peers expected their wives to tolerate their extramarital affairs, but for some reason Duchess Elizabeth was unable or unwilling to do so. She justified her behavior by explaining that her husband had chosen her "for love."[122] She insisted that he, not her family or friends, had taken the initiative in courting her: "it was my Lord my husband's suit to my Lord my father, and never came of me nor none of my friends."[123] Therefore, she implied, he had no right to treat her as if theirs had been only a marriage of convenience. Whether the duchess had interpreted her husband's feelings correctly is an unanswerable question. Only fifteen at the time of her wedding, she may well have misunderstood her

35-year-old suitor. Perhaps she fell in love with him and mistakenly assumed he shared her feelings. In any case, she could not, or would not, look the other way when he lived openly at his main residence, Kenninghall, with Bess Holland.

In explaining her outrage, the duchess also claimed that she deserved better treatment because she had given birth to five of Norfolk's children, thus fulfilling one of a wife's major functions. Furthermore, she had always been faithful to him and had guarded her reputation. "I have lived always a good woman, as it is not unknown to him. I was daily waiter in the Court sixteen years together, when he hath lived from me more than a year in the King's wars. The King's Grace shall be my record how I used myself in my younger days: and here is a poor reward I have in my latter days for my well doing." [124] Her comments suggest that chastity could not be taken for granted among the aristocratic women at Henry VIII's court. The episode involving one of her Stafford aunts and Sir William Compton supports her judgment on that point. [125]

The duchess of Norfolk expressed particular anger at losing her husband to a woman of inferior social rank. She referred to his mistress contemptuously as "washer of my nursery," "that harlot," "a churl's daughter," and "that drab." [126] In fact, Bess Holland probably came from the minor gentry. Her father was the duke of Norfolk's steward, an office normally held by a man of gentle status. [127] Even the duchess acknowledged that the Hollands claimed some social standing through their kinship to Lord Hussey, although in her eyes Hussey was only a "late made" peer. [128] Bess Holland eventually became one of Anne Boleyn's ladies-in-waiting. [129] Even with Norfolk's great influence, she could hardly have held this position if she had not been of gentle birth.

Elizabeth's reaction to her husband's infidelity raises some interesting questions about the double standard, particularly as it affected wives. Most historians have analyzed it from the husband's point of view. Lawrence Stone claimed that extramarital affairs were common among noblemen because this was the only way for society to make the arranged marriage acceptable to them.[130] However, the prevalence of extramarital affairs in our own society, where marriages are almost universally arranged by the couple concerned and where most people claim to be marrying for love, casts serious doubt on his hypothesis. According to Keith Thomas, husbands insisted on exclusive sexual possession of their wives because they considered them a species of property devalued by other men's use. In his opinion, the insistence on female chastity had much less to do with men's desire to ensure that their estates passed to their rightful heirs than with the assertion of this property right.[131] Perhaps Baldassare Castiglione, who wrote during the period under discussion, came closest to the truth when he described the double standard as a blatant exercise of male power: "we men have arrogated to ourselves a license, whereby we insist that in us the same sins are most trivial and sometimes deserve praise which in women cannot be sufficiently punished."[132]

Both Stone and Thomas have assumed that women had so little emotional and romantic investment in their marriages or were so socialized to subordination to their husbands that they passively accepted social arrangements created by men for their own convenience. In the duchess of Norfolk's case, at least, this was simply not true. Since very little evidence from the early Tudor period touches on women's reactions to their husbands' infidelities, there is no ground for automatically dismissing her feelings as unique. Indeed, we have seen in Duke Edward's letter to the Fitzwalters some suggestion that her own mother, Alianore, duchess of Buckingham, had reacted angrily to what may have been one of *her* husband's extramarital affairs.[133] What was unusual in the duchess of Norfolk's case was the openness with which she protested against her husband's behavior, as well as her willingness to destroy her marriage rather than tolerate his infidelity.

Relations between the Howards deteriorated steadily until their quarrels became public knowledge. The duchess's uncontrolled anger and unrelenting protests against her husband's behavior made it more and more difficult for the couple to live together. By the early 1530's, Norfolk, who was unwilling to give up Bess Holland, decided that his only choice was to divorce or separate from his wife. He may have felt free to take drastic action because his wife's father had been attainted and the whole Stafford family was in disgrace. In 1533, both Norfolk and Thomas Cromwell wrote to the duchess's brother, Henry Stafford, asking whether the duchess could live with him.[134] His replies indicate that this was not the first time the request had been made.[135]

Stafford completely rejected their suggestion in two very explicit letters, one to Norfolk and one to Cromwell. He made clear that his sympathies were with his brother-in-law, not with his sister. In what appears to be an astonishing display of male solidarity, he blamed her "wild language," not the duke's infidelity, for the collapse of their marriage. She carried "this continual contention" so far as to "make him [Norfolk] to absent her company." Henry unquestioningly accepted the double standard and expected his sister to do the same. He never seems to have questioned the acceptability of male infidelity in marriage or considered its incompatibility with Christian morality.

What aroused Stafford's anger was the imprudence of his sister's behavior from a practical point of view—an imprudence that affected her relatives as well as herself. By constantly railing against a situation she ought to accept, she was ignoring the advice of "the best and wisest of her kin," and, even worse, "the gentle advertisement that his highness hath sent to her divers times." Instead of cavalierly throwing away the advantages of her marriage to the highest-ranking peer in the realm, she should call "to remembrance the great honour that she is come to by that noble man her husband, and in what possibility she was in to do all her friends good, if she had followed the king's highness' pleasure." Her unfortunate stubbornness made her husband "nothing to tender the preferment of any of her friends," and brought her "the king's high displeasure, which is to every true heart death, and her poor friends an continual hinderance, whereof our Lord knows they have no need."[136]

Henry Stafford expected, indeed demanded, that Duchess

Elizabeth recognize that the main purpose of her marriage was not her personal happiness but the social, political, and economic advancement of her kin. All her relatives stood to gain by her brilliant match; all consequently felt aggrieved by her intemperate behavior. It is hard to imagine a clearer statement of the reality of the extended family as a social unit, or of Miriam Slater's point that its solidarity depended on the recognition of the group's common interests.[137] The duchess of Norfolk was asserting her emotional needs against the interests of her kin in an environment that supported a different hierarchy of values.

In light of her past behavior, Henry Stafford rejected Cromwell's suggestion that he might be able to influence his sister for the better if she lived with him and that "a quietness and tranquillity between [husband and wife] might ensue and continue." On the contrary, Stafford felt he would only be making matters worse: "[I would be putting] myself in great jeopardy to match myself with her, that by her wild language might undo me and all mine, and never deserving the same."[138] He was clearly furious with Norfolk for even suggesting that he take his sister in.

Now I perceived you would constrain me to speak further than I thought to have done, or else I must grant that that should be my utter undoing—which is to put your grace in remembrance of her accustomed wild language, which lieth not in my power to stop whereby so great danger might ensue to me and all mine, though I never deserved it. Wherefore, I beseech your grace to pardon me, though I think [it] unkindness in your grace to desire that wherein your grace is assured by long experience, I can do no good, but put me and mine in great jeopardy.[139]

Henry Stafford's panic at the idea of being saddled with the duchess may seem excessive until one remembers that his father, the duke of Buckingham, had been executed in 1521 for saying things later construed as high treason. He was understandably sensitive about potentially dangerous talk.

His sister compounded her errors by openly opposing Henry VIII's divorce from Catherine of Aragon. In January 1531, Chapuys reported that "the duchess of Norfolk sent to tell the Queen that her opponents were trying to draw her over to their party, but that if all the world were to try it she would remain faithful to her."[140] A few months later, she was driven from court at Anne Boleyn's request "because she spoke too freely, and declared herself more than they liked for the Queen."[141] In 1533 the duchess refused to attend Anne's coronation "from the love she bore to the previous Queen."[142] How much she acted out of loyalty to Catherine of Aragon, how much out of empathy with a wife in a situation similar to her own, how much out of a vindictive desire to embarrass her husband, it is impossible to know. But contemporaries certainly recognized the parallel between her situation and the queen's. For example, a Mrs. Amadas was arrested for saying, among other "ungracious rehearsals," that "there was never a good married woman in England except prince Arthur's dowager [Catherine of Aragon], the duchess of Norfolk and herself," and that because "the king had foresaken his wife, he suffers her husband to do the same, but the good Emperor will deliver all good wives when he comes, which shall be shortly."[143] With such dangerous sentiments circulating, it is no wonder that cautious Henry Stafford wanted no part of his intemperate, free-speaking sister.

The duchess, for her part, remained unintimidated. Shortly after Anne Boleyn's coronation, she resisted still another mission from her relatives. On this occasion, the king sent her brother-in-law, Lord Bergavenny, to make an arrangement between her and her husband. Norfolk, who had just returned from France, was afraid to see his wife until after Bergavenny approached her for him. Bergavenny promised her "that the Duke should henceforth be a good husband," but what this assurance meant is unclear since Norfolk had no intention of giving up Bess Holland, the cause of all the trouble between them.[144]

According to the duchess, her husband had threatened her life and behaved violently toward her during their furious quarrels. She claimed that when she had been recovering from the birth of her daughter Mary, he had pulled her out of bed by the hair, dragged her around the house, and wounded her with a dagger.[145] In three separate letters to Thomas Cromwell, she repeated words to this effect: "he set his women to bind me till blood came out at my finger ends; and pinacled me, and set on my breast till I spit blood; and he never punished them."[146] She said that she had never recovered from this abuse.[147] After she and her husband separated, she expressed fear that if she returned home, her life "should be but short"[148] and that she "should be poisoned for the love that he beareth to the harlot Bess Holland."[149] How true these accusations were is impossible to tell. Norfolk explicitly denied the story that he had abused his wife while she was recovering from the birth of their daughter. "She had the scar in her head fifteen months before she was delivered of my said daughter. . . . Surely I think there is no man on live that would handle a woman in childbed of that sort, nor for my part would not so have done for all that I am worth."[150] In another letter he protested, "apparent false lies were never contrived by a wife of her husband that she doth daily increase of me."[151]

In March 1534, the Howards finally separated, a step apparently taken on the duke's initiative, since the duchess always referred later to the fact that he had put her away.[152] According to her, the final break occurred after he had been away and returned in a temper: "he came riding all night, and locked me up in a chamber, and took away all my jewels and all my apparel."[153] From then on, she lived in a house rented from the crown in Redbourne, Hertfordshire,[154] and referred to herself as being like a prisoner: "None comes at me but such as he appointeth."[155] Elsewhere she wrote, "I am so shamefully handled, and have so poor a living, that no gentlemen nor gentlewoman dare not come at me; but as my Lord appoints to know my mind, and to counsel me after his fashion."[156] Again, in 1539: "I am so well used to imprisonment I care not for it; for he will suffer no gentlemen to come to me . . . and very few gentlewomen."[157] She obviously had no freedom of movement, since in 1541 she wrote to her brother-in-law, the earl of Westmorland, "I pray God that I may break my prisonment that I have had this seven year, that I may come abroad and see my friends."[158]

The duchess's isolation during these years was emphasized by her estrangement from her elder son and her daughter, both of whom sided with their father. She considered them ungracious, unkind, and unnatural;[159] on one occasion she referred to them as "*his* children."[160] In a society where an important function of the family was to allocate economic goods controlled by the father, their behavior was predictable. Furthermore, however the duchess saw her situation, she had ignored the behavioral norms of her social milieu and persistently rejected the advice of her monarch and kin. In such circumstances she was probably unrealistic in expecting support from her children. Her daughter had particularly cogent reasons for dissociating herself from her troublesome mother. Through her father's influence, she married Henry VIII's illegitimate son, the duke of Richmond. When he died prematurely at the age of 17, she became completely dependent on her royal father-in-law for her jointure. Duchess Elizabeth's correspondence indicates that Mary had great difficulty securing her financial rights, despite Anne Boleyn's promise that she would have £1,000.[161] Mary was in no position to defy the king.

During the early years of their separation, the duchess sought a reconciliation with her husband. In her correspondence with Thomas Cromwell, she referred to "two gentle letters" that she had written to Norfolk but that he had not answered.[162] In June 1535 she approached the king when the court was at Dunstable "and put my matter to his Grace to make an end."[163] But since Henry VIII was unlikely to force her husband to get rid of Bess Holland, and the duchess was no more willing to accept his mistress than before, there was very little the king could do about the fundamental problem. Perhaps the duchess simply hoped that he would force Norfolk to release her from imprisonment or to make some satisfactory financial arrangement with her. In any case, "by the King's commandment," she wrote her husband still a third "gentle" letter.[164] When he once again failed to answer, she resolved: "from this day forward I will never sue to the King, nor to none other, to desire my Lord my husband to take me again." She well knew that if he took her back, there would be only one reason: "it is more for the shame of the world than for any love he beareth me." Her husband would never give up Bess Holland, who still lived at Kenninghall. Therefore, if the duchess returned home, the bitter quarrels between her and her husband would simply begin again. Rather than that, she preferred to remain where she was. "I have been well used, since I have been from him, to a quiet life, and if I should come to him, to use me as he did, he [i.e. it] would grete me worse now than it did before; because I have lived quiet these three years, without brawling or fighting."[165]

Nonetheless, despite the duchess's comment, the conflict between the Howards continued. The central point of contention shifted, however. The duchess's main concern now was to receive an adequate living from her husband. She seemed even more interested in that than in ending her state of semi-imprisonment. Although she had been promised a jointure of 500 marks at the time of her marriage, Norfolk was giving her an allowance of only 300 marks a year. She claimed that her allowance did not adequately support her household of twenty.[166] She also wanted the clothes and jewels that her husband had taken from her. The duchess knew that only the king would be able to force the duke to return them; she counted on Thomas Cromwell to persuade Henry VIII to act on her behalf despite her defiance of the king on a number of occasions. Most of our information about the Howards' marriage comes from the letters that the duchess sent to Cromwell in connection with her suit.

In the first of these letters, written in August 1535, the duchess referred to a book of articles and a letter that she had sent Cromwell "to entreat my lord my husband to have a better living."[167] The articles have not survived but, judging from Elizabeth's subsequent correspondence, they probably contained a lengthy recitation of all her grievances against Norfolk and a defense of her own conduct. As was usual when she acted in her own behalf, the duchess embarrassed and antagonized her relatives. One of her aunts, Anne Hastings, countess of Huntingdon, wrote asking her to rescind the articles. Henry VIII and

Cromwell did the same. But the duchess was as stubborn as ever and wrote in December 1536, "I will never deny the said two articles during my life. And so I pray you shew my Lord my husband, that I will never deny them, for no ill handling that he can do to me: nor for no imprisonment . . . seeing that I will not do it at the King's commandment, nor at your desire. I will not do it for no friend nor kin I have living."[168]

For five years, the duchess of Norfolk deluged Cromwell with entreaties for his help in getting her jointure. He encouraged her enough so that she believed she had his promise to help her with her suit. But, despite her flattery, "you be called so true of your promise," neither her letters nor her gifts to him did any good.[169] At one point Cromwell advised her to return home on whatever terms she could, advice she rejected out of hand. "I pray you, my lord, take no displeasure with me, although I have not followed your lordship's good counsel, and your letters, as touching my lord my husband for to come home again, which I will never do during my life."[170]

Meanwhile, the duke of Norfolk was furious at the duchess for continuing to air her grievances against him publicly. Thinking she would behave more submissively if she lived in someone else's household rather than her own, he wrote to Cromwell, before setting out on a journey: "I require you by your wisdom to find the means my wife may sojourn in some honest place, and I shall help her with some better living if she so do—and surely if she do not, and continue in her most false and abominable lies and obstinacy against me, if God bring me home again, I shall not fail, unless the king's highness command me to the contrary, to lock her up."[171] The duchess firmly resisted all pressure on this point. She felt that although her husband had promised to give her more money if she agreed, his real intention was "to keep me barer than I am." He would also expect anyone she lived with "to bring me to his purpose and rule me." Past experience of the duchess's sojourns in other people's homes showed that she could not be influenced that way. The end result, therefore, would only be to cause trouble between Norfolk and her hosts. With admirable self-possession, she wrote: "I am of age to rule myself, as I have done these five years, since my lord my husband put me away. Seeing that my lord my husband reckoned me to be so unreasonable, it were better that I kept me away, and keep my own house still, and trouble no other body, as I am sure I should so."[172]

One of Norfolk's purposes during this period was to secure his wife's agreement to a divorce.[173] In return for her consent, he offered her all her jewels and clothing, "and a great part of his plate, and of his stuff of household." The duke wrote to Elizabeth in his own hand about the matter, and the duchess was well aware that "he had liever than a £1,000 he could have brought me to have been divorced." But once again the duchess proved obdurate, resisting a suggestion "to put me to shame."[174] On this point alone, she proved successful; she remained Norfolk's legal wife until his death in 1554.

The duchess's remarkable letters to Cromwell ended in 1539, when he was struggling desperately to maintain his position in the government. After his fall, she did not correspond with anyone else at court about her difficulties. Since she had been away from court for years, she may not have known anyone with great influence whom she felt she could trust. Or, perhaps, after years of controversy, she had become resigned to her situation and tired of expending so much time and energy on fruitless quarrels with her husband.

In any case, the only one of her letters from the 1540's that has survived reflects a mood of tranquillity and goodwill. A short note to her brother-in-law, the earl of Westmorland, thanked him for all the efforts he had made on her behalf over the years, and asked him to make no further suits to her husband for her. Along with the letter, she sent gifts for him, for her sister Catherine, and for her niece Dorothy. She asked to be remembered to her aunt and uncle, the earl and countess of Huntingdon, should Westmorland see them, and expressed the hope that someday she would be free to leave Redbourne to visit her friends.[175]

At some point, Elizabeth and her brother, Henry, were reconciled. Sometime before 1547 Henry sent one of his many daughters to live with her. In an undated letter to him, the duchess reported that her niece Susan was "in good health and merry." But Duchess Elizabeth clearly preferred her niece Dorothy and tried to persuade Henry to send her in Susan's place. "If you send me any of your daughters, I pray you to send me my niece Dorothy, for I am well acquainted with her conditions already, and so I am not with the others; and she is youngest, too; and if she be changed, therefore, she is better to break as concerning her youth." [176] The comment about breaking Dorothy if her behavior had changed for the worse reveals the harsh discipline characteristic of some members of the early Tudor peerage. The phrase is noteworthy because the concept of breaking the child's will is often associated with the Puritans of the Elizabethan and Jacobean periods. [177]

Whether Duchess Elizabeth succeeded in exchanging Susan for Dorothy is unknown, but she apparently was exceedingly generous to whichever girl remained with her. Henry wrote her a warm letter in 1547 thanking her for her kindness and generosity toward his daughter. The duchess not only had paid her living expenses, but also had bought her clothes and given her spending money. [178] Henry told his sister that he planned to go to London after Easter and that he hoped to visit her at that time. The duchess had obviously expressed a great longing for his visit since he closed by saying, "And thus I praye god send your grace your noble herte desyre." [179] Significantly, Henry's visit was planned after her husband had been arrested and imprisoned in the Tower of London. [180]

Eleven years later, when Elizabeth wrote her will, she named Henry her residual heir and sole executor. She left his wife, Ursula, affectionately described as her "suster Stafford," all her apparel and jewelry, including her "best Frenche hode [and her] best sadle, with the cover of velvett, and all that belongith therto." [181] In turn, Henry Stafford wrote an exceedingly flattering epitaph for her tomb, which included these lines: "Thou was to me, both far and near, A Mother, sister, a friend most dear." [182]

One would hardly guess that he was writing about the sister he had once characterized as having a "sensual and wilful mind."[183]

The letters growing out of Elizabeth's unhappy marriage raise serious questions about the belief that emotional distance and coolness between husband and wife characterized the arranged marriages of the early Tudor period; and that members of the nobility, particularly women, accepted the predominance of the economic and political interests of family and kin over their interests as individuals. The marriage of the duke and duchess of Norfolk was clearly an emotionally explosive one. The duchess expected love and fidelity from her husband, and she defied the king, her relatives, and the social conventions of her age when she received neither. That the duchess's behavior was considered eccentric and outrageous is beyond doubt; all the contemporary sources make that clear. What is not clear, however, is how different her expectations and emotions were from those of other women of her class. Women, after all, did not invent or benefit greatly from either the arranged marriage or the double standard. They had little choice about acquiescing in these institutions, but that does not mean they accepted the values on which they were based.

Duchess Elizabeth's life also illustrated the powerlessness of women within the noble family. Women might occasionally act on the public stage, particularly when crises occurred in their husbands' absence (as her sister Catherine did), but they had no meaningful control over their own lives. The duke of Buckingham viewed his daughters as interchangeable pieces in a complicated game whose object was to marry them off in the interests of the Stafford lineage. The fact that peers' daughters brought huge dowries into their spouses' families gave them little leverage, since their husbands or fathers-in-law controlled the money. After more than twenty years of marriage, the duke of Norfolk was able to throw his wife out of his home, take away her clothes and jewels, imprison her for years, and probably even physically abuse her. Although there is no suggestion in the sources that the duchess's large and influential kin group felt her marriage had removed her from the Stafford family, none of her relatives did anything to alleviate her situation, because they were either unwilling or unable to do so. Perhaps if the duchess's father had still been alive, her husband would not have dared to treat her as callously and brutally as he did.[184] As the story stands, however, it is hard to imagine a more dramatic example of the reality of patriarchal power in the early sixteenth-century aristocratic family.

## CHAPTER FOUR

# The Great Household at Thornbury

The third duke of Buckingham's lifetime fell squarely within the period that David Starkey has astutely called "the age of the household."[1] For the magnates, the household performed four functions: it provided the lord and resident members of his family with the necessities of life, it testified to his social and economic position through its size and splendor, it administered the estates on which his wealth depended, and it provided the core of his political and military power. At the center of the household stood the biological family. Past generations of the family had accumulated the property and titles that gave the current head of household his status, wealth, and power; the present generation functioned to preserve his position and transmit it to his heirs.

The households of the nobility were designed to turn the ordinary activities of daily life into visual and ceremonial forms that demonstrated the political, social, and economic hegemony of their class. The ethos of the peerage placed a high value on magnificence, the visual expression of a man's worth.[2] In the late fifteenth and early sixteenth centuries, the household was the chosen vehicle for demonstrating that magnificence. Conspicuous consumption was a hallmark of nobility, and largesse, or openhandedness, was one of the most admired qualities of the age.[3] A large household advertised its lord's wealth and provided the foundation of his public power by drawing large numbers of people of all classes into his service. At the same time, its permeability to outsiders turned it into a stage for displaying the high status of its lord and his family. Elaborate ceremonials regulated daily life, particularly the service of meals, which became a form of theater.[4] Magnates who did not live in an extravagant and public style sacrificed their dignity and lost the respect of both their peers and their social inferiors.

To achieve the desired degree of magnificence, Buckingham maintained a household that consisted of about 125 people. In addition to members of his family, residents included the duke's councillors, chaplains, personal attendants, domestic servants, visiting estate officials and tenants, members of the local gentry, artisans in temporary employment, traveling minstrels, and beggars. In his account for the year 1504, Richard Mynors, treasurer of the household, stated that the household included 130 persons.[5] A household book covering the period from November 5, 1507, to March 22, 1508, shows that at least a hundred people (and usually something more like 125) ate at the duke's expense each day.[6] A roll of the duke's servants drawn up shortly after his son's wedding in 1519 listed 148 persons;[7] even when he was traveling, Stafford's entourage usually included at least sixty.[8] A dozen or more servants were attached to the duchess, who rewarded thirteen gentlewomen in the fiscal year ending March 1517.[9] The nursery employed a staff of five, including three gentlewomen and a laundress.[10] Although these numbers seem large to us, they were not unusual among the early Tudor nobility. Buckingham's brother-in-law, the fifth earl of Northumberland, had a household of 166.[11] Paul Jones, who studied eighteen household accounts and regulations for the period 1462–1640, estimated that noble households usually numbered between 75 and 140.[12]

Within this huge establishment, the Staffords surrounded themselves with hordes of liveried retainers and servants, dispensed alms generously, wore lavish clothing, accumulated large stocks of jewelry and gold and silver plate, and offered hospitality to anyone coming to their doors. The duke's servants contributed to the visual splendor of the household by wearing the black-and-red Stafford livery. In December 1515, the duke gave cloth for uniforms to 149 persons, 80 of whom were members of the household.[13] A similar list of 199 persons who received livery cloth in the year ending March 30, 1517, includes 84 household servants.[14]

One of the most striking forms of extravagance in Buckingham's household was the consumption of huge quantities of food. On an ordinary day, Stafford, his family, his guests, and his servants ate 220 loaves of bread, 9 quarts of Gascon wine, 81 flagons of beer, 12 rounds of beef, 4 sheep, ½ deer, ½ pig, 2 geese, 2 suckling pigs, 3 capons, 7 rabbits, 3 woodcocks, 1 mallard, 6 swans, 8 lambs, 60 eggs, and 4 dishes of butter.[15]

During holidays the size of the duke's household doubled or tripled. Although the feasts at Thornbury on Christmas 1507 and Epiphany 1508 are famous among historians of the early Tudor period, they were probably not atypical and would seem less remarkable if descriptions of other feasts had survived. On Christmas Day, 294 persons dined at Thornbury; on Epiphany, 459.[16] The quantity of food consumed on Epiphany was astounding: 678 loaves of bread, 8 gallons and 6 pitchers of wine, 259 flagons of beer, 36 rounds of beef, 12 sheep, 2 calves, 4 pigs, 1 dried ling, 2 salt cod, 2 hard fish, 1 salt sturgeon, 3 swans, 6 geese, 6 suckling pigs, 10 capons, 1 lamb, 2 peacocks, 2 herons, 22 rabbits, 18 chickens, 9 mallards, 23 widgeons, 18 teals, 16 woodcocks, 20 snipes, 9 dozen large birds, 6 dozen small birds, 3 dozen larks, 9 quail, ½ fresh salmon, 1 fresh cod, 4 dogfish, 2 tench, 7 small beams, ½ fresh conger, 21 small roaches, 6 large fresh eels, 10 small whitings, 18 flounders, 100 lampreys, 3 plaice, 400 eggs, 24 dishes of butter, 15 flagons of milk, 3 flagons of cream, 2 gallons of frumenty, and 200 oysters.[17] Buckingham and his family clearly conformed to the pattern of behavior noted by an Italian visitor to England in this period. "They take great pleasure in having a quantity of excellent victuals, and also in remaining a long time at table. . . . They think no greater love can be conferred, or received, than to invite others to eat with them, or to be invited themselves."[18]

The Stafford household consumed these enormous quantities of food in an atmosphere of almost boundless opulence. The duke and his family dressed in the finest silks, satins, and velvets, adorned themselves with jewels and furs, and drank from gold and silver cups. The best evidence of the magnificence of Buckingham's lifestyle comes from two extant wardrobe accounts that list everything other than food purchased during 1503–4 and 1514–15. William Cholmeley's account for the twelve months ending in March 1504 recorded the purchases of 6 pearls from Cyprus, 8 pairs of French gloves, an ivory comb, 3 pairs of ivory beads, yards of silk ribbon, a collar of gold powder, 5 gold crucifixes, 17 gold tokens, a gilt sword, 5 gilt daggers, a gilt wooden box, 2 black velvet coats with goldsmiths' work, diverse sorts of feathers, a huge amount of fur (including 4 ermine skins), and yards and yards of expensive textiles, such as velvet, satin, and fustian. In all, the duke spent £125 on cloth, £226 5s on textiles, £62 13s on "precious things and jewels," and £25 2s on furs and skins.[19] Thomas Bridges's account for the year ending in 1517 shows a marked rise in the duke's expenditures. He reported outlays of £147 14s on cloth, £429 18s on textiles, £150 14s on jewels and other valuable items, and £13 14s on furs.[20] In September 1520, an inventory valued the duke's plate at £2,494. The collection included flagons, pots, bottles, cups, saltcellars, crucifixes, goblets, chafing dishes, shaving basins, candlesticks, and gold, silver, and gilt chapel plate.[21]

The kind of conspicuous consumption that characterized Buckingham's entire life was carried to its extreme in the clothes he wore on great state occasions. In 1500, when Henry VII met Archduke Philip at Calais, a richly dressed company accompanied him, "especyalle the duke of Buckyngham, in soo large and so riche a gowne of clothe of golde, his courser richly trapped, and the trapper enramplished with littel prety belles of silver and gilt, of a very goodly fascyon."[22] The next year he appeared at the wedding of Prince Arthur and Catherine of Aragon in a gown "wroughth of nedyll work and sett upon cloth of tyssu furrid wyth sablys," a gown valued at £1,500.[23] Nine years later, after Henry VIII's marriage to Catherine, the king entered London accompanied by "many well apparaylyd Gentylman, But in esspeciall the duke of Bukkyngham . . . In a Goune of Goldsmythys werk a thyng of grete Rycchesse." [24] The duke appeared in his most splendid outfit in 1513 when Henry met Emperor Maximilian in France. All the noblemen who had gone on the campaign were there, all "gorgiously apparrelled," all outshone by Buckingham, who wore "purple Satten, his apparel . . . full of Antelops and Swannes of fine gold Bullion and full of Spangles, and little Belles of golde, marueylous costly and pleasant to behold." [25]

The household of an early Tudor nobleman was designed to emphasize the master's high status and dignity, as well as to display his enormous wealth. To maintain the decorum appropriate to his rank, he conducted his daily life with formality and ceremony. Household regulations set out in the greatest detail such matters as the number and rank of those attending the lord and his family during the day, and the seating arrangement and serving order for meals. [26] A major concern in all these regulations was to distinguish between people of different ranks and to ensure that they were treated accordingly. The hierarchical concept of the great chain of being permeated social life at all levels. The effect, of course, was to further exalt the lord and his family, since they occupied a status higher than that of anyone else in the household.

The preoccupation with drawing social distinctions spatially and visually was most obvious at mealtime. People of different ranks ate at different tables, and seating at each table was carefully arranged. In the duke of Buckingham's household, tables were set up in both the great chamber and the hall. The duke and his family ate in the great chamber. [27] Another table or "knights' board" probably was set up there for any knights, gentlemen, and gentlewomen who were present. [28] Everyone else ate in the hall, where the treasurer, marshall, and clerk of the kitchen each headed a table. The rank of everyone eating in the house was carefully recorded each day. Regular members of the household were classified as gentry, yeomen or valets, and grooms or garcons. Strangers (i.e. nonresidents) were also carefully listed. People of high status were listed by name with the number of their servants; those of lower status were referred to solely by their occupational titles.[29]

The elaborate service at meals and the huge quantity of food consumed meant that eating took up a good part of the day. At the home of Buckingham's brother-in-law, the fifth earl of Northumberland, dinner lasted from 10:00 A.M. to 1:00 P.M., supper from 4:00 to 7:00.[30] Nonetheless, a magnate did not spend his entire life at table. Unless he was completely feckless, he had to set some time aside on a regular basis for business of one sort or another—supervising the management of his property, checking household and estate accounts, keeping an eye on his overall financial position, solving the endless problems and disputes arising among his household servants, estate officials, and tenants, attending to his complicated legal affairs, and cultivating his political position on both the local and the national level. But because he had a large staff to assist him, a peer still had plenty of time for leisure activities.

To entertain his huge household, Buckingham maintained minstrels, a bear, and an idiot. He also welcomed the itinerant entertainers who continually made their way to Thornbury. The cofferer's accounts for 1508 show rewards to the minstrels of the king, the earl of Oxford, the earl of Arundel, and Lord Dacre, to the waits of Warwick and London, to a harpist named William Esgate, to a Welsh harpist, to two wrestlers, and to two groups of anonymous minstrels.[31] Two minstrels, six trumpeters, four waits from Bristol, and four players sent by the earl of Northumberland were present during the feast of the Epiphany that year.[32] In 1520, the cofferer recorded the presence of a female tumbler, "certain Egyptians," and "certain Frenchmen and two Frenchwomen playing the passion."[33]

When Buckingham first came of age, he lived at Penshurst in Kent and Bletchingley in Surrey.[34] He soon made Thornbury, Gloucestershire, his principal residence, although his household still retained some of the itinerant quality of an earlier age. From time to time, he took up residence at one of his other manors. He also attended the king for a month or more each year. Records of his presence at court exist for every year except two between 1498 when he came of age and 1521 when he died.[35] Buckingham, whose religion expressed itself in a scrupulous attachment to external forms of piety and ritual, also spent a month or more around Easter visiting local shrines and relics. Finally, great state occasions, military campaigns, diplomatic meetings, and festivals at court regularly drew him from home.

In 1503, for example, Buckingham's household moved between Thornbury, Newport, and London.[36] Records for 1508, 1519, and 1520 give us an idea of his movements in a typical year. In 1508, he was at court or in progress from January 28 through February 28, at the monastery of Kaynsham in Somerset and nearby religious shrines from March 29 to June 30, and at court again from July 2 to August 1. He was not back at Thornbury until September, for on August 27 he paid a visit to Hatfield Broadoak, one of his manors in Essex.[37] In 1519, he was with the king from at least July 9 to August 11, when the court made its celebrated visit to Penshurst.[38] From there he moved to Bletchingley, where he was in residence from September 10 to October 2.[39] In 1520, he was at Bletchingley in January and February, probably stopping on the way either to or from court.[40] On May 10 he was in London, and on the 27th and 28th at Canterbury for the meeting between Henry VIII and Charles V.[41] Immediately following this conference, he crossed the Channel with the king for the month-long festivities at the Field of Cloth of Gold.[42] In July he was at Gravelines, still on the other side of the Channel, for a second meeting between Henry VIII and Charles V.[43] From September until the following February he was back at Thornbury, but then he began a month of movement between the shrines at Tewkesbury, Winchecombe, and Haile.[44]

Like most men of his class, Buckingham was an enthusiastic hunter. His accounts show him pursuing this sport in the king's woods on the way from London in 1508, during his visit to the relics at the abbey of Glastonbury later in the year, and at the abbey of Gloucester in March 1521.[45] Indeed, during his annual progresses at Easter, he spent as much time hunting as visiting religious shrines.

Something of Buckingham's great interest in the hunt comes through in the lengthy instructions he gave to his estate officials in 1504. He wandered from the melancholy business of raising his revenue to remind them to see to "the keping of the almaner [of] oure game." Every year after Easter they were to inspect his parks and game, and charge the keeper with any damage to wood or deer. Above all, "nooman undre the degree of a lord [is to] be suffred to have shot, sute ne course withoute oure speciall warraunt."[46] The 23 well-stocked deer parks on the duke's estates when he died testify to the vigilant enforcement of this policy.[47]

The articles directed his officials "that ye doo [order] almaner of hawkes . . . to be saved for us and meane devised how they may be sent us from yere to yere."[48] Satisfying the duke in this matter required constant supervision and care by his bailiffs, as a book of information compiled from their reports in 1516 makes clear. John Walhed, bailiff of Kneshall, reported that he had surveyed all Buckingham's lands in Nottinghamshire but found only one nest of lanards in Radcliffe upon Soar. He showed them to the bailiff and the duke's other servants at that manor and charged them "with the saufe kepynge and conveyinge of them to my lord's use."[49] The book also contains the statements of two inhabitants of Bletchingley that lanards had never bred there before 1515. Apparently, officials of the duke's manor had sent him some lanards for the first time that year, and he was checking to make certain that he had not been cheated on earlier occasions.[50]

His passion for hunting turned Buckingham into a notorious encloser, for he was continually enlarging the deer parks at Thornbury. According to the 1517 inquisitions of enclosure and depopulation, he enclosed 172 acres of demesne and 98 acres of land occupied by copyholders to form New Park in 1508. Seven years later he enlarged it by adding 116 acres of demesne and 47 of pasture, the pasture again occupied by customary tenants. At the same time, he added 164 acres of demesne and 16 of pasture to the older Marlewood Park.[51]

The duke had secured a license from the crown in 1510 to make 1,000 acres at Thornbury a park and another for a further 500 acres in 1517, so these enclosures were not illegal.[52] They were, however, exceedingly unpopular with his tenants, who complained both to the commission appointed in 1517 to inquire into enclosures and to the crown officials surveying Buckingham's lands after his death. The commission's returns for Gloucestershire included reports on the duke's enclosures at Thornbury.[53] The surveyors of 1521 discussed the plight of the dispossessed tenants.

The late duke of Bukkingham haith enclosed into the said [New] parke divers mennes landes aswell of free hoolde as copyhoode and noe recompense as yet is made for the same. And lately he haith also enclosed into the same park two fair tenements with barnes and other houses well buylded with stoon and slate with 500 acres of lande and as yet the tennents contynue in the same. Wherin of necessities some redress muste be aither in amoving the said tenements from oute of the parke with convenient recompense or elles in taking ynne the pale as it stoode afore.

They estimated that rents and farms worth £48 19s 3d were decayed because of the enclosures.[54] Henry VIII was apparently in no hurry to remedy the situation and failed to act on the tenants' petition. In desperation, they asked Sir John Daunce to intercede with the king for them.[55] They claimed that 28 customary tenures, parts of 40 others, and 2 freeholds had been taken into Buckingham's parks to "the utter undoyng of your pouer compaynaunts, the kyngs tenaunts."[56]

In other parts of his estates, Buckingham's enclosures were on a much smaller scale. He added twenty acres to the park of Bremkamyck in Huntingdonshire; thirteen of these acres had been pasture, six arable land.[57] In Staffordshire, he enclosed some waste lying between the parish church of Forebridge and the inhabitants' houses.[58] Here he was careful to leave enough common land for the tenants and the adjoining highway. Finally, in the East Riding of Yorkshire, he converted 100 acres of land into pasture, without, according to the commission of 1517, damaging any house or arable land.[59] He wanted to enclose the forest at Hatfield Broadoak, but the tenants objected "that it was never enclosed nor they whyll not assent to the closure."[60] The duke bowed to the opposition, and the forest was still in its original state when he died two years later.

Buckingham also spent a considerable amount of time supervising the rebuilding of his manor at Thornbury, an ambitious project that was still incomplete in 1521. He secured a license to castellate Thornbury in 1510, but evidence exists that work had actually begun some years earlier.[61] His intention was to create an appropriate setting for his lavish style of life in a building that retained many of the defensive features of the traditional castle.

Historians do not agree on the significance of the defensive military features at Thornbury. The main gate had a portcullis and towers, the ground floor of the outer court had openings only for crossbows and guns, and the inner court was surrounded by a massive wall with battlements. W. D. Simpson called Thornbury "the last great baronial house in England to be built in the old castellated style, retaining something of the serious purpose of medieval fortification";[62] Lawrence Stone noted that it was the "last private castle to be built from scratch in England."[63] Both Simpson and Stone underscored the continuity of Thornbury with the past, an emphasis that supports the more general interpretation of Buckingham as an overmighty lord in the tradition of the late middle ages. K. B. McFarlane, on the other hand, had a very different view. He considered Thornbury indefensible and regarded the military features "only as romantic adjuncts of nobility."[64] The oriel windows on the external walls of the inner court belied a serious military purpose.

The truth probably lies somewhere between these two views. As A. D. K. Hawkyard pointed out, the oriel windows and the side gate without a portcullis suggested that Thornbury was not designed as a center of war and rebellion.[65] On the other hand, the military features at Thornbury might well have been adequate for defensive purposes in a small-scale emergency. The duke was probably planning for just such a contingency. Thornbury was located on the borders of the tumultuous Welsh marches, where Buckingham was an unpopular absentee landlord and an obvious target in the event of a popular rebellion.[66]

Furthermore, building a fortified manor like Thornbury did not make the duke an anachronism or prove that he had dangerous ambitions, as both Simpson and Stone suggested. In this case, as in so many others, neither 1485 nor 1509 marked a definitive landmark in English history. Sir William Paulet received a license to fortify Basing in 1530, Sir William Fitzwilliam a license to fortify Cowdray in 1534, and Sir Thomas Wriothesley a license to fortify Titchfield Abbey in 1542.[67] As late as the 1570's, the earl of Leicester modernized and heavily fortified Kenilworth.[68] Nonetheless, Stone and Rawcliffe are probably correct that the duke's plans for castellating Thornbury contributed to Henry VIII's doubts about his loyalty.[69]

Thornbury was planned around two courts.[70] The outer opened directly on the countryside and had no openings on the ground floor except gunports and loopholes for crossbows. The only entrance was through a gatehouse with portcullis topped by a tower. An inscription over the gateway stated, "Thys Gate was begon in the Yere of oure Lorde Gode MCCCCCXI, the ii yere of the reyne of Kynge Henri the VIII, by me Edw Duc of Bukkyngha. Erlle of Herford. Stafforde and Northampton."[71] The court housed the duke's officers and servants; it had stables on the ground floor and living quarters, reached by exterior wooden stairs, above. W. D. Simpson described it as "a veritable barracks." He remarked that "from the exterior, its long array of walls and towers, well provided with crosslets and gunloops, gives the impression of a town enceinte."[72] The court contained an area of about two and a half acres.

The inner court, or main castle, was approached through a second gatehouse, again equipped with a portcullis. Crowning the archway was the shield of Stafford, bearing a chevron of gold and the four badges of the family: the golden knot, the silver swan, the blue-ermined mantle, and the spotted antelope. This court contained an area of about half an acre. A porter's lodge with a dungeon underneath, the duke's and duchess's wardrobes, two steward's chambers, and four other rooms with chimneys adjoined the gatehouse leading into this court. The buildings in this part of the castle had large oriel windows on the ground floor and lacked the characteristics of military structures, yet even they were protected by a massive, embattled outer wall.

Along the left side of the court were all the cooking facilities needed to provide for a huge household—a wet and a dry larder, a bakehouse, the great kitchen, and a privy kitchen—with lodgings above. The lodgings included four rooms called the earl of Stafford's lodgings, which may well have been occupied by the duke's son and heir. Opposite the entrance to the court was the great hall, which Buckingham retained from the old building and which still had a central open hearth. A gallery connected the hall with the kitchen. Entered from one side of the hall, the castle chapel was a building large enough to contain stalls for 22 "priests, clerks and queristers."[73] The main floor of the chapel had a large space for worshipers. Over it were two private rooms, where the duke and duchess could sit when they worshiped in the chapel.

The duke's and duchess's living quarters, on the right side of the inner court as one entered, were the only parts of Thornbury completed before Buckingham's death. The ground floor contained the duchess's living apartments. A stairway from the great hall to the first floor of this wing led through an anteroom to the great chamber, the duke's dining room, his private room, and his bedroom. A private garden of about a third of an acre adjoined these private quarters. Finally, a group of thirteen isolated rooms known as the earl of Bedford's lodgings, probably used for guests, adjoined the right side of the hall. The whole area within the castle walls was about twelve acres.

A notable feature of the arrangement of the inner court was the duke's alteration of the traditional castle plan to secure greater privacy for himself and his family. Stone dated the increasing importance of privacy among the upper classes from the seventeenth century, but the plan of Thornbury indicates that Buckingham felt something of this impulse in the early sixteenth.[74] Usually, the lord's dining room adjoined the great hall, with free

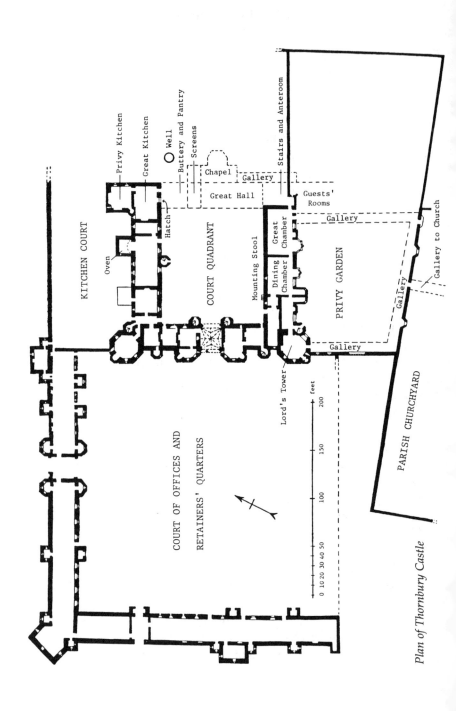

Plan of Thornbury Castle

KITCHEN COURT

Privy Kitchen
Great Kitchen
Well
Buttery and Pantry
Screens
Oven
Chapel
Gallery
Great Hall
Stairs and Anteroom
Hatch
COURT QUADRANT
Mounting Stool
Guests' Rooms
Gallery
Dining Chamber
Great Chamber
PRIVY GARDEN
Gallery
Lord's Tower
Gallery
Gallery
Gallery to Church
COURT OF OFFICES AND RETAINERS' QUARTERS

PARISH CHURCHYARD

feet
0 10 20 30 40 50    100    150    200

movement between the two rooms. Here, however, they were separated by the great chamber, to which access was restricted by the interposition of an anteroom. Furthermore, by means of a gallery running from the great chamber to the chapel, the duke could attend religious services without passing through the public rooms of the castle. Once there, he worshiped apart from other members of his household in the small private rooms reserved for his use.[75]

Thornbury was built in the late Gothic style, which dominated English architecture from the reign of Henry VI until well into the sixteenth century.[76] Contemporary architects and craftsmen sought novelty in the exuberant development of decorative features, especially brick chimney stacks and windows.[77] Although the chimneys at Hampton Court are probably the most widely known example of the extravagance and variety that could be achieved in this style of architecture, the main shaft at Thornbury, completed in 1516, was "not only among the finest, but also among the earliest that survive."[78] The oriel and bay windows were also outstanding, even in a period that expended an unusual amount of energy on this form of decoration. Authorities on early Tudor homes praise the windows at Thornbury for "the diversity of their plans and the skill exhibited in carrying out such difficult masonry." They were "the most elaborate and the most successful of all that have survived."[79] Simpson considered Thornbury "one of the most vivid and charming examples left to us of the latest phase of English gothic."[80]

It would be interesting to know how much money Buckingham spent on rebuilding Thornbury, but the documentation has not survived. The duke's cofferer's accounts show expenditures of £147 in 1508;[81] £823 in 1514;[82] and £100 in 1521.[83] Unused timber worth £20 and stone worth £17 10s were found at the site after Stafford was executed in 1521.[84] These figures suggest that the duke spent several thousand pounds on the portion of the castle completed before his death.[85]

Although Buckingham spent most of his time on worldly activities and pleasures, he was also concerned with the state of his soul. By the standards of his time and class, he was a pious man. As we have seen, he spent at least a month around Easter visiting religious shrines in the neighborhood of Thornbury. In 1508 he stopped at the monasteries of Kaynsham, Glastonbury, and Henton in Somersetshire, and St. Augustine in Bristol, as well as the shrine of St. Anne in the Wood just outside the city.[86] In addition to the monasteries of Haile, Tewkesbury, and Winchcombe, all in Gloucestershire, his progress in 1521 included the shrine of the Holy Rood on the outskirts of Gloucester.[87] His frequent journeys to court always included visits to shrines along the way. On his last progress to London, in April 1521, he stopped long enough to make offerings at the monastery of Reading and at the shrine of Our Lady of Grace in Windsor.[88]

In the last months of his life, Buckingham even contemplated making a pilgrimage to Jerusalem, although it is not clear how serious he was about the matter. In October 1520 he told his council, "Ye see I wear a beard, whereof preadventure ye do marvel: but marvel not of it, for I made vow unto God that it shall never be shaven unto such time as I have been at Jerusalem: and if I may obtain the king's license to perform my promise and advow, it were more to my comfort than if his grace would give me £10,000; yea, more glad than if his grace would give me £10,000 land to me and mine heirs." He said that his almoner, George Poley; his chaplain, John Dellacourt; and his master of the works, Sir William Curtis, had promised to go with him. While he was away, he planned to entrust his affairs to his chancellor, Robert Gilbert; the dean of his chapel, Thomas Wotton; his receiver general, Thomas Cade; and his surveyor, John Jennings.[89]

When Buckingham was in residence at Thornbury, he frequently heard mass and sermons in his private chapel. His large collection of jewels and plate contained enough chapel plate to ensure that service would be conducted in an atmosphere matching the opulence of everyday life at Thornbury. Buckingham's favorite preacher, or at least the one he heard most frequently, was Dr. Mandeville, prior of the Black Friars in Bristol.[90]

Charity was an integral part of Buckingham's religious life, as well as one of the recognized obligations of men of his wealth and status. As W. K. Jordan has noted, most noblemen gave a large part of their charity as random alms to the poor on a daily basis.[91] Buckingham was no exception. At Christmas 1508, for example, he distributed two loaves of bread as alms; at the great revels of Epiphany, four.[92] He frequently gave small sums to persons described as idiots. At the suggestion of Nicholas Hopkins of the charterhouse at Henton, he undertook to support a fourteen-year-old child named Francis, who was in the care of the prior of St. John's of Jerusalem and wanted to become a priest.[93] Fragments of accounts for 1519, 1520, and 1521 record payments for Francis's board, clothes, medical care, laundry, ink, and writing paper. At Shrovetide in 1519 the duke gave 7d "for a hen . . . for Frauncis to sport hym with the chylder [children]." In August 1520, the duke sent him the substantial sum of 40s as a reward in addition to his living expenses.[94] The arguments that Hopkins, who knew the duke well, used to persuade him to support Francis probably give a clear indication of the duke's motives in performing good works. "I trust verily ye shall have of him a good and virtuous religious man, and also a true and trusty beadman. And moreover, after my confident feeling, I believe it shall be to your Lord's grace as charitable deed before Almighty God, and as well accept as ever was deed of charity by your noble Grace's power done."[95]

Buckingham also conformed to the pattern of charitable giving typical of the nobility by contributing to the construction of churches and chantries.[96] In July 1508 he gave the sum of £20 for vaulting the collegiate church at Windsor.[97] Six years later, he alienated land valued at £60 per annum to the monastery of St. Mary in Tewkesbury and founded a chantry at Thornbury with an endowment of £300.[98] He rebuilt the aisle of the parish church in Eastington, Gloucestershire, which is still decorated with his badges.[99] The duke is also credited with building the great hall of Buckingham College, a Benedictine priory in Cambridge, in 1519. Extant accounts contain no evidence that he did so; however, his portrait still hangs in the hall of Magdalene College (the priory was refounded as Magdalene College after the Reformation).[100]

A great household like Buckingham's at Thornbury inevitably functioned as a regional center of political, economic, and social power. Its standing in the counties of Gloucestershire, Somerset, and Wiltshire was much like that of the royal court in England as a whole. Thornbury was a major factor in the local economy both because it consumed so many goods and services and because it employed so many people of all social classes. It was also the basis of Buckingham's political power. As David Starkey has stated, "Public power lay in the command of men, and the household was the institution through which that command was bought."[101] When men entered the duke's service, they officially recognized him as their lord, a relationship symbolized by their wearing the Stafford livery. Service meant more than simply filling a particular post. It meant, rather, acting loyally in the duke's interest at all times. In return, Buckingham promised to be a "good lord" to his dependents: to use his resources and power to give them generous rewards, patronage, and protection.

As a source of potential political power, Thornbury was particularly important because it acted as a magnet to the local gentry. The duke's public and extravagant lifestyle provided many opportunities for friendly social contacts that might develop into or reinforce more concrete political and economic ties. At the feast of the Epiphany in 1508, for example, his guests from Gloucestershire included Sir Anthony and Sir Robert Poyntz, two members of a leading county family; Sir William Kingston, a servant of the king's; and three Berkeleys—Sir Maurice, his brother James, and Richard, head of the Stoke Gifford branch of the family.[102] Two knights from Somerset, Sir John Rodney and Sir Edmund Gorges, were also present, as well as three less eminent gentlemen: Hugh Boughey, who lived near the duke's manor of Maudley in Staffordshire; William Kemys of Began, Wentloog, in Wales; and Robert Partesoil of Riseley, Bedfordshire.[103] William Kemys, Hugh Boughey, and Robert Poyntz all held offices on Stafford's estates.[104]

Buckingham's household provided many opportunities for employing members of the gentle classes. Of the 45 members of the duke's council and staff identified in Appendix A, 26, or 58 percent, were gentlemen, a very high percentage in a period when no more than 3 percent of the population at large fell into this category.[105] In addition, Stafford employed a number of gentlemen as personal servants. An account for 1517 or 1518 lists George Grey, Thomas Kemys, John Ratcliffe, and Ambrose Skelton as gentlemen of the household.[106] Grey, a brother of the marquess of Dorset, was related to the duke by marriage: his mother was married to the duke's brother, Henry, earl of Wiltshire.[107] Kemys and Skelton both received substantial annuities of £6 13s 4d from the duke and held positions as park keepers on his estates.[108] Finally, twelve gentlemen who wore Buckingham's livery during the period 1515–17 seem to have been retainers in the classic sense.[109] They did not fill any specific household offices and were rewarded either by receiving an annuity from the duke or by holding an administrative position on his estates.[110]

To keep his large and magnificent household functioning smoothly, Buckingham maintained an elaborate organization headed by a council that included his most trusted advisers and such major administrative officials as his chancellor, treasurer, auditor, cofferer, comptroller, steward, almoner, keeper of the wardrobe, secretary, master of the works, and chaplain. The body was a fluid one; at a given time only a portion of the councillors were in residence at Thornbury. When they were in attendance, they received a daily allowance of 3s 4d.

Underneath this council were the working departments themselves: wardrobe, jewelry, bedchamber, armory, artillery, stables, chapel, and household proper, which handled meals. Each of these departments was in itself an elaborate structure. The household, for example, had three subdivisions: the great household, at Thornbury or wherever the duke was living, the household of his son and heir, and the traveling household.[111] A brewery, a bakehouse, a buttery, a cellar, a kitchen, a spicery, a saltcellar, and a chandlery supplied the needs of the three households.[112]

In addition to the leading councillors and senior officials, the household staff included grooms of the wardrobe, grooms of the wardrobe of the bedchamber, yeomen of the bedchamber, gentlemen of the chapel, gentlemen ushers, a herald, and, finally, the liveries.

Buckingham's councillors and senior household officers were typical of the gentlemen bureaucrats who played a growing role in running the households and estates of magnates in the later middle ages.[113] Of the 58 advisers and household servants known by name, 26, or approximately 45 percent, were of gentle birth or rose into the gentry. More than half were either lawyers (13) or clergymen (19); 9 of the lawyers were members of the Inns of Court, and 13 of the clerks had attended a university.[114] Buckingham had actually paid for the Oxford education of one of the clerks, Thomas Moscroff, who later served as his receiver general, secretary, and councillor.[115] Training a loyal future servant may well have been the duke's motive for supporting Francis, the boy mentioned earlier in this chapter, for Nicholas Hopkins assured him Francis would become his "true and trusty beadman."[116]

Despite the significant number of trained bureaucrats among his key advisers and household servants, some of Buckingham's most important officials fell outside this category. Clearly, the duke sought and rewarded competence and loyalty wherever he found them. Men from the gentry and yeomanry entered the households of great lords in the early 1500's as they had for centuries, and in some cases turned themselves into professional administrators through their work. This was true of John Russell, Buckingham's secretary from 1499 to 1507, William Cholmeley, his cofferer from 1503 to 1521, and William Walwyn, his auditor from 1507 to 1521.[117]

The large number of lawyers on Buckingham's payroll is especially noteworthy. During his lifetime, his councillors and administrative staff included at least thirteen lawyers. Many of them, such as John Scott, Richard Brooke, and Christopher Hales, rose to the very top of their professions. Others, such as Thomas Jubbes, who became recorder and member of parlia-

ment for Bristol, and Robert Turberville, who was a Hertfordshire landowner and member of parliament, were important at
the local level. The duke even employed Edmund Dudley, one of
Henry VII's most influential advisers.[118] In addition to these
men, who formed the core of his legal advisers, he hired other
lawyers, such as John Cowper, to represent him in specific courts
or to serve as justices on the itinerant commissions he sent into
Wales.[119] Sir Andrew Windsor, who rose to be keeper of Henry
VIII's great wardrobe; John Kingsmill, a member of the court of
common pleas; John Yaxley, a serjeant-at-law; Richard Littleton,
a member of the Inner Temple from an important Shropshire
family; and William Huntley and Walter Rowdon, two Gloucestershire landowners and members of the Inns of Court, all served
him on itinerant commissions. Two other lawyers, Walter Luke,
who rose to be a justice of the court of king's bench, and John
Skilling, a master of the bench at the Inner Temple, held offices
on his estates.[120]

The increasing professionalism of the men who worked in the
households of magnates like Buckingham meant that they often
placed career advancement over loyalty to their employer. When
a better opportunity presented itself, they felt no compunction
about leaving one employer for another. Carole Rawcliffe has
suggested that the duke had difficulty ensuring administrative
continuity in his household for this reason. She has specifically
cited the case of Humphrey Bannaster, Buckingham's treasurer
in 1508, who entered the duke of Suffolk's service sometime before 1515.[121] There are similar examples: Laurence Stubbes joined
Cardinal Wolsey's household after seven or more years working
for Buckingham; Richard Mynors, the duke's treasurer from 1502
to 1507, was a member of the earl of Shrewsbury's household by
1513. John Russell successfully sought employment under the
crown after a dozen years in the duke's service, eight of them in
the important position of secretary. By 1525, Russell was secretary to Princess Mary.[122]

Nonetheless, historians should not overestimate the impact of
this trend on the efficiency of great households like Bucking-

ham's. Except perhaps for Bannaster, all the men mentioned above worked for the duke for considerable periods before they left his service. Overall, his household servants and councillors were a stable group. Of the 58 persons known to us by name, sparse records prevent us from saying almost anything definite about 13. Of the remaining 45, 23—more than half—were in Buckingham's service for more than five years, 13 for ten years or more, and 7 for more than fifteen years. Rawcliffe's reference to his "constantly changing administrative personnel" hardly seems justified.[123]

Buckingham's enthusiasm for employing lawyers was in part a testimony to his litigious and somewhat vindictive nature. Like most of his rich and powerful contemporaries, he regarded the law as a means to achieve private ends that he could not attain in any other way, or as a method to be combined with direct personal action.[124] He was an example of a type that Lawrence Stone found increasingly common in the Elizabethan period: the nobleman who sublimated at least some of his aggressive instincts into lawsuits, instituting legal actions when his ancestors would have committed breaches of the peace.[125] During his lifetime, he instituted the staggering number of 128 lawsuits in the courts of common pleas and king's bench. Very few of these actions concluded satisfactorily from the duke's point of view: of the 106 cases decided before his death, he won only six.[126] Since he must have known that he was unlikely to win favorable verdicts in the common-law courts, the persistence with which he instituted suits strongly suggests that he had some other goal in mind. Probably he was using the law to harass his opponents and intimidate them into settling with him favorably out of court.

In addition to pursuing his lawsuits, the lawyers on Buckingham's payroll probably had a great deal of routine legal business to do for him. Great nobles used members of the bar to write their wills, to act as executors of their estates, to arrange jointures for their daughters and sisters, to superintend the purchase or sale of land, to act as feoffees, and to arbitrate their quarrels. More importantly, lawyers were the leading experts in

estate management and performed many functions that would
be taken over by other professionals in later centuries. Indeed,
Eric Ives has suggested that when large landowners put lawyers
on their payrolls, they were more interested in securing fiscal
officers to work on their estates than barristers to pursue their
affairs in court. As we shall see in the next chapter, Stafford employed lawyers on his estates regularly enough and on a scale
large enough to support Ives's generalization.[127]

Unfortunately, Buckingham's litigious nature affected the way
he managed his large household staff. When his servants failed
to carry out their duties satisfactorily or refused to settle a dis-
agreement with their employer on his terms, he sued them as
readily as he did anyone else. The duke regularly used the law
to punish inefficient and negligent officials.[128] Over the years,
he sued at least eleven of his household servants. He actually
brought eight separate actions seeking recovery of £1,561 18s
against one of his treasurers, Richard Mynors.[129]

The ugliest legal battle between the duke and one of his senior
officials took place in the court of Star Chamber between the
duke and his former secretary John Russell. Russell had been
raised in the household of Buckingham's stepfather, the duke
of Bedford, and entered Buckingham's service soon after his
first patron's death in 1495.[130] He served Buckingham in various
positions, holding the important post of secretary from 1500
to 1507.[131] During this period he handled large sums of money
for his employer. When he was discharged, his account was
not settled.

In 1513, Russell filed a bill of complaint in the court of Star
Chamber alleging that he had been trying in vain to settle his account with the duke for eight years, two of which he had spent
in constant attendance on the itinerant nobleman and his auditors at great cost to himself; that he had bound himself to the
duke for 1,000 marks to follow a certain timetable in ending the
dispute and had complied with it; that Buckingham had initiated
a suit against him in London despite Russell's sincere effort to
conclude the matter out of court; that the duke had sued him in

chancery for 1,000 marks on the false ground that he had not fulfilled his obligations under that bond; that Buckingham had
seized his property in Surrey and Hereford and was trying to
have him arrested; and, finally, that the duke had ignored the
impartial judgment of the lord of St. John's, the dean of St. Paul's,
and Sir Andrew Windsor that Russell owed him nothing.[132]

Buckingham's answer to this bill overflows with contempt for
his social inferiors. After accusing Russell of outright lying and
slander, he recounted his lowly origin "of a simple and very
pore and nedy kyndred."[133] Buckingham claimed that Russell
had resisted settling his account for the period March 1500–
March 1507 on one excuse or another, despite frequent entreaties
from his master; that his suspicions had been aroused when he
learned that Russell "did were in his garments and apparell as
fyne velvet and silks in his dobletts and jakets and cloth in his
gownes . . . as the seid duke did" and kept his family "as gen-
telfolks . . . which were tofore right pore and nedy"; that he had
instituted his suit in London only when Russell had misused a
further period of grace to marry without the duke's knowledge;
that when Russell had bound himself for 1,000 marks to termi-
nate the matter by a given date, Buckingham had graciously
allowed him to discharge the sureties made necessary by the
lawsuit and had cancelled an earlier bond for 2,000 marks; that
Russell had not lived up to the terms of his bond and the duke
had therefore rightfully secured an execution on his property;
that the former secretary could not account for all the money he
acknowledged having received; and that the mediators Russell
cited were hardly impartial or well informed, since they had not
asked the duke to present his side of the case. Buckingham
frankly accused his former secretary of stealing money and
goods worth £3,315 from him.

If eny person hadd delyvered twenty pounds to oon of his most trusty
servaunts to provyde twenty yerds of sylke at 20s the yerde And if his
seid trusty servaunt asked allowance of the said 20 yerdes by hym so
provided and bought and delivered therof to the seid maistrs use but 10
yerds hit were nether right nor conscience . . . and for such matier and

the seid Russell's sumptious lyvyng and fynding his seid nedy fader moder britherne and kynesfokes to kepe hymself and all thoder aforesaid otherwise thenne did becom theym to leve . . . ys the very and most cause of his dett.

He concluded his answer with an impassioned plea that "such an untrue servaunte among noble men be remembered according to his deserts and demerits." [134]

If Star Chamber ever issued a decree in this case, it has not survived. Without this relatively impartial source, it is almost impossible to determine where right lay and which of the facts alleged by the litigants were true. Only three facts can be corroborated independently: Russell did pay some of his arrears before he left Buckingham's service, [135] the duke's auditors did audit his account and conclude that Russell owed their master £3,315 15s 3½ d, [136] and Buckingham did seize Russell's land and take the income. [137] Three years after the case was brought before the Star Chamber, two of the duke's estate officials reported about lands in Surrey "wych my lord's grace hath in execucion for such money as John Russell is indetted to hym," an indication either that the matter was still unsettled or that the court had decided in favor of Buckingham and awarded him the property until the debt was repaid. [138] The duke was also receiving the income from Russell's land in Brent Pelham, Hertford, "by reson of a statute." [139]

Whatever the truth about the case, Buckingham's answer to the bill of complaint reveals a great deal about him and is a valuable historical source on that account. It contains several brutally frank statements of the social pride implicit in the duke's conduct and bearing. Buckingham referred repeatedly—and with considerable exaggeration—to Russell's lowly origins, as if this alone were enough to condemn him and make it incomprehensible that anyone would take his word against that of so exalted a nobleman as the duke. He also expressed outrage at the presumption of any commoner who tried to imitate his lavish way of life. To Buckingham, wealth and luxury were outward manifestations of nobility. Thus the very fact that Russell and his family had, in his opinion, been guilty of breaching the social order by living "too well" for their station in life was enough to convince him that they must have been stealing from him. The answer also illustrates the duke's assumption that his rank conferred the right and the ability to dispense justice. It apparently never occurred to him, any more than it would have to Henry VIII, that his auditors were just as susceptible to improper bias as those Russell selected.

The conviction that his high rank entitled him to have his own way made it difficult for Buckingham to acquiesce when he could not get satisfaction in the courts. He obviously did not regard legal action as an impartial means of settling issues fairly. When the law did not grant him what he wanted, he readily turned to other methods, even if they were illegal. On one occasion, for example, he unlawfully imprisoned his auditor, John Seintgeorge, for failing to carry out his duties, while a suit was pending against Seintgeorge in the court of common pleas. He was probably trying to force his auditor to accept an unfavorable settlement out of court.[140] For an unknown reason, Buckingham seized the goods of Elizabeth Knevet, who had been a lady-in-waiting in his household, after her death.[141] In November 1520 he ordered the arrest of two chaplains for "departynge from us contrary to . . . [their] oath."[142] He also ordered the imprisonment for debt of his receiver general, John Pickering, and the seizure of "suche [of] hys goods that ye kanne have knowledge off."[143]

Buckingham's harsh and arbitrary behavior had the inevitable result that few of his household officers felt much affection for or loyalty to him, even when they remained in his service for many years. Instead, his methods bred insecurity, fear, and distrust. In the end, he paid a high price for his arrogant and arbitrary conduct: three of his household servants played crucial roles in his downfall.

The duke's semiregal life at Thornbury and his extravagance on public occasions increased his annual expenses to what were, in early Tudor times, staggering heights. His annual expenditures were recorded in three kinds of financial statements: household, wardrobe, and cofferer's accounts. The household account listed outlays on food and fuel for the duke's establishment; the wardrobe accounts, purchases of nonedible goods. The cofferer's account contained occasional expenses, such as offerings at mass or religious shrines, payments to priests delivering sermons, rewards to persons bringing messages and gifts, salaries of councillors in attendance, and outlays for building and repairs.[144]

Fortunately, enough of these records survive to make it possible to estimate Buckingham's expenses in 1504, in the half year ending September 30, 1517, and in the last three complete fiscal years of his life. The household and wardrobe accounts for these five periods amount to £3,478 14s or £2,827 13s for 1504; £1,339 18s for the last six months of 1517; £5,048 1s for 1518; £6,286 18s for 1519; and £7,098 12s for 1520.[145] There are cofferer's accounts only for 9 months in 1508 and 7 months in 1521. In 1508, expenses averaged £72 4s 5d per month; at that rate the cofferer would have spent £866 13s annually.[146] In 1521, the cofferer spent £99 19s 7d per month, which suggests annual expenses of £1,199 15s.[147] If the estimate of the cofferer's annual expenses for 1508 is added to the sum of the 1504 wardrobe and household accounts, the result is £4,345 7s or £3,694 6s, probably a fairly accurate estimate of Buckingham's expenses in 1504. Adding the estimated cofferer's outlay for 1521 to the household and wardrobe accounts for each period from 1517 through 1520 results in comparable estimates for those years: £1,939 15s for the last six months of 1517; £6,247 16s for 1518; £7,486 13s for 1519; and £8,298 7s for 1520.[148]

The striking thing about these estimates is the great increase in Buckingham's cost of living in the last three years of his life. His expenses in 1518 were £2,000 more than in 1517, representing an increase in his rate of spending of about 60 percent.[149] In 1519 his outlay increased by another £1,200 and in 1520 by another £800.

The increase in Buckingham's expenses was not due to a steady rise in everyday household expenses. Household accounts for 1503, 1504, and 1518 indicate that expenses for food and fuel were relatively stable. In 1504 they were £2,061 2s or £2,712 3s; in

### Expenses of the Third Duke of Buckingham

| Year ending: | Household | Wardrobe | Subtotal | Cofferer (estimate) | Total (estimate) |
|---|---|---|---|---|---|
| Mar. 1504 | £2,061 2s[a] | £766 11s[b] | £2,827 13s | £866 13s[c] | £3,694 6s |
|  | £2,712 3s[d] | — | £3,478 14s | — | £4,345 7s |
| Mar. 1517 | — | £976 7s[e] | — | — | — |
| Sept. 1517 | £1,062 7s[f] | — | — | — | — |
| Apr.–Sept. 1517 | £1,002 15s[g] | £337 3s[h] | £1,339 18s | £599 17s[i] | £1,939 15s |
| Sept. 1518 | £2,634 4s[j] | £2,413 7s[k] | £5,048 1s | £1,199 15s[l] | £6,247 16s |
| Sept. 1519 | £3,700 14s[j] | £2,586 4s[k] | £6,286 18s | £1,199 15s[l] | £7,486 13s |
| Sept. 1520 | £2,898 9s[j] | £4,200 3s[k] | £7,098 12s | £1,199 15s[l] | £8,298 7s |

Sources: (a) SRO, D641/1/3/8. (b) SRO, D641/1/3/7. (c) PRO, SP1/22, ff. 66–88; see n.148, p. 281. (d) BL, Add'l Mss., 40859B. (e) SRO, D641/1/3/9. (f) BL, Royal Mss., 14 BXXXVB. (g) PRO, E101/518/5, pt. 2. (h) BL, Royal Mss., 14 BXXXVC. (i) PRO, E36/220, passim; see n.148. (j) BL, Royal Mss., 14 BXXXVB. (k) BL, Royal Mss., 14 BXXXVC. (l) PRO, E36/220, passim; see n.148.

1518 £2,634 4s.[150] Wardrobe expenses grew from £766 11s in 1504 to £976 8s in the year ending March 1517, a significant but hardly ruinous increase.[151] Outlays in the wardrobe from April through September 1517 were only £337 3s.[152] In 1518, however, the expenses of the wardrobe more than doubled, to £2,413 17s.[153] Expenditures in the wardrobe remained at this high level in 1519 (the exact figure was £2,586 4s), while the cost of the household soared to £3,700 14s.[154] In 1520, expenses in the household fell to £2,898 9s, not too much more than the 1518 level, but the wardrobe spent £4,200 3s—over four times the figure for the year ending March 1517.[155]

The dramatic increases in the costs of Buckingham's household and wardrobe during this three-year period were due to the convergence of a number of extraordinary personal and public events in his life. In 1519 Buckingham's son married Ursula Pole; the duke paid all the costs of the wedding except that of the bride's dress.[156] That year his daughter Mary also married George Lord Bergavenny, which meant the beginning of payments for her dowry, as well as certain wedding expenses. Since the marriage contracts have not survived, there is no evidence about the obligations Buckingham undertook, but his accounts do show a payment of £123 19s to Mary's husband, Lord Bergavenny, for "his wedding gear, velvet and cloth of silver."[157] In August 1519 the visit of the king and court to Penshurst caused still another heavy drain on the duke's resources.[158] In 1520, on top of all this, Buckingham accompanied the court during Charles V's visit to Canterbury, during the meeting with Francis I at the Field of Cloth of Gold, and during the second meeting between Henry and Charles, at Gravelines. The size of his entourage at the Field of Cloth of Gold goes a long way toward explaining the staggering costs of his wardrobe that year. The entourage included 5 chaplains, 10 gentlemen, 55 servants, and 30 horses.[159]

The chroniclers who recorded Buckingham's magnificence on great state and diplomatic occasions knew he was the largest private landowner in England, and assumed his wealth was inexhaustible. Unfortunately, the truth was quite different. By 1520 the duke was forced to sell large amounts of land to cover the huge expenses he had incurred between 1518 and 1520. He could not afford the extravagance of the previous three years because inefficient management had kept the income from his property far below its estimated value. In the next chapter, we shall move out from Thornbury to Buckingham's far-flung estates to look more closely at the primary source of his financial difficulties.

## CHAPTER FIVE

# The Stafford Estates

The third duke of Buckingham's income came from a vast inheritance that sprawled through 24 English counties and the marches of Wales.[1] His estates included 124 manors, 12 castles, 9 hundreds, 11 boroughs, and 65 other properties. He owned woods valued at £4,525 1s. More than 8,000 deer roamed his 9 forests and 24 parks. He also held the advowsen of 58 churches and religious foundations.

After Buckingham's property was forfeited to the crown in 1521, the king appointed Thomas Magnus, a royal servant, and William Walwyn, the late duke's auditor, to survey it.[2] The document they drew up, known as a valor, was a statement of the income anticipated from the estates. It estimated that they were worth £5,061 18s per annum after deducting operating costs, routine expenses for repairs, and salaries.[3] None of Buckingham's peers could boast of owning such valuable property. The Stanley earls of Derby came closest, with estates worth between £4,000 and £5,000 per annum.[4] The duke's brother-in-law, Henry Percy, fifth earl of Northumberland, whose land had a clear value of £3,900, was next.[5] No other nobleman had lands worth even £3,000 a year.[6]

Unfortunately, when the young duke came of age in 1498, he found that his actual annual income fell far short of the anticipated £5,000. As we have seen in the accounts of Jasper Tudor, duke of Bedford, and Margaret Beaufort, countess of Richmond, who administered the estates during Buckingham's minority, profits had been far below that level for years.[7] This situation was the cumulative effect of Glyn Dŵr's rebellion,[8] minorities in the

Stafford family totaling 47 years between 1403 and 1498,[9] turmoil in Wales in the 1480's,[10] and the usual difficulties of managing a huge conglomeration of properties in the fifteenth century. In this unfavorable situation, Buckingham not only had to struggle to extract enough money from his estates to support his lavish style of life, but also had to repay enormous debts to the crown.[11] He had no choice, therefore, but to turn his attention to problems of estate management and to take whatever steps he could to raise his income.

Buckingham preserved the impressive administrative structure that he had inherited from his father.[12] His lands were divided into nine groups: the general circuit, which included property in Warwick, Nottingham, Rutland, Northampton, Huntingdon, Suffolk, Norfolk, Essex, Buckingham, Bedford, Cornwall, and London; the Stafford inheritance in Stafford, Chester, and Shropshire; the Gloucester receivership of lands in Gloucester, Wiltshire, Hampshire, and Somerset; the Kent and Surrey receivership; the lordship of Holderness in York; the lordship of Caus in the Welsh marches; the marcher lordship of Newport; the receivership of the Welsh lordships of Brecon, Hay, and Huntingdon; and, finally, the Welsh receivership of Cantref Selyf, Penkelly, and Alexanderstone. Each of these groups had a receiver to collect money due from individual manors and carry it to the duke's cofferer. The receiver for the general circuit was called the receiver-general.

Each county had a steward, ostensibly the duke's leading administrative official in the area, who received a salary of anywhere from 26s to £20 per annum.[13] Since Buckingham regarded his lands as a source of political power as well as of income—an attitude very common among the late medieval nobility—his goal in filling these stewardships was to strengthen his personal and political ties within the peerage rather than to maximize his income or improve the management of his estates.[14] He treated the positions as sinecures and appointed dukes and earls as stewards. These noblemen undoubtedly delegated the responsibilities of stewardship to subordinates, if they took them seriously at all; they obviously were not going to pay close attention to administering his property.

The officials who actually ran the duke's estates cannot be arranged into a neat hierarchical structure. Most manors had a steward, a bailiff, and a reeve, who was responsible for the account submitted at the end of each year. There were also keepers for each park and forest, and constables and porters for each castle. Where the duke's property was not part of a manorial unit, there were officials variously known as bailiffs, beadles, reeves, approvers, and collectors. All in all, Buckingham's payroll included 164 estate officials receiving annual wages of £493 13s in an average year.[15]

Three different systems of administration existed side by side on Buckingham's manors. The duke leased out or farmed 43 manors for a fixed annual rent. The lessee or farmer was completely responsible for the operation of these estates, and Buckingham's position was reduced to that of a rentier. He administered the rest of his estates directly, but restricted his personal participation in the actual operations of the manor as much as possible. He leased out all or part of the demesne lands on at least 39 of his manors, as well as leasing out all mills, meadows, pastures, mines, rabbit warrens, dovecotes, and rights of agistment, herbage and pannage.[16] The remainder of these manors was parceled out among countless tenants; the more fortunate held their land by copyhold or lease, the rest at the duke's will. Finally, in a third group of manors, the demesne, or part of it, remained "in hand," and the duke's tenants and employees engaged in farming.

The primary function of the duke's officials was to collect the revenues due him under these arrangements and to ensure that farmers, leaseholders, and tenants did not do permanent damage to the properties. In 1516, for example, William Cooper, bailiff of the manor of Disining in Suffolk, reported that "the farmor of desnynge called Robert Holde is not mete to contynewe in the same farme for his lyght behaivyor makyng . . . wast in my lords wodds suffryng the howsis of the farme to fall into grete ruyn, not withstanding the greate charge of reparacone that my lords grace hath of late . . . there." [17] Two years later, John Pickering, the receiver general, reported that in Oakham and Langham, both in Rutland, many of the duke's houses and cottages were "sore in dykaye for lake off reparacyon." He ordered the reeve of Langham to seize the unharvested grain until the tenants "fynde souerty that the howsis and cotages [will] be reparyd at ther proper [own] coste and charges." [18] In order to collect occasional revenues such as entry fines and heriot, the officials held frequent manorial courts. [19]

The officers also had to prevent trespasses on the duke's parks and woods, which offered constant temptation to the local inhabitants. Reports from various officials in 1515 and 1516 indicate that this was a wearisome task. On Easter Monday in 1516, for example, Thomas White and 59 others broke into the rabbit warren at Disining in Suffolk and killed 38 rabbits. [20] The bailiff of Radcliffe upon Soar in Nottingham reported that "oone Martin Lees of Keyworth yoman destreyeth my lord's waren of Radcliffe with grehoundes and ferretts." [21] In Essex, John Burrell and his friends repeatedly hunted deer in the forest of Hatfield without permission. [22]

In 1518–19, John Pickering reported that John Plaisted had occupied four of the duke's cottages in Buckinghamshire without authority "thys 20 yeres and above." [23] Even more contemptuous of his rights was Lady Barrington, who stole 40 loads of wood from the forest of Hatfield Broadoak and sold "as much as she toke" for £12 "after that the auditors and I dyd for bydde hyr the wod." Pickering beseeched his master to deal with her "a cordyng to the law for she wyll not be rowled nolder [neither] bi keper nor balory [bailiff] but too do as it plese her." [24]

When the duke engaged in demesne farming, his officials also had to direct agricultural operations. Some manors, such as Haverhill and Horsham in Suffolk, and Brecon in Wales, had a special officer known as the harvest overseer, who received an annual salary of 6s 8d. [25] The duke depended for farm labor on serfs and customary tenants. Only where the demesne was leased out does a manor's account show annual payments for commutation of work service.

On property that was not part of a manorial unit, the functions of Buckingham's officials varied with the nature of his rights. In many cases his only right was to collect rent; his representatives, called collectors, did just that. They did not receive salaries and were probably paid in the form of a free house or piece of land. In some such places, Yalding prepositura and Bletchingley bedellary, for instance, Buckingham's rights paralleled those on his manors, and he administered them in the same way.[26] Finally, the duke was the lord of nine hundreds. Here he collected rents and had judicial rights. His officers held the hundred court and took the revenue as part of his personal income.

Surviving manorial accounts give the impression that the income from manors and lands that were farmed out, or "in farm," approached the anticipated value more frequently than the income from estates that Buckingham administered directly. Yet the duke did not lease out a growing portion of his property. In the eleven cases where accounts of lands in farm survive from the early years of the duke's majority and from the last years of his life, a change in the method of administration occurred only in the cases of the manor of Policott, in Buckinghamshire, and of the honor of Gloucester, in Northampton. Each had been farmed in the earlier year but was administered directly in the later. At Policott the change had little effect,[27] but at the honor of Gloucester the farm of 100s in 1505 gave way to an income of only 33s in 1521.[28]

In some cases, Buckingham may have resisted leasing his lands in order to maintain the personal character of his lordship, a motive consistent with his tendency to treat his estates as a political asset as well as a source of income. Often, however, his motives were purely economic: he continued to administer his property directly when he considered the rents offered him for leases and farms inadequate. In 1500, for example, he rejected an offer from the mayor and burgesses of Newport for £20 a year for the profits of the city. Under Henry VI the annual fee-farm had been £32; the duke probably had that figure in mind. He should have taken the burgesses' protest that this was "the highest ferme that they may endure to paye" more seriously than he did, however, for his decision to administer the city directly proved to be unwise. In 1504, the income was only £18 10s, less than the sum he had disdained four years earlier.[29] In the same year the duke ordered his receiver general and auditor to determine

wheithre it shal stand beest with oure prouffite and suertie of oure inheritaunce to let oure lordships of Writle, Hatfild, Boyton and Aymoundisham with al casulties, as hathe been heretoforn used [i.e., to farm them], orelles t'appoinct baillifes accounptable in every lordship, wherebie it is thought great avauntaige shal rise of the casualties.[30]

His officers must have advised against the change. It was made only in the case of Writle, where profits did increase from £87 2s in 1499 to £111 9s in 1521.[31]

Buckingham presided over this amorphous structure with a firm determination to exact all his rights. That his tenants found his effort to revive practices and exactions fallen into disuse during the minority oppressive was no concern of his. His attitude was summed up perfectly in an instruction given to his officers in 1504: "Dryve thayme in their covenauntes asmouche to oure prouffite as ye can."[32] When tenants of Nether-Gorddwr, in the lordship of Caus, petitioned to be discharged from a duty called *porthean bagle*, which they claimed had not been levied "tyme out of mynd," he replied firmly,

As touching our duetye . . . callid 'Portheant bagull,' forasmouche as our auncestors and other for the season havying the proffictis of our lordship of Caurse have bin answerid therof of old tyme and lately, in the dayes of Kingis Henry the VI, Edward the IIIIth and Henry the Sevenynthe, nowe oure soveraigne lord . . . we therfor, not willing to put our inheritance in furder doute ne tryall then our auncestoures have hertofore don, woll now that ye . . . make us undelaied payment therof.[33]

Buckingham frequently intervened in the administration of his estates in attempts to increase his income. Soon after he attained his majority, he made a personal tour of the Welsh lordships, a sign of his determination to end the chaos that had reigned there for more than a decade. The tour also afforded an opportunity to collect the *primo recognito*, a customary payment made to the marcher lord when he took possession of his lands. It amounted to £838 7s, payable over three years. The duke also exacted £140 from the inhabitants of Newport for a pardon of their arrears.[34] From time to time, he visited his other lordships, though with what frequency it is impossible to say. Furthermore, he regularly entertained his estate officials at Thornbury. These occasions gave him a chance to encourage them to squeeze even more money from his tenants and to turn over whatever cash was in their possession. In 1508, for instance, Buckingham extended his hospitality at Epiphany to the receivers of Newport and of Kent and Surrey, and to the bailiffs of Hatfield Broadoak, Oakham, Naseby, and Rothwell.[35] It is significant that in 1520–21 the cofferer's receipts were unusually high during the holiday months of December and January.[36]

Buckingham also regularly employed his brother, Henry, earl of Wiltshire, to assist him in managing his estates, particularly those in Wales. In 1500 Henry headed a commission to survey the duke's properties in Wales, Thornbury, and Bedminster;[37] in 1502 he was present at an audit of the Gloucestershire estates.[38] He returned to Wales in 1503 on the panel appointed to hold the Great Sessions in Newport and Brecon.[39] At Buckingham's death in 1521, he was steward of the Welsh lordships of Newport and Caus.[40]

Ultimately, however, the burden of increasing Buckingham's income fell on his leading councillors, who made periodic circuits through his lordships to improve the efficiency with which they were exploited. On these occasions the duke issued detailed instructions, or articles, that explained his policy on each aspect of estate management and asked questions about specific problems. He issued such articles to his brother and to the other councillors in 1500, and to Robert Turberville, his receiver general, and John Gunter, his auditor, in 1504. The articles drawn up on these occasions reveal the numerous difficulties facing Buckingham and the steps he took to remedy them.[41] The books of information compiled in the general circuit in 1515–16 and in 1518–19 may have been the result of similar commissions, although no instructions from these years survive.[42]

First and foremost, Buckingham had to find out such basic facts as what the names of his tenants were, how they held their land, whether they owed entry fines, and so forth. During the long minorities of the fifteenth century, records relating to the lordships had been neglected. Since the temporary administrators had had little interest in the long-term prosperity of the estates, they cared little when old court rolls were lost, when officials stopped taking periodic rentals, and when stewards grew lax about holding manorial courts. For the young duke the result was disastrous. How was he to collect his income if he did not know who owed it? The situation was summed up by the receiver of Brecon, who told the commission sent out in 1500 that a new rental must be made as soon as possible, "for he seith that diverse parcelles of rent, aswele yn his charge as yn the reves charge, be not levable, nor knowen where for them to distreyne, yn default of evidence."[43]

The articles of both 1500 and 1504 insisted on the urgency of remedying this situation. The stewards must compile books containing the names and holdings of all customary tenants, copyholders, and free tenants, and send them to the duke;[44] they must compile another of all those who held land by knight service or socage, "declaring plainly what quantite every man holdith and of what honnour and manoure";[45] they must examine old rentals where they survived and "take and here th'infourmacions of old men" so they could discover all lands that were concealed, encroached upon, or decayed;[46] they must measure the duke's lands wherever they bordered on the property of freeholders "so that non incrouchement be made upon any parte";[47] and, finally, they must survey the woods "to see what therof stondeth yn tymbir and what yn underwode . . . and how many freholders have wode within the boundes of my lorde's forest."[48] In the general circuit, the death of William Gibbons, Buckingham's first receiver general, caused additional problems. His officials were to find out which tenants had arranged entry fines with Gibbons and how many of the fines had been paid. The duke cautioned his representatives "by youre discrecions to comon with thayme in the same covenauntes, lest thei wil clayme more then thei aught, by reason that Maistre Gibons is deceassed." [49]

He urged that every precaution be taken to prevent such chaos from developing again. The officers in Wales were instructed to make a duplicate copy of each court roll and each recognizance taken since the duke's entry into his lands, and send him the original. [50] In the future, duplicate copies were to be made of all court rolls. [51] All grants of new leases were to be recorded in a book to be delivered to Buckingham. [52] In the general circuit, where some records survived, they were to be carefully inventoried and then kept "in oure manor or surest ferme place in every lordship in a coufre with 3 lokkes." [53] Buckingham was concerned enough about the safety of his estate and legal records to include a muniments room when rebuilding Thornbury. For safety, the room was located on the top floor of a tower in the inner court; it held six large storage chests. [54]

Enunciating these policies was a good deal easier than executing them. If lands worth £8 15s were uncovered in the manor of Haresfield by 1502, [55] the officials of Forthingbridge, Hereford, still could not collect a rent of 16½d in 1516, "for as moche as it is not knowen wher the land lies that the seid [rent] ys charged uppon." [56] In 1516, the bailiff of Staffordshire was still trying to find out who held various knights' fees and three of the duke's officials were collecting information about the occupants of the manor of Hope, in the lordship of Caus, going back to the time of the duke's father. [57]

The receiver general, John Pickering, admitted in 1518–19 the failure of his effort to discover how much of Buckingham's land John Barrington, a ward of the duke of Norfolk, held and whether it was by knight service or by socage. "I cannot cume to the knowledge ther offe," Pickering said, "for ther is no man canne schew me." The only one who knew the truth was John's mother, and she would not divulge it. Pickering suggested that "sche must be compelled by the law to schew, for oder remedy is ther none."[58] That same year, the receiver general was thwarted when he tried to inspect the copyholds of the tenants of the manors of Wells, Warham, and Sheringham, in Norfolk.[59] When he arrived at the lordships, he found to his "gret payne" that "almost all your tenants . . . is in iseland [Iceland]." He held a court "but it was to none affecte lakkyng ther apparens and ther copys." Furthermore, Gregory Morgan, who had custody of the duke's records, was in London, "wher for we couyd come to lytell knowledge." Yet in spite of these difficulties, the duke's efforts did not end in complete failure. The 125 court rolls and manorial accounts that survive from his lifetime are ample testimony to his success in securing records of transactions on his estates.

Buckingham's careful inquiries into the obligations of his tenants included questions about which of them were "bondmen of blood," or serfs.[60] He fully intended to extract traditional servile duties from them or to charge them for the privilege of manumission.[61] The duke's policy was both reactionary and unpopular, since serfdom had ceased to be a significant social and economic institution in England in the century and a half after the Black Death. The end of large-scale demesne farming and the consequent commutation of labor services, the relative abundance of land compared to the number of prospective tenants, the pressure from the peasantry, including the withdrawal of serfs from manors and the failure of heirs to take up bond holdings, and the natural attrition as lords failed to replace serf families who died out—all these had contributed to the decline of serfdom.[62] As one might expect, Buckingham's tenants were even more uncooperative than usual when his officials held inquisitions to identify serfs. After a survey of Wales and Thornbury in 1500, for example, the duke's officials reported that "Inquisicion hath been made for bondemen of blode withyn the lordship of Neuporte, wherunto the tenauntes sey ther be none such withynne the lordship, wherfore it is thought necessarie that better serche be made yn my lorde's recordes for the same."[63] At Thornbury too, "speciall inquerry was made for bonde men and none presented." [64]

The search went on. As late as June 1517, the understeward of Wiltshire reported that the Pynchons, "as he hereth say, be Bondmen to my lords grace to his manor of Thornbury," and undertook "to inquier further of ther fadders and graunde fadders and whether they or any of them came owte of the lordship of Thornbury or from whens they came." [65] Two years later, John Pickering reported with satisfaction that he had "seissed [the duke's] bondman John Dyx of Padbury and taken surety for his body and goods by obligacion in fourty pounds." The unfortunate Dyx offered to buy his liberty for 53s 4d. [66] Pickering also ordered Henry Jervis to seize John Okeham, a serf worth £200 who had escaped to the town of Grimston. [67]

The people concerned naturally resisted being returned to servile status as best they could. When the duke required various members of the Mors family, of his manor of Rumney, to perform bond service, they refused and demanded "a trialle off the country." [68] They in fact secured trials on three separate occasions; on each, the verdict went against them. Even then, however, they did not resign themselves to their fate. In 1527 they sued the duke's widow, who held Rumney as part of her dower, for wrongfully demanding bond service of them. [69] Despite such persistence, the duke was ultimately successful in many of his claims. When he died there were serfs on his manors in the counties of Gloucester, Northampton, Norfolk, Nottingham, Buckingham, Oxford, York, and Rutland, as well as in Wales. [70]

Incomplete records were only one of the causes of poor management on the duke's estates. Another was the unreliability of his officials: the majority were local inhabitants with stronger ties to the tenants than to their lord. The temptation to connive at their friends' and neighbors' cheating was not easy to resist, especially since they might be able to secure some of the concealed profits for themselves. When the duke's officers arrived at Thornbury in 1500, for example, their inquiry was held up because the feodary failed to appear, "wherfore none examinacion cowde be hadde of knightes' fees, nor of tenauntes holding their landes by knightes' service."[71]

One of the main functions of the circuits through Buckingham's lordships was to check up on his estate officials. The articles drawn up for the commission of 1500 prohibited the officers of Newport from assessing fines or giving safe-conducts to felons;[72] too much bribery at Buckingham's expense was occurring in connection with these functions. During their progress through Wales, the duke's councillors took action against individual officers who had cheated their master or neglected their duty. They discharged the ringild of Nether-Gorddwr for "slak payment,"[73] fined the former coroner of Wentloog 100s "for his mysbehavour yn the same office," and fined his successor 40s "yn default of his attendaunce upon the same."[74]

Four years later, in the general circuit, Buckingham ordered Robert Turberville and John Gunter to examine all the leases his stewards had granted since he had entered into his lands, "to enqueire if we have bee deceived by means of any suche leases or nat"[75] and to investigate whether any park keepers "hathe mysbehavyed his houthe [oath] unto us by wast of wood or othre meane."[76] In the future, manorial and county stewards were not to make leases on their own authority but were to take the advice of the receiver general and the auditor, who could be consulted at the audit held each year after Easter.[77] The duke's officers also had to deal with William Pell, formerly an official at Kimbolton in Huntingdonshire, "aswel for his fyne for concilement . . . asfor the repaiement of al such sommes as in his handes restith yet unansuered."[78]

In Haverhill, Suffolk, the duke almost lost his judicial rights because of the neglect of his officials. The understeward did not hold the court because, he said, "he hathe nothyng for his payne," and the bailiff was equally negligent. The abbot of Bury took advantage of the situation and issued his own warrants in the duke's lordship. "Thus by twyx the bayley and hyme [Buckingham's] tenaments is in gret decay and [his] Ryalte almost lost."[79]

Periodic visits by Buckingham's councillors were not enough

to guarantee the honesty of local officials. He was therefore in the habit of taking recognizances from them: he ordered the commission of the general circuit in 1504 to insist that "al and every baillif, fermour and othre accomptaunt finde sufficiaunt sureties bounden to Robert Turbreville, Richard Mynores, John Gounter, and John Russell, to oure use, by obligacion in greater sommes then their charge."[80] There is insufficient evidence to determine whether this policy was actually implemented in all his lordships, but it certainly was applied in Wales. The commissioners in Wales in 1500 reported that the former steward of Newport, Sir Morgan John, was bound by two bonds at his death and that the ringild of Over-Gorddwr, Caus, had at last found sureties.[81] In 1521, Thomas Morgan, receiver of Newport and constable of Newport Castle, was bound by a recognizance for 500 marks (£333 6s 8d).[82]

As important as it was for Buckingham to secure full and accurate information about his inheritance and to minimize the opportunities for dishonesty and neglect on the part of his officials, his policies on these matters were not ends in themselves. Their real goal was to increase the flow of hard cash into his coffers. One obstacle damming this flow was arrears, or the money that an official rendering an account owed to his employer but did not pay. Arrears often resulted from the discrepancy between the value assigned to a particular piece of property on the basis of an outdated assessment and its real value. But arrears also included cash that the official kept, with or without permission; money the official should have collected but didn't, because of either laxity or corruption; rents and dues the tenants could not or would not pay; allowances and deductions not recognized elsewhere in the account; and some bad and unrecoverable losses. Arrears thus originated from two different sources: administrative officials themselves and tenants. The entry for arrears in the official's account included arrears from previous years, as well as the current one, and might even include the debts of previous bailiffs and receivers.

The problem of arrears was a stubborn one. The great landlord of the late medieval period, who expected loyalty and political support as well as income from his tenants, was traditionally indulgent when they were lax about paying their rents and farms. This indulgence was part of the whole concept of good lordship. Estate officials, for their part, were accustomed to retaining a portion of what they owed their employer. This portion appeared as arrears on the charge side of the annual account.[83] These sums had a way of accumulating rapidly, and it frequently became clear that the arrears would never be collected. The lord acknowledged this situation by "remitting" these arrears to the official concerned, and the account was made to balance, although he had not received the money due him. One should not, however, automatically equate arrears with irretrievable losses. Some would eventually be collected, often in installments over a long period. A great landlord dependent on the income from his estates to support a lavish style of life obviously could not afford to have too much of his annual income deferred for too long. In judging the efficiency of estate administration, therefore, one should consider the length of delay in ministers' payments, the tendency of arrears to increase or decrease, and the percentage of projected annual income lost completely.[84] According to K. B. McFarlane even landlords on the best-administered estates were having difficulties collecting income by 1490. A pattern of mounting arrears was far from uncommon.[85]

Such was the pattern on the duke of Buckingham's estates. In 1498 there was a great deal of slack to be taken up because arrears had accumulated during the minority; arrears in Brecon alone amounted to more than £600. If Stafford could collect even a part of this money while preventing his own officers from amassing arrears, it would be a major victory. In 1504, therefore, he ordered the commission for the general circuit "that by youre best policies ye set to the good and quike levie of al oure arreragis within that circuite." They were to take bonds one-third greater than the sum owed from anyone who did not pay his debt.[86]

To change the traditional pattern, however, proved beyond the capacity of the third duke of Buckingham. Recurring arrears in all his receiverships were one factor in a persistent gap between the anticipated income and the actual income from his estates.

Arrears in Brecon, for example, were £491 3s in 1502,[87] an improvement on the £2,426 6s owed in 1496, but still a large sum.[88] In 1504, arrears in Newport were £577 14s,[89] and in the Gloucester receivership £419 3s.[90] In 1506, unpaid income in Kent and Surrey amounted to £482 11s.[91] For 1508 and 1509 in York, arrears were £298 9s;[92] and for 1512 in the Stafford receivership, £412 2s.[93] By 1512, they had risen to £1460 12s in Newport, five times the estimated annual income of the lordship.[94] In 1516, the nearby Welsh lordships of Brecon, Hay, Huntingdon, Cantref Selyf, and Penkelly reported arrears amounting to £776 14s.[95] Arrears in 1517 in the lordship of Caus were £374 19s.[96] In 1519, Roland Bridges still owed £548 19s, which he had incurred in Brecon more than a decade earlier.[97] At Buckingham's death, arrears in the general circuit stood at £385 14s.[98] These figures are necessarily impressionistic, based as they are on fragmentary records, but they do come from each of Buckingham's receiverships and show the huge sums that accumulated as arrears.

The only area for which anything like complete figures have survived is the Stafford receivership. Accounts exist for twelve of the 22 years after the duke took control of his estates. There were no arrears when he attained his majority in 1498,[99] but they grew steadily, to £412 2s in 1512.[100] Sometime after this, the duke either received substantial payments or, more probably, remitted a good part of this debt, since in 1519, the next year for which an account survives, arrears had fallen to £180 5s.[101] Yet the upward pressure was relentless; they had already risen to £258 14s in 1521.[102]

The persistence of substantial arrears in his accounts was not the only obstacle to Buckingham's efforts to increase his income. Equally, if not more, important was the necessity of extracting reasonable rents from his tenants. In this period, rent consisted of two elements: the rent proper, or annual payment, and the entry fine, a lump sum that the tenant paid when he took up his holding. During the sixteenth century, entry fines tended to increase as a proportion of the tenant's total payment.[103] Where large entry fines were combined with low rents for long-term leases, copyholds, or customary tenures, the landlord in effect extracted capital from his estate up front at the expense of his (or his heir's) future annual income. The advantage of entry fines was, of course, that they put significant amounts of cash into the landlord's hands in a period when cash liquidity was a persistent problem.[104]

From the outset, Buckingham suspected that his lands, woods, mills, and other assets were not being let on the best possible terms. In both 1500 and 1504, he ordered his commissions "to see what landes, pastures, milles or other fermes been to be let-tyn or [are] redy letten not to full value, that proclamacion be made to se who will moste geve for the same, so they be lettyn as ner as can."[105] It is difficult to know what the duke meant by full value. In some cases, that of the town of Newport, for example, he clearly meant the traditional rent,[106] but in others he ob-viously wanted to raise customary payments. At the same time, he ordered his commissioners to shift the burden of repairs to his tenants and take "as large fynes . . . as may be dryven."[107] The duke's policy was to maximize both rent proper and entry fines. There is no indication in his instructions that he recog-nized that the two payments tended to move in opposite direc-tions, one rising while the other fell or, at best, remained the same, nor is there evidence that he favored one form of income over the other.

Two obstacles to the immediate implementation of Bucking-ham's policy were existing leases and customary tenures. In the case of existing leases, he simply waited until they expired. De-spite the wording of his instructions, which hinted that he would break unfavorable agreements, there is no evidence that he ever did so.

In dealing with customary tenures, the duke tried to persuade the tenants to convert their tenures into copyholds, that is, ten-ures recorded in the manorial courts. The records do not make clear whether he envisioned copyholds of inheritance, under which the tenant and his heirs had a legal right to the land at the terms recorded in the manorial court, or copyholds for life or lives or a term of years, under which the tenant had to make a new agreement each time his term ended.[108] Copyholds for specified terms were much more favorable to the landlord, since they gave him periodic opportunities to raise the rent. The great resistance to copyholds that Buckingham encountered may indicate that this was the arrangement he had in mind. Even if he granted copyholds of inheritance, he undoubtedly intended to raise rents in the process.

The advantage to his tenants of having proof of their title and the terms under which they held their land specified in writing was not great enough to induce them to agree to the proposed change. In Naseby, Northampton, Pickering reported that "they wyll not consent therto; they had lever to departe the lordshipp, for they say they wyll pay the rent from yere to yere acordyng to ther old custom. And other wayes they wyll nott."[109] In another lordship, many of the tenants replied they "hadde lever dy" than convert their tenures to copyhold.[110] Buckingham's tenants obviously felt in a strong enough position to resist his demands. Apparently, land was so plentiful that their threat to vacate their holdings would be taken seriously.

The response of the commissioners in Wales in 1500 to the instruction to raise rents was not encouraging; the increases they reported were hardly on a scale to make much difference in Buckingham's accounts. His officers were able to lease the herbage of Newport Park to Jankyn Watkins for twelve years at 40s per year; in 1498 and 1499 it had "yelded to my lorde no peny," and in 1500 Watkins had paid only 26s 8d for it.[111] In Brecon, the Great Forest was leased to the officers of the lordship for £94 3s 4d, an improvement over the previous lease of £24 3s 5d; however, half the increase was temporarily remitted until the new lessees could petition for an increment of only £12 1s 8d.[112] Whether or not the duke granted their request, the payment certainly had been raised to the full £94 3s 4d by 1519.[113]

At Hay, demesne lands that had previously been let for 4 marks were leased at the "full farm" of £4 13s 4d, an improvement of £2.[114] Decayed land in Caus was "revyved" and rented for 33s 4d, and the rent of the demesne increased by 6s 8d.[115] The total gain was £14 15s. Against these small successes must be set the council's pessimistic report that in Brecon "ther is none in-crece of rent offred at this tyme for medowes, pastures nor other lands,"[116] that in Huntingdon "decayes were examyned and as yet can not be founde no meanes of approwment other then ys above made of the demaynes,"[117] and that Watkyn Vaughan held for 3s 4d the demesne in Hay, "whiche myght be better letten, as it ys thought."[118]

Despite this inauspicious beginning, Buckingham continued his efforts to raise rents. Over the years he managed to increase the leases on the mills of Tonbridge and the manors of Tillington, Bayhall, Dacherst, and Edenbridge by £22 14s.[119] On the other hand, when the leases on the mills in Radcliffe upon Soar ran out in 1518–19, Thomas Jackson offered 40s plus repairs on a property let for £5 in 1505–6.[120]

In 1520 the duke launched a new campaign to let unoccupied land. A proclamation read at the manorial court of Forebridge— and presumably elsewhere—announced that he had authorized John Jennings, his surveyor general, and David Young, his au-ditor, to rent

all suche our fermes and copy holdys in the counties of Staffede Salop and Chester And our lordship of Holderness and Caurs as be nowe in our hands unlettyn . . . payeing the olde rent and for suche fynes or in-crement as any person or persons willing to take or have any of our said fermes and copy holdes shall agree with our said surveor and auditor.[121]

Despite his eagerness to let all his unoccupied property, Buck-ingham frequently refused offers he considered inadequate in the hope of securing better ones. Naturally, the results of this tactic varied. Thomas Harrison proposed to rent the manors of Thorpe and Thorpe Hall in Essex for 40 marks plus repairs but eventually agreed to £25 plus repairs, an improvement of more than £3.[122] John Bence leased the herbage of Haresfield Park for £1 more a year than he had originally anticipated.[123] On the other hand, Pickering, the receiver general, could not find any better offer than Richard Norris's for some tenements in Buckingham-shire, and strongly urged his master to accept it.[124]

Despite Buckingham's efforts, the new or increased rents listed in the valor of 1521 amounted to only £82 6s 8d, small comfort in the face of a deficit of more than £4,800 in 1520.[125] There is evidence that much of the land was still under-rented. After it was forfeited to the crown, John Baynam offered 26s 8d and a fine of 40s for a close in the lordship of Burbage and Savage that had previously been let for 13s 4d,[126] and Robert Hobbes offered an increase of £5 for the demesne of Willesford Manor.[127] The king was frequently able to raise the rents on leases for other lands as well.[128]

Rising entry fines failed to compensate for the low rents on Buckingham's estates. In 1500, for example, the duke ordered his officials in Wales to investigate "what custume laundes have be taken by fyne syn my lorde's entre and if they be truely fyned fore or not." Wherever they were owed, fines were to be taken "accordynge to the olde custume," that is, at a noble (8s 6d) per acre.[129] The commissioners reported that fines were due on 280 acres in Newport but that the tenants "aunswered that they in no wise can be of power to make their fynes of old tyme acustomed . . . but they offer to pay 2 shillings for the fyne of every acre, or 2d. of the encrece for an acre, and not above." The duke's officials rejected this offer and informed the tenants they would have to pay at the old rate or vacate their lands by Michaelmas. Since Buckingham had not given them any discretion to bargain with the tenants, they could do little else. Nevertheless, they were convinced that the inhabitants could not pay at the old rate. They recommended in their report that the fine be reduced, reminding the duke that his customary tenants were "yerely charged with gaddrynge of the lorde's rent, mayntenynge the see wallis, clensynge water courses and with many other custumarie werkes . . . [and] owe to graynde al ther cornes at my lorde's mylles."[130] In Caus, the council levied a fine of 53s 4d [131] and in Huntingdon one of 25 marks,[132] but this £19 6s 8d was all that could be made from entry fines in the other Welsh lordships.

Whether a similar order to the commission of 1504 in the general circuit proved more profitable is unknown, since the report submitted to the duke has not survived.[133] Certainly at a later date resistance in the general circuit was great. In 1518–19, Pickering reported that the inhabitants "have no joye to offer no fyne, by reason that they stande 2 or 3 yere and nott fynysshed," an indication that the entry fines were a heavy burden on the duke's tenants.[134] In some cases, Pickering had to seize the tenants' lands to force them to pay their fines.[135]

Normally, entry fines were levied at the manorial court and were included in the annual account under the heading "prerequisites of the court." From the accounts for Staffordshire and Gloucestershire, the two counties with the most complete records, it is clear that in the first years after the duke entered his lands, he collected fines that had been neglected during the minority as well as those currently due whenever possible. He reaped substantial profits from this source. At the manor of Madeley, for example, the income of the court was rarely higher than 37s, yet in the first year of Buckingham's majority it rose to £4 17s.[136] During his minority the revenues of the courts of Eastington and Alkerton had reached 72s on only one occasion, but in 1500 they were £25 3s, of which £24 was from entry fines.[137] In 1498–99, the first year after he entered his lands, the duke managed to raise the income from the court of Mars from 4s to £7 19s.[138] The court of Rendcombe normally yielded £1 10s, but in 1500 the profits were £12 2s, a figure that included fines.[139] The most spectacular success was in the Thornbury bedellary, where £103 17s was levied in fines in a court whose usual profit was between £6 and £15.[140]

Buckingham's inability to raise his income from rents must be seen in the context of general price movements during his lifetime so that it is not ascribed unfairly to his personal failures as a landlord.[141] The great inflation of the sixteenth century did not begin until after his death.[142] Eric Kerridge's study of rent indicated that income from land did not start to rise before 1530; indeed, rent was lower in the 1520's than in 1510 on the Herbert and Seymour estates he examined.[143] More recently, Ian Blanchard has shown that rents were falling in the first two decades of the sixteenth century. Vacant holdings, decayed buildings, and reversion of arable land to pasture or waste characterized the period.[144] Studies of the estates of the earls of Shrewsbury, the earls of Northumberland, and the bishops of Worcester confirm Kerridge's and Blanchard's generalizations about the movement of rent and suggest that Buckingham's inability to raise the rents on his properties was rooted in general economic conditions.[145]

Furthermore, the experience of Henry Clifford, first earl of Cumberland, underscores the untenable position of a magnate who wanted both to maximize his income and to maintain his regional power. Clifford's inability to control Westmorland and Cumberland during the Pilgrimage of Grace was at least partly due to the fact that he had alienated both the peasantry and his mesne tenants in an effort to raise rents. The duke of Norfolk explicitly told Thomas Cromwell that Cumberland would have to be less greedy if he wanted to serve the king in the western marches. It is significant that Cumberland's heir restored the rents of the Clifford mesne tenants to their level during the reign of Henry VI.[146]

The movement of rents did not correspond to the trend of food prices, which were rising from the turn of the century.[147] Although most historians assume that an increase in population lay behind the rising cost of food, Blanchard has concluded that the population did not actually begin to grow until the second decade of the sixteenth century. Hence, the upward trend in rent did not occur until the 1520's or 1530's.[148]

Rent was only one of the kinds of income that Buckingham collected from his property. There were many sources of occasional revenue, or income that varied from year to year. Among these were knights' fees: Buckingham had rights to wardship and marriage if the heir to the fee was a minor, to relief when the fee passed from generation to generation, to the traditional feudal aids, and to fines from those who failed to do homage for their lands. In both 1500 and 1504, he ordered his commissioners to start a process of distraint against those guilty of failure to do homage and to fine them 6s 8d a year.[149] His councillors were also to appoint a feodary in each county to ensure that the duke received all the rights due him as overlord.[150] In Newport, the commission of 1500 began a legal process against seven tenants "and the launde holders of the manor of Yolton."[151]

Since those who held land by knight service had as great an interest in concealing that fact as Buckingham had in uncovering it, it was not easy for him to enforce his claims. In 1516, officials in Hereford were still trying to find out "what gentlemen holdith lands of his grace by knyghts service."[152] An official in Rutland complained that Lord Mountjoy, Lord Zouche, and Sir John Hussey all held knights' fees of the duke but "never came to doo his homage."[153]

Nor was the duke's intention of having a feodary in every county ever carried out: records of these officials exist only for Warwick, Stafford, Shropshire, Chester, Kent, and Surrey, and even these did not submit regular accounts to the duke. Only the feodary of the Stafford receivership was able to collect substantial sums. In 1507, Thomas Slade collected £148 14s in relief. His successor levied some £12–£14 a year, although he was not always able to collect it.[154] In 1512, Buckingham exacted an aid for the marriage of his eldest daughter. There is not enough information to estimate how much profit the aid yielded, but if Gloucestershire is at all typical, the income was considerable. In the lordship of Thornbury his feodaries collected £2 10s, and in the honor of Gloucester, £25 9s.[155]

Of all Buckingham's privileges as feudal overlord, probably the most profitable was his right to the wardship and marriage of the minor heirs of tenants who held their land by knight service. When Buckingham died, he had custody of at least a dozen wards, and was therefore receiving the income from their lands. One ward's property was worth £50 and another's 40s—not huge sums by Buckingham's standards, but certainly a welcome addition to his coffers.[156] He also received £4 a year for a ward named

Haklet, whom the king had sold to John Brainton of Hereford-shire,[157] and the baron of Burford owed him an unknown sum for another ward, Edmund de la Warre.[158]

From the scant available data it is impossible to tell how much money Buckingham collected by virtue of his rights as feudal overlord or whether the amount was a significant one. Consider-ing the dearth of feodary accounts for years and counties for which we have manorial records, I doubt very much that he re-ceived anything like the potential value of this source of income.

The duke was somewhat more successful in exploiting another financial resource—his woods, which were valued at £4,525 in 1521. The valor done in that year listed 9 forests, 28 manors or lordships that included woods, and 24 parks, many including woodlands. Woodlands yielded income from two sources: pay-ments for rights of agistment, herbage, and pannage in the for-ests, and profits from the sale of wood. The valor of 1521 esti-mated the amount paid for the former rights at £66 9s 7d a year, but the duke's actual profits were not much more than £50.[159]

Selling wood was more profitable, but required great care if it was to be accomplished without exhausting the capital value of the forests. The duke instructed the commissions of 1500 and 1504 to survey the woods in the lordships they visited to ascer-tain "what sale withoute distruccion myght be made of the same and yn what yeris."[160] The councillors in Wales had the melan-choly task of reporting the damage done during the minority. In Machen and Coed Meredydd forests in Newport, "gret and yn maner extreme wast and distrucction hath be doon yn the seid woodes yn yeres passed before my lorde's entre, and cannot be knowen as yet apparauntly by whome." There was "nother un-derwode, nor but littell faire tymbre" left, and the prospects for future sales of wood were virtually nil.[161] In Brecon, too, "gret defaultes [were] fownde," and Buckingham's councillors insti-tuted an inquest to discover the guilty parties.[162] Happily, things were much better in the lordships of Hay and Huntingdon, "wheryn no gret waste [was] doon."[163]

Because the evidence is incomplete, estimates of how much

the duke earned each year from sales of wood are impossible. It is clear, however, from the scattered facts at our disposal that substantial sales went on regularly. Annual profits probably never fell below £100. Naturally, the income varied a great deal from year to year: in the general circuit, for example, it was £45 in 1513 and £347 17s in 1514.[164] Regular sales from certain forests added some stability to profits from this source; underwood worth £13 6s 8d was sold each year in the lordship of Kimbolton.[165] Cumulative sales made in the years immediately preceding Buckingham's death amounted to £302 2s, without counting the unknown profits from a wood called Ongar Park in Essex and from two acres in Maxstoke.[166]

The valor of 1521, which included a great deal of detail about the woods, made it clear that the duke did not exploit this resource to the fullest. The surveyors reported that in the lordship of Caus there was "myche wood and tymber but litle sale for the same, howe be it for oon pece called Pontes Cliff is offerde £11. Other parcelles of wood there be that may be soolde and necessary it is thay soe be, for . . . thay be dailly waisted and made a way bi nere neighbors."[167] They recommended a sale of £300 from the lordship of Kimbolton, commenting that the "woodes [would be] myche the better for the same."[168] Unfortunately, when the officers of lordships did not entirely neglect their duty in regard to wood sales, they frequently proved to be poor bargainers. Pickering reported in 1518–19, for instance, that wood sold by Thomas Cade and Thomas Celar for £60 was later resold for more than £126.[169]

In addition to the sources of income common to all his lands, Buckingham had one further resource in his Welsh lordships: his judicial rights as marcher lord. As the supreme legal authority in the lordships of Brecon, Newport, Hay, Huntingdon, Cantref Selyf, and Penkelly, he appointed all legal officers and received the fines collected from criminals and wrongdoers. During the survey of 1500, his commissioners administered justice and collected what revenue they could for their lord. They commanded the coroner of Newport to take sureties from "all rietous and suspect persones, of their apparaunce and gode aberynge." For a fine at the customary rate of 2s, they pardoned all outlaws who surrendered themselves and took bonds for their future good behavior, "whiche was done upon this consideracion, that all tenauntes and resiauntes stondying owte of the lordship shulde come yn . . . so to lyve under the lawes."[170] In Hay they took bonds from all "suspecte persons," and in Huntingdon they held a hundred court in Kington, "one of the Englishrie and another for the Walsherie."[171] The duke's councillors levied fines totaling £123 12s 4d during the circuit. Unfortunately, only a small portion of it ever reached Buckingham.[172] His officers claimed a large portion—half in Brecon—as their prerequisites. Furthermore, since the duke could not afford to antagonize influential tenants whose cooperation was essential for administering his estates, many offenders were excused from paying all or part of their fines. Morgan ap Howell's debt of 50 marks was reduced to 10, and Thomas Morgan of Machen was completely excused from paying the fine of 40s that he owed for his failure to appear as coroner.[173]

In fact, large profits were to be made not from the routine administration of justice but from the Great Sessions, a special commission sent out by Buckingham to supersede the regular courts and to provide swift and effective justice. In theory (as explained in Chapter 1), the sessions resembled the eyres of royal justices throughout England in the twelfth and thirteenth centuries. Traditionally, Great Sessions were held every three years, though Buckingham might have held them more often. Members of the commission were carefully selected from among the duke's closest advisers, important members of the West Country gentry, and lawyers in his service. In 1503, Stafford's brother headed the list of judges sent to Brecon and Newport. Also serving as judges were his secretary, John Russell; his receiver general, Robert Turberville; his treasurer, Humphrey Bannaster; and his auditor, John Gunter. The list included three practicing lawyers, John Kingsmill, John Yaxley, and John Scott; and three members of the Inns of Court, Andrew Windsor, Richard

Littleton, and Walter Rowdon. The remaining members were two Gloucestershire gentlemen, William Dennis and William Huntley; two from Hereford, Roger Bodenham and Walter Vaughan; and a Warwickshire landowner, Thomas Slade.[174]

Despite the great number of lawyers deployed on these occasions, little legal business was actually conducted. At Brecon in 1503, eighteen persons were indicted for criminal offenses, but only one was brought to trial, and it is not clear that even he was punished. On the civil side, the justices heard eight cases and decided three. If the purpose of the Great Sessions had really been to administer the law, they would have been a complete failure. In fact, however, the duke's motive in sending his justices into Wales was not to see that his Welsh tenants obeyed the law but to collect a fine from them for redeeming the sessions, that is, for excusing them from attending.

It was the custom in the Welsh marches to take a recognizance from every adult male to ensure that he attended his lord's court. The original purpose was to guarantee that wrongdoers would appear for punishment, but as we have seen, little legal business was actually conducted at the Great Sessions in Buckingham's domain. After a week or more of attendance, the tenants would become justifiably indignant at being called from their homes and occupations for no purpose, and their clamor for permission to leave would grow louder. At this point, the duke's officials would make it clear that they could return home only after they had agreed to pay Buckingham a fine for dissolving his court.[175]

The Welshmen rightfully grumbled at having to pay the fines, which totaled £2,102, in order to save a criminal minority from punishment, and it was never easy to collect them.[176] On one occasion the duke was actually driven to ask Henry VII for help in collecting the money due from Brecon. This proved to be a great mistake since, like most noblemen, he gained little from his financial dealings with the first Tudor. The king insisted that he pardon the inhabitants of 1,200 marks of the 2,000 they owed and then claimed 300 marks of the remaining debt for himself.[177] Among the Lansdowne manuscripts is the duke's bond for 300 marks "delivered for the kingis gracious favor in the recovering of the 800 marks assessed upon the towne of Breknok."[178]

The accounts for the fiscal year 1520–21, which ended a few months after the duke's death, are a fitting postscript to Buckingham's unsuccessful efforts to increase the income from his lands. All his English estates except those in York together yielded £1,890 17s, less than half the value of £3,943 11s assigned them in the survey of 1521.[179] If the returns from the York and the Welsh properties bore a similar relation to the profits estimated in the valor, his total income that year was about £2,500. If the earnings for York and Wales reported in receivers' accounts for other years is added to the figure of £1,890 17s, the resulting figure, £3,416 16s, has no significance for any particular year, but supplies another rough estimate of Buckingham's actual yearly income.[180] Both these figures fall far short of the £5,000 estimated as the value of the property in the survey of 1521. Worse still, even the higher of the estimates falls far short of the duke's annual expenses, by £250 to £900 in 1504, £2,800 in 1518, £4,000 in 1519, and £4,800 in 1520.[181] Throughout his adult life, Stafford was living beyond his means. Although he made no apparent effort to reduce his expenses, he could not ignore the unpleasant facts of his finances, and he struggled to come to terms with them.

From the beginning, Buckingham kept capital expenditure on the estates to a minimum except at Thornbury. He instructed his officials to shift the responsibility for repairs onto his tenants wherever possible. But this policy had only limited success. Even where the land was farmed out rather than administered directly, he frequently had to pay for any improvements made. For example, he spent 57s 2d at Agmondesham in 1504, and 104s 1d at Hatfield Broadoak and 22s 2½d at Boynton Hall in 1520–21.[182] All these manors were in farm.

The surveyors of 1521 estimated that routine repairs would come to about £126 a year,[183] but clearly this amount was not enough to keep the properties in working order and the manor houses and castles inhabitable. In 1499–1500, the duke spent £191 2s 4d at Bletchingley and Penshurst alone.[184] It cost £120 to repair seawalls in the lordship of Newport in 1501.[185] During the last year of the duke's life, £75 11s was spent in the general circuit and an additional £17 10s on Bletchingley and on the Manor of the Red Rose, in London.[186] Considerable outlays were also made at Brecon, where the hall received a roof "newly and costuly made with pendanntes after a goodly facon."[187]

The run-down condition of much of Buckingham's property in 1521 shows that expenditures, though substantial, were inadequate. The bailiffs and farmers of individual manors were not allowed to make any repairs without the approval of the steward or understeward of the lordship.[188] Evidently, they did not give their approval readily. Of all his property, only Thornbury, Tonbridge, and Brecon castles, Bletchingley and Penshurst manors, and the town of Oakham did not require immediate repairs. The others were in different stages of deterioration. At Newport, the castle had a "faire hall proper loggings . . . and many houses of office. Howe be it in maner all is decaied in covering and floores specially of tymber work."[189] The other Welsh castles were in even worse states. Hay, with the town around it, was described as "an oolde ruynous decaid thing."[190] Bronllys, the castle of the lordship of Cantref Selyf, and Huntingdon were "decaied and mete for noe thing but for prisonners."[191] Caus, though "standing veray goodly upon height," was "in grete ruyne and decay."[192]

Except for Thornbury and Tonbridge, which the surveyors thought "the strongest forteres and mooste like unto a castell of any other that the duke hadde," the castles in England were not in a much better state.[193] Oakham was "an oolde castell all ruynous," although it stood in "a market tonne propurly buylded and the best tonne in ale Rutlandshire."[194] Kimbolton, built for the most part by Duke Edward's great-grandmother, contained "lodgings and all houses of office sufficient for keping of a duks house in a right stately manner." Yet a great many repairs were urgently required: "by occasion of the oolde mantill wall the hall ther . . . is likely to perisshe and thorow [throughout] the said castell is and wolbe great decays by occasion ther is no reparacions doon nor haith not bene doon by many yeres specially in covering."[195] Margaret, countess of Richmond, had improved the castle of Maxstoke during Buckingham's minority, but it "wanteth fynysshing in sondery wises, specially with plaister floring and walling and thoroughly with glassing." The crown surveyors thought it could be made fit for the king for £100.[196] At Stafford Castle, they discovered many defects in the lead covering on the roof and floors, "and the seid enbatelling woolde be better pointed and filled with lyme which with weder is worne away."[197]

Many of the uncastellated manors were also in a state of decay. As early as 1516, William Cooper, the bailiff of Disining, had called the duke's attention to the poor condition of the manor of Cavenham.[198] In 1521, Disining itself was fit "oonly for a fermer and for noon other pleasur to lye at."[199] The surveyor's description of Hatfield Broadoak was almost identical.[200] Naseby was "for lacke of tymber . . . in grett ruyne and lyke to fall" in 1518–19.[201] Writtle was a fine manor, "albe it hit decaieth much by occasion of noe reparacions haith bene doon upon hit by a long tyme."[202] The manor of Brustwick, in York, was "utterly in decay and ruyne," without even lodgings for estate officials, who "for want of necessary lodgings be soone wery and glad shortly to depart from thennes."[203] Here the duke's neglect was pure folly; it diminished his chances of administering his estates in the county of York profitably. His neglect had a similar result in Radcliffe upon Soar. Not only the manor but also the mills and the tenements in the town were in decay.[204] His property in Calais had fallen into ruin and ceased entirely to produce an income.[205]

As the years rolled by and his expenses grew heavier, Buckingham not only neglected the upkeep of his property but also fell deeper into debt. He regularly delayed paying the merchants from whom he bought cloth, textiles, fur, armor, spices, jewels, plate, and other goods. In March 1504, he owed various tradesmen £131 15s for goods delivered to the wardrobe.[206] Twelve years later, these debts had risen to £425 5s.[207] The department of the household was also usually behind in its payments. At the end of 1500 it owed £548 1s; four years later, £243 4s.[208]

For the merchants, collecting the money the duke owed them was a delicate matter. They were eager to keep his business and probably well aware that he was easily offended. Even if they resorted to the courts, they would be beset by difficulties. As a peer of the realm, Buckingham was immune from arrest in matters of debt and consequently was difficult to pressure in this way. If the merchant had taken the precaution of insisting that one of the duke's servants or friends give him a bond for the debt, he still had to face Buckingham's impressive coterie of lawyers. William Butter, a mercer of London, eventually did lose patience. In 1508, he sued John Richard, Buckingham's valet of the robes, for silks delivered to him for the duke's use "long afore." The matter was settled out of court, and Butter withdrew his action when he received the 106s 2d due him.[209]

For larger sums of money, Buckingham turned to the king, peers, ecclesiastics, his estate officials, merchants, and anyone else with cash on hand. The duke was in debt to the king from the day he came of age to the day he died. In 1519, he still had not paid £1,655 10s of the fine levied on him for suing his lands out of livery.[210] He also owed another £1,000 from Henry VII's reign.[211] A memorandum of May 31, 1518, mentioned £1,322 3s, "by which certain lordships are bound," giving a grand total of £3,977 13s.[212] Although Henry VIII did not charge Buckingham interest on the money he owed the crown, he did force him to mortgage some of his property as security for his debts. On one occasion, the king actually foreclosed on mortgaged land worth £1,650.[213]

Buckingham's other debts were on an equally large scale: in 1518 they amounted to £1,676 13s. His creditors included the duke of Suffolk; his son-in-law, Thomas Howard, earl of Surrey; the earl of Arundel; the bishop of London; the abbot of Glastonbury; Robert Amadas, a citizen of London and master of the jewels; Brian Tuke, the king's secretary; Richard Smith, a merchant tailor of London; and William Paulet of London.[214] By the next year, these debts had more than doubled, to £4,160 16s. His

new creditors included the bishop of Durham; the abbot of Westminster; the dean of Wells; the prior of St. John's of Jerusalem;
the abbots of Bury and of St. Augustine's in Bristol; Sir Thomas
Lovell; Sir William Compton; John Haslewood; Thomas Bridges,
his master of the wardrobe; Anthony Vivaldi, an Italian merchant; and William Lok, a mercer of London.[215] He borrowed still
more in 1520. By March he owed £9,201 7s 4d, including his
debts to the crown, and by November a grand total of £10,535
10s.[216] A memorandum drawn up in March noted that £2,500 was
due on Christmas 1520, £2,300 the next year, and £1,500 in 1522.[217]

Clearly Buckingham could not go on borrowing on this scale
indefinitely. There was a limit to the land he could mortgage, to
the gold chains and plate he could use as security for loans, and
to the willingness of friends to guarantee his debts. By 1520 he
was driven to selling some of his property. Sir Richard Sacheve-
ell bought the manor of Radcliffe upon Soar, in Nottinghamshire, for 850 marks.[218] The duke drove a hard bargain: although
the manor and town were in ruin, he received £100 more than
the capital value figured at twenty years' purchase.[219] In the same
year, he sold the manors of Tysoe, Much Wolford, Little Wolford,
and Whatcote, all in Warwickshire, to Sir William Compton for
£1,640, almost twice the twenty-year purchase price of £887 8s.[220]
The last sale was to Sir Thomas Kitson, a mercer of London, who
paid £2,340 for the manors of Hengrave, in Suffolk, and of Colston Bassett, in Nottinghamshire, some £352 more than the normal sale value of £1,987 12s.[221] Buckingham netted £4,546 13s 4d
from these transactions, enough to meet the debts due at Christmas, but far short of the amount necessary to liquidate all his
obligations or to meet his current expenditures.

The king's visit to Penshurst and the Field of Cloth of Gold
were probably the two most important causes of the duke's rising
expenses and debts in 1519 and 1520;[222] and that financial crisis
was in turn a cause of his growing political dissatisfaction, a subject I will explore in greater detail in Chapter 7. Magnates were
often expected to spend large sums participating in the diplo-

matic and social life of the court; in return they expected the offices, gifts, and annuities from the crown that would allow them to pay for the enormous outlays appropriate to their rank. Buckingham felt, with good reason, that Henry did not extend "good lordship" to him in this respect. He was intemperate enough to give voice to his grievances, behavior that undoubtedly led to a deterioration of his position at court and helped to pave the way for the political debacle of 1521.

## CHAPTER SIX

# Patronage and Local Power

In the late middle ages, the ownership of land was the key to political power as well as to wealth. Magnates employed hundreds of men to run their huge households and to administer their far-flung estates. Furthermore, they often used significant portions of their income to grant annuities to those whose friendship and support they wanted. Through this kind of patronage, the nobility drew many members of the gentry, the landowning class that increasingly dominated government and society at the county and local levels, into their orbit. A magnate's household servants, estate officials, and pensioners constituted the core of his affinity, the complex network of dependents to whom he owed "good lordship" in return for loyalty and service. This patronage network enabled a magnate to dominate large areas of the countryside and, on occasion, to assert his claim to power at the center. Even in the fifteenth century, however, a great noble's retinue functioned "less [as] a private army than [as] a combination of an estate bureaucracy and a series of quasi-business alliances with the gentry, for mutual profit and for the control and discipline of the countryside."[1] As we have seen, estate policies designed to maximize the lord's income often clashed with those designed to strengthen or extend his affinity.[2]

The third duke of Buckingham followed the pattern of his class and exploited his estates to maintain a large and impressive patronage network. The enormous household at Thornbury stood at the center of his affinity. Of the 125–150 people employed there at any given time, about 80 wore the Stafford livery.[3] The most important members of this group were the duke's leading councillors—the men who held the highest offices in his household—and those who served him personally. As we saw in Chapter 4, many of them were members of the gentry and therefore helped to forge links between Buckingham and that class. The duke's councillors included numerous lawyers, all gentlemen. A large percentage of them rose to the highest positions in their profession. The duke also found places in his household for men who were related to him by marriage, particularly a number of his brother's Grey stepsons.[4]

Buckingham's network of client/patron relations spread outward from Thornbury to his estates, which provided even more opportunities for drawing members of the gentry into his affinity than his household did. There were 164 estate officials on his payroll receiving annual wages of £493 13s in 1520–21.[5] The most important positions were the county stewardships, which the duke granted to noblemen and gentlemen whose friendship he sought. Buckingham's brother-in-law, Henry Percy, earl of Northumberland, was steward of the duke's property in the lordship of Holderness; one son-in-law's father, Thomas Howard, second duke of Norfolk, of his lands in Suffolk and Essex; George Talbot, earl of Shrewsbury, of his estates in Staffordshire, Shropshire, and Cheshire; and another son-in-law's brother, Sir Edward Neville, of his Kent and Surrey properties. During the duke's lifetime, his county stewards also included five other knights (Sir Thomas Lovell, one of Henry VII's leading advisers; Sir Walter Luke, a prominent lawyer; Sir John Seymour; Sir Thomas Wodehouse; and Sir Andrew Windsor, keeper of Henry VIII's wardrobe), two squires (John Skilling and Walter Vaughan), and a prominent lawyer (Richard Littleton).[6]

As Appendix B indicates, leading members of the gentry held a wide variety of other positions on Buckingham's estates. They served as receivers, deputy stewards, park keepers, foresters, and bailiffs. A dozen sat on the itinerant commissions that supervised local officials, collected revenues, and tried to improve administration on the duke's properties. The social and political importance of these men is indicated by the fact that eleven of them were knights, nine squires.[7] Many played significant roles in governing their counties: twelve served on commissions of the peace, seven as sheriffs, and nine as members of parliament. Six—Sir William Dennis, Sir Edward Guildford, Sir Thomas Lovell, Sir Henry Owen, Sir John Seymour, and Sir Andrew Windsor—were servants of the crown and hence at least potentially useful as contacts at court. More than a third of the group— 14 of 36—were lawyers; eight of these served on the itinerant commissions. The seven who were serjeants-at-law and/or judges of the common-law courts—John Brooke, Richard Brooke, Christopher Hales, John Kingsmill, Sir Walter Luke, John Scott, and John Yaxley—would have been useful not only in looking after Buckingham's general legal affairs, but also in furthering his interests with the royal government. Five estate officials— John Brooke, Christopher Hales, John Russell, John Scott, and Robert Turberville—were also key members of the duke's council and held important positions in his household. Buckingham probably granted them offices on his estates to reward them for their service.

In addition to these prominent members of the gentry, Buckingham employed more than twenty gentlemen who had standing and influence in their communities, but were not key figures in county politics and probably had no connections at court.[8] They invariably lived in the county where they held office, often in the same hundred or village. Their goodwill and vigilance were probably helpful in preventing trespasses on Buckingham's parks and forests and, to a lesser extent, in expediting payment of the rent and other dues owed him. The duke often employed more than one member of a family, trying either to create or to perpetuate permanent ties with them. The Lavingtons of Willesford, Wiltshire, and the Cholmeleys of Bletchingley, Surrey, were typical of this group.

Over his lifetime, Buckingham also granted annuities to more than forty people in an effort to create or reinforce ties with them.[9] The largest of these annuities, which ranged in size from £2 to £20, went to Sir Thomas Wodehouse, who also held an

office on the duke's estates.[10] Thomas Denton, a leading Oxfordshire landowner who eventually served as sheriff of his
county, received the generous annuity of £10.[11] The duke also
gave large pensions to three distant relatives by marriage: Sir Edward Neville, Lord Bergavenny's brother, received £5 a year; Sir
John Grey, a younger brother of Thomas, marquess of Dorset
and Buckingham's brother Henry's stepson, £7; and Sir William
Herbert, brother of the duke's brother-in-law, £10.[12] It is significant that Buckingham did not exploit the annuity to create connections at court. Only two servants of the crown, Sir Thomas
Wriothesley, garter king of arms, and Sir William Norris, a squire
of the body to Henry VIII, received annuities from him. Norris
had participated in the second duke of Buckingham's rebellion
against Richard III and fled to Brittany when it failed, returning
to England with the first Tudor monarch in 1485.[13] There may
also have been a long-standing tie between Buckingham and
the Wriothesley family, since he was a godfather of Sir Thomas's
younger brother Edward.[14] Fifteen of the gentle recipients of the
duke's annuities were members of his household or officers on
his estates.[15] Three lawyers who had no other office or reward
from him received annuities of £2, apparently the sum necessary
to retain them as legal counsel.[16]

Buckingham granted his livery, the external sign that a man
had entered his service, to large numbers of his household and
estate officials. A list for the year 1515–16 contains the names of
149 persons who received red and black cloth for the Stafford
livery, and a list for 1516–17 contains 199 names. About 80
people on each list were members of the household; the rest
were estate officials.[17] Wearing a peer's livery indicated a level of
dependence and subordination inappropriate to the duke's relationship with the knights and other leading gentlemen who
acted as his councillors and held offices on his estates. Consequently, except for the clerks, few of the men listed in Appendixes A, B, and C, or whom I have mentioned in this chapter,
appear on either list. None of the serjeants at law or lawyers who

practiced in the common-law courts at Westminster wore the duke's livery, with the possible exception of John Brooke.[18]

On the other hand, such gentle members of the household as Thomas Jubbes, Giles Greville, Ambrose Skelton, and Humphrey Fowke did wear the Stafford livery. Of the county gentry who held offices on Buckingham's estates, only John Corbet of Leigh, Hugh Marvyn, John and Thomas ap Morgan, and Walter Vaughan appeared on either list. It is significant that these men all owned land in Wales or in English counties relatively close to Thornbury. As might be expected, proportionately more of the local gentry among the duke's estate officials received his livery. This group included William Bedell, John Cholmeley, three members of the Kemys family, James Newell, Edward Osborne, and William Wodegate. Of the gentlemen who received annuities from the duke, only Thomas Denton and Thomas Lewis wore his livery.

The formal ties of office, annuity, and livery that created client/patron relations between Buckingham and members of the gentry represented only one side of his connections to that class. Continual, informal social relations included the extension of hospitality at Thornbury and the exchange of gifts.[19] Thomas Bridges's wardrobe account for the year ending in March 1517 contains a list of thirteen knights and gentlemen who received presents from the duke.[20] Two of the recipients were leading members of his council, Giles Greville and Thomas Jubbes; two others, liveried members of the household, Thomas Lewis and William Colson; and a fifth, one of his leading legal advisers, John Brooke. Buckingham gave gifts to four men who also held annuities from him: Thomas Denton, Thomas Lewis, Sir William Herbert, and Sir Thomas Wriothesley. Only two crown officials appeared on the list: Wriothesley, garter king of arms, and Sir William Dennis, a knight of the body to Henry VIII. Dennis had served on the itinerant commission to Brecon in 1503.[21] Buckingham also gave presents to two important Gloucestershire gentlemen, Sir John Walshe and Sir Edward Wadham, both of whom served as sheriff of the county. Walshe was married to a daughter of Sir Robert Poyntz, who was at Thornbury for the holidays in 1508 and was another member of the county gentry.[22] Still another gift went to William Herbert of Troy, an important Welsh landowner.

The duke's cofferer's accounts give a further indication of his social relations with members of the gentry. In 1508, for example, Sir Edmund Gorges, who had been at the great Epiphany feast earlier that year, sent Buckingham a buckhound as a gift.[23] During the duke's visit to local shrines in the Easter season of 1508, he visited the home of one of the Hungerfords, a leading West Country family, near the charterhouse at Henton.[24] Sir Anthony Hungerford would represent Gloucestershire as knight of the shire in 1553; his sons John and Edmund would represent Great Bedwynd, Wiltshire, in 1553 and 1554, respectively. The duke was godfather to one of Sir Anthony's children in 1521 and rewarded his wife's midwife and nurse with 10s.[25]

In 1519, Stafford visited Sir Henry Guildford's home, where he rewarded the wife of a minstrel. Sir Henry was a courtier and favorite of Henry VIII's; his half brother, Sir Edward, held an office on the duke's estates.[26] Lady Guildford (it is not clear whether the wife of Sir Henry or Sir Edward) supplied a nurse when Buckingham's daughter-in-law, Ursula, gave birth to her first child.[27] She sent the duke a greyhound in 1520.[28] Sir Edward Darrell of Littlecote, Wiltshire, a member of an old and important family in that county, gave the duke a lanner and a lanneret, another gift connected to his passion for hunting.[29]

Buckingham's tenantry formed the outer ring of his affinity. He depended on them for manpower, along with his servants and friends among the gentry, when he assembled an army for his own or the king's service. Whatever the early Tudors' feelings about being dependent on private retinues of this sort, they had little choice, given the limited financial resources of their government. As late as 1536, Sir John Thimbleby "assembled all his tenauntes, frendes and servantes together under the colour to do the kinges service," and then employed them in the Pilgrimage of Grace.[30]

In this context, Buckingham, who commanded a vast tenantry, in addition to his household and estate staff of almost three hundred, was a potential source of considerable strength. There is even some evidence that the duke tried to secure tenants who could equip themselves for war. In 1517–18, for example, when Richard Norris wanted to rent a piece of land in Burton, Buckinghamshire, he not only offered a higher rent than anyone else, but also promised "to fynd a man, horse, and harness and 20 shillings in his purse when your grace comands in the kynngs serves."[31]

The *manred* of Buckingham's tenants—that is, the number liable to military duty—numbered 4,840 in 1521.[32] But he was never able to raise that number. In 1513–14, he contributed 550 men to the army in France, considerably less than his brother's 1,500 or Lord Bergavenny's 984.[33] There is no way of knowing whether this represented the maximum number he could bring into the field but, considering his hostility to France and his persistent desire to outdo his peers, it probably did.

The duke's serious financial difficulties and unpopular estate policies accounted in large measure for his inability to bring anything like five thousand men to the war. Particularly important was the fact that of the tenants liable for military service, 2,766 were Welshmen. Buckingham was such a detested figure in Wales that he could not even maintain his rights there without the help of the crown.[34] Indeed, on a number of occasions, he assembled his retinue for the purpose of using it against his Welsh tenants. On one occasion he allegedly sent John ap Morgan, Thomas ap Morgan, Roger Kemys, and two hundred others to collect some disputed rents from the manor of Holton, in Wales. When the tenants refused to pay, his men seized twelve of them and imprisoned them in Newport Castle.[35] And in 1520, Buckingham wished to assemble a private army of three or four hundred men to take into Wales for the express purpose of intimidating his rebellious tenants.[36]

Just as Buckingham's policies as a landlord undermined his relations with his tenants, his behavior toward the gentry and his staff thwarted his efforts to win their loyalty through traditional forms of patronage and social relations. His proud nature was captured perfectly in the title that appears at the head of his accounts: "the right high and mighty prynce, Edward duc of Bukyngham, erle of Hereford, Stafford and Northampton." He was as sensitive as the Tudors themselves to divided allegiance among his servants and to affronts to his dignity. In 1520, for example, he ordered the arrest of Sir John Coke and one Gamme when they tried to leave his service.[37] Christopher Villers claimed that the duke deprived him of his office as keeper of Kneesall Park, Nottinghamshire, when he entered the royal service.[38] The duke's tactless outburst when he thought one of Henry VIII's courtiers was trying to seduce one of his married sisters expressed his condescending attitude toward the new dynasty explicitly: "Women of the Stafford family are no game for Comptons, no, nor for Tudors either."[39]

When angry, Buckingham was vindictive and stubborn, and had no qualms about using the considerable resources at his disposal to force anyone who had crossed him into submitting to his will. He was particularly likely to resort to the common law for this purpose. These characteristics were frequently evident in his treatment of his household and estate officials. During his lifetime, he instituted 49 separate suits in the court of common pleas against members of his own staff.[40] On other occasions, he seized their goods or imprisoned them in his castles. It is not surprising, therefore, that a number of them betrayed him in 1521.

Buckingham's conduct was not much better when he was dealing with members of the peerage or the gentry. According to John Smyth of Nibley, for example, there was a long-standing feud between the duke and Maurice Lord Berkeley. Although Smyth did not explain the cause of the feud, it may well have been property, since both men owned land in Thornbury. The quarrel apparently descended to a rather low level: Buckingham called Berkeley's wife "false chorle and wiche" and told Maurice "that hee shall be faine to feed piggs . . . which is more meet for him than any other person, or for any goodness or vertue that is in him, save false covetousness and false desire of that hee hath noe right to." Perhaps the continual legal battles that Berkeley fought to regain his inheritance appeared to Buckingham to be symptoms of covetousness, but his insults ill became someone who frequently resorted to the courts himself in similar matters.

The friction between the two men was common knowledge in Gloucestershire. On one occasion, the citizens of Tetbury shut their gates to Buckingham, "hopeing belike to please therby this lord Maurice." In 1519 an unsuccessful effort was made to reconcile the two men: the duke visited Berkeley and lost £6 13s 4d at dice to his host. Smyth even suggested that Berkeley "had a finger in removing the Duke's head from his shoulders," but whether this was speculation or based on something more solid is not known.[41]

Inquisitions in 1505 and 1506 reveal that Buckingham committed a number of trespasses on property in Berkshire, Worcester, and Essex inherited by Edmund Lord de Roos from Eleanor, the late duchess of Somerset.[42] Eleanor had been married twice: the first time to Thomas Lord de Roos and the second to Edmund, duke of Somerset. Edmund Lord de Roos, her grandson by her first marriage, was her heir. By her second marriage, she had eight children, including Buckingham's grandmother.[43] Buckingham laid claim to the manor of Bedminster, Somersetshire, which was part of the late duchess's estates. According to the duke,

by an untrue office it was found in Somersetshire that Elinor late dutches of Somerset shoud dye seased of the manor and hundred of Bedmynster in the said county, the same manor and hundred then being in my possession, by reason that I came of one of the daughters of the said Eleanor and by her will and feoffment. By the said untrue office, I was put out of possession of the same.[44]

It is unlikely that the duke was ever seized of the manor in question, since there is no record of it in the accounts prior to 1508.[45] Yet that he had some interest in the late duchess's property is indisputable, for an act of 1491 restoring the duchess's lands to her grandson and heir contained a proviso protecting his rights.[46] In 1508, Buckingham received a pardon from the king for his trespasses. From then on, Bedminster appeared regularly in his accounts.[47] Buckingham had evidently proved his title, although we do not know the details of the settlement.

On another occasion, Buckingham laid claim to the manors of Haughton, Offley, and Doxesy, in Staffordshire, and of Send, in Wiltshire. They belonged to John Bourchier, Lord Berners, another nobleman from an old family to which the duke was distantly related. Shortly after the duke's death, Bourchier petitioned the crown for the return of these manors. According to Berners, the late duke had sued him for them on the basis of a false title. "Fering the extremyte of thexecucion of the same and also in the eschuynge of the greate importunable coosts and charges and other inconvenyannces that therof myght have ensued," Berners had agreed to exchange the manors with Buckingham for the duke's manor of Upper Clatford, Hampshire, and 300 marks. Since the duke had paid Berners only 100 marks before his death, he maintained that the bargain was void and that his manors should be returned to him.[48]

Whether or not Berners's explanation of the transaction is accurate, some exchange had certainly taken place. The survey of Buckingham's lands made in 1521 noted that Berners had lately occupied the manor of Upper Clatford, Hampshire.[49] On November 26, 1520, the duke had instructed his chancellor to treat with Berners "in regard to certain debts."[50] It is also a matter of record that Haughton and Send, the two manors I have been able to trace, were part of Bourchier's rightful inheritance.[51] The two men had a common great-great-grandmother, and certain portions of the Stafford inheritance that she had held after the death of her first husband, the earl of Stafford, had descended to the offspring of her subsequent marriage to Sir William Bourchier. This complicated situation was probably the basis of the duke's claim.[52] Through Cardinal Wolsey's good offices, Berners's petition met with a favorable response.[53] The king's officials did not include the four manors in question in their accounts of Buckingham's lands, and Upper Clatford was in the crown's hands until 1528.[54]

The duke appeared in a particularly unfavorable light in his suit against Sir Edward Darrell for 500 marks in October 1514. Sir Edward had stood as a surety for Sir Walter Herbert when Herbert had signed an agreement to marry the duke's sister Anne in 1500 and to settle specific pieces of property worth 300 marks a year on her as her jointure. Herbert had died in 1507. Buckingham claimed that Herbert had not fulfilled the agreement, because although Anne's jointure lands were worth 300 marks, they were not the specific properties mentioned in the original contract. On the basis of this technicality, he asserted that Darrell had forfeited his 500 marks. After five years of delay and postponements in the court of common pleas, the duke settled with Darrell out of court.[55]

About the same time, Sir Amias Paulet submitted a dispute about various trespasses and offenses he had committed against Buckingham to the arbitration of the duke's brother, Henry, earl of Wiltshire. Both parties bound themselves by obligations of 1,000 marks to abide by his decision. Paulet, a member of an important Somerset family, served as both sheriff and justice of the peace in the county. The *DNB* described him as "a very active and officious country gentleman." He had been attainted after the second duke of Buckingham's rebellion and restored in 1485, so there had probably been some previous connection between him and the Staffords.

The arbitration procedure could hardly have been a fair one, since the decision was left in the hands of the brother of one of the parties. Furthermore, the judgment was handed down with the explicit provision that "if the said Duke be contented and pleased with this my awarde that then yt stande and be in full strength and vertue, or else be voide and of no effect." Sir Amias had no such veto power. He had obviously agreed to the procedure to avoid the cost and inconvenience of a long-drawn-out legal battle with Buckingham. The award explicitly stated that both parties had agreed to arbitration "by mediacion of their friends in eschying furder trouble costs and charges that might ensue." Paulet, however, was clearly taking a greater risk than the duke. Wiltshire ruled that his brother must drop all his legal actions against Sir Amias, and that Sir Amias had to pay the duke 400 marks. Since the award contains no information about the dispute, and I have not found any independent source, it is impossible to evaluate the fairness of Wiltshire's judgment.[56]

With the possible exception of his legal actions against his former secretary John Russell, discussed in Chapter 4, Buckingham's suits against Thomas Lucas showed him at his worst.[57] Lucas began his career in the household of the duke's stepfather, Jasper Tudor, duke of Bedford. After Bedford's death in 1495, he entered the royal service, eventually becoming solicitor general and a member of Henry VII's council learned in the law.[58] After Bedford's death, while the duke was still a minor and a royal ward, Lucas was also receiver of his property in Gloucestershire.[59]

Buckingham's hostility toward Lucas went back to 1499, when Lucas was appointed royal escheator for land held from the king by the two minor coheirs of Sir Thomas Darrell. Buckingham claimed that Lucas had secured the king's right by a false *inquisition post mortem*, that this right belonged to him, and that, in consequence, he had suffered losses of £1,000. He instituted an unsuccessful action against Lucas in the court of common pleas. In anger, at some point, he also seized some of Lucas's property in Suffolk.

In 1512, the duke again sued Lucas, this time for libel under the statute *De Scandalis Magnatis*. He alleged that the defendant had said "that he sett not by the duke two pens and that the seide duke hathe no more conscience than a dogge and so the seid duke may have good he fains not howe he come thereby." The defendant denied ever having spoken these words. He admitted, however, to having said "that by the duke's feyned accyon I sett not two pens" at the time of Buckingham's first suit against him. Furthermore, he acknowledged having complained when Buckingham seized his property in Suffolk "that the seid duke has small conscience so to deal with me and so the said duke may have goods and land by those weys it semythe he careth not."[60] Though the duke won his case, he received little satisfaction from his victory: he had claimed damages of £1,000, but the court awarded him only £40.[61]

The duke sued Lucas still another time for libel, on this occasion in Star Chamber, and offered the record of the previous judgment in his favor as evidence.[62] It would be interesting to know how the court responded to this attempt to convict Lucas for his libel a second time, but once again we are thwarted by the disappearance of the court's decrees. In any case, the episode reveals how easily the duke permitted legal actions that began about financial matters to become feuds.

Buckingham's quarrels, legal actions, and arbitrary behavior probably offset much of the goodwill and support he might have gained from distributing the patronage at his disposal. He was never as powerful a figure as the number of his household servants, estate officials, annuitants, and tenants suggested. As great a disparity existed between his potential and actual political resources as between his potential and actual economic or military resources.

Furthermore, while the duke gained relatively little from his activities as a patron, they probably had a negative effect on his relations with the crown. Both Henry VII and Henry VIII were instinctively suspicious of magnates who lived on estates in outlying areas of the kingdom and created affinities as their fathers and grandfathers had done in the fifteenth century. Living amid the splendors of Thornbury, surrounded by scores of household servants and liveried retainers, Buckingham was a prime example. On his side, because of political insensitivity or misplaced personal and family pride, the duke did nothing to reassure Henry VII and Henry VIII that his highest loyalty was to them and that his economic and political resources were at the service of the crown. This failure was a major element in the troubled and ultimately tragic relationship that evolved between Buckingham and the early Tudors.

## CHAPTER SEVEN

# The Duke of Buckingham and the Crown

Looking at the third duke of Buckingham in the setting of his household, his estates, and his patronage networks highlights aspects of the life of the nobility characterized by a great deal of continuity in the fifteenth and early sixteenth centuries. The duke maintained patterns of family relationship, consumption, and lordship with deep roots in the past, and seemed to dominate large areas of the West Country and the marches of Wales in much the same way that his father and great-grandfather had. Nonetheless, despite these continuities, the political environment was undergoing significant change as Henry VII and Henry VIII redefined the opportunities open to the nobility for influencing policy and exercising power on both the regional and the national level.

Both Henry VII and Henry VIII wanted to establish a new balance between monarchy and nobility and to gain greater control over England than any of their fifteenth-century predecessors had enjoyed.[1] Their goal was to resolve the political crisis of the fifteenth century by tying the aristocracy to the crown.[2] To succeed, they had to accumulate political, legal, and financial resources sufficient to establish their supremacy over even the greatest lords. Slowly but steadily, they increased their administrative control over the nobility's activities; they also used both rewards and coercion to force the peers to use their power in the service of the central government. In this way, the magnates slowly learned that royal patronage was a reward for loyalty, good service, and obedience.

What neither Henry VII nor Henry VIII would tolerate was the magnate who thought of himself as the king's equal and pursued ambitions defined independently of the crown's. They rejected the concept of government as a dialogue between the monarchy and the great lords. Nor would they tolerate magnates who created disorders to intimidate the king if he withheld the offices and rewards they considered their due.[3]

Although both Henry VII and Henry VIII were determined to redefine the relationship between crown and nobility by strengthening the monarchy and central government, neither king envisioned destroying the peerage or excluding it entirely from political power and social preeminence. Indeed, they were not strong enough to do so had they wanted to. The limitations of central government forced them to rely on the peerage—and therefore indirectly on the peers' affinities—to control and govern the countryside. They also depended on the nobility to supply them with the men to fight their wars. The crown's military commanders were usually members of the pre-Tudor peerage, such as the earls of Surrey and of Oxford, and Lord Edward Howard. On a social level, the king lived in the company of dukes, earls, and other noblemen, whose presence he required to maintain the dignity and ceremony of the monarchy and to participate in the great festivals for which the early Tudor court was to become famous.

Although Henry VII and Henry VIII had similar ideas about the proper relationship between crown and nobility, the differences in their personalities and in the political circumstances of their reigns created obvious contrasts in the way they translated these ideas into concrete policies and specific behavior. During the reign of the first Tudor, the convergence of a number of factors undermined the nobility's power and influence: the king's personal control of both policy and the everyday business of government, his general distrust of a class with independent sources of wealth and power, his reluctance to grant new titles, his greed, and the fact that the peerage did not include any of his close relatives after the death of his uncle, the duke of Bedford, in 1495.[4] Henry VII paid lip service to the importance of the nobility and required the peers' presence at court on important occasions, but gave them little real weight in his government. Except for the duke of Bedford, the earl of Oxford, and Henry's stepfather, the earl of Derby, few peers outside the royal household had much influence with him. Throughout his reign as a whole, a quarter of the members of Henry's council were noblemen, although none were among his leading advisers. Between 1485 and 1509, however, the number of noblemen on the council declined.[5]

In outlying areas of the kingdom, traditionally the strongholds of the most independent peers, Henry VII combined the tactics of undermining the great families, relying on nobles of lesser rank or on those from outside the region, and creating new offices and institutions directly dependent on his council. When it was absolutely necessary to build up his supporters in turbulent areas, he was extremely cautious about granting them estates and franchises; during his entire reign, only Robert Willoughby and Giles Daubney received titles in these circumstances.[6]

The king tried to limit the autonomy of the peerage by curbing the practice of retaining and granting liveries, but his dependence on the retinues of the nobility to maintain order and to raise an army severely limited his scope of action. When he ascended the throne, there were already two statutes against these practices.[7] A statute passed under Richard II in 1390 allowed only peers the right to grant liveries to non-household servants, and then only to knights and esquires.[8] Edward IV's statute of 1468 restricted retaining to legal counsel, household servants, and estate officials. There was an exception to this prohibition, for "lawfull service,"[9] but whatever the intent of the exception, most historians agree that Edward's statute was little more than an ambitious declaration of intent.[10]

In 1485–86, Henry VII required the nobility to take an oath not to retain or give livery contrary to the law. Common-law judges and lawyers took the view that this requirement outlawed retaining any nonresidents, but such a restrictive interpretation was never enforced. Indeed, there is considerable evidence for the widespread existence of sizable retinues in the early part of the reign.[11] A statute of 1504 prohibited royal officials and tenants from becoming the retainers of anyone else.[12] The statute once again exempted household servants, estate officials, and legal counsel from its general prohibition against retaining, although it omitted the exemption for lawful service of the 1468 statute. A license from the king was required to retain anyone outside the exempted categories.[13] In effect, the practice of retaining continued, limited somewhat by a system of royal licensing that enabled the crown to act against any peer whose loyalty was suspect.[14] However restricted its impact, the statute of 1504 challenged the fundamental right of the nobility to retain followers and thus constituted a direct attack on feudal privilege.[15]

From time to time, the early Tudors punished violations of these laws to remind the nobility that they now commanded men at the sufferance of the state and that the crown would not tolerate rival centers of power. In the most spectacular prosecution of Henry VII's reign, the court of king's bench convicted George Neville, Lord Bergavenny, Buckingham's future son-in-law, of illegally retaining 471 men below the rank of knight or esquire. No one in England would have been able to pay the fine of £76,760 imposed by the court. Eventually, the king agreed to accept £5,000, payable in equal installments over ten years; even this much-reduced sum was a heavy burden on an ordinary baron in the early sixteenth century. In addition, Bergavenny had to acknowledge debts of £100,000 "or thereabouts" to the crown. Since they were payable at the king's pleasure, he remained at Henry VII's mercy. Fortunately for Bergavenny, Henry VII died in 1509, a year after receiving the first payment. Henry VIII canceled all Bergavenny's bonds and indentures after he ascended the throne. By that time, the unlucky lord had probably paid only £1,000 of his fine.[16] Another spectacular prosecution took place when Henry VII fined the earl of Oxford 15,000 marks (£10,000) because of the large number of retainers on display when the king visited him at Henningham.[17]

The first Tudor monarch used bonds and recognizances even more often than the statutes against retaining to terrorize the no-

bility and ensure their obedience. He thus expanded and inten-
sified a practice already in use during the reign of Richard III.[18]
Extracted on a wide variety of pretexts, these obligations involved
fines and other payments that were frequently suspended on condition of future good behavior and loyalty. Between 1483 and
1509, only fifteen or sixteen of the 62 peerage families escaped
financial threats by recognizance. In addition, many peers gave
bonds and recognizances for the good behavior and obligations
of other noblemen.[19]

Henry VII's relationships with individual noble families also
demonstrated that obedience, loyalty, and service to the crown
were the only sure bases for wealth, prestige, and power. As
D. M. Loades has pointed out, the king's strategy often involved
multiplying the number and precision of tasks entrusted to
members of the peerage, rather than excluding nobles from positions of responsibility. "By this means they became more dependent upon royal patronage and more closely associated with the
operation of royal authority."[20] The gradual restoration of the
Howards to their lands and titles in return for their cooperation
illustrated this lesson and effectively turned them into courtiers
and servants of the crown.[21] On the other hand, Henry never
trusted the fifth earl of Northumberland and consistently tried
to undermine his regional power, thus demonstrating the fate of
the family of a peer who was unwilling or unable to mobilize his
resources in the service of the new dynasty.[22]

The third duke of Buckingham's relationship with Henry VII
and the duke's political position during his reign must be understood in this broad context. As we have seen, Buckingham was
the single largest private landowner in the kingdom. His income
was immense even though it regularly fell below the anticipated
level. Furthermore, a good deal of his property was concen-
trated in the Welsh marches and the border region of Gloucestershire, Herefordshire, and Shropshire. His predominance in
an area of the kingdom that was traditionally disorderly and
difficult to control increased the importance of his response to
the crown's policies and made any passive or active resistance to

them on his part appear very threatening to the king. Henry VII's own invasion of England through Wales certainly heightened his awareness of the importance of controlling this area of the kingdom.

Buckingham's place in the early Tudor state was further complicated by his blood-relationship to the king. Like Henry VII, he was descended from Edward III through the Beauforts: John of Gaunt's son John Beaufort, earl of Somerset, was their common ancestor. Kinship with the king was, of course, a double-edged sword. Sometimes it was the basis for royal favor and for loyal service to the crown. Henry VII's uncle, Jasper Tudor, duke of Bedford, spent his life advancing the interests of his nephew, a dedication undoubtedly facilitated by the fact he had no sons of his own. When he died in 1495, both the titles and estates he had received from Henry reverted to the crown. On the other hand, close relatives of the king could pose a threat to the reigning dynasty, particularly one—such as the Tudors'—that was not successful in producing male heirs. Gossip at Calais in 1503, for example, mentioned Buckingham as a possible successor to the throne. At the time, Henry VII's heir was only twelve years old. The officers speculating about the future completely ignored the possibility of a minor inheriting the crown.[23]

Although these facts encouraged Henry VII to regard Buckingham with suspicion, the young duke had a legitimate claim to royal favor as the son of the first magnate to die fighting in the Tudor cause. To a certain extent the king acknowledged this debt soon after he assumed the crown. As we saw in Chapter 2, the first parliament of the reign reversed the attainder of the second duke and restored his property to his son. The king placed Edward in his mother Margaret Beaufort's household, both a mark of Edward's high rank and a sign of the king's desire to bind him to the new dynasty. Since Edward was only eight years old at Henry's accession in 1485, the king certainly had ample opportunity to try to create a warm relationship with the young nobleman. Instead, he exploited the duke's wardship ruthlessly, ultimately extracting £6,600 from him.[24] His need for money and his suspicions of potentially dangerous members of the peerage were stronger than any affection or gratitude he felt toward Buckingham or his father.

Henry VII's general distrust of the greater peers and the specific factors complicating his relationship to Buckingham virtually ensured that he would exclude the duke from any significant political role or influence. Buckingham did lead a contingent of West Country gentlemen against Perkin Warbeck at Taunton in 1497, but this was a testimony to his regional power and to the crown's military dependence on the nobility rather than a sign that he had any real political weight.[25] He subsequently participated in state trials that exploited the presence of high-ranking noblemen to legitimize verdicts already decided upon by the king and his closest advisers. The duke was a member of the courts that convicted William Stanley in 1495, the earl of Warwick in 1499, and Sir James Tyrell in 1501.[26]

The only time Buckingham played a major role during Henry VII's reign was at the feasts, tournaments, and pageants that marked coronations, weddings, major diplomatic events, and the maturation of the king's sons. Despite his reputation for frugality, Henry VII was well aware that magnificence was expected of great rulers and was necessary to persuade observers at home and abroad to take him seriously. As G. R. Elton has observed, "The Tudor court, with its red-coated guard and its vast expenditure on silks, satins, and velvets, was always a gorgeous affair, and ceremonial was one thing on which Henry invariably spent in a prodigal manner."[27] The lavishness of the court demonstrated visually the superiority of the king over even the greatest of his subjects. Furthermore, Henry never participated in court entertainments such as jousts and revels, but increased the distance between himself and his subjects by attending as chief spectator.[28]

Buckingham's participation in a court ceremony or pageant augmented the splendor of the occasion, and invariably cost him a great deal of money he could ill afford, thus reinforcing the more direct ways in which the king exploited and undermined him financially. As in the case of the fifth earl of Northumberland, Henry apparently hoped to turn the young nobleman into a courtier who found sufficient outlet for his energies and ambition in conspicuous expenditure for the benefit of the new dynasty.[29]

Buckingham played his first role at the Tudor court at Henry VII's coronation, when he was only eight years old. The king gave him new bridles for the horses he rode during the ceremonies and dubbed him Knight of the Bath.[30] Nine years later, he participated in the festivities when Prince Henry was created duke of York.[31] This celebration was the most elaborate of the reign, except for the marriage of Prince Arthur and Catherine of Aragon. The banquets, dances, and jousts were designed to emphasize the unity of the houses of Lancaster and York, to assert that the previous duke of York was dead, and to convince everyone that Perkin Warbeck was an impostor.[32] In 1497, while he was still under age, Buckingham attended the king when he received the new Venetian ambassador at Woodstock.[33] The significance of the duke's blood-relationship to the king and the importance that his presence lent state occasions was made clear in 1499, when the Milanese ambassador reported the reception of an envoy from France. "Has not heard the cause of Luis's coming, though it cannot be unimportant, because the Bishop of Durham, the king's Privy Seal, has been several times to his house; and subsequently . . . the King's near relative, the Duke of Buckingham and the Duke of Suffolk, entertained him with stately banquets."[34]

As an adult, Buckingham appeared regularly at court for important state occasions and celebrations in splendid costumes that dazzled contemporary chroniclers, who described them in loving detail. In 1500, for example, when Henry VII met Archduke Philip of Austria at Calais, the duke's lavish costume stood out even in the richly dressed company that attended the king.[35] The next year he appeared at the wedding of Prince Arthur and Catherine of Aragon in a gown valued at the staggering sum of £1,500.[36]

The tournaments to celebrate the marriage included processions of knights into the lists complete with pageant cars, pavilions, and masques. Ever since the thirteenth century, tournaments had been developing as a form of artistic expression, often approaching drama, in which the actual combat was subordinated to the elements of display and masquerade.[37] On this occasion, Buckingham, who was the chief challenger, appeared at the tilting ground "in a chappell hangid or curteynyd abowth whyth white and grene satyn palid, brawderid Right goodly upon every side and ende whith iiij grete Rede Rosis, and the coveryng thereof payntid with azure, and set at every corner whyth a gilt pynnakyll."[38] The duke's splendid entrance foreshadowed his triumph in the contest: at the end of the day, he won "the pryse and honor."[39] The chronicler Hall reported that Buckingham and the marquess of Dorset, "wyth their aydes and compaygnions, bare theim selfes so valyauntely that they obteyned great laude and honoure, bothe of the Spanyardes and of their countrymen."[40]

During the final years of Henry VII's reign, Buckingham continued to participate in the pageantry and ceremonies that characterized social and political life at the court. In 1503, for example, he attended the marriage of the king's daughter Margaret to James IV of Scotland.[41] In 1505, he again accompanied the king to greet Archduke Philip, whom a storm had forced to land in England.[42] He was part of the "honourabyll company of lordys spirituell and Temporall" who joined the king to celebrate St. George's Day that same year.[43]

The duke's most spectacular appearance in these years, however, was at the enthronement of William Warham as archbishop of Canterbury in 1504. Buckingham assumed the office of Lord High Steward as service for the lordship of Tonbridge, which he held of the see of Canterbury.[44] He received the white staff of office "in curteous maner professyng his duetie, saying . . . that there was never gentleman of his noble progenie before hym, neither after hym ever, shoulde do or execute his office with better whyll and diligence than he would." At dawn on Passion

Sunday, when Warham formally entered the city, Buckingham greeted him at the Church of Saint Andrew "with great reverence and an honorable retinue." From there they proceeded to Canterbury Cathedral to pray to St. Thomas and say mass. A magnificent banquet followed at the episcopal palace. The duke headed the procession to serve Warham on horseback, head bared, a pious expression on his face, the white staff of office in his hand. Without doubt, he "proved ryght well" the lofty promises he had made on assuming his post and thus earned the sobriquet "mirror of all courtesy." [45]

Buckingham's splendid appearance at court ceremonies and on great state occasions did not give him any political influence with the king or secure him a meaningful role in Henry VII's government. His choice of Thornbury, Gloucestershire, on the Welsh border, as his chief residence symbolized his peripheral position in the government. Certainly Buckingham could have lived closer to the court and center of government had his regular presence there been necessary or of interest to him. Indeed, in the first two years after he came of age, he resided at Penshurst, in Kent, and Bletchingley, in Surrey, both within easy traveling distance of the capital. In 1499–1500, he spent £191 2s 4d on repairs at these two manors; Penshurst was still suitable for entertaining the king and court in 1519. Two years later, the manor at Bletchingley was described as "propurly and newly builded with many goodly lodgings and houses of office. . . . The hall, chapell, chambers, parlours, closetts and oratories be newley seiled, with waynescott rooves, floores and walles, to thentent they may be used at pleasure without hanggings." [46] In addition, the duke possessed an impressive castle at Tonbridge, Kent, described as his strongest fortress in England or Wales. [47]

As one might expect given his lack of political power and influence at court, Buckingham received few favors from the crown. Henry VII granted him the Manor of the Red Rose in London, but that was the only property he received from the king during the entire reign. [48] The king also gave him a large diamond during the festivities to celebrate Catherine of Aragon's arrival in London in 1501. The gift was probably a way of impressing the Spanish and the public and of repaying the duke for his enormous expenses in connection with the wedding, rather than a sign of extraordinary royal favor.[49]

The endemic disorder in Buckingham's Welsh lordships must have confirmed the king's belief that the duke was not a suitable servant of the crown. Because the king's writ did not run in the marches and because the duke continued to redeem the Great Sessions, his Welsh domain was notorious as a center of crime and disorder.[50] Felons and other wrongdoers habitually slipped over the border from England to avoid prosecution in the counties where they had committed their offenses. The situation provided the duke's officials with innumerable opportunities for profit in the form of bribes from those fleeing justice.

Henry VII was determined to restore order in Wales and in the neighboring English counties, but his policy was essentially a conservative one that attempted to make the existing machinery work. He permitted the marcher lords to retain their jurisdiction over felons and murderers, but forced them to sign indentures in which they promised to enforce the law and to prevent their domains from serving as refuges to criminals.[51] In 1504, Buckingham signed an indenture in which he promised to enforce the law in Brecon, Newport, Hay, Huntingdon, Kingston, and Caus on pain of forfeiting £100. He agreed to extradite both tenants and nonresidents who fled to his lordships after committing crimes elsewhere, and to return stolen goods and cattle brought into his domains. He would also proclaim as felons any of his officials or inhabitants who "shall favour, secour ne mainteigne with mete, drinke ne money, ne herbroughe any outlaw or notarely knowen fellow nor rebel." Finally, he undertook to put all the residents of his lordships under surety for their good behavior.[52]

Despite the indenture of 1504, conditions in Buckingham's Welsh lordships did not improve, because the duke was either incompetent or uncooperative, or a combination of both.[53] From Henry VII's point of view, the situation underscored the way the inherited rights and liberties of the nobility obstructed his efforts to enforce the law and consolidate control over his kingdom. It also illustrated the difficulty of using a magnate like Buckingham to implement royal policy.

Henry VIII's accession to the throne in April 1509 seemed to usher in a new era. With his exuberant personality, his zest for life, his appetite for pleasure, and his evident distaste for the routine business of government, the young king could not have been more different from his father. Life at court seemed to settle into an endless round of celebrations, masques, revels, pageants, tournaments, and banquets, interspersed with long days of hunting and hawking. Unlike Henry VII, who had remained studiously aloof, Henry VIII participated enthusiastically in all the activities and entertainments at court, including jousting. He fought in the lists for the first time after his accession in June 1510, when he and Sir William Compton appeared in disguise; although both men won praise for their skill, Compton was nearly killed.[54] A group of courtiers gathered around the king who shared his tastes and included Thomas Boleyn, Henry Bourchier, earl of Essex, Charles Brandon, Francis Bryan, Nicholas and Peter Carew, William Compton, Edward and Henry Guildford, Edward Howard, Thomas Knevet, Edward Neville, John Peachy, Edward Poyntz, and Lord Henry Stafford, the duke of Buckingham's younger brother.[55] Henry VIII staffed the privy chamber with his favorite boon companions rather than the modest gentlemen who had served his father.[56]

With the arrest of Edmund Dudley and Richard Empson, who were subsequently executed for treason, Henry lost no time repudiating the unpopular financial policies of his father. During the next few years he pardoned many peers of all or part of the fines, bonds, and recognizances levied on them during the previous reign. He also distributed gifts, titles, and other favors with an openhandedness that contrasted dramatically with his father's stinginess.[57] The duke of Buckingham and his family were among the recipients of this unaccustomed royal largesse. In December 1509, Henry VIII canceled four recognizances of

£160 each that Buckingham, his brother, and his sister Anne had signed and delivered to Sir Thomas Lovell, Sir Henry Wyatt, and Edmund Dudley.[58] The next month he canceled two other obligations of £400 each: the duke and three of his servants, Robert Gilbert, Humphrey Bannaster, and William Walwyn, had signed the first; the duke, Sir John Guise, William Bedell, and Robert Partesoil the second.[59] In 1510, the king granted the title of earl of Wiltshire to Buckingham's younger brother, an unusual mark of favor to a family already holding a dukedom.[60] Some years later, in 1514, the king remitted part of the duke's still unpaid fine for suing his lands out of livery, specifically "to obtain his good will."[61] He also granted Buckingham two valuable wardships: that of Ralph, fourth earl of Westmorland, in 1509, and that of Thomas Fitzgerald, son of the late earl of Kildare, in 1518.[62] In 1518, he also gave the duke "a goodly courser, a rich gown, a like jacket doublet, and hosen."[63] In 1519 he honored Buckingham by visiting him at Penshurst, a visit that was apparently successful since Richard Pace reported to Cardinal Wolsey that "Buckingham makes him [the king] excellent cheer."[64]

Despite these obvious contrasts between Henry VII and Henry VIII, there was actually far more continuity than difference in the way the first two Tudor monarchs governed. Although the second Tudor willingly gave over the routine business of government to others, he never relinquished control over policy. It is significant that, in the very first year of his reign, he wrote to reassure his father-in-law, King Ferdinand of Spain, that while he was enjoying "jousts, birding, hunting, and other innocent and honest pastimes, also . . . visiting part of his kingdom," he was not neglecting "affairs of state."[65] Henry revealed his exalted notion of himself as king when he referred to his prerogative as "his most noble and mighty power" in 1516.[66] He saw no diminution of the majesty of the crown in the fact that he left most of the actual business of government to his able minister, Thomas Wolsey. Indeed, as G. R. Elton has observed, "those who reckoned that [Wolsey's] years of power could be called the reign of the cardinal made a mistake not shared by the cardinal himself."[67]

In order to raise the monarchy to heights unattainable by any of his subjects, Henry sought to centralize politics and the distribution of patronage at the court. He was as intolerant and suspicious as his father had been of rival centers of political loyalty. Within a few years of his accession, he succeeded in making the Tudor court the focus of social and political life. The careers of Sir William Compton and a somewhat less eminent figure, Sir Ralph Egerton, show how dependent ambitious gentlemen were on the king's favor and how much that favor depended on frequent, personal access to him.[68] In a parallel development, the monarchy asserted its right to grant and confirm honorable status itself through state-supported heraldic visitations. The nationalization of the honor system, as Mervyn E. James calls it, contrasted with the traditional view of honor as a quality that was inherited through the blood and confirmed by individual behavior and was thus self-authenticating.[69]

There was no room in Henry VIII's conception of the monarchy for peers who thought of themselves as the king's equals, assumed they had an inherent right to political power and royal patronage, or obstructed the implementation of Tudor policy in the regions they dominated.

In this context, the outcome of the struggle for control of the council that broke out in the opening months of Henry VIII's reign is instructive.[70] Thomas Howard, earl of Surrey, sought to wrest control of the council from Bishop Fox and Henry VII's other intimate advisers. Surrey's allies included George Talbot, earl of Shrewsbury; Thomas Ruthal, bishop of Durham; Sir Henry Marney; Charles Brandon; Thomas Lord Darcy; and Archbishop Warham. His position was undoubtedly strengthened by the fact that his son Edward and his son-in-law Thomas Knevet were among the king's favorite companions. The arrest of two members of Henry VII's inner ring, Empson and Dudley, must have made Bishop Fox aware of his vulnerability. To shore up his position, he considered an alliance with two magnates who were not associated with Surrey, the duke of Buckingham and his brother-in-law, the earl of Northumberland. In August 1509, Lord Darcy reported to Bishop Fox,

It is the saying of every market man from London "that the Lord Privy Seal [Fox], seeing of his own craft and policy he cannot bring himself to rule the king's grace and put out of favour the Earl of Surrey, and Earl of Shrosbere [Shrewsbury], the bishop of Dorisme [Durham], Mr. Mernye [Marney], Mr. Brandon, and the Lord Darcy, now he will prove another way, which is to bring in and bolster himself to rule all with the Duke of Bukyngham and the Earl of Northumbr."[71]

In the event, however, Bishop Fox saved his position not by bringing in two magnates, but by adding Wolsey to the council. By 1514, Wolsey had clearly defeated Surrey in the struggle for power. At the center of Tudor government, therefore, there was no "noble reaction."

Although Wolsey's rise to power was undoubtedly due to his extraordinary capacity for business and his competence, it also suited the predilections of a king somewhat suspicious of the nobility. Henry's attitude surfaces from time to time in the state papers. In April 1518, for example, when the dukes of Buckingham and of Suffolk were with the king at Woodstock, Henry ordered John Clerk, who had brought letters from Wolsey, "that in no wise he should make mention of London matters before his lords."[72] In a mysterious undated letter, the king ordered Wolsey to keep a watch on the dukes of Buckingham and Suffolk, and the earls of Northumberland, Wiltshire, and Derby.[73] Many years later, in the aftermath of the Pilgrimage of Grace, Henry exploded at the duke of Norfolk for even suggesting that he ought to rely on peers to govern the North. "We thank you for your opinion of the Marches, but we doubt not you will conform your mind to find out the good of that order which we have therein determined and cause others to perceive the same; for we will not be bound to accept the service of none but lords."[74]

Henry VIII clearly preferred relying on men like Charles Somerset, earl of Worcester, Sir John Russell, and Sir William Compton, whose territorial position depended on grants from the

Tudors, to relying on peers from families that had ruled in their regions for generations. Neither the duke of Suffolk nor the second or third duke of Norfolk, who played such large roles at Henry VIII's court, were independent magnates in the fifteenth-century sense. Suffolk had been raised from the gentry largely because he was a favorite companion of the king's; no one forgot that his father was a mere gentleman. The Howards had been transformed into courtiers and servants of the Tudors in the long period of probation between their attainder in 1485 and the final restoration of the dukedom of Norfolk in 1513.

The similarity of Henry VIII's attitude to his father's is evident in his dealings with the Cliffords and the Percies. Henry Clifford, first earl of Cumberland, was reared with the king and always had a hold on his affections. After Henry ascended the throne, he showered Clifford with favors, including elevation to the earldom of Cumberland in 1525 and the marriage of the earl's son and heir to the king's niece, Eleanor Brandon. Nonetheless, as Mervyn James has shown, the king took advantage of Cumberland's willingness to exchange the reality of regional power for land, titles, and status symbols and used it to extend his control over the counties of Cumberland and Westmorland.[75]

Henry's treatment of the Percies was far more ruthless, probably because he trusted them less. Cumberland was always loyal, whatever his other faults. Henry VII had tamed the fifth earl of Northumberland by fining him £10,000 in a case of ravishment of a ward; the younger Tudor apparently turned him into "a model Henrician courtier," by imprisoning him in the Fleet for abducting a ward in 1516.[76] Subsequently, in a series of transactions worthy of his father, Henry VIII convinced the incompetent, childless sixth earl of Northumberland, who was estranged from both his wife and his heir, Sir Thomas Percy, to bequeath to the crown all that remained of the Percy estates after his extravagant and irresponsible life.[77]

Despite Henry VIII's promise to end the onerous financial exactions of his father's reign and to redress the grievances of those who had been wronged, the reform was much more limited than royal propaganda suggested.[78] In 1506, for example, Thomas Stanley, second earl of Derby, owed Henry VII £4,133 for various fines. Henry VIII did not pardon him of this debt; in March 1512, Derby still owed the king £3,333 6s 8d. Two years later Henry charged Derby another £414 14s for the right to enter the lands of his mother, Joan Lady Strange, and in 1516 he fined him £900 for using force against Sir Thomas Butler. When Derby died in 1521, he still owed the king more than £3,000. Although Henry VIII received more than 3,600 marks from the Stanley lands during the third earl's minority, he would not allow any of that money to be applied to the second earl's debt.[79]

Henry was no more generous with Richard Grey, third earl of Kent. A series of complicated transactions in the previous reign, culminating in the infamous recognizance of August 1507, had left the entire Grey inheritance at the mercy of the crown. By the time the pathetic earl died in 1524, a sizable portion of his inheritance had passed into the hands of the king and his influential courtiers. Kent's half brother and heir, Henry, was unable to recover the Grey patrimony despite complaints in Star Chamber, suits in chancery, and direct appeals to Henry VIII and Wolsey.[80]

Henry VIII was somewhat more generous with the duke of Buckingham, who owed the crown more than £6,000 when Henry VII died in 1509. Nonetheless, Buckingham was far from satisfied with the cancellation of the recognizances mentioned above. He formally petitioned for restitution of the £3,000 fine he had paid to sue his lands out of livery and systematically recounted his other financial grievances against the late king.[81] When Henry VIII failed to respond to the petition, the duke grew impatient. In 1515 he sued the late king's executors for recovery of the £3,000 fine. The king's council and a majority of the royal judges heard the case; they ruled against the duke on the ground that since special livery was a favor, the recipient had to pay whatever price the king demanded for it. Nevertheless, Henry restored £1,000 to the duke "to obtain his goodwill."[82]

Henry VIII's government took the offensive against a number of nobles and knights in the spring of 1516. In April, the crown imprisoned Henry Percy, fifth earl of Northumberland, in the Fleet for abducting a ward.[83] In May, the king excluded three nobles from the council: Thomas Grey, second marquess of Dorset; Thomas Howard, earl of Surrey (Buckingham's son-in-law); and George Neville, Lord Bergavenny (also Buckingham's son-in-law). The next month the crown brought charges for illegal retaining against Dorset, Bergavenny, Hastings (Buckingham's brother-in-law), Sir Edward Guildford, and Sir Richard Sacheverell, despite the fact that the statute of 1504 had expired on Henry VII's death.[84] Sometime the same year the earl of Derby was fined £900 for using force against Sir Thomas Butler.[85]

The situation at court during the spring and summer of 1516 was evidently very dangerous, if the letters of Thomas Alen to George Talbot, earl of Shrewsbury, are to be believed. Although it is difficult to be sure from Alen's cautious comments, he was probably witnessing a final stage in Wolsey's consolidation of power. Wolsey had become lord chancellor about six months earlier, after pressuring Archbishop Warham to resign from office. In May 1516, the very month the crown took action against so many peers, Bishop Fox resigned as lord privy seal. The office went to one of Wolsey's allies, Thomas Ruthal, bishop of Durham.[86] Alen reported on the prosecutions for retaining and noted that Shrewsbury was as guilty as those who had run afoul of the law. He also worried that those who were in disgrace would try to deflect attention from themselves by turning on Talbot: "I fer som ther be wold take a thorn out of theyr own fote and put hit yours."[87] He was convinced that Shrewsbury would be safest if he stayed away from court and engaged in an extended series of maneuvers to prevent the king from demanding his attendance. The only good news Shrewsbury's informants reported during that gloomy month concerned the duke of Buckingham. On May 16, Richard Sacheverell commented that Buckingham was "in great favour"; on May 31, Thomas Alen wrote that the duke "went home yesterday; hath all his desires, with great thanks from the King."[88]

Although Buckingham avoided trouble during the crisis of 1516, he was involved in a major case against illegal retaining in Star Chamber in November 1520. Henry VIII personally attended a dramatic session of the court to prosecute Sir William Bulmer for breaking the law that forbade a servant of the crown from being retained by anyone else. The king delivered a stinging rebuke to the terrified knight, a sworn royal servant who had appeared at court wearing the badge of the Staffords: "He would none of his servauntes should hang on another mannes sleeve. . . . he was aswell able to maintein him as the duke of Buckingham: and . . . what might bee supposed by the duke's retaining, he would not then declare." Bulmer fell to his knees and pleaded for mercy, but Henry was in such a temper that "never a noble man there durst entreate for him." Finally, when the court had dealt with all the other matters on the agenda for the day, the king, "moved with pitie," forgave him. He closed the session with a homily that was probably meant for Buckingham much more than for Bulmer: "We will that none of our servauntes shalbe long to any other person but to us, nor we wil not that our subjects repine or grudege at suche as wee favoure, for our pleasure will have in that cace as us liketh, for one we will favor now and another at such tyme as us shall like."[89]

Henry apparently humiliated the duke further by ordering Wolsey to reprimand him directly for his misdemeanor. In a memo dated November 26, the duke referred to "how my lord Cardinall hath handlede us."[90] In all likelihood, this was the occasion when Wolsey warned him that although "he used to rail upon [Wolsey] . . . yet that he should take heed how that he did use himself towards the King's highness."[91] Sir William Fitzwilliam, the ambassador to France, probably had the rebuke to Buckingham in mind when he spoke to Francis I shortly after the duke's sudden arrest in April 1521. Fitzwilliam recounted the conversation with Francis to Wolsey:

I said I thought he was a highminded man, 'and a man that would speak sometimes like a man that were in a rage . . . Then I showed him the

King's grace had given him good lessons . . . and so good that, an [i.e. if] he had had any grace, he would not have deserved [to have] been there . . . I showed hym I knew his grace had given him warning, as well by your grace as by his own. . . .'[92]

In light of Henry VIII's attitude toward the nobility, it is not surprising that he continued his father's practice of excluding Buckingham from political power. Although the duke remained on the king's council, he rarely attended its meetings. There are records of his participation in its decisions on only two occasions. It is significant, given the crown's continued military dependence on the peerage, that both had to do with military matters: in 1509, he signed a proclamation ordering the people to prepare in case of war; in 1512, he participated in a discussion about the disastrous expedition to Spain, which had ended in mutiny and the precipitous return of the officers to England.[93] The duke sat with the council in Star Chamber only five times between November 1509 and May 1516, although the court met regularly on fixed days during term time. He also attended the three parliaments of the reign that met during his lifetime—in 1510, 1512, and 1515—and served as a trier or receiver of petitions in all three of them.[94] At the opening of Henry VIII's first parliament, he even carried the cap of state.[95]

As one would expect, Buckingham did participate in the French wars of 1513–14. He supplied 550 men for the king's army and served during the siege of Therouanne.[96] On the night of August 13, he joined the earl of Essex, the marquess of Dorset, Lord Bergavenny, Lord Willoughby, and 6,000 men to prevent any attempt by the French to relieve the city, "where they were all night in order of battaille, awaityng the rescue of the citie, but the Englishmen were ascryd [seen], and so the Frenchmen brake their purpose for that time: and so the Duke of Buckyngham and his companions returned to the campe."[97]

Buckingham also continued to play a leading role in court ceremonies and at major diplomatic events. He filled the office of lord high steward at Henry VIII's coronation feast.[98] The following June he rode through London with the king after his marriage to

Catherine of Aragon.[99] The duke was also present, gorgeously appareled as was his wont, at Henry's meeting with Emperor Maximilian in France in 1513.[100] When the king and Wolsey reversed their foreign policy the following year, the duke witnessed the betrothal of Henry VIII's sister to Louis XII of France.[101] At the ball following the ceremony, he and the king danced in their doublets.[102] Four years later, Henry renewed the French alliance by betrothing his daughter to the dauphin, and Buckingham had a place of honor at the banquet that followed.[103] The duke had signed the Treaty of Universal Peace a few days earlier.[104]

Buckingham, who preferred a pro-imperial, anti-French foreign policy, was probably far happier with his duties when Charles V visited Canterbury in May 1520. During the meeting, the duke accompanied the French ambassador to services in the Cathedral. At the banquet held in Archbishop Warham's palace, the duke held the office of sewer. He entered the banqueting hall "upon a whyte hobby, and in the midest of the hall was a partition of boordes, at which partition the Duke alyted from his hobby, and kneeled on his knee, and that done, tooke agayne his horse backe, until he was almost halfe way unto the table, and there alyghted, and dyd the lyke as before, and then rode to the table, where he delivered his hobby, and served kneelyng at the table where the Empereur was."[105] This was also the famous occasion when the dukes of Buckingham and Suffolk, who performed the service of holding a bowl in which the royal family and the imperial guests could wash their hands, were humiliated by having to extend the courtesy to Cardinal Wolsey as well.[106]

Henry VIII embarked for his meeting with Francis I at the Field of Cloth of Gold as soon as this meeting was over. Buckingham accompanied him with the sizable entourage of 5 chaplains, 10 gentlemen, 55 other servants, and 30 horses. His wife attended the queen with 4 gentlewomen, 6 gentlemen, several servants, and 12 horses.[107] But Wolsey triumphed once more: his entourage was larger than the combined retinues of the archbishop of Canterbury and the dukes of Suffolk and Buckingham.[108] On June 7, the duke accompanied the Spanish ambassador to the meeting between the two kings.[109] Twice he rode back to French territory with the French king after Catherine of Aragon had entertained Francis in her tent.[110] Buckingham also acted as a judge on the English side at the tournament held to celebrate the occasion.[111]

The duke's last public appearance was at Henry VIII's second meeting with the emperor at Gravelines, immediately following the conclusion of the meeting at the Field of Cloth of Gold. Buckingham's modest retinue on this occasion consisted of only ten men on horse, but he distinguished himself nonetheless by his cordial reception of the imperial envoy, the marquis d'Arschot.[112]

Evidently, then, the duke of Buckingham's political position did not change substantially after Henry VIII's accession to the throne: the duke continued to be a prominent figure at court and a decorative participant in the ceremonies and pageants that marked sixteenth-century diplomacy, but he had little real political power or influence. What did change was his readiness to express his discontent over his limited political role and to criticize specific royal policies. The duke, who was in his early thirties in 1509, may have felt more secure about expressing his views than he had when he was younger. Since he was more than ten years older than Henry VIII, he may have found it easier to criticize him than he had Henry VII, who had been considerably older than the duke. Finally, because of his age, he probably felt that if he did not win adequate recognition early in the new reign, he never would.

Buckingham's decision to sue Henry for recognition of his hereditary position as high constable of England in 1510 must be understood in this context. The office, which carried with it command of the armed forces and the right to hold a court to punish treason, was potentially a powerful one. The duke claimed the right as heir to Humphrey Bohun, earl of Hereford, who had held the manors of Haresfield, Newnham, and Whytenhurst, all in Gloucestershire, in return for carrying out the duties of this office. At the time of the suit, Buckingham held the manors of Haresfield and Newnham; Whytenhurst had reverted to the crown on the marriage of Humphrey's daughter and co-heir Mary to Henry IV. The judges ruled in the duke's favor on the ground that if he did not fill the office of high constable, he would hold the manors without rendering any service for them. In the event, however, Buckingham's victory did him little good. Henry VIII refused to be coerced into giving Buckingham the post and responded to the ruling by allowing the constableship to lapse.[113]

Buckingham's complaints about the exclusion of the nobility from power were directed against both Cardinal Wolsey and the king's minions, a group of adolescent boys who became the king's boon companions in 1515 and gentlemen of the privy chamber in 1518.[114] The duke was probably referring to them when he complained that "he had done as good service as any man, and was never rewarded; and that the King would give his fees, offices, and rewards rather to boys than to noble men."[115] He also felt, with some justification, that Wolsey was hostile to the peerage, commenting, "My lord Cardinal is so sore with noble men, that they would be all in his top if the king's grace were displeased with him. . . . He would undo all noble men if he could."[116] Furthermore, pride in his royal and noble lineage made it unbearable for him "to be subservient to so base and un-civil a fellow."[117] He resented performing a menial task for the cardinal, as he was forced to do during Charles V's visit to England in 1520.

Buckingham bitterly opposed the pro-French foreign policy that emerged in 1515. He rightly blamed Wolsey for it. Many years earlier, the Spanish ambassador had accurately reported that "the Duke of Buckingham and many others are mortal ene-mies of the French."[118] The duke was in regular contact with the Spanish and the Venetian ambassadors. In 1511, for example, the doge and senate of Venice instructed their envoy to "avail himself of all the friends of the Signory, and especially the Duke of Buckingham."[119] On July 14, 1519, Buckingham received both the Spanish and the Venetian ambassadors.[120]

From the moment he heard of it, the duke criticized the meeting between Henry VIII and Francis I at the Field of Cloth of Gold. He considered it too costly, too much associated with Wolsey, and an undesirable affirmation of the detested French alliance. He was furious that "so expensive and serious an undertaking had not been set on foot with the consent of the council."[121] According to Polydore Vergil, he "grudged the great expenses involved. . . . He did not know, so he repeatedly asserted, what could be the cause of so great an expenditure of cash, unless it was for the future spectacle of foolish speeches, or for a conference of trivialities."[122] He protested against the short notice he and the other peers were given to prepare "as the time was fixed without consulting them."[123]

Buckingham's complaints about the cost of the expedition were due to the fact that he knew he could not afford the huge and elaborate retinue expected of him. We have seen that in 1520, the year of the meeting, his debts rose to £10,535 10s and he was forced to sell land worth £4,546 13s.[124] It was also in 1520 that his brother-in-law, Henry Percy, fell deepest into debt.[125]

Aside from foreign affairs, the issue that caused the most contention between Buckingham on the one hand and Henry VIII and Wolsey on the other was the situation in the duke's Welsh lordships. Law and order had all but disappeared there, despite the indenture of 1504. The duke's high-handed methods of dealing with his tenants and his efforts to raise his income, involving as they did a revival of serfdom and the continual imposition of huge fines for redeeming the sessions, had brought the inhabitants to the brink of rebellion. As early as 1516–17, the fines levied at the Great Sessions in Cantref Selyf, Penkelly, and Alexanderstone soared to £7,195. The fines for redeeming the sessions in these lordships were only £100 1s. The rest of the debt, which clearly was never collected, represented fines for crimes or recognizances forfeited by people who failed to appear at all.[126] When the duke's officers tried to collect his arrears, the tenants responded with force, boycotted the sessions, and actively interfered with the execution of decisions made by the courts.[127] The inhabitants of Brecon forfeited recognizances totaling £15,858

18s for boycotting the sessions.[128] Collections of both fines and land revenues were so poor in Brecon in 1518 that arrears rose to £27,574 14s.[129]

In June 1518, Henry VIII sent a stinging letter to his "right trustie and right entierlie welbeloved cousyn" rebuking him for the disorder in his Welsh lordships. He reminded the duke that it was the custom to bind every man between the ages of 18 and 60 with sureties for his appearance at court and his good behavior.

> We are now crediblie informed that in Lordshippes to you belonging within our saide marches few or no persons be put under anie such bondes but remain clerely at libertie contrarie to the usage accustomed which thinge is in your default and negligence. And by meane thereof many and diverse murders, Rapes, Roberies, Riottes and other misdemeanors have bene of late and dailie be committed and left clerlie unpunished within the same to the high displeasure of God, the disorder and transgression of our lawes, the great hurte, damage and inquietnes of our subjectes, and to our no litle displeasure and myscontentacon.

He commanded Buckingham to rectify the situation, "all doubtes and dilacions put aparte," and to certify that he had done so by the last day of August.[130]

Buckingham did not admit he was wrong easily. It was probably after he received this letter that he filed a bill against the tenants of Hay in Star Chamber accusing them of boycotting the Great Sessions and regular courts and of committing various riots, rescues, and misdemeanors.[131] In their answer, the inhabitants denied all the charges and expressed their willingness to attend Buckingham's courts, but lamented the inequity of the system of redeeming the Great Sessions.[132]

By the fall of 1518, it was clear that the crown would have to intervene to restore order. On November 26, Cardinal Wolsey, the duke of Norfolk, the earl of Surrey, Lord Bergavenny, the bishop of Durham, and Sir Thomas Lovell issued detailed ordinances in Star Chamber to settle "almaner variaunces, controversies and debates heretofor mooved and nowe depending bifore the said lordes bitwene the duc of Buckingham and his tenauntes of his severall lordships of Brecknock [and] Haye." The decree ordered the duke's tenants to refrain from interfering when his officials tried to collect money or to enforce the law, and commanded them to attend the sessions and other courts "peseablye . . . without having or wering of ony harnes or wepon there." It also carefully regulated the convening of future Great Sessions. Once those currently under way were dissolved, none might be called before October 1, 1521. They were never to be held more than twice a year, and no single session was to last more than eight days. Nor were the sessions to be called between the middle of March and the end of September, a time of year when the tenants found court attendance particularly burdensome—and hence when the duke was inclined to convene the court, "to the'entent to coarce theim to redeme his said sessions." Furthermore, the duke could only collect the fine for dissolving the sessions if he "forbere his said sessions in eyr from 3 yere to 3 yere."

In addition, Wolsey and the king's other councillors tried to suppress some of the arbitrary methods Buckingham employed in his dealings with his Welsh subjects. They commanded him and his officers not to imprison persons suspected of committing murder or other felonies if the accused could find sufficient sureties for their appearance at the next sessions. They also ordered the duke's officers to refrain from arresting, or seizing the goods of, people suspected of forfeiting their bonds for good behavior or of breaking the peace unless they had had a trial by jury, as long as the suspects found adequate sureties. Finally, in return for the 2,000 marks and £140 granted respectively by the inhabitants of Brecon and Hay, the duke was required to agree to pardon all crimes committed before October 1, 1518, except proven cases of murder, and to remit all debts except arrears of rent. Since the canceled obligations included all the recognizances forfeited during the boycott of the Great Sessions, which amounted to well over £15,000, the duke had made a substantial concession. Should the tenants fail to obey these ordinances, they would forfeit 1,000 marks *to the king* for each offense.[133]

If Henry and his councillors hoped that this judicious decree would solve the problem of Buckingham's Welsh lordships, they were sadly disappointed. Two years later, Wolsey had to intervene in the case of William Vaughan, indicted as an accessory to murder in Brecon. Before the trial, Vaughan was sent to Westminster to be examined by the council about a "riotous rescue." While he was there, he complained that he could not get a fair hearing in Brecon because the duke's officers were partial. The council sent some royal commissioners to participate in the trial and to warn Buckingham that Vaughan "must be indifferently tried, setting apart all rancor and malice." [134]

Sometime between 1518 and 1521, to give another example, a group of tenants from the lordship of Penkelly petitioned Wolsey for writs of habeas corpus and for subpoenas against some of the duke's officers. The plaintiffs claimed that Buckingham had imprisoned them, contrary to the ordinances of 1518 for the better government of his Welsh lordships. They specifically stated that they were appealing directly to the cardinal because they "be not of power to sue for theyr remedy by the cours of the comen lawe." [135]

Buckingham, for his part, was no more satisfied than his tenants with the situation in Wales. In the fall of 1520, he proposed to visit his lordships in person, "whyche jorney shalbe moche proffitable unto us as well for the knowlege whyche shalbe gyven by our tenents to my Lady at here fyrst commynge thyther as forleveynge of our rents and farmes and lawfull casualtysc, whyche woll not be leved onlasse we be there present." In November, he directed his chancellor, Robert Gilbert, to seek a license from the king permitting him to take three or four hundred armed men with him. [136] His timing could hardly have been worse. Earlier that very month, Henry had personally reprimanded the duke for illegally retaining Sir William Bulmer. In these circumstances, the king's refusal to allow Buckingham to take a private army into Wales was to be expected; what is surprising is the duke's lack of political sensitivity in making such a request at that juncture.

Although Buckingham grumbled about his exclusion from political power, complained about Wolsey, and opposed his pro-French foreign policy, contemporary evidence does not sustain Eric Ives's view that he "stood at the center of a powerful group of councillors and courtiers" who constituted a cohesive faction at court.[137] Wolsey's effective control over both policy and patronage left very little room for a faction to maneuver in. As long as no one could compete with Wolsey for the king's ear, the inadequate supply of royal grants encouraged aspirants to seek his favor rather than to oppose him.[138]

Buckingham was acutely aware of the conflicting interests and mutual suspicions that prevented the nobility from acting together. According to his chancellor, Robert Gilbert, the duke had openly complained that "it would be well enough if the nobles durst break their mind together, for few of them were contented, they were so unkindly handled, but they were afraid to speak."[139] In November 1520, Buckingham expressed fears that someone in his own household was "misreporting" him to the king and revealing the deliberations of his council at court.[140]

None of the evidence suggests that Buckingham's political fortunes were consistently related to those of any other members of the nobility or that he was regularly associated with any other peers in expressing his views. For example, though the duke enjoyed cordial social relations with all three of his brothers-in-law, Northumberland, Hastings, and Fitzwalter, their political fortunes were very different.[141] During the struggle for control of the council in 1509, Buckingham and Northumberland were considered political allies and potential supporters of Bishop Fox.[142] Yet, in 1516, while the duke was in great favor at court, Northumberland was imprisoned in the Fleet and Hastings was prosecuted for illegal retaining.[143] The undated letter from Henry VIII to Wolsey (calendared by J. S. Brewer with documents from 1519) once again links Northumberland and Buckingham, this time in a group of nobles under suspicion for some unstated reason.[144] The name of Robert Radcliffe, Lord Fitzwalter, does not appear in the evidence about any of these events at court.

Despite their connection through marriage, Buckingham and his two sons-in-law, Thomas Howard, earl of Surrey (the future third duke of Norfolk), and George Neville, Lord Bergavenny, seem to have been antagonists at court more often than allies. Although nothing in the sources explains the hostility between them, Surrey recollected, many years after Stafford's death, that "the duke of Bukyngham confessed . . . that of all men living he hated me most." [145] Both Surrey and Bergavenny were part of the group that tried in 1509 to wrest control of the council from Bishop Fox, while Stafford supported Fox.[146] The struggle was not, as Eric Ives has suggested, between Buckingham and Surrey on one side, supported by the king's closest companions at court, and Henry VII's bureaucrats on the other.[147] In 1516, when the duke was basking in the king's favor, both his sons-in-law were thrown out of the council and Bergavenny was prosecuted for illegal retaining.[148] At the time the undated letter mentioned above was written, the scene had shifted somewhat. Henry included Bergavenny, but not Surrey, in the group of suspected nobles.[149] Bergavenny again found himself in serious trouble at the time of his father-in-law's arrest.[150] Buckingham's third son-in-law, Ralph Neville, fourth earl of Westmorland, was a minor and played no role in court politics.[151]

The duke had friendly relations with three of the other leading noblemen at court—Charles Brandon, duke of Suffolk; George Talbot, earl of Shrewsbury; and Thomas Howard, second duke of Norfolk (Surrey's father)—but these friendships do not seem to have carried over into court politics. Brandon, Howard, and Talbot all accepted that service to the crown and acquiescence in Tudor policy were the keys to power and prosperity more easily than Buckingham. In any case, Brandon and Howard were much more dependent on Henry VIII than Buckingham was for their positions. The fact that Shrewsbury and Norfolk held stewardships on the duke's estates does not, therefore, seem to have had much political significance.[152] Buckingham did trust Norfolk enough to ask him to intervene at court for him in November 1520, when he was in disgrace for retaining Sir William

Bulmer and wanted a license to take armed retainers into Wales. Whether he was exaggerating or not, he instructed his chancellor to tell Norfolk and his wife that he had "as grete truste in them as eny chyld they have."[153]

Buckingham's relations with Shrewsbury underscore how wrong it is to assume that friendships among the peers are a reliable indication of their political alignments. In 1509 Shrewsbury supported Surrey against Bishop Fox for control over the council; Buckingham supported the bishop. Both men were also apparently in different factions during the crisis of May 1516: Shrewsbury faced considerable danger while Buckingham was in great favor. Yet during that very month, the duke proposed cross-marriages between his son and the earl's daughter, and the earl's son and his own daughter.[154] Shrewsbury refused on the ground that he could not afford the dowry Buckingham expected,[155] but the real reason was that he preferred to marry his daughter to the earl of Northumberland's son. According to George Bernard, Shrewsbury was pursuing a deliberate policy of marrying his children into leading northern families as the center of the Talbot estates shifted from Shropshire and Wales to Yorkshire and Derbyshire.[156]

The surviving documents thus make clear that by the end of 1520, Buckingham had emerged as a fairly outspoken critic of Wolsey, of certain aspects of Tudor foreign policy, and of the exclusion of the greater nobility from a predominant role in the king's council. There is no proof, however, that he was the leader of a coherent aristocratic faction. Unlike Norfolk, Shrewsbury, and Suffolk, who were far more successful politically at court than Buckingham, the duke apparently had no idea how dangerous it was to criticize the regime so openly and so persistently. Whether he recognized it or not, when Buckingham attacked Wolsey, he was attacking both the king's policy and his right to choose his first minister. Nor did he recognize Henry's strong will and potential ruthlessness. Perhaps he was deceived by the king's devotion to pleasure and his apparent unwillingness to assume the routine burdens of government.

Buckingham's criticism of the meeting at the Field of Cloth of Gold, his persistent misconduct in Wales, his breach of the law about retaining, and his expressed desire to raise a private army undoubtedly aroused all Henry VIII's instinctive suspicions of heads of old magnate families. Yet many other peers had broken the laws against retaining or otherwise offended the king without having to face charges of high treason. As we shall see, Buckingham's fate must be understood less as a reflection of the king's exaggerated fears of a potentially dangerous nobleman than as one of the earliest manifestations of the dynastic concerns that were to play such a large role in the religious and political revolution of the 1530's.

## CHAPTER EIGHT

# The Fall of the Duke of Buckingham

The duke of Buckingham retired from court almost immediately after the conclusion of Henry VIII's meeting with Charles V at Gravelines in July 1520. Except for short visits to local religious shrines, he remained at Thornbury until the king summoned him in April 1521. There is evidence that by the fall of 1520 the duke was deeply worried about his position at court and suspected that members of his household were fomenting trouble between him and the king. About Michaelmas (September 29) 1520, he summoned his council to discuss visiting his Welsh lordships with an armed escort of three or four hundred men. He reported that he had sent some of his councillors to court to ask Henry for permission to arm his retainers. When they arrived at court, the king already knew about his request. Buckingham said that "he knew not whom he should mistrust to have disclosed that, except only his receiver [Thomas Cade], for that he was nigh unto Sir William Compton [Henry VIII's favorite], which had rule about Burforde," where the receiver was vicar.[1]

Then, in November, Buckingham fell into disgrace for retaining Sir William Bulmer.[2] On the 26th, he wrote a long series of directions to his chancellor, Robert Gilbert, in his own hand. An examination of this memorandum reveals how deeply worried he was about his relationship with the king. The first item directed Gilbert to

deliver our letters of credence to my lord of Norffolk and to my Lady hys wyfe . . . praynge them evere to be meane to furder us in all our causes and suets to the Kynges grace and my Lord Cardinall, and yf ther be eny thynge that they shal here that shal be agenst our honoure, or surty, that they woll advertyse [us] theroff wyth theyre good advyses what is best for us to doo.[3]

He also asked Gilbert to "speke wyth Sir Henry Owen . . . to knaw of hym what he hath hard of Mayster Bryane how [whether] the kyngs graceys [is] good lord unto us."[4] Sir Henry, who was on Buckingham's payroll as keeper of Postern Park, Kent, held a position at court and was probably one of the duke's sources of news.[5] The Master Bryan referred to may well have been the king's favorite, Francis Bryan.

The instructions of November 26 also reveal the duke's continuing suspicion that members of his household were betraying him. It was at this time that he told Gilbert to find out if Margaret Geddynge, whom he had discharged sometime before, "have not made mysreporte to hym [the Cardinal] of us." If she were innocent, Gilbert should "take the advyse of my lady Fytzwater [the duke's sister] whether we shal take the sayd Margarete to our servyce agene." He wanted to know specifically "how Margarete Geddynge hath appon her othe declared here sylff, and what she sayth of Charles Knevet."[6]

The final item in the instructions was an anxious discussion of the necessity of his taking an army into Wales. Buckingham expressed concern about whether the king and Cardinal Wolsey would help him to reassert control over his Welsh lordships:

for that yt ys well knowne to all the Kyngs commissioners that have bene ther, and to our counsayle, that we kanne not be ther for our suerty with owt iij. or iiij. hundred men. . . . And forasmuche as we trust that the Kyngs Hyghnes and my lord Cardinall wold not have us cast away, we desyre my lord Cardinall to be meane to the Kyngs Grace that we have licens to have our harnnes secretly convayed wyth us, and not to have yt worne but in tyme of nede for our suerty.[7]

On April 8, 1521, a message came from the king that summoned Buckingham to Greenwich and abruptly ended all his worried musings about his position at court and about the treachery of his servants.[8] Demonstrating his usual largesse, the duke rewarded the royal envoy with one mark.[9] He set out almost immediately, apparently unaware that Sir William Compton, Sir Richard Weston, Sir William Kingston, and numerous sergeants at arms were trailing him on the king's orders. The duke did not begin to suspect he was being followed until he reached Windsor. After spending an uneasy night, he called to Thomas Ward, a royal servant, and asked why he was loitering about. Ward answered that his office lay there, by the king's commandment. Buckingham was thunderstruck. He was so upset that, in Hall's words, "as he was at breakfast his meat would not doune." He set out for London at once. When he arrived at Wolsey's palace near Westminster, his apprehensions were confirmed: the cardinal's servants told Buckingham their master was sick and could not see him. Without losing his composure, the duke replied, "Well, yet will I drynke of my Lord's wine or [ere] I pass," and refreshed himself in Wolsey's cellar. As he approached London on his barge, Sir Henry Marney, captain of the king's guard, and a hundred yeomen boarded without warning. Sir Henry arrested Buckingham in the king's name and led him through Thames Street to the Tower of London.[10]

Once Buckingham was imprisoned in the Tower, the king lost no time in setting the machinery of government in motion against him. On May 8, the duke was indicted for high treason at the Guildhall before a jury that included the lord mayor of London. The bill of indictment charged that Buckingham, intending to exalt himself to the crown, had imagined and compassed the deposition and death of the king, and cited as evidence words spoken and acts committed between March 10, 1511, and November 4, 1520. The majority of the charges referred to conversations or messages between Buckingham and Nicholas Hopkins, a monk at the Carthusian priory at Henton, Somersetshire. Hopkins had predicted on various occasions that the king would have no male heir and that the duke would therefore have all—that he would be king of England. Hopkins had also advised Buckingham to cultivate the goodwill of his countrymen. The bill noted that on April 16, 1515, Buckingham had given the priory an annuity of £6 for wine and a gift of £20 for a water conduit, of which he had then and there "traitorously" paid £10. On other occasions he had given Hopkins smaller payments.

The indictment also recorded two treasonous conversations

between the duke and his Neville sons-in-law. In 1515, he had told Ralph, earl of Westmorland, that if anything but good should happen to the king, he, the duke of Buckingham, was next in succession to the crown. Four years later, Buckingham had complained about the king's councillors to George Neville, Lord Bergavenny, and had said that if the king should die, he meant to rule England, whatever the opposition.[11]

Buckingham allegedly had also made traitorous comments to his servants Robert Gilbert and Charles Knevet, both of whom appeared as witnesses against him at the trial. Only a few months before embarking for the meeting at the Field of Cloth of Gold, he had revealed to Gilbert that he would wait for a more convenient time to execute his treason, but that it could be accomplished if the lords of the kingdom cooperated with one another. He had also disclosed that he possessed a document under the great seal containing an act of parliament that legitimized the duke of Somerset, one of the king's ancestors. At one time, he had intended to give it to Henry, but now he would not do so for £10,000. Worst of all, Knevet claimed that the duke had bragged that if the king committed him to the Tower for retaining Sir William Bulmer, "the principal actors therein should have little joy of it, for he would have done what his father intended to do to Richard III at Salisbury, when he made suit to come to the King's presence, having upon him secretly a knife, so that when kneeling before the King he would have risen suddenly and stabbed him." At this point, according to Knevet, the duke traitorously put his hand on his dagger. Buckingham had also told his former steward that if he ever became king, he would behead Cardinal Wolsey and Thomas Lovell. (Lovell had been a leading adviser of Henry VII and a county steward for Buckingham).

In addition to this evidence that the duke desired and intended to succeed Henry VIII, the indictment endeavored to prove that he had taken steps to fulfill his purpose. It asserted that on numerous occasions he had distributed cloth of gold, silver, and silk to soldiers of the king's guard in an effort to win their adherence, that he had appointed many new officers in his

lands to obtain followers, and that he had sought a license to retain certain of the king's subjects in Herefordshire, Gloucestershire, and Somerset and to lead them armed into Wales with a
view to fortifying himself there against the king. The charge that
Buckingham was suborning the king's guard must have weighed
heavily against him in light of the well-publicized incident concerning Sir William Bulmer.[12]

Buckingham's trial for high treason began on May 13, only five
days after his indictment, at 8 o'clock in the morning. The secretary to the Venetian ambassador reported that he was taken from
the Tower to Westminster by water, under a strong guard, to prevent any rescue attempt by his numerous followers in London.[13]
As a nobleman with the privilege of trial by his peers, Buckingham appeared before a court composed of twenty lords.
Thomas, duke of Norfolk, was appointed Lord High Steward of
England for the occasion.[14]

The trial began with a charge by the king's counsel:[15] "Sir Edward Duke of Buckyngh hold up thy heade, thou are endited
of high treason, for that thou traitorously hast conspired and
ymagined as farre as in thee lay to shorten the life of our sovereigne lorde the kyng: of this treason how wilt thou acquite thee."
The duke replied, "by my Peres." The prosecution then read the
indictment. Buckingham responded firmly, "It is false and untrue, and conspired and forged to brynge me to my death." He
defended himself against the charges as best he could. The king's
attorney then cited the confessions of the witnesses against
him. When the duke demanded that they be brought before
him, Knevet, Gilbert, Dellacourt, and Hopkins appeared in
court. Knevet repeated his evidence orally and the duke tried to
answer it. The prosecution concluded its case by reading the
depositions.

If the only extant deposition, Robert Gilbert's, is typical, most
of the "evidence" simply repeated allegations made in the indictment. The remaining portion consisted of general statements of
discontent that Buckingham had made in Gilbert's hearing, or of
specific instances in which the duke had committed the trea-

sonous acts ascribed to him. Gilbert claimed, for example, to have heard the duke say that although he had done as good service as any man for Henry VIII, he was never rewarded, for the king preferred to give his fees, offices, and rewards to boys rather than to noblemen. He also charged that Buckingham had said that God had punished the Tudors for putting the earl of Warwick to death by preventing the king from having a male heir. Gilbert greatly expanded on Buckingham's alleged hostility to Wolsey. He claimed that he had heard the duke say that the cardinal had consulted a spirit on how to retain the king's favor and thus was an idolator, that Wolsey helped the king find pleasing women, and that the life king and cardinal led together was so abominable that God would punish them for it. According to Gilbert, Buckingham had also frequently said that the cardinal would undo all noblemen if he could.[16]

As soon as all four depositions were read, the witnesses returned to the Tower under guard. The duke of Norfolk then informed the defendant that the king had expressly ordered him to administer the laws favorably to the duke and that, therefore, if he had anything to say in his defense, he would be heard. Buckingham spoke for more than an hour, refuting the charges with such eloquence that everyone in the courtroom was deeply moved.

Then, while Edward Stafford awaited his fate, the jury of his peers considered the evidence. Apparently they had a difficult time reaching a verdict, for Hall reported that they conferred a great while. The difficulty was probably due to a sentimental reluctance to convict Buckingham rather than to any scruples about his guilt. Chief Justice Fyneux had already settled the legal question of whether the words and deeds attributed to the duke constituted treason by ruling that "it is not felony if there is no act committed. But if one intends the death of our Lord the King, it is high treason because it is the will of the commonweale."[17]

Accordingly, when the lords returned to their places in the courtroom and the duke of Norfolk asked them each in turn, "What say you of Sir Edward Duke of Buckyngham touching the high treasons?" they replied unanimously, "He is giltie." But when Buckingham returned to the courtroom, the jury was so moved that no one was able to pass sentence on him. Proud in adversity as well as good fortune, he urged them to speak, assuring them that he knew it was the king's will he should die, and that he was content to accept the punishment, "not for the crime laid to his account, which was utterly false, but for his very great sins." [18]

Buckingham's willingness to accept execution for a crime he denied having committed expressed an attitude that Mervyn James has called the "moralization of politics" and that he has connected to the consolidation of the early Tudor monarchy. According to James, the traditional code of honor valued the spirit in which a man acted—particularly his consistency in standing by a position once it had been assumed with a public gesture, such as an oath—rather than his particular acts and their consequences. The code left judgment on the defeated to God. In the Tudor period, however, men increasingly subscribed to a providentialist view of history, which viewed the results of acts as vehicles of divine judgment. As a result, condemned traitors such as Buckingham routinely admitted their guilt and said that they deserved their fate, even if they denied committing the specific crimes for which they were convicted. [19]

Finally, the duke of Norfolk spoke: "Sir Edward, you have heard how you be endited of high treason, you pleaded thereto not giltie, puttyng your selfe to the Peres of the realm, the which found you giltie." Then Norfolk, weeping, pronounced the horrible sentence reserved for traitors. To these words, the condemned man replied with dignity,

You have sayd as a traytor should be sayd unto, but I was never none, but my Lordes I nothing maligne for that you have done to me, but the eternal God forgeve you my death and I do: I shall never sue to the kyng for life, howbeit he is a gracious prince and more grace may come from him than I desire. I desire you my Lordes and all felowes to pray for me.

Sir Thomas Lovell then led Buckingham back to a barge on the Thames with the edge of an ax turned toward him as a symbol of his sentence. The duke refused the cushions that Lovell offered him in words that Shakespeare later turned into poetry: "Nay, for when I went to Westminster, I was duke of Buckyngham, nowe I am but Edwarde Bowhen the mooste catiffe [wretched] of the worlde." [20] The barge landed at the Temple; from there Sir Nicholas Vaux and Sir William Sandys led him through the City, arriving at the Tower about four o'clock in the afternoon.

Four days later, on the morning of May 17, two sheriffs and a guard of 500 infantrymen led the third duke of Buckingham to Tower Hill. [21] Despite the entreaties of Queen Catherine, the king had not granted the pardon for which Buckingham was too proud to ask. [22] He had, however, mitigated the penalty in view of the duke's high rank: the duke was to be beheaded, not hanged, drawn, and quartered like a traitor of common birth. From the scaffold, the duke addressed the assembled crowd. He told them that he had offended the king through negligence, warned all other nobles to heed the example of his fate, begged everyone to pray for him, and said that he trusted to die the king's true man. After reciting the penitential psalms, he called on the executioner to dispatch him quickly. He took off his gown, had his eyes blindfolded, and laid his head on the block. "And thus," to quote the Venetian ambassador's secretary, "miserably, but with great courage, did he end his days on the 17th of May." [23]

Three weeks later, an elaborate ceremony took place in St. George's chapel at Windsor Castle, expelling the deceased duke from the Order of the Garter, "to the intent that all other noble men thereby may take ensample hereafter, not to committ any such haynous and detestable treason and offences." A herald carried out the expulsion in symbolic terms by throwing Buckingham's crest, banner, and sword from the loft of the chapel into the choir. The officers of arms of the order then dragged them through the church and out the west door, depositing them finally in a nearby ditch. [24]

Even more important than this ceremony in completing the destruction of the late duke of Buckingham was the action that Henry took in the parliament of 1523, the first to meet after the duke's execution. An act of attainder stated that on "the xxiiij[ti] day of Aprill in the fourth yere of the reign of oure sovereign Lord the King that nowe is and dyvers tymes after, [Buckingham] ymagyned and compassed trayterouslie and unnaturally the distruccion of the moost roiall persone of oure seid Sovereigne Lord the Kyng contrarie to hys allegiaunce," convicted him posthumously, and declared all his personal and real property forfeit to the crown.[25]

Events had thus proved that Buckingham's fear of betrayal by his servants was well founded. Charles Knevet, a former official on his estates; Robert Gilbert, his chancellor; John Dellacourt, his chaplain; and Nicholas Hopkins, his favorite priest and confessor, provided the sole evidence against him at his trial. Both Henry Stafford, the duke's son, and Polydore Vergil named Knevet, a distant relative of the duke's, as the initial and principal informer against him.[26] They both thought that Knevet betrayed Buckingham for having dismissed him from a position on his estates.[27] According to one account, the duke discharged him in the spring of 1520 because his tenants complained about his "Exactions and other oppressive Methods."[28] The duke's son Henry told a more plausible version of the story. "My fathire had discharged [him] of all his fyies [fees] becaws he disteaned [cheated] him in one matier of 200 marks."[29]

Knevet himself is said to have explained the dismissal differently: "the chief cause of his putting away was for disclosing certain matters to Mr. Lark, to be opened unto [Wolsey]."[30]

An anonymous letter to Wolsey discussed at length how Knevet could be persuaded to betray his former employer.

Please it your Grace to be remembered; as touching the matter that I showed unto your Grace at More of Charles Knyvet, & c., wherein ye advertised and commanded me that I should handle it further. . . . So it is that I have communed with him divers times the last term, and persuaded him in the matter as far as I might, in such wise that he should not suspect my meaning therein. . . . He answered me how he labored to be the King's servant, and if he were once sworn and admitted, then durst he speak boldly, and would tell all. And further he said, "Then will I speak, by Saint Mary, for it toucheth the King in deed." . . . Your Grace should send for Charles to come before you, showing unto him that ye have heard he should be [put] from the Duke, wherof ye much marvel, considering the great service that he hath done him, and how near he is of blood. And thereupon I think that Charles will be plain. . . . If not, your Grace then may show unto him that ye have heard, by divers servants that the Duke hath lately put from him, that in his fumes and displeasures he will oftimes rail and misuse himself in his words, as well against your Grace as against the King's highness; and ye doubt not that he hath been so great and secret with him, and in so great trust, that he hath heard and knoweth much more of his inward mind an any other; charging him therefore to be plain.[31]

J. S. Brewer assumed that whoever wrote this letter was the initial informer against Buckingham and that since Knevet was not its author, he was not the guilty party.[32] An entirely different but equally logical construction can, however, be put upon the letter. The author may well have been a servant of Wolsey's assigned to investigate suspicious rumors about the duke, and not an independent informer at all. Since the author specifically stated that Knevet had already disclosed certain matters to Mr. Lark, Brewer's conclusion that Knevet was not the first accuser appears unwarranted. Furthermore, Knevet played the role of star witness at the trial.[33] There is insufficient evidence to draw a definitive conclusion about whether or not he was the first to speak against the duke.

The remaining suspects are the three other witnesses at the trial—Gilbert, Dellacourt, and Hopkins—and Margaret Geddynge, who was not a witness. Nicholas Hopkins is most easily exonerated from being either the author of the letter or a willing informant. The letter was not in his handwriting. Furthermore, there is evidence of his deep attachment to Buckingham in the contemporary belief that he died of a broken heart because his prediction that the duke would succeed Henry VIII had contributed to his death.[34] John Dellacourt had served as an intermediary between Buckingham and Hopkins ever since 1511 and was therefore almost as thoroughly implicated in the priest's dangerous prophesying as his master.[35] It is therefore unlikely that he would have divulged anything about them to Wolsey. Nor is there any known reason why he would have betrayed the duke in 1521 after a full decade of loyal service. A final piece of evidence establishes almost beyond doubt that Hopkins and Dellacourt were, at best, reluctant witnesses: Henry sent them both to the Tower for having been "privy to the Duke's treason."[36]

The evidence concerning Margaret Geddynge is both less conclusive and more incriminating. Geddynge had been in Buckingham's service at least since 1502, when she was receiving an annuity of £6 13s 4d from the receivership of Kent and Surrey.[37] In November 1520, she was no longer in Buckingham's service. As we have seen above, the instructions issued to Gilbert on the 26th of that month discussed the duke's suspicions about her.[38] The anonymous letter to Wolsey specifically mentioned "divers servants that the Duke hath lately put from him" who had dangerous things to say about him.[39] Geddynge may well have been one of these servants. The connection between her and Knevet in the duke's instructions may even indicate that he suspected them of working together.[40]

On the other hand, it is possible to read the evidence concerning Margaret Geddynge in a completely different light. As was explained in Chapter 3, there is some indication that she was involved in a dispute between Buckingham and his wife and was discharged from, or voluntarily left, his service on that account. In the memorandum of November 26, 1520, the duke asked Gilbert to tell his sister, Lady Fitzwalter, about his wife's demeanor and to ask her help in finding a new servant for the duchess.[41] The mysterious reference to what Margaret said about Charles Knevet may mean that she was betraying him, not working with him.[42]

Whether or not Margaret was guilty of informing against Buckingham, she had regained his confidence shortly before his arrest. He received a message from her on January 4, 1521, and took her back into his service by March 26.[43] The posthumous survey of Buckingham's property listed her as the lessee of demesne lands in Eastington and Alkerton, Gloucestershire.[44]

The fifth member of Buckingham's household suspected of betraying him was his chancellor, Robert Gilbert. Gilbert, a priest, entered the duke's service by 1508 at the latest, though possibly as early as 1500, when the duke gave him an annuity as "scholar and chaplain," from Little Brickhill, Buckinghamshire.[45] The anonymous letter to Wolsey referred to Gilbert in the third person, which rules him out as its author.[46] The chronicler Hall, on the other hand, named him as "fyrst accusor," which strengthens the supposition that Brewer was incorrect in concluding that the anonymous letter writer and the initial informer were the same person.[47]

Aside from Hall's explicit statement, the evidence against Gilbert is purely circumstantial. Gilbert was at Magdalen College, Oxford, at the same time as Wolsey and therefore almost certainly knew him.[48] Since he frequently went on errands to London and the court for Buckingham, he had ample opportunity to deal privately with the cardinal. It may be significant that Gilbert delivered Wolsey's warning to Buckingham to "take heed how that he did use himself towards the King's highness."[49] It is also noteworthy that Gilbert was not imprisoned with Hopkins and Dellacourt for being "privy to the Duke's treason," since the indictment makes it clear that he knew about the priest's predictions for some time before the trial.[50]

On the other hand, no contemporary document explains why Gilbert would have betrayed the duke after almost two decades of service or suggests that a quarrel had simmered between them. Despite all the suspicions plaguing him in late 1520, Buckingham continued to trust his chancellor. When he arrived at Wolsey's palace on his last journey to the capital, he "mervailled" that Gilbert, who was already in London, did not come to meet him.[51] Gilbert may have been the servant who took the initiative in betraying Buckingham, but, as in the case of Knevet, there is not enough evidence to support a conclusion either way.

Whatever their roles in giving evidence against Buckingham, a final piece of evidence establishes almost certainly that Della-court, Geddynge, Gilbert, and Hopkins were innocent of writing the anonymous letter to Wolsey. The author was almost certainly a lawyer or royal servant, since he mentioned some indentures he had drawn up between Henry VII and Sir Nicholas Vaux and referred to the last term of the courts at Westminster.[52]

An examination of contemporary evidence relating to Knevet, Hopkins, Dellacourt, Gilbert, and Geddynge does not solve the puzzle of who initially betrayed Buckingham. Thomas Cade, who entered Wolsey's household sometime after the execution, may not have been as innocent as he protested at the meeting of the duke's council in late September 1520.[53] Or another of Buck-ingham's servants whose name does not appear in the available evidence may have taken the initiative in instigating his fall. Fi-nally, the search for a traitor within the duke's household may be misguided. The author of the anonymous letter specifically men-tioned that the cardinal had ordered him to deal with Knevet, which suggests that Wolsey may have initiated the inquiries into the duke's conduct and approached Buckingham's servants only after he had some leads to follow.[54]

Conventional accounts of Buckingham's trial and execution describe them as thinly veiled acts of judicial murder, totally un-anticipated by contemporaries and carried out with great speed to forestall protest and minimize criticism.[55] In his biography of Henry VIII, for example, A. F. Pollard wrote: "In this, as in all the great trials of all ages, considerations of justice were subordi-nated to the real or supposed dictates of political expediency. Buckingham was executed not because he was a criminal, but be-cause he was, or might become, dangerous: his crime was not treason, but descent from Edward III."[56] Authorities as distin-guished as J. S. Brewer, Kenneth Pickthorne, H. A. L. Fisher, and Garrett Mattingly shared this view, and in a recent essay, Mortimer Levine took essentially the same position.[57] These his-torians have contended that the court that tried Buckingham was an instrument of royal despotism, that the procedure followed at the trial guaranteed conviction whether or not the defendant was guilty, and that the form of treason for which the duke was condemned was of dubious legality. However, the conventional judgment is anachronistic, applying legal standards to the duke's trial that did not evolve until long after the early Tudor period. In reality, Buckingham was convicted according to established criminal procedure, for a recognized form of treason, before a tribunal that had shown it could be independent enough of the crown to bring in a verdict of not guilty if the evidence warranted.

Buckingham was tried in the court of the Lord High Steward of England, which heard cases involving peers of the realm when parliament was not in session. L. W. Vernon Harcourt, who wrote the most complete history of the court, considered it "a fraudulent device for the degradation of the nobility . . . intended to supersede and altogether deprive them of trial in parliament." [58] Since the king summoned a small number of lords to serve as jurors, he could, according to Harcourt, manipulate the composition of the court to secure conviction. Furthermore, he could intimidate the members of the jury much more easily than he could the entire peerage assembled in parliament. Levine quoted and reiterated Harcourt's point of view in his essay, and G. R. Elton referred to the Lord High Steward's court as "a bastard institution, a sort of invention." [59]

Actually, the record of the court belies Harcourt's assertion that the tribunal was a rubber stamp for the crown. Only four trials had taken place in this court before Buckingham's in 1521. The first, in 1415, convicted Richard, earl of Cambridge, and Henry Lord Scrope for high treason. Under Henry VI, the court brought in a verdict of not guilty in the case of Thomas, earl of Devonshire, also tried for high treason. In 1499, the Lord High Steward's court convicted Edward, earl of Warwick, for high treason. Finally, in 1503, Edward Sutton, Lord Dudley, was tried for a felony and either acquitted or pardoned. The first trial after Buckingham's was that of William Lord Dacre of the North, who was acquitted of high treason in 1532.[60] In its first six cases, therefore, the court brought in three verdicts of guilty, two of not guilty, and one that is unknown but was favorable to the defendant—hardly a record that justifies Harcourt's blanket condemnation.

It is difficult to know how much weight to place on the fact that there had been so few trials in the Lord High Steward's court before Buckingham's. In his book on the law of treason in the later middle ages, J. G. Bellamy emphasized the wide variety of tribunals used to try treason cases, which included the court of king's bench, courts held under special commissions, the court of the steward of the royal household, the king's council, various courts of chivalry, the court of chancery, and parliament. In fact, there was a trend away from hearing treason cases in parliament during the fifteenth century. "Impeachment disappeared after 1459, appeal of treason in parliament had been forbidden in 1399 and bill of attainder except in a single instance was never part of an actual trial. Sensibly the king realized that the days of parliament as the scene of the state trial were over."[61] Seen in this light, Harcourt and the historians who have relied on him have erred in speaking of the "newness" and "illegitimacy" of the Lord High Steward's court.

Furthermore, there is no evidence that Henry VIII packed the jury that tried Buckingham. Besides the duke and his close relatives, there were eleven English noblemen above the rank of baron in 1521. The king summoned all of them except the earl of Arundel, who was over 70 and possibly exempt on that account.[62] He appointed the highest ranking, the duke of Norfolk, to preside as Lord High Steward.[63] It is reasonable to suppose that one of Henry's chief concerns was to secure as impressive a jury as possible. The other members of the panel were Thomas Dowcra, prior of St. John's of Jerusalem, who represented the Church, and nine barons. Dowcra and Buckingham had had cordial relations over a long period. Of the nine barons, only one came from a family that owed its title to the Tudors. Henry even excluded two barons, John Lord Berners and Maurice Lord

Berkeley, who had openly feuded with the duke.[64] Thus, of the 49 peers in 1521,[65] just under 40 percent served on the jury that condemned Buckingham, including all those above the rank of baron who were not closely related to him or of an extremely advanced age.

Even if Henry VIII did not directly pack the jury that tried Buckingham, it is still questionable whether any panel chosen from the tiny early Tudor peerage could have been genuinely impartial in a treason trial. Members of the nobility were very dependent on royal favor for their prosperity and advancement and must have felt very vulnerable when called upon to give their verdicts. From this point of view, it made little difference whether Buckingham was tried in the Lord High Steward's court or in parliament, although Harcourt attached great importance to the venue of his trial. On the other hand, there is no evidence that Henry VIII ever took reprisals against noble jurors who brought in verdicts of not guilty, although reprisals were common in the case of ordinary petty jurors.[66]

Aside from the question of whether any panel of noblemen in this period could be genuinely impartial, modern notions of justice are offended by the spectacle of hand-picking a jury to try a particular case. This practice was in fact common to all treason cases, not just those in the Lord High Steward's court, and distinguished treason cases from felony cases.[67] According to Sir John Fortescue, defendants charged as traitors who were tried in courts of oyer and terminer could challenge jurors up to the number of 35. Although he implied that the accused frequently exercised this privilege, there is no evidence of their doing so in the fifteenth and sixteenth centuries.[68] As for the selection of the jury, defendants in the court of the Lord High Steward were not, therefore, treated more severely than those tried for treason at common law during that period.

Criticism of the procedure followed at Buckingham's trial has focused on the fact that he had no lawyer, no prior knowledge of the case against him, and no right to cross-examine prosecution witnesses or to call witnesses of his own. J. S. Brewer described this aspect of the trial in a tone of condemnation that many other historians have echoed.

The depositions of the witnesses were read . . . but if we may draw any conclusion from the silence of Hall, no opportunity was afforded the Duke of confronting and cross-examining the witnesses in person, or of producing evidence in his own defense. He was allowed no counsel: and no other course was open to him for establishing his innocence, beyond the bare denial of the offence. . . . As trials for treason were conducted in those days, it was little better than a question of personal credibility—assertion against assertion. . . . The king had already pronounced judgment: he had examined the witnesses, encouraged and received their confidence, and expressed his belief in the Duke's guilt. Who was to gainsay it? Who should be bold enough to assert that the King had arrived at a false conclusion, and that such methods of procedure were fatal to justice? In a court also, constituted of men who were not lawyers by profession, who had received no training for such nice questions, who understood nothing of the salutary laws of legal evidence, what hope could there be for the accused? . . . The only lawyer employed was the attorney-general in behalf of the Crown. But in those days attorney-generals regarded themselves as the servants of the Crown, who had to earn their wages by establishing the guilt of the prisoner.[69]

Brewer and the historians who share these views have based their opinion on modern ideas about the rights of defendants in criminal cases. To understand the significance of Buckingham's trial, however, it is necessary to understand how people living at that time thought treason trials ought to be conducted and how they embodied these ideas in courtroom procedure. Two contemporary lawyers, the yearbook reporter of Buckingham's trial and Sir William Stanford, described the normal procedure followed in the Lord High Steward's court. Sir Edward Coke, writing two or three generations later, also discussed it in *The Third Part of the Institutes of the Lawes of England*.

These sources agree that, following an elaborate series of opening ceremonies, the defendant was led to the bar, the clerk of the court read the indictment, the prisoner pleaded, the king's lawyer gave his evidence, the defendant answered, the defendant was led from the courtroom, the lords deliberated about the verdict, and, finally, the lords announced their decisions individually, beginning with the nobleman of the lowest rank and progressing in order to that of the highest. A majority sufficed to convict or acquit. There is no mention of permitting the defendants to confront and cross-examine the witnesses against them or to produce witnesses and evidence of their own. Coke stated explicitly that because only evidence beyond argument or doubt sufficed to secure conviction, persons indicted for capital crimes had no right to counsel. The judges were expected to advise the defendant on how to conduct his case and to ensure that the law was strictly followed; Chief Justice Fyneux was present at Buckingham's trial to perform these functions.[70] Recent scholars writing on the subject agree that no defendants in treason or felony cases were allowed the privilege of counsel, the right to testify under oath, the power to summon witnesses or to produce evidence, or the privilege of cross-examining government witnesses.[71]

The most striking difference in procedure between the Lord High Steward's court and ordinary common-law courts was that juries in the former could convict by majority vote, whereas common-law courts required unanimous verdicts. Since no records of the deliberations of juries in the Lord High Steward's court have survived, there is no way of knowing how this difference affected the outcome of any specific case. At Buckingham's trial, the verdict was unanimous. Nonetheless, this departure from normal common-law practice lends the only support for Harcourt's condemnation of the court.

The other major procedural difference between the Lord High Steward's court and common-law criminal courts characterized treason trials before all types of tribunal. Although royal judges on regular assize circuit sat in felony cases, the government specifically chose the justice who would preside over a treason trial.[72] Judges acted as advocates for the king and often cajoled or browbeat defendants.[73] There is no evidence that Chief Justice Fyneux behaved in this manner at Buckingham's trial. However, this deviation from common-law procedure demonstrated the crown's determination to convict defendants in treason cases.

Another unique characteristic of treason trials was the presence of prosecuting counsel for the crown, usually the attorney general. As John Langbein has emphasized, private citizens—not government lawyers—prosecuted most criminal cases until the Marian reform of 1555.[74] Like the handpicking of the presiding justice, the unusual practice of employing royal counsel to prosecute traitors stemmed from the crown's interest in securing convictions. Even the charges were drawn up with more precision than usual.[75] The care taken in presenting the king's case undoubtedly reduced the defendant's chance of acquittal, particularly since the accused had no lawyer. There is no evidence, however, that the role of the crown lawyers infringed on any of the defendant's recognized legal rights. At Buckingham's trial, the king's attorney presented the case against the defendant as he would at any treason trial.

In general, the duke's trial conformed closely to the procedures described above as customary in the Lord High Steward's court, though there were two departures from traditional forms. First, the lords announced their verdicts beginning with the highest ranking, the duke of Norfolk, working downward to the lowest ranking, rather than vice versa. This change saved a mere baron from being the first to pronounce judgment on the highest-ranking nobleman in the realm and probably facilitated a verdict of guilty, although there is no evidence on this point. Second, Norfolk agreed to the defendant's request that the prosecution witnesses be brought into court, contrary to usual practice. Whether anything approaching cross-examination occurred is doubtful, since Buckingham had had neither legal training nor advance notice of what would be said against him. Nonetheless, this change in procedure was clearly to the duke's advantage and justified Norfolk's subsequent assertion that he had administered the law favorably to Buckingham.

From the foregoing analysis, it is clear that Buckingham's trial was carried out according to the legal norms of his own day. His trial was conducted according to procedures that characterized prosecutions for treason at common law as well as in the Lord High Steward's court. The crown's increased involvement in treason cases was to be expected, given the nature of the offense. The careful framing of the indictment, the selection by the government of judge and jury, and the employment of lawyers for the prosecution distinguished treason trials and made conviction much more likely than in ordinary felony cases. Behind these vigorous methods stood the king's personal interest in preventing treason and the intense horror that the crime inspired in the early Tudor period. As has been mentioned above, the only instance in which the Lord High Steward's court departed from procedures followed in common-law treason trials was in permitting conviction by majority vote. The change hardly justifies condemning the tribunal completely as a kangaroo court.

In addition to the procedural issues that led Brewer to condemn Buckingham's trial, there was a question, raised at the trial itself, about the particular form of treason for which he was convicted. The duke was found guilty of compassing and imagining the death of the king on the basis of verbal evidence. Edward III's treason statute of 1352 included compassing and imagining the death of the king among its definitions of high treason, but required an overt act as proof.[76] A statute passed in 1397 permitted conviction for compassing the death or deposition of the king without an overt act, but was repealed a few years later as being too vague and elastic.[77] Nonetheless, when the lords trying Buckingham asked Chief Justice Fyneux whether a person could be convicted on the basis of words alone, he answered, "it is not felony if there is no act committed. But if one intends the death of our Lord the King, it is high treason."[78] The yearbook reporter left no doubt that this ruling forced the jury to find the duke guilty.

Whatever the meaning of the statute of 1352, Chief Justice Fyneux's ruling did not alter existing law. An examination of treason cases going back to the early years of Henry IV's reign indicates that treason by words was a recognized crime in fifteenth-century England. In 1402, the defendants in four cases were convicted for spreading the rumor that Richard II was alive and would return shortly to reclaim his kingdom.[79] Under Edward IV, Oliver Germain was found guilty for predicting that Henry VI would reconquer England from Scotland, regain his throne, and murder Edward IV.[80] In 1477, Thomas Burdett was condemned for compassing and imagining the death of the king on the evidence that he had calculated the nativities of Edward IV and his heir and then predicted their imminent deaths "to the intent that by revealing and making known these matters, the cordial love of the people might be withdrawn from the king; and the king, by knowledge of the same, would be saddened thereby, so that his life would be shortened." He had also distributed complaints, seditions, and treasonable arguments for this nefarious purpose.[81] A third case in the same reign convicted a citizen of London, Walter Walker, who lived at the sign of the crown in Cheapside, for telling his child that, if he would only be quiet, he would make him heir to the crown.[82] Finally, under Henry VII, William Stanley was condemned for saying that "if he were sure that the young man [Perkin Warbeck] was King Edward's son, he would never bear arms against him."[83] In short, fifteenth-century judges regularly construed words that predicted or expressed a desire for the death of the king or an alteration of the succession as an overt act of treason within the meaning of the statute.[84]

What is so troubling to modern notions of legality is the apparent discrepancy between the statute of 1352 and case law. Nonetheless, there can be little doubt that the act was not regarded as an exhaustive definition of treason in the fifteenth century.[85] Bellamy described the fifteenth-century conviction for treason of words as a "novel and important construction," implying that this form of treason was not covered by the statute.[86] Isobel Thornley believed that during this period a common law of treason, which included treason by words, existed side by side with the statute of 1352. The statute supplemented and defined, but did not supersede, common law. Samuel Rezneck disagreed sharply with her theory. He questioned "the supposed existence of a mysterious and rather mystifying common-law doctrine of treason by words" and asserted, rather unconvincingly, that words constituted an overt act under the statute.[87] Among more recent authorities, Elton has agreed with Thornley that the act of 1352 "by implication . . . left the door wide open for other treasons at common law," though Bellamy has denied the existence of any recognized common law of treason in the fourteenth and fifteenth centuries.[88] Whatever the fifteenth-century judges' legal reasoning, which cannot be conclusively analyzed since they did not explain themselves in writing, their view of treason by words is incontestable: "si home ymagyn le mort de Roy et ne fait pluys il serra traye et pend et disclos."[89] They implemented this interpretation consistently in the numerous cases cited above.

In the early sixteenth century, legal and constitutional opinion began to shift. Increasingly, lawyers and political theorists held that the government could not do anything not expressly sanctioned by statute. In 1533–34, an effort to prosecute the Nun of Kent broke down because her crime consisted of words alone. This may explain the explicit provision for treason by words in the infamous Treason Act of 1534.[90] In 1521, however, when Fyneux ruled on the issue of treason by words, he based his interpretation of the law on precedent, rather than on the newer legal doctrines emerging in the early Tudor period.

In light of the cases discussed above, statements attributed to Buckingham in the indictment and in the depositions offered as evidence at the trial undoubtedly constituted high treason. Establishing that fact does not, however, completely dispense with the criticisms of the trial voiced by historians. It is impossible to ignore the enormous contrast between the legal standards of our own time and those of the late medieval and early Tudor periods, and it is certainly legitimate to ask why that era enforced a law that condemned a man to death for what we would regard as a loose tongue and a bad temper. In this connection it is significant that all the convictions for treason by words alone and all the trials in the Lord High Steward's court occurred during the reigns of Henry IV, Henry VI, Edward IV, and Henry VII. None of these kings had an undisputed claim to the throne; all faced the plots and rebellions of rivals and pretenders. These facts suggest that both treason by words and the Lord High Steward's court were legal instruments designed to suppress opposition to the monarchy in times of dynastic instability. Thus, Edward Stafford's trial raises the questions of whether the period of the early 1520's was—or was believed to be—such a period and whether the duke posed a threat to Henry VIII's throne. To answer these questions, it is necessary to turn from the trial itself to the political context in which it took place.

# Conclusion

The earliest political explanations of Edward Stafford's trial and execution go back to the sixteenth century, when a number of chroniclers and historians laid the blame for his tragic fate at the door of Cardinal Wolsey. Nothing less than the malice of Henry's all-powerful minister seemed adequate to account for the duke's sudden and unexpected ruin. The contemporary sources of this tradition were Buckingham's son, Henry; Polydore Vergil; William Roy, author of the ballad "Rede me and be nott wrothe"; and the anonymous composer of a ballad called "An Impeachment of Wolsey."[1] Early authorities such as Raphael Holinshed, Edward Lord Herbert of Cherbury, Francis Godwin, William Shakespeare, William Dugdale, and David Lloyd, and modern historians such as Theodore Maynard and Garrett Mattingly have perpetuated the tradition.[2] The open enmity between the two men gave the explanation credibility.

There is, however, good reason to doubt this version of Buckingham's fall. The four contemporaries who held Wolsey responsible for the duke's death all had an ax to grind and hence were not reliable witnesses. The duke's son made the charge many years later in a letter to Queen Mary seeking her favor. Since the queen's mother, Catherine of Aragon, regarded Wolsey as her mortal enemy and held him responsible for putting the idea of a divorce into Henry VIII's head, Wolsey was an obvious scapegoat for Lord Henry in recounting his own troubles to Mary.[3] Furthermore, he probably shared his father's aristocratic contempt for the cardinal. Polydore Vergil, as J. S. Brewer pointed out, also detested Wolsey and seized any opportunity to discredit him.[4] The two ballads were written in 1528, when the cardinal's position was tottering, and were contributious to the virulent propaganda campaign launched to ensure his ruin. The ballad writers blamed Wolsey for everything they thought had gone wrong during Henry VIII's reign, greatly exaggerating contemporary political discontent and social distress in order to blacken his reputation. Their works are closer to outright libel than to accurate historical evidence.

> Of the prowde Cardinall this is the shelde,
> Borne up between two angels of Sathan,
> The sixe bloudy axes in a bare felde,
> Sheweth the cruelty of the red Man
> Which had devoured the beautiful Swan.[5]

Apart from legitimate skepticism about the sources of the belief that Wolsey plotted to destroy Buckingham, other contemporary evidence raises some doubts about Wolsey's culpability. Hall, certainly no friend of the cardinal's, did not accuse Wolsey in his narrative of the duke's arrest, trial, and execution.[6] An anonymous undated ballad, "Lament of the Duke of Buckingham," alluded to the duke's treacherous servants but made no mention of Wolsey.[7]

Brewer thought that the anonymous letter to Wolsey discussing how the cardinal could induce Charles Knevet to reveal what he knew about the duke's "inward mind"[8] indicated that the author of the letter, not Wolsey, wanted to frame Buckingham.[9] However, since the cardinal had asked the author to deal with Knevet in this matter, the author was probably Wolsey's agent rather than an independent informer. As we have seen, the letter also mentioned that Knevet had already spoken to Mr. Lark, one of Wolsey's servants, and that the cardinal had previously heard incriminating information from other servants of the duke. The crucial question is whether Wolsey had instigated the original investigation.

Since no evidence on this point exists, different historians' answer to the question depends on their general interpretations of Wolsey and Buckingham's relationship. That the two men heartily disliked each other is beyond doubt. The evidence cited to the contrary—that the duke made suits to the crown through Wolsey, that he discussed his son's marriage with the cardinal, that he once thanked him for his good offices—is testimony to Wolsey's preeminence after 1515, not to cordial relations between them.[10] Buckingham openly complained about the necessity of being "subservient to so base and uncivil a fellow,"[11] and Wolsey, for his part, apparently enjoyed humiliating the duke. When he had—or thought he had—a completely free hand in arranging the meeting at the Field of Cloth of Gold, he excluded the duke from the tournament;[12] when the opportunity arose to discipline the duke in the Bulmer case, he did so with relish.

Yet the distance between this open hostility and a plot to eliminate Buckingham is considerable. Unless historians simply assume, with Henry Stafford, Polydore Vergil, and William Roy, that the cardinal was vindictive, ruthless, and bloodthirsty, they must, at the very least, supply a plausible motive. The most obvious explanation—that Wolsey felt politically threatened by Buckingham—is hardly credible. The cardinal, an astute and shrewd politician, must have known that the duke had little real political power or influence with the king.

Rumors of a plot to assassinate Wolsey, current during the last years of Buckingham's life, may be the missing piece in the puzzle. The bishop of Worcester reported early in 1518 "that there was a party in England plotting, in conjunction with France, to depose Wolsey."[13] Fear of such a conspiracy may have been the reason Henry VIII told the cardinal to keep his eye on Buckingham and four other peers.[14] When the Venetian ambassador to Charles, Gasparo Contarini, explained Buckingham's execution in 1521, he referred to a "report the Duke had plotted to assassinate Cardinal Wolsey."[15]

Whether or not Wolsey instigated the investigation that led to Buckingham's arrest, the anonymous letter discussed above clearly establishes that he played a role in collecting preliminary evidence against the duke. His involvement at that stage, however, does not prove that he was behind the inquiry to start with. Given his position as the king's leading servant, and the delicacy of any question of treason that implicated a noble of Buckingham's rank and lineage, it seems clear that Wolsey neither could nor would have proceeded with an investigation of this sort without the explicit or tacit approval of the king. His power depended completely on Henry's confidence in his executive and administrative ability; as Wolsey himself well knew, the king always retained ultimate control over political decisions.[16]

That Henry took an active interest in the bishop of Durham's examination of Buckingham's servants is beyond doubt.[17] That he was convinced of the duke's guilt long before the trial is also clear.[18] But the central question—why Henry exploited Buckingham's rash words to send him to his death—still remains. The king certainly knew that the duke was no threat to the crown. Lawrence Stone was mistaken in suggesting that some perceived threat was a significant factor in Henry's decision to eliminate him.[19] The duke threatened Henry VIII in only one way: as a potential claimant to the throne in the event that Henry left no male heir. Only Buckingham's death could remove that danger. This dynastic consideration was the key to the king's decision to prosecute the duke for treason.[20]

By 1521, Henry VIII was deeply troubled that he had no male heir. There seemed little chance that Catherine would still give him a son, since she was already 36 years old and her last recorded pregnancy had been in 1518. In view of the experience of the only previous English queen, Henry I's daughter Matilda, the king had little confidence that his subjects would accept Princess Mary as their ruler. His sense of insecurity was all the greater because his family had so recently ascended the throne. Henry thus had good reason to fear Buckingham, his nearest living male relative in the Lancastrian line. The king's and duke's grandmothers were first cousins and were great-great-granddaughters of Edward III.[21] Therefore, Buckingham did pose an alternative with a semblance of legitimacy should Henry die without a son.

Since the modern historian knows that the story ended happily for the Tudors—that Henry VIII successfully imposed a political and religious revolution on his subjects, that Edward VI and then Mary carried out radical religious policies without sacrificing the throne, that Elizabeth emerged triumphant from her struggle against the Counter-Reformation—it is very difficult to appreciate the dynastic fears that plagued Henry VIII in the early 1520's. His strong hold on the affections of his subjects seems obvious at a distance of four and a half centuries. Yet even a cursory survey of the plots and unrest during Henry VII's reign and the early years of Henry VIII's shows how mistaken it would be to assume that the duke's contemporaries shared this view.

Henry VII had surmounted the most serious threats to his throne by his defeat of Lambert Simnel's backers at Stoke in 1487, his successful dealings with Perkin Warbeck, and the execution of the earl of Warwick in 1499. Nevertheless, his last years were not free of dynastic worries. There are hints of conspiracies in 1502 and 1503.[22] In 1503, the officers at Calais spoke "'of the world that shoudbe after hym yf hys grace hapned to depart.' . . . Some of them spake of my lorde of Buckyngham saying that he was a noble man and woldbe a ryall ruler. Other ther were that spoke of your troytor Edmund De Pole, but none of them . . . of my lord prynce."[23] The problem of the de la Poles was not resolved finally until 1506.[24] Any plot was potentially dangerous because, in J. D. Mackie's words, there was "a spirit of disaffection among the old families."[25]

On the day after Henry VIII succeeded to the crown, he sent the duke of Buckingham's brother Henry to the Tower on a charge of treason.[26] The younger Stafford, who was found innocent, was released in early 1510. The king created him earl of Wiltshire at his first parliament.[27] This last episode has never been satisfactorily explained, but it may have been a move on the new king's part to ensure the good behavior of his closest rival to the throne. The only clue to the duke's activities in this period is the letter from Lord Darcy to Bishop Fox in August 1509, reporting that "my lord of Northumberland's servants said that 'my lord of Buckingham should be protector of England.'"[28]

Although Henry VIII tried to conciliate the nobility in the first years of his reign, he did not trust them with political power any more than his father had. With the rise of Wolsey—whom peers from old families regarded as their mortal enemy—and the renewal of prosecutions in Star Chamber for illegal retaining, noblemen became increasingly discontented with their position under Henry VIII.[29] Once again, suggestions of disloyalty and plots appear in the state papers, although they were never as serious as those that had plagued Henry VII. In 1518, the bishop of Worcester commented on a plot against Wolsey,[30] and Contarini repeated a similar rumor three years later.[31] In June 1519, Archbishop Warham wrote a letter to Buckingham containing the enigmatic remark, "I had lever lose 500 marks than that the matter that is intended should take none effect."[32] Three months later, Sebastian Giustinian wrote that the duke was "very popular" and "were the King to die without heirs male, he might easily obtain the crown."[33] It was during this period that Henry ordered Wolsey to watch the group of five noblemen that included Buckingham.[34]

The duke's provocative behavior undoubtedly exacerbated the suspicion and fear Henry felt toward him during these years. As we have seen, he enraged the king in November 1520 by breaking the laws against livery and maintenance by retaining a royal servant, Sir William Bulmer. The tongue-lashing Henry personally administered to Bulmer in Star Chamber was clearly meant for Buckingham as much as for Sir William: "what might be thought by his [Bulmer's] departyng and what might bee supposed by the duke's retaining, he would not then declare."[35] It was probably on this occasion that Wolsey warned the duke "that he should take heed how . . . he did use himself towards the king's highness."[36] We have also seen that according to Charles Knevet, the duke exploded after being rebuked and actually threatened to assassinate the king if he was arrested;[37] at about the same time, Buckingham petitioned the king for permission to lead a few hundred armed retainers into Wales to suppress disorders in his lordships there.[38] The king, furious about the Bulmer incident and generally suspicious of the duke, flatly refused his consent. He was undoubtedly struck by the parallel between Buckingham's plan and the behavior of his father, the second duke of Buckingham, who had withdrawn to Wales shortly before he rebelled against Richard III. The petition was cited as evidence of treasonous intent in the indictment against him.[39]

In light of the Bulmer incident, the projected expedition into Wales, and the public's inclination to regard Buckingham as a potential heir to the throne, Henry took reports that the duke threatened to alter the succession very seriously. The decision to prosecute him for words that undoubtedly constituted treason under the law was understandable, and, in the circumstances, almost inevitable. The king's willingness to execute the duke for a form of treason that involved such a large discrepancy between crime and punishment reveals the depth of his dynastic fears as early as 1521. Buckingham's death showed how perilous it was to speculate about the cause of the series of disasters that had carried off so many of Catherine of Aragon's children.

Henry's action also served as a warning to members of the peerage of the danger involved in openly criticizing Wolsey, complaining about the exclusion of noblemen from office, and denying full support for the goals of the early Tudor monarchy. On the scaffold, Buckingham warned all noblemen to beware of his fate.[40] The duke's absolute helplessness in the face of Henry's wrath made the folly of incurring the king's displeasure abundantly clear: family connections, wealth, and affinity were of no use to him at the critical juncture of his life. His position underscored the enormous disparity between the power of the crown and the power of even the greatest lords. The ease with which Henry VIII eliminated Buckingham was a mark of the early Tudors' success in strengthening the monarchy and raising the king to heights unattainable by any of the nobility.

The Nevilles and the Poles, families connected to the Staffords by marriage, found themselves in a particularly precarious position at this time. Margaret Pole, countess of Salisbury, fell into disgrace and was temporarily replaced as Mary Tudor's governess, though no punitive action was taken against her "on account of her noble birth and many virtues."[41] The king took punitive action against all her sons: the eldest, Henry, Lord Montague, was sent to the Tower; Arthur was expelled from the court; and the king told the Venetians that they "must not make so much" of Reginald, then studying at Padua, "lest he prove disloyal like the others."[42] The Poles probably suffered as much for their royal blood as for their connection with the duke, but certainly the relationship did them little good at this juncture.[43]

The hostility and political rivalry that had long existed between Buckingham and his son-in-law George Neville, Lord Bergavenny, did not save Bergavenny from being implicated in the duke's fall. The king sent him to the Tower of London for misprision of treason because he had not reported Buckingham's traitorous conversation with him. To gain his freedom, Neville, who was still in prison in 1522, had to sell King Henry the manor of Birlyng, pay a fine of 10,000 marks, surrender all his offices under the crown, and sign a recognizance of 10,000 marks for his good behavior in the future.[44] He had, to use Chapuys's colorful phrase, "lost his feathers."[45] Henry also banished Bergavenny's brother, Edward Neville, who had received a pension from the late duke, from court.[46] Surprisingly, Henry VIII explicitly exonerated Henry Percy, the earl of Northumberland from any involvement in Buckingham's treason, despite his close longtime political and social relationship with his brother-in-law.[47] Nonetheless, it was a dangerous time for English noblemen, who adopted the safe course of bowing to the storm: there is no record that even one of them uttered a word of protest against the treatment accorded the late duke of Buckingham.

Both the duke's dramatic death and his long-term relations with Henry VII and Henry VIII suggest the need for refining, if not revising, our interpretation of the position of the nobility in the early Tudor state. Until about 1960, historians worked within a framework that assumed 1485 was a crucial turning point in English history, drew a sharp contrast between the new monarchy of Henry VII and Henry VIII and that of their medieval predecessors, and saw the destruction of the old nobility and its replacement by men of gentle or even common birth as a key element in the new order. Many historians considered the battle of Bosworth the boundary between medieval and modern times; the Tudor regime appeared as a modern form of absolutism that replaced the medieval constitutionalism of the Lancastrian period. As recently as 1950, these assumptions underlay Stanley Bindoff's elegant contribution to the Pelican series on the history of England. Bindoff considered Henry VII an innovator both in the use he made of the council and in his choice of advisers. His discussion emphasized the displacement of the great nobles who had dominated government in the fifteenth century by "men of lower rank and smaller fortune," "minor peers, knights or squires," "'new men,' who in turn were wholly dependent for their position and prospects."[48]

In the last 25 years, historians have challenged all the assumptions of this interpretation. The significance of 1485 as a watershed in English history has disappeared in the work of scholars such as S. B. Chrimes, J. R. Lander, A. J. Slavin, and B. P. Wolffe, who have emphasized instead the continuity between Yorkist and early Tudor methods of government.[49] Some historians have abandoned the concept of the "new monarchy" altogether; others have extended it backward to the reign of Edward IV. One of the most influential students of the period, K. B. McFarlane, has even asserted emphatically that "the only New Monarchy that England ever had came in with William the Conqueror."[50] According to McFarlane, vigorous kings controlled "overmighty subjects" and depended on churchmen and laymen of the official class to run their governments throughout the medieval period. G. R. Elton has contributed to this revision from the opposite direction, by placing the transition from medieval to modern government in the 1530's, thereby reducing the significance of 1485 and the reign of the first Tudor. All these historians have seen Henry VII as a "medieval" king, though a competent and unusually successful one.

These scholars have also emphasized the survival and continuing influence of the nobility. They have noted the lords' continued presence at court as the king's social companions, their domination of high office, their key roles in ceremonies at court, and in most cases their membership on the king's council. Because of the limited financial resources of the monarchy, neither Henry VII nor Henry VIII could wage war without the service of the nobility and their retainers, a fact that explains why the crown licensed the granting of liveries instead of enforcing its stated policy of repressing livery and maintenance altogether. At the local level, peers performed essential services in preserving law and order and in implementing royal policy while they dominated economic and social life by their vast ownership of land and the employment of enormous staffs in their elaborate households.

The revisionists are undoubtedly correct when they assert that Henry VII adopted Yorkist methods of government and that there was little institutional change before the 1530's. Recognizing this continuity, however, should not blind historians to the real differences between Edward IV's government and that of the first Tudors. Even on an institutional level, Henry VIII made a significant impact by making the Star Chamber a regular court in the first decade of his reign. And as Charles Ross has underscored in his recent biography of Edward IV, Edward's policies toward the aristocracy were quite different from those later adopted by Henry VII and Henry VIII.[51] An analysis that minimizes the real conflicts between crown and nobility and emphasizes their mutual interests and cooperation cannot account for the experience of the peerage in the early Tudor state.

Edward Stafford's life furnishes an exemplum. His position under both Henry VII and Henry VIII becomes explicable only when one recognizes that both kings harbored deep suspicions of the nobility, particularly members of old magnate families that dominated unruly, peripheral areas of the kingdom. At the same time that they burdened Buckingham with expensive ceremonial and diplomatic duties at court, the Tudors consistently excluded him from influential and lucrative offices. When combined with the heavy fines Henry VII imposed on Buckingham during his minority, this unrewarded yet costly service to the state forced him into debt, both to the crown and to private creditors. By the last year of his life, as we have seen, the duke was forced to sell substantial amounts of land. The Tudors' policy of weakening the peerage through financial pressure seemed to be working.

The Tudors' unsuccessful efforts to compel Buckingham to maintain order and enforce the law in Wales highlight another area of conflict between crown and nobility. Both Henry VII and Henry VIII clearly felt that the security of their dynasty depended on establishing law and order throughout the realm. They rightfully considered the continued lawlessness in the duke's Welsh lordships a serious threat to their policy of gaining control over every corner of their kingdom. Buckingham's behavior strongly suggested that he did not identify his interests with the crown's and that he was unwilling or unable to implement this policy. On his side, the duke undoubtedly considered the Tudors' interference in his Welsh lordships an attack on his position as marcher lord and another sign of their hostility toward great nobles. Similar conflicts of interest bedeviled the Tudors' relations with the Percies and Cliffords in the north and the Neville Lords Bergavenny in the South.[52]

The facts of Edward Stafford's life thus make it clear that reducing the power of the nobility was a key element in the process of consolidating the power of the early Tudor monarchy. His experience also shows how difficult it was for members of magnate families with roots deep in the past to adapt to the new roles Henry VII and Henry VIII created for the peerage as courtiers and servants of the crown. Unlike the Talbot earls of Shrewsbury and the Howard dukes of Norfolk, Buckingham could not adjust to the demands of the new order. His life should caution historians against uncritically accepting an interpretative framework that overestimates the continuity between Yorkist and early Tudor monarchies and underemphasizes the real conflict between crown and nobility in the reigns of Henry VII and Henry VIII.

*Appendixes*

# Buckingham's Household Staff and Councillors

Councillors indicated by asterisks were members of the gentry.

## Clerks

Thomas Bridges, clerk of the wardrobe, 1514–16 (SRO, 641/1/3/9), chaplain, 1521 (PRO, E101/518/6); master of the wardrobe, 1521 (PRO, E36/220, m. 22): Godshouse College, Cambridge, 1499–1503 (A. B. Emden, *A Biographical Register of the University of Cambridge to A.D. 1500*, Cambridge, 1963, p. 101).

Henry Bullock, clerk of the wardrobe, 1513–15 (SRO, D641/1/3/9; Carole Rawcliffe, *The Staffords, Earls of Stafford and Dukes of Buckingham, 1394–1521*, Cambridge, 1978, p. 198): fellow of Queens' College, Cambridge, 1507–13, 1515–1524/25 (Emden, *Cambridge*, p. 105).

Thomas Cade, receiver general, 1511; farmer of Dodington, Staffordshire, 1511–12 (SRO, D641/1/2/89); receiver of Staffordshire, 1512–15; surveyor and councillor by 1514; was sued for breaking his contract, 1514, but reappointed receiver general, 1519: steward of Cardinal Wolsey's household, 1528 (Rawcliffe, *The Staffords*, p. 229, except as otherwise indicated).

William Curtis, receiver of Gloucestershire, Wiltshire, and Hampshire, 1519–20; master of the works, 1520–21; treasurer of the household and councillor, 1521 (Rawcliffe, *The Staffords*, p. 229).

John Dellacourt, chaplain, 1512–18 (*L&P, Henry VIII*, vol. III (1), pp. 490–91); auditor, 1516; councillor by 1520: fellow of Magdalen College, Oxford, 1498; testified against Buckingham at his trial (Rawcliffe, *The Staffords*, p. 229, except as otherwise indicated).

William Gibbons, clerk of the household, 1497, 1499–1500 (SRO, D641/1/3/5); receiver of Staffordshire, 1497–1502; receiver general, 1499–1502: Oxford scholar; served on many conciliar commissions (Rawcliffe, *The Staffords*, p. 229, except as otherwise indicated).

Robert Gilbert, retained by 1500; member of household by 1508 (PRO, SP1/22, f. 77); chancellor by 1514: fellow of Magdalen College, Oxford, by 1487 (A. B. Emden, *A Biographical Register of the University of Oxford to A.D. 1500*, Oxford, 1957, vol. II, p. 767); received an annuity of £5, Dec. 1500; received a number of benefices in Buckingham's gift—Newton Blossomville, Buckinghamshire, 1502–3; Bradley, Staffordshire, 1503; Amersham, Buckinghamshire by 1518; Worthen, Herefordshire, 1518 (ibid.; *VCH, Staffordshire*, vol. IV, London, 1958, p. 86); testified against Buckingham at his trial in 1521 (Rawcliffe, *The Staffords*, pp. 229, 242, except as otherwise indicated).

John Golde, clerk of the wardrobe by Mar. 1499 (Rawcliffe, *The Staffords*, p. 198); master of the wardrobe, 1508 (PRO, SP1/22, f. 63): fellow of Magdalen College, Oxford, 1502–3; expelled 1507 for contumacious conduct in withdrawing from a visitation of the college (Emden, *Oxford*, vol. II, p. 781).

John Gregory, clerk of the household by Mar. 1506 (Rawcliffe, *The Staffords*, p. 198); still in duke's service in 1508 (*L&P, Henry VIII*, vol. III (1), 1285, p. 498): M.A., Magdalen College, Oxford; fellow of Eton College, Mar. 1512 (Emden, *Oxford*, vol. II, p. 818).

John Jennings, receiver of Gloucestershire, Hampshire, and Wiltshire, 1511; surveyor general and councillor by 1520: doctor of civil law, 1499; practicing attorney in court of arches, 1510 (Rawcliffe, *The Staffords*, p. 229).

John Llandaff, keeper of the wardrobe, 1511 (SRO, D641/1/3/9).

Thomas Moscroff, receiver general, 1519; secretary and councillor by 1520 (Rawcliffe, *The Staffords*, p. 230); fellow of Merton College, Oxford, 1510; degrees include B.A., M.A., B.Med., B.D., D.D.; physician; Wolsey's physic reader, 1522; vice-chancellor of Oxford, 1523 (Joseph Foster, *Alumni Oxonienses, 1500–1714*, Oxford, 1891–92, vol. III, p. 1040); Buckingham gave him an annuity of £10 in 1519 (PRO, SP1/29, f. 183).

Anthony Nowers, comptroller of the household, 1517–21 (Rawcliffe, *The Staffords*, p. 196).

Humphrey Ogull, keeper of the wardrobe, 1512–13 (Rawcliffe, *The Staffords*, p. 198).

George Poley, wore livery by 1515–16 (SRO, D641/1/3/9); keeper of the jewels, 1515–17; treasurer, 1515–20; was sued for debt, 1516, but still made almoner and councillor by 1520: Cambridge scholar, 1500; fellow of Jesus College, 1510 (John Venn and J. A. Venn, *Alumni Cantabrigienses*, Cambridge, 1927, vol. I, p. 379); University Preacher, 1509–10 (Rawcliffe, *The Staffords*, p. 230, except as otherwise indicated).

Richard Pooley, clerk of the household, c. 1514; wardrober by 1506–7 (Rawcliffe, *The Staffords*, p. 198).

Henry Sleford, surveyor general, 1501–6; councillor by 1505; receiver of Holderness, 1505–8: Cambridge scholar in canon law; rector of Amersham, Buckinghamshire, in duke's gift, by Dec. 1504 (Emden, *Cambridge*, p. 533; Rawcliffe, *The Staffords*, p. 230).

Laurence Stubbes, member of household, 1507; conciliar commissioner, 1508; receiver of Gloucestershire, Hampshire, and Wiltshire, 1508; secretary, 1511–14: distinguished fellow of Magdalen College, Oxford; rector of Fobbing, Essex, in Buckingham's gift, 1511 to death (Emden, *Oxford*, vol. III, p. 1809); joined Wolsey's household by 1515 (Rawcliffe, *The Staffords*, p. 230, except as otherwise indicated).

Thomas Wotton, receiver of Gloucestershire, Hampshire, and Wiltshire, 1513–18; master of works, 1514–19; councillor, 1518–19 (PRO, SC6/Henry 8/4775); dean of chapel and councillor, 1520: bachelor of canon law, 1511–12 (Venn and Venn, *Alumni Cantabrigienses*, vol. IV, p. 476).

*Lawyers*

*John Brooke, awarded Stafford livery by 1503; itinerant justice in Brecon, 1503; involved in various collusive suits as Buckingham's feoffee, 1513; in attendance at Thornbury to give counsel, 1521: son of Thomas Brooke of Redcliffe, Bristol; member, Middle Temple; serjeant-at-law; on commission for enclosing land in Somersetshire, 1517; steward of Bedminster, Somersetshire (Rawcliffe, *The Staffords*, p. 227; PRO, E36/150, f. 109; J. Bruce Williamson, *The Middle Temple Bench Book, A Register of Benchers of the Middle Temple*, 2d ed., London, 1937, p. 50).

*Richard Brooke, councillor by 1508; Buckingham's feoffee, 1513–14; collector of Stretton Audley, Oxfordshire, 1506–7 (PRO, SC6/Henry 7/5808): son of Thomas Brooke of Leighton, Cheshire; member, Middle Temple; served on many commissions of the peace; serjeant-at-law, 1510–20 (S. T. Bindoff, *The House of Commons 1509–1558*, London, 1982, vol. I, p. 503); recorder and MP for London, 1510–15; justice of common pleas, 1520; chief baron of exchequer, 1526 (Rawcliffe, *The Staffords*, pp. 227–28, except as otherwise indicated).

*John Carter, Buckingham's attorney at exchequer, 1498–1509; farmer of Agmondesham, Buckinghamshire, by 1521 (Rawcliffe, *The Staffords*, p. 228): received an annuity of 66s 8d; described as gentleman (PRO, SP1/29, f. 187).

*Sir Humphrey Coningsby, retained 1500, when already employed by Buckingham: also in service of crown; member of Inner Temple; justice of King's Bench, 1509; received an annuity of £2 (Rawcliffe, *The Staffords*, pp. 228, 242; Edward Foss, *Judges of England*, London, 1848–64, vol. 5, p. 185; Bindoff, *The Commons*, vol. I, pp. 680–81).

*Edmund Dudley, councillor by 1498–99; Buckingham's feoffee, 1501

(Rawcliffe, *The Staffords*, p. 228): one of Henry VII's most important advisers.

* Sir Thomas Frowyck, retained by 1502: member of influential Middlesex family; member of Inner Temple; justice of common pleas, 1502; received an annuity of £2 (Rawcliffe, *The Staffords*, pp. 228, 242; Foss, *Judges of England*, vol. 5, p. 283).

* William Greville, retained 1504; feoffee for Buckingham's sister, 1505; received an annuity of £2: serjeant-at-law by 1503 (*CCR, Henry VII*, London, 1955, 1963, vol. II, 384); became justice of common pleas, 1509 (Rawcliffe, *The Staffords*, p. 228).

* Sir Christopher Hales, Buckingham's attorney general by 1521: from a Kentish family; member of Gray's Inn; MP, Canterbury, 1523; Henry VIII's solicitor general, 1525; attorney general, 1529; Master of the Rolls, 1536; knighted, 1538 (Rawcliffe, *The Staffords*, p. 228; *DNB*, vol. VIII, pp. 910–11; Bindoff, *The Commons*, vol. I, p. 274).

* Thomas Jubbes, awarded Stafford livery, 1503; involved in collusive suits as Buckingham's feoffee, 1512–14; councillor, 1520; received an annuity of £2 (PRO, SP1/29, f. 183): member Middle Temple (Sir Henry F. MacGeagh and H. A. C. Sturgess, *Register of Admissions to the Honourable Society of the Middle Temple*, London, 1949, p. 2); influential in Gloucestershire as recorder and MP for Bristol; on commissions of peace, Somersetshire, and subsidy commissions, Bristol (Bindoff, *The Commons*, vol. I, p. 456). (Rawcliffe, *The Staffords*, p. 228, except as otherwise indicated.)

Thomas Matston, retained 1517; member council 1520–21; received an annuity of £2 (Rawcliffe, *The Staffords*, p. 228): member of Middle Temple (MacGeagh, *Register of Admissions*, p. 2); described as gentleman (*CCR, Henry VII*, vol. II, 544, 684).

* John Scott, attorney general, 1498–1515; councillor from 1501 (SRO, D1721/1/1); itinerant justice in Brecon, 1503; receiver of Kent and Surrey, 1505–6 (PRO, SC6/Henry 7/1076); parker of Bletchingley, Surrey, 1506; keeper of South Park, Surrey, 1520–21 (*L&P, Henry VIII*, vol. III (2), 1532); farmer of Camberwell and Peckham, Surrey: member of Middle Temple; granted office of chief baron of exchequer in reversion but never obtained possession; one of jurors who indicted Buckingham in 1521; granted Camberwell and Peckham, Surrey, after the duke's attainder (Rawcliffe, *The Staffords*, pp. 228–29, and T. B. Pugh, ed., *The Marcher Lordships of South Wales, 1415–1536: Select Documents*, Cardiff, 1963, pp. 296–97, except as otherwise indicated).

* Robert Turberville, treasurer of household to 1502; then steward of household; receiver general, 1503–8; itinerant judge in Brecon, 1503; involved in many suits for debt on Buckingham's behalf; received an

annuity of 5 marks, 1509–21: influential Hertfordshire landowner, lawyer, knight of the shire (Rawcliffe, *The Staffords*, p. 230; Pugh, *Marcher Lordships*, 297).

*William Walwyn, auditor general, 1507–21; councillor, 1518–19 (PRO, SC6/Henry 8/4775); Buckingham's surety in dealings with the crown; brought actions for debt on his behalf: member of Lincoln's Inn; crown auditor for South Wales (*The Records of the Honourable Society of Lincoln's Inn*, vol. I, *Admissions from 1420–1799*, London, 1896, p. 30; Rawcliffe, *The Staffords*, p. 231).

## Other Officers

*Humphrey Bannaster, esquire, itinerant justice, Brecon, 1503; councillor by 1505; comptroller of household, 1506; involved in many suits for debt on Buckingham's behalf, 1506–11; treasurer, 1508; Buckingham sued him for debt, 1511: of Tonbridge, Kent; joined household of Charles Brandon, duke of Suffolk, by 1515 (Rawcliffe, *The Staffords*, p. 229; *CCR, Henry VII*, vol. II, 822).

*William Cholmeley, cofferer, 1503–21 (SRO, D641/1/3/7; *L&P, Henry VIII*, vol. III (1), pp. 495, 501); clerk of the wardrobe, 1506 (SRO, D641/1/3/9); received an annuity of £6 13s 4d (PRO, SP1/29, f. 183): from yeoman stock (Rawcliffe, *The Staffords*, p. 89); but described as gentleman, 1523 (*L&P, Henry VIII*, vol. III (2), 3695); admitted Lincoln's Inn, 1528 (*Records of Lincoln's Inn*, vol. I, p. 43).

*Humphrey Fowke, wore livery by 1515–16 (SRO, D641/1/3/9); master of horse, 1516 (SRO, D641/1/3/9): from Staffordshire family; went with Buckingham to Thornbury (Harleian Society, vol. XXI, *Visitation of County of Gloucester, 1623*, p. 245).

*Giles Greville, treasurer, 1515 (Rawcliffe, *The Staffords*, p. 229); wore livery, 1516–17 (SRO, D641/1/3/9); was sued for failure to account, 1512 (Rawcliffe, *The Staffords*, p. 248): described as esquire (*CCR, Henry VII*, vol. II, 537).

*John Gunter, originally in service of dowager Duchess Anne, widow of Humphrey, first duke of Buckingham, and Henry, second duke; itinerant justice in Newport, 1476 and 1503 (Rawcliffe, *The Staffords*, pp. 226, 242); auditor of third duke, 1500–1506 at least; annuity of £5; involved in cases of debt on Buckingham's behalf: land in Surrey, Sussex and Hay, Wales (Pugh, *Marcher Lordships*, p. 290).

*Humphrey Hervey, retained and received an annuity of £2 by 1503; councillor by 1508; (Rawcliffe, *The Staffords*, p. 228): from Bristol; MP for Wells, 1483, 1484–85, 1489–90, JP, Somerset, 1488–1512 (Josiah C. Wedgewood, *History of Parliament: Biographies of Members of the Commons House, 1439–1509*, London, 1936, p. 447).

*Sir William Knevet, chamberlain and councillor to Buckingham at £36
    10s per annum (Rawcliffe, *The Staffords*, p. 227): great-uncle of third
    duke of Buckingham (see Chapter 2, n. 5); retainer of second duke
    and involved in rebellion of 1483 (*Rolls of Parliament*, vol. VI, p. 254);
    involved in escape of third duke from Richard III's men (SRO, D1721/
    1/11, ff. 241–43): important landowner in Norfolk; also owned lands
    in Suffolk, Cumberland, Huntingdonshire, and Nottinghamshire
    (Wedgewood, *Biographies*, pp. 520–21).

*Richard Mynors, treasurer, 1502–7; conciliar commissioner, 1504 (SRO,
    D641/1/5/4) and 1505; brought many actions for debt on duke's be-
    half, 1505–11; was sued for failing to account for receipts of £1,562,
    1507–12: of Treago, Herefordshire (Bindoff, *The Commons*, vol. II,
    p. 651); joined the earl of Shrewsbury's retinue by 1513; sheriff of
    Hereford; described as esquire (PRO, *Lists and Indexes*, vol. IX, *List of
    Sheriffs*, p. 61; Rawcliffe, *The Staffords*, p. 230, except as otherwise
    indicated).

*John Pauncefoot, conciliar commissioner, 1511; comptroller of the house-
    hold, 1514: Gloucestershire landowner and crown administrator
    (Rawcliffe, *The Staffords*, p. 230).

*Richard Pole, receiver general and steward of the household, 1495,
    while Buckingham still a minor; reappointed steward and made
    councillor by 1514: influential courtier and Herefordshire knight
    (Rawcliffe, *The Staffords*, p. 230).

*John Russell, clerk of the kitchens, 1495; secretary, 1499–1507; receiver
    of Gloucestershire, Hampshire, and Wiltshire, 1501–4; Buckingham's
    feoffee, 1501; itinerant justice in Brecon, 1503; on general circuit,
    1504 (SRO, D641/1/5/4); brought many suits for debt on duke's be-
    half, 1505–11; was sued for embezzlement, 1508–11: rose in service
    of crown, becoming secretary to Princess Mary by 1525; Worcester-
    shire landowner; JP in Herefordshire and Shropshire (Rawcliffe, *The
    Staffords*, p. 230; Bindoff, *The Commons*, vol. II, p. 232).

*John Seintgeorge, auditor, 1506–14; Buckingham sued him for failing to
    carry out his duties, 1515, and imprisoned him illegally in Glouces-
    tershire Castle (Rawcliffe, *The Staffords*, pp. 167, 200, 248).

*William Tracy, bailiff of Policote, Buckinghamshire, 1517–18 (West-
    minster Abbey, 5470) and 1520–21 (*L&P, Henry VIII*, vol. III (2), 3695);
    treasurer of household, 1521 (PRO, E36/220, f. 29); received an an-
    nuity of 40s (PRO, E36/220, f. 27): probably the William Tracy of Tod-
    dington, a member of an old Gloucestershire family, who served as JP
    and sheriff (Bindoff, *The Commons*, vol. III, p. 471); described as "a
    substancyall man and a goode payer" (PRO, SP1/29, f. 181).

Listed below are auditors or clerks of the household about whom no other information is available and who do not seem to have played an important role in Buckingham's household or on his council (for the dates of their employment, see Rawcliffe, *The Staffords*, pp. 198, 200).

| | | |
|---|---|---|
| William Becke | William Hobson | William Sharp |
| William Bradbolt | Richard Palmer | John Snow |
| John Buttys | John Rosse | Walter Thomas |
| Robert Cade | William Sandes | David Young |
| Edward Edgar | | |

# County or Upper Gentry Who Held Office on Buckingham's Estates

Persons indicated by asterisks were lawyers.

Roger Bodenham, esquire, itinerant judge, Brecon, 1503 (BL, Egerton Rolls, 2203): important member of gentry in South Wales and Hereford; from 1485, on commissions of peace and gaol delivery; sheriff of Hereford 1489–90 (T. B. Pugh, ed., *The Marcher Lordships of South Wales, 1415–1536: Select Documents*, Cardiff, 1963, p. 238).

*Roland Bridges, receiver of Brecon, 1508 (PRO, SP1/22, f. 61): of Clerkenwell, Middlesex, and Ley, Weobley, Herefordshire; a lawyer of gentle birth; commissioner of gaol delivery, Hereford Castle, 1511; MP for city of Hereford, 1512; JP, 1531–32 (Stanley Thomas Bindoff, *The House of Commons, 1509–1558*, London, 1982, vol. I, pp. 535–36).

*John Brooke, itinerant judge, Brecon, 1508 (PRO, SP1/22, f. 77), and steward of Bedminster, Somersetshire, 1520 (PRO, E36/150, f. 109); also a member of duke's council (see Appendix A).

*Richard Brooke, collector of Stretton Audley, Oxfordshire, 1506–7 (PRO, SC6/Henry 7/5808); also a member of duke's council (see Appendix A).

Sir Edward Chamberlain, approver of woods in Kent and Surrey, 1520–21 (PRO, E36/150, f. 40): of Shirburn, Oxfordshire; JP, Oxfordshire, 1509–37; sheriff of Oxford and Berkshire, 1506–7, 1517–18; esquire of the body by 1509; knighted 1520 at Field of Cloth of Gold and Gravelines; served Henry VIII in military capacity; MP for Wallingford, Berkshire, 1529; held office in Catherine of Aragon's household at Kimbolton (*DNB*, vol. IV, p. 71; Bindoff, *The Commons*, vol. I, pp. 614–15).

John Corbet of Leigh, receiver and forester of Caus, 1520–21 (*L&P, Henry VIII*, vol. III (2), 3695); wore duke's livery 1516–17: eldest son of Thomas Corbet of Leigh, Shropshire; member of branch of most powerful family in county; JP, Shropshire, 1521–54; sheriff 1526, 1537; servant to countess of Salisbury before he entered service of the duke of Buckingham and Lord Stafford; MP for Shropshire, 1530; uncle with same name shared lease of demesne of Caus in 1500 and was duke's deputy steward and receiver there (SRO, D641/1/3/9; Bindoff, *The Commons*, vol. I, pp. 697–98).

Sir William Dennis, itinerant judge, Brecon, 1503 (Pugh, *Marcher Lordships*, p. 118): member of important Gloucestershire family; member of Henry VII's household; knight of body to Henry VIII; sheriff of Gloucestershire, c. 1519 (Pugh, *Marcher Lordships*, p. 290; Bindoff, *The Commons*, vol. II, p. 36).

Sir Edward Guildford, keeper of Northfrith Park, Kent (PRO, SP1/29, f. 182): son and heir of Sir Richard; elder half-brother of Henry Guildford, comptroller of Henry VIII's household; on commissions of peace in Kent, Northampton, and Surrey; on subsidy commissions in Kent; esquire of the body, 1509; sheriff of Lincolnshire, 1511; knight by 1514; constable, Dover Castle, and lord warden, Cinque Ports, 1521–34; constable (with Sir Henry) of Reeds Castle, Kent, 1531–34; councillor by May 1534 (Bindoff, *The Commons*, vol. II, p. 262).

*Christopher Hales, receiver for London and Middlesex (PRO, SP1/29, f. 183); also Buckingham's attorney general by 1521 (see Appendix A).

*John Haslewood, keeper of Writtle Park with Mistress Philips (*L&P, Henry VIII*, vol. III (2), 3695), received two annuities, one of £10 and another of £6 13s 4d, 1520–21 (ibid.); he and Mistress Philips lent the duke over £1,800 by 1520: of Waltham, Essex, and London; lawyer and member of the Middle Temple; a teller at the exchequer; MP for Buckingham, 1529 (Bindoff, *The Commons*, vol. II, pp. 314–15).

*William Huntley, esquire, itinerant judge, Brecon, 1503 (BL, Egerton Rolls, 2201): from a distinguished Gloucestershire family; member of Inner Temple (Pugh, *Marcher Lordships*, p. 291). A John Huntley, in the duke's service in some unspecified position in 1504 (BL, Add'l Mss., 40,859B), may have come from his family too.

*John Kingsmill, itinerant judge, Brecon, 1503 (BL, Egerton Rolls, 2203): from Hampshire and Wiltshire; member of Middle Temple, 1489; MP from Heytesbury, Hampshire, 1491–92; tried cases in court of requests, 1493–94; king's serjeant, 1497; justice of common pleas, 1503 (Pugh, *Marcher Lordships*, p. 293; Josiah C. Wedgewood, *History of Parliament: Biographies of Members of the Commons House, 1439–1509*, London, 1936, p. 516; A. B. Emden, *A Biographical Register of the University of Oxford to A.D. 1500*, Oxford, 1957, vol. II, p. 1074).

William Leighton, receiver of Caus, 1516–17 (BL, Egerton Rolls, 2200): wore duke's livery 1515–16 (PRO, E101/631/20); probably a member of the prominent western Shropshire family of that name that held land of barony of Caus (Bindoff, *The Commons*, vol. II, p. 518).

*Richard Littleton, steward of Stafford, 1502–3 (SRO, D641/1/2/83); itinerant judge, Brecon, 1503 (SRO, D641/1/4U/1, m. 1): of Pillaton, Staffordshire; from legal family; son of Thomas Littleton, judge; inherited wide estate in Shropshire from mother; JP, Salop, 1485–1504 and 1511–16; also JP in Staffordshire and Shropshire; MP for Ludlow, Shropshire (Wedgewood, *Biographies*, p. 547).

Sir Thomas Lovell, steward of Norfolk (*L&P, Henry VIII*, vol. III (2), 3695): leading figure in Henry VII's government and early years of Henry VIII's.

*Sir Walter Luke, steward of Huntingdonshire (PRO, SC6/Henry 8/5853, m. 5): of Copley, Bedfordshire; member of Middle Temple; on commissions of peace in Bedfordshire and Huntingdonshire; serjeant-at-law, 1531; justice of King's Bench, 1532 (Rawcliffe, *The Staffords*, p. 228; Edward Foss, *Judges of England*, London, 1848–64, vol. V, p. 417).

Hugh Marvyn, esquire, bailiff of Lalleford, Warwickshire, 1501–21 (SRO, D641/1/2/278, 279; PRO, SC6/Henry 7/867–69; PRO, SC6/Henry 8/3718); bailiff of Maxstoke and parker of Warwickshire (PRO, E36/150, f. 115); deputy steward of Warwickshire (ibid.); receiver of Cantref Selyf, Penkelly, and Alexanderstone, 1516–17 (BL, Egerton Rolls, 2195); wore duke's livery, 1516–17 (SRO, D641/1/3/9); receiver for Brecon, Cantref Selyf, Hay, and Huntingdon, 1520–21 (PRO, E36/220, f. 3): described as "able and substanciall esquire" (PRO, SP1/29, f. 178).

John ap Morgan, esquire, deputy steward of Newport (PRO, SP1/29, f. 174); wore duke's livery, 1516–17 (SRO, D641/1/3/9).

Thomas ap Morgan, esquire, deputy steward and receiver of Newport, and constable of castle (PRO, SP1/29, f. 174); wore duke's livery, 1516–17 (SRO, D641/1/3/9): described as "an honeste and a trewe esquier" (PRO, SP1/29, f. 174).

Henry Myle, esquire, substeward of Cantref Selyf, 1521 (*L&P, Henry VIII*, vol. III (2), 3695): sheriff of Hereford, 1499, 1508, 1512 (PRO, *Lists and Indexes*, vol. IX, *List of Sheriffs*, p. 61).

Sir Edward Neville, steward of Kent and Surrey (PRO, SP1/29, f. 182; E36/150, f. 38): brother of George Neville, Lord Bergavenny, husband of Buckingham's daughter Mary.

Sir Henry Owen, keeper of Postern Park, Kent (PRO, SP1/29, f. 182): knighted at Tournai; present at meeting at Field of Cloth of Gold; king's sewer; served on embassy to France; on subsidy commission for Sussex (*L&P, Henry VIII*, vol. I, 4468; vol. II (1), p. 1708; vol. III (2), p. 1362; *Rutland Papers*, ed. William Jerdan, Camden Society, vol. XXI, London, 1918, p. 33).

*Walter Rowdon, itinerant judge, Brecon, 1503 (BL, Egerton Rolls, 2203; SRO, D641/1/4U/1, 1) and 1508 (PRO, SP1/2, f. 78); bailiff of the honors of Hereford and Gloucester, in Gloucestershire, 1499–1502 (SRO, D641/1/2/201–2): a member of Lincoln's Inn; mayor of Gloucester, 1492 and 1503; JP in Gloucestershire; steward of the duchy of Lancaster (Pugh, *Marcher Lordships*, p. 296).

John Russell, receiver for Gloucestershire, Hampshire, and Wiltshire, 1501–4 (PRO, SC6/Henry 7/1075; Pugh, *Marcher Lordships*, p. 296); itinerant judge, Brecon, 1503 (BL, Egerton Rolls, 2203); itinerant judge, general circuit, 1504 (SRO, D641/1/5/4); also Buckingham's secretary (see Appendix A).

*John Scott, receiver for Kent and Surrey, farmer of Camberwell and Peckham, and keeper of Bletchingley Park, 1515–16 (PRO, SC6/Henry 7/1076); keeper of South Park, Surrey, 1520–21 (*L&P, Henry VIII*, vol. III (2), 3695); also attorney general and leading councillor (see Appendix A).

Sir John Seymour, steward for Wiltshire, 1503–21: of Wolf Hall, Wiltshire; constable and doorman of Bristol Castle with son Edward; father of Jane Seymour; sheriff many times between 1498 and 1507; JP, Wiltshire, 1499–1536; knight of the body to Henry VIII, 1509; MP, Heytesbury, 1529 (Bindoff, *The Commons*, vol. III, p. 293; *L&P, Henry VIII*, vol. III (2), 3695).

*John Skilling, esquire, receiver of Hampshire and Wiltshire, 1498–99 (BL, Additional Charters, 26,873); steward of Wiltshire, 1498–1502 (Rawcliffe, *The Staffords*, p. 211): of Lainston, in Hampshire, and Salisbury; MP for Chippenham, 1491–92; member of Inner Temple, 1507; JP, Wiltshire, 1510–13; sheriff of Wiltshire (PRO, *Lists and Indexes*, vol. IX, p. 153; Wedgewood, *Biographies*, p. 771).

Thomas Slade, surveyor general, 1499 (Rawcliffe, *The Staffords*, p. 200); feodary in Warwick, 1501–2 (SRO, D641/1/2/278), and in Stafford receivership, 1506–7 (PRO, SC6/Henry 7/1077); itinerant judge, Brecon, 1503 (BL, Egerton Rolls, 2203): held estate of Buckingham in Maxstoke, Warwickshire, by knight service; held lands valued at £70 17s 2d per annum; on commission of peace in Warwick, 1506 and 1507 (*CPR, Henry VII, 1485–1509*, London, 1914, 1916, vol. II, 663; Pugh, *Marcher Lordships*, p. 297).

*Robert Turberville, receiver general, 1503–8 (Pugh, *Marcher Lordships*, p. 281; PRO, SP1/22, f. 61); itinerant judge, Brecon, 1503 (BL, Egerton Rolls, 2203); leading councillor (see Appendix A).

John Uvedale, esquire, keeper of Brasted Park, Surrey, 1520–21 (*L&P, Henry VIII*, vol. III (2), 3695): from influential and wealthy family connected with Surrey from 1304 to 1654 (Lambert Uvedale, *Bletchingley*, Guildford, Eng., 1959).

Walter Vaughan, esquire, receiver of Hay and Huntingdon, 1497–98

(Pugh, *Marcher Lordships*, p. 298); steward of Huntingdon, 1497–99 (Rawcliffe, *The Staffords*, p. 207); itinerant judge, Brecon, 1503 (BL, Egerton Rolls, 2203): originally in service of second duke; of Hergest Court, Hereford; son and heir of Thomas Vaughan (Pugh, *Marcher Lordships*, pp. 297–98).

Robert Whitgreve, receiver of Staffordshire, 1510–11 (SRO, D641/1/2/88): members of his family served Staffords throughout fifteenth century; owned substantial amount of land in county (Pugh, *Marcher Lordships*, p. 299; *VCH, Stafford*, vol. V, London, 1959, pp. 88–89).

*Sir Andrew Windsor, steward of Hampshire, Bedfordshire, Buckinghamshire, and Northamptonshire (*L&P, Henry VIII*, vol. III (2), 3695); itinerant judge, Brecon, 1503 (BL, Egerton Rolls, 2203): member of Middle Temple; on many commissions of the peace, subsidy, etc.; MP, for an unknown constituency, 1510, and for Buckinghamshire, 1529; keeper of king's wardrobe for 37 years; created Lord Windsor of Stanwell, 1529 (Pugh, *Marcher Lordships*, p. 299; GEC, vol. XII (2), pp. 792–93; Bindoff, *The Commons*, vol. III, p. 634).

Sir Thomas Wodehouse, steward of Norfolk, 1520–21 (PRO, SP1/29, f. 180); received an annuity of £20 from duke (PRO, SP1/29, f. 183): on commissions of peace and subsidy in Norfolk (*L&P, Henry VIII*, vol. I, 1172; vol. III (2), p. 1366).

*John Yaxley, itinerant judge, Brecon, 1503 (Pugh, *Marcher Lordships*, p. 118): owned land in Suffolk; serjeant-at-law; JP in Suffolk, 1485–1505; MP for Ipswich, 1491 (Wedgewood, *Biographies*, p. 978).

# Parish or Lesser Gentry Who Held Office on Buckingham's Estates

John Archer, constable of Maxstoke Castle, Warwickshire, 1520–21 (*L&P, Henry VIII*, vol. III (2), 3695): from family of Archer in Tamworth, Warwickshire, with three successive generations named John in sixteenth century; in 1519 John Archer held manor of Botley of Buckingham. This identification is difficult because John Archer died on Apr. 16, 1520. Yet it is possible that no new appointment was made between then and Buckingham's execution in May 1521, especially since the duke was away for much of the spring and summer of 1520 and was agitated about the Bulmer affair and the situation in Wales in the fall (Harleian Society, vol. XII, *Visitation of Warwick, 1619*, p. 309; *Memorials of Families of the Surname of Archer*, London, 1861, pp. 8, 11–12; *VCH, Warwick*, vol. III, London, 1945, p. 214).

Ranulph Bagnull, collector of Titensore and Barleston, Staffordshire, 1506–7 (PRO, SC6/Henry 7/1077, f. 8d) and 1520–21 (PRO, SC6/Henry 8/5804, f. 12): from a Barleston family of local influence (*VCH, Stafford*, vol. VIII, London, 1965, pp. 42, 184; Harleian Society, vol. LXIII, *Staffordshire Pedigrees*, p. 13).

William Bedell, bailiff of Kimbolton, Huntingdonshire, 1517–18 (W'min Abbey, 5470); bailiff of Kimbolton and keeper of the park, 1520–21 (*L&P, Henry VIII*, vol. III (2), 3695): a number of references to men of this name appear in records connected to Buckingham, and it is difficult to tell if they all refer to the same person. A William Bedell of Kimbolton, co. Huntingdonshire, gentleman, was undoubtedly the duke's estate official. He was probably the same William Bedell who wore the duke's livery in 1516–17 (SRO, D641/1/3/9). There is no way of knowing if he was the person granted an annuity of 5 marks in 1504, but it is certainly possible. The same doubt applies in identifying him with the treasurer of the countess of Richmond's household (*L&P, Henry VIII*, vol. II, 4183), who was remembered in her will (*L&P, Henry VIII*, vol. I, 236), although Buckingham was raised in her household and may well have employed Bedell after the countess's death.

John Bennett, farmer of Knoak, Nottinghamshire, 1498–99 (BL, Additional Charters, 26,873): the Bennetts were a prosperous family in the
village of Norton Bavant, Warminster Hundred; a John, clothier,
flourished in the late fifteenth century and was succeeded by his son
John in 1509; they were described as gentle (*VCH, Wiltshire*, vol. VIII,
London, 1965, pp. 7–8; *Genealogist*, New Series, 11, pp. 249–50).

Hugh Boughey, bailiff of Forebridge, Staffordshire, 1501–2 (SRO, D641/
1/2/82, m. 8), 1516 (Book of Information, f. 8d, bound in SRO, D1721/
1/6), 1517–18 (SRO, D641/1/94, m. 4): a younger son of family of
Boughey, lords of the manors of Whitmore, Biddulph, Anesley, and
Bucknall; his nephew Sebastian was a member of the duke's household and wore his livery in 1516–17 (Walter Chetwynd, "Collections
for a History of Pirehill Hundred," *Collections for a History of Stafford*, William Salt Society, New Series, 12 (1914), 18, 197, 200; SRO,
D641/1/3).

Thomas Brooke, bedell of Thornbury, Gloucestershire, 1520–21 (PRO,
E36/220, f. 3): probably the father of Sir Richard Brooke, who was
also in Buckingham's service: of Leighton, Cheshire (*DNB*, vol. II,
p. 1296).

John Cholmeley, bailiff of Bletchingley, Surrey, 1503–4 (BL, Add'l Mss.,
40,859B), beadle of Bletchingley, 1505–6 (PRO, SC6/Henry 7/1076,
m. 10): wore Buckingham's livery in 1515–16 (PRO, E101/631/20);
owned lands worth £6 and goods worth £5 in 1522; conveyed additional lands to his sons Richard and Henry; "substantial, if not a
wealthy, man"; son Richard a tanner (Uvedale Lambert, *Bletchingley*,
London, 1921, vol. II, p. 501).

Richard Cholmeley, bedell and bailiff of Bletchingley, Surrey, 1520–21
(*L&P, Henry VIII*, vol. III (2), 3695): son of John; assessed on £40 worth
of goods in 1523; a gentleman tanner, according to Lambert. Granville Leveson-Gower says the family was the principal middle-class
family in Bletchingley. Whatever their strict legal status, the family
was an influential one in Bletchingley at this period and therefore
useful to the duke. (Granville Leveson-Gower, "Manorial and Parliamentary History of Bletchingley," *Surrey Archaeological Collections*, 5
(1871), 222; Lambert, *Bletchingley*, pp. 501–3; Stanley Thomas Bindoff,
*The House of Commons 1509–1558*, London, 1982, vol. I, p. 711).

Richard Cole, feodary in Gloucestershire (*L&P, Henry VIII*, vol. III (2),
3695).

William Cole, bailiff of Eastington and Alkerton, Gloucestershire, 1501–
2 (SRO, D641/1/2/202), 1511–12 (SRO, D641/1/2/205), 1520–21
(PRO, E36/220, f. 3); bailiff of Haresfield, Gloucestershire, 1520–21
(*L&P, Henry VIII*, vol. III (2), 3695): both Richard and William Cole

were probably members of the family that owned a large estate in Gloucestershire. Walter Rowdon, who was also in the duke's service and a more important member of the county gentry, was the patron of another member of this family (Bindoff, *The Commons*, vol. I, p. 672).

John Cotton, keeper of Southwood Park, Disining, Suffolk, 1520–21 (PRO, SP1/29, f. 180): described as gentleman; admitted as king's servant by 1523 (ibid.); probably a member of family with lands in Cambridge, Suffolk, and Essex; nephew of same name was an MP (Bindoff, *The Commons*, vol. I, p. 711).

Richard Fane, feodary in Kent and Surrey, 1505–6 (PRO, SC6/Henry 7/1076, f. 13): of Tudley, Kent; esquire; died in 1540 (Edward Hasted, *Kent*, London, 1797–1801, vol. II, pp. 250, 265, 315).

Walter Grymston, escheator and coroner of Holderness, York, 1520–21 (PRO, SP1/29, f. 177): described as "very substantial gentleman"; on commission of sewers in York (ibid.; *L&P, Henry VIII*, vol. I, 481, vol. II (2), 4250).

John Harcourt, receiver of Stafford, 1509–10 (PRO, SC6/Henry 8/5803, 11): of Renton, Staffordshire; on subsidy commission in Staffordshire, 1523 (*L&P, Henry VIII*, vol. III (2), p. 1363).

Thomas Harcourt, receiver of Stafford, 1506–7 (PRO, SC6/Henry 7/1844): father of John (Josiah C. Wedgewood, "Harcourt of Ellenhall," *Collections for a History of Stafford*, William Salt Society, 1914, pp. 189, 200; Bindoff, *The Commons*, vol. II, p. 295).

Roger Kemys, reeve of Newport Burgus, 1503–4 (PRO, SC6/Henry 7/1665).

Thomas Kemys, keeper of Horsfirth Park, Essex, 1520–21 (*L&P, Henry VIII*, vol. III (2), 3695).

William Kemys, collector of Stowe, 1503–4 (PRO, SC6/Henry 7/1665, m. 7d).

Kemys family. The family originally settled at Began on the Glamorgan border of Newport. Jevan Kemys of Began, who flourished at the beginning of the fifteenth century, had seven sons, three of whom served the first duke of Buckingham. Branches of the family were found subsequently at Began, Newport, and Stowe, Wales; Syston, Gloucestershire; and Bedminster, Somersetshire. It is almost impossible to identify individual members of the family because the stock was so prolific and certain names recur frequently; there were, for example, two or three Williams living at the time of the third duke. The genealogists do not agree. In 1515–16 John, Morgan, Henry, and David Kemys wore the Stafford livery (PRO, E101/631/120, 20). Thomas also was a gentleman of the duke's household in 1517–18

(PRO, E101/518/5, pt. 1) and received an annuity of £6 13s 4d in 1520–21 (PRO, SP1/29, f. 183). The latter document described him as a gentleman. By 1523 he was one of the king's gentleman officers (ibid., f. 181; on the Kemys family, see T. B. Pugh, ed., *The Marcher Lordships of South Wales, 1415–1536: Select Documents*, Cardiff, 1963, pp. 291–93; Harleian Society, vol. XXI, *Visitation of Gloucester, 1623*, pp. 98–99; Frederic William Weaver, *Visitations of the County of Somerset, 1531 and 1573*, Exeter, 1885, pp. 118–19; Sir Joseph Bradney, *A History of Monmouthshire*, London, 1929, vol. IV, pt. 1, p. 130).

John Lavington, reeve of Willesford, Wiltshire, 1498–99 (BL, Additional Charters, 26,873).

Robert Lavington, reeve of Willesford, 1511–12 (BL, Additional Charters, 26,874). Family of this name established in Willesford according to Harleian Society, vols. CV and CVI, *Wiltshire Visitation Pedigrees, 1623*, p. 108.

James Newell, wore duke's livery, 1515–16 (PRO, E101/63/20); receiver of Stafford, 1518–19 (SRO, D641/1/2/96) and 1520–21 (PRO, E36/220, f. 13): family had been in Stafford from thirteenth century (Chetwynd, "Pirehall Hundred," p. 66).

Edward Osborne, wore duke's livery, 1517–18 (SRO, D641/1/3); bailiff of Rothwell, Northamptonshire, 1517–18 (W'min Abbey, 5470) and 1520–21 (PRO, SP1/29, f. 79): described as a gentleman (ibid.).

William Tracy, bailiff of Policote, Buckinghamshire, 1517–18 (W'min Abbey, 5470), and 1520–21 (*L&P, Henry VIII*, vol. III (2), 3695); also treasurer of duke's household, 1521 (see Appendix A).

William Wodegate, keeper of Kimbolton Castle, Huntingdonshire, and Penshurst Park, Kent (*L&P, Henry VIII*, vol. III (2), 3695): member of old Kentish family; owned land in Penshurst, Chidingstone, Sunridge, and Chevening (G. Woodgate and G. M. G. Woodgate, *A History of the Woodgates of Stonewall Park and of Summerhill in Kent*, privately printed, n.d., p. 79).

# *Abbreviated Stafford Genealogy*

The purpose of the Stafford genealogy on the following pages is to clarify the text by showing the descent of the senior male line of the family from the fourteenth to the sixteenth century, and the connections between the Staffords, the royal line of the Plantagenets, and other leading noble families.

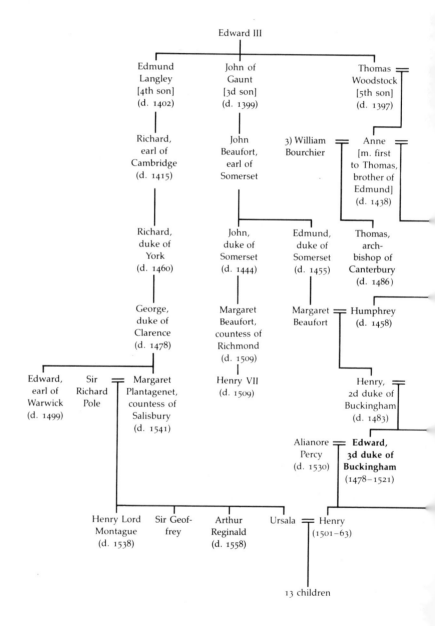

Edward III

Edmund
Langley
[4th son]
(d. 1402)

John of
Gaunt
[3d son]
(d. 1399)

Thomas
Woodstock
[5th son]
(d. 1397)

Richard,
earl of
Cambridge
(d. 1415)

John
Beaufort,
earl of
Somerset

3) William
Bourchier

Anne
[m. first
to Thomas,
brother of
Edmund]
(d. 1438)

Richard,
duke of
York
(d. 1460)

John,
duke of
Somerset
(d. 1444)

Edmund,
duke of
Somerset
(d. 1455)

Thomas,
arch-
bishop of
Canterbury
(d. 1486)

George,
duke of
Clarence
(d. 1478)

Margaret
Beaufort,
countess of
Richmond
(d. 1509)

Margaret
Beaufort

Humphrey
(d. 1458)

Edward,
earl of
Warwick
(d. 1499)

Sir
Richard
Pole

Margaret
Plantagenet,
countess of
Salisbury
(d. 1541)

Henry VII
(d. 1509)

Henry,
2d duke of
Buckingham
(d. 1483)

Alianore
Percy
(d. 1530)

Edward,
3d duke of
Buckingham
(1478–1521)

Henry Lord
Montague
(d. 1538)

Sir Geof-
frey

Arthur
Reginald
(d. 1558)

Ursala

Henry
(1501–63)

13 children

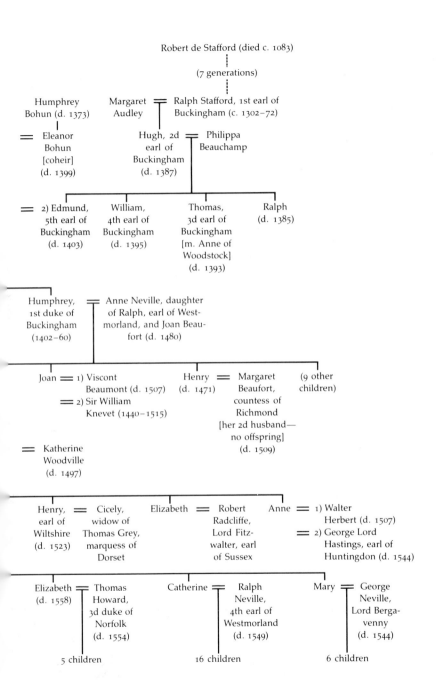

Robert de Stafford (died c. 1083)

(7 generations)

Humphrey
Bohun (d. 1373)

= Eleanor
Bohun
[coheir]
(d. 1399)

Margaret = Ralph Stafford, 1st earl of
Audley        Buckingham (c. 1302–72)

Hugh, 2d = Philippa
earl of        Beauchamp
Buckingham
(d. 1387)

= 2) Edmund,          William,          Thomas,          Ralph
5th earl of        4th earl of        3d earl of        (d. 1385)
Buckingham        Buckingham        Buckingham
(d. 1403)          (d. 1395)          [m. Anne of
                                        Woodstock]
                                        (d. 1393)

Humphrey,          = Anne Neville, daughter
1st duke of            of Ralph, earl of West-
Buckingham            morland, and Joan Beau-
(1402–60)              fort (d. 1480)

Joan = 1) Viscont          Henry = Margaret          (9 other
          Beaumont (d. 1507)  (d. 1471)  Beaufort,        children)
     = 2) Sir William                      countess of
          Knevet (1440–1515)               Richmond
                                            [her 2d husband—
= Katherine                                no offspring]
  Woodville                                (d. 1509)
  (d. 1497)

Henry,     = Cicely,          Elizabeth = Robert          Anne = 1) Walter
earl of        widow of                      Radcliffe,              Herbert (d. 1507)
Wiltshire      Thomas Grey,                  Lord Fitz-         = 2) George Lord
(d. 1523)      marquess of                   walter, earl             Hastings, earl of
               Dorset                        of Sussex               Huntingdon (d. 1544)

Elizabeth = Thomas          Catherine = Ralph          Mary = George
(d. 1558)      Howard,                      Neville,              Neville,
               3d duke of                    4th earl of           Lord Berga-
               Norfolk                       Westmorland           venny
               (d. 1554)                     (d. 1549)             (d. 1544)

5 children                  16 children                6 children

# Property of the Third Duke of Buckingham

The properties listed below were administrative and fiscal units. Unless otherwise indicated they were manors. Many of these manors had appurtenances not mentioned separately that were casually referred to as manors by contemporaries (in *inquisitions post mortem*, for example), but they were not independent units. Thus, this list does not include every property listed in sixteenth-century sources.

*Bedfordshire*

Honor of Gloucester

*Buckinghamshire*

Amersham
Bourton
Buckingham, Borough
Essington
Honor of Gloucester
Little Birkhill
Policott

*Cheshire*

Cristellon, rents
Macclesfield, rents

*Cornwall*

Caliland

*Essex*

Barnemarsh
Boynton
Chignal
Estlee
Fobbing

Hatfield Broadoak with
  Bromeshbury
Haydon
Norton
Ongar ad Castrum
Ongar and Harlow Hundreds
Piggesland, Biggesland and
  Botteleys
Poolmarshe
Stanford Rivers
Suttons
Thorpe and Thorpehall
Writtle
Writtle, rents

*Gloucestershire*

Cerney and Woodmoncote lands
Eastington and Alkerton
Haresfield
Honor of Gloucester
Honor of Hereford
Mars, lands
Newenham Borough
Rendecombe
Thornbury, bedellary

Thornbury, manor
Thornbury, borough

*Hampshire*

Cornhampton
Fordingbridge, rents
Mapledurham
Petersfield, borough
Upper Clatford

*Huntingdon*

Bakenhow
Hardewick
Honor of Gloucester
Kimbolton, bailiwick and castle
Kimbolton, office of reeve
Kimbolton, bedellary
Kimbolton, approver of the
  woods
Southoe
Swineshead
Tillbrook

*Kent*

Bayhall
Brasted
Chepstede
Dacherst
Hadlow
Hilden
Oxsted
Penshurst
Southborough
Tonbridge, town and castle
Tonbridge, lardmar
Tonbridge, camera
Tonbridge, farm of meadows and
  pastures
Tonbridge, farm of mills
Tonbridge, liberty
Yalding, office of reeve
Yalding, bedellary

*London*

Thames Street, rents

*Norfolk*

Sheringham
Stratford Barningham
Warham
Welles
Wiveton

*Northampton*

Clapthorne
Haculton and Pedington
Honor of Gloucester
Naseby
Rothwell
Rothwell, hundred

*Nottingham*

Colston Basset
Kneesall
Ratcliffe upon Soar

*Oxfordshire*

Stretton Audley

*Rutland*

Egelton
Langham
Oakham with castle

*Shropshire*

Bridgenorth, rents

*Somerset*

Bedminster

*Staffordshire*

Blymhill
Dodington, rents
Dorlaston

Eton

Forbridge, rents
Holditch nigh New Castle
Madeley
Norton in the Moors
Pakington
Stafford with castle
Stafford, rents
Tillington
Tittensor and Barleston

*Suffolk*

Crosieners, Talmages, and
   Pashelow
Disining
Haverhill and Horsham
Helion Haverhill
Hengrave
Shardlow

*Surrey*

Bletchingley, bedellary
Bletchingley, borough
Camberwell and Peckham
Edenbridge
Essingham
Oakham
Porkeley Upwood, Halingburie,
   Gatiers Catterham
Tillingdon
Titsey

*Warwick*

Lalleford
Maxstoke
Ringby
Sheldon
Tyshoo
Whatcote
Wootton Wawen
Great Wolford
Little Wolford

*Wiltshire*

Bedwyn, borough
Burbage and Savage
Fordingbridge, rents
Hide next Domerham, rents
Knoak
Kynwardeston, hundred
Lapsall, rent
Orcheston
Stratton St. Margaret
Wexcombe
Willesford

*York and Lincoln*

Barrow, rents
Bonde Brustwick, rents
Brustwick
Burton Pidsea, rents
Cleton
Dunceley, rents with castle
Elstrowick, rents
Essington, rents
Hedon
Helpston, rents with castle
Holderness, escheator
Kayingham, rents
Kayingham, meadow and pasture
   of manor
Kayingham, stockman
Kelnesey, rents
Lamwath, rents
Lelley and Dike, rents
Little Humbre, rents
Moys, rents
Outherne and Withorne, rents
Pawleflete, rents
Preston, rents
Skesteling, rents
Skipse, rents
Skipse Ballin, rents
Sproatley, rents
Tunstall, rents

*Brecon Lordship, Wales*

Brecon manor and castle
Brecon receiver
Hay borough with castle
Hay English
Hay Welsh
Huntingdon English with castle
Huntingdon Welsh
Huntingdon Bailiwick
Kington Villa

*Alexanderstone, Cantref Selyf,
   and Penkelly, Wales*

Alexanderstone
Bronllys Castle
Cantref Selyf
Penkelly, English
Penkelly, Welsh

*Caus, Marches of Wales,
   and Shropshire*

Aston
Caus with castle
Caus, borough

Haburley
Hay Forest
Heathe, bailiwick
Hope
Minsterley manor
Minsterley park
Nether-Gorddwr
Over-Gorddwr
Worthen, burgh
Worthen, manor

*Lordship of Newport, Wales*

Dowlais
Dyffryn
Machen manor
Machen Forest
Machen, bedellary
Newport borough with castle
Penkerne
Romney
Sealand, rents
Stowe
Wentloog

*Reference Matter*

# Abbreviations

All citations of asterisked items refer to the item number, not the page, unless otherwise indicated.

BL: British Library.
    Add'l Mss.: Additional Manuscripts.

*CCR: *Calendar of Close Rolls.*

CPR: *Calendar of Patent Rolls.*

*CSP: *Calendar of State Papers.*

DNB: *Dictionary of National Biography*, ed. Sir Leslie Stephen and Sir Sidney Lee. New York, 1908–9.

GEC: George E. Cokayne, *Complete Peerage of England, Scotland, Ireland*, ed. Vicary Gibbs, H. A. Doubleday, G. H. White, and R. S. Lea, rev. ed., 12 vols. London 1910–59.

HMC: Historical Manuscripts Commission.

*L&P, Henry VIII: *Letters and Papers of Henry VIII*, ed. J. S. Brewer, James Gairdner, and R. H. Brodie. London, 1862–1910.

PRO: Public Record Office.
    E36: Exchequer, Miscellaneous Books, Treasury of Receipt.
    E101: Exchequer, King's Remembrancer Accounts.
    SC6: Special Collections, Minister's Accounts.
    SP1: State Papers, Henry VIII.

SRO: Stafford Public Record Office.
    D641: Lord Stafford's Manuscripts.
    D1721: Bagot Manuscripts.

VCH: *Victorian County History.*

W'min Abbey: Muniments Room, Westminster Abbey.

# Notes

## Introduction

1. Carole Rawcliffe, "A Tudor Nobleman as Archivist: The Papers of Edward, Third Duke of Buckingham," *Journal of Society of Archivists*, 5, no. 5 (1976), 294–300.

2. Cambridge, Eng., 1978.

## Chapter One

1. K. B. McFarlane, "Extinction and Recruitment," in *The Nobility of Later Medieval England* (Oxford, 1973), pp. 143–51. "As a group the earls in 1400 were mostly newcomers to their rank. And in this—you will have to take my word for it—1400 was no way exceptional. The highest ranks of the nobility rarely deserved the epithet 'old.' The turnover was always rapid, the eminence short-lived, the survivors invariably few." Between 1300 and 1500, members of 357 families received writs of summons to parliament. Of these only 61 families survived in unbroken male descent until 1500. Of 136 who received summonses from Edward I, only 16 survived in 1500 (ibid., pp. 143–45). Much of McFarlane's book is an illustration and elaboration of this point. See also J. R. Lander, "The Crown and the Aristocracy in England, 1450–1509," *Albion*, 8, no. 3 (Fall 1976), 206, 207. Joel T. Rosenthal notes that of the 740 persons who received summonses to the House of Lords between 1295 and 1500, one-third were the first members of their immediate families to attend. *Nobles and the Noble Life, 1295–1500* (New York, 1976), p. 23. On the other hand, the fluidity of movement in and out of the peerage should not be exaggerated. Of the 21 peerages continued via heiresswives, many went to younger sons of peers, so that actual upward mobility was minimal in these cases (ibid., p. 35). Furthermore, between 1453 and 1509, 64 percent of the attainders, a major reason for the termination of peerages, were reversed. J. R. Lander, "Attainder and Forfeiture, 1453–1509," in *Crown and Nobility, 1450–1509* (London, 1976), p. 129.

2. McFarlane, "Extinction," pp. 156–67.

3. GEC, vol. XII (1), pp. 168 and n. a, 169, n. c. SRO, D1850/4/2, R. Trappes-Lomax, "House of Stafford." BL, Add'l Mss., 36,542, ff. 138–40, "Copy of a Tabul Hanging at Stone Priory in the County of Stafford." The Stafford inheritance eventually descended to de Toeni's great-granddaughter Millicent, whose husband took the family name and the title of baron de Stafford.

4. Ralph, son and heir of Hugh, second earl of Stafford, was murdered in 1385. Edmund, fifth earl, died fighting at Shrewsbury in 1403. Humphrey, first duke of Buckingham, died in 1460 at the Battle of Northampton. Henry, second duke, was executed for rebellion against Richard III in 1483. Edward, third duke, was executed for high treason in 1521. Thomas, third earl, and William, fourth earl, both died prematurely, of natural causes. Humphrey, fifth son and heir of the first duke, died of the plague in 1458.

5. McFarlane, *Nobility*, pp. 201–3.

6. Trappes-Lomax, "House of Stafford," f. 6.

7. Ibid., f. 7. GEC, vol. XII (1), p. 175 and n. j.

8. GEC, vol. XII (1), p. 175.

9. McFarlane, *Nobility*, p. 202.

10. Ibid. Also Carole Rawcliffe, *The Staffords, Earls of Stafford and Dukes of Buckingham, 1394–1521* (Cambridge, Eng., 1978), p. 10.

11. Rawcliffe, *The Staffords*, pp. 8–10.

12. Ibid., p. 8. For a complete list of these properties, see pp. 191–92.

13. Ibid., p. 10.

14. GEC, vol. XII (1), p. 176; Rawcliffe, *The Staffords*, p. 10.

15. GEC, vol. XII (1), pp. 177–78.

16. McFarlane, *Nobility*, p. 203; Rawcliffe, *The Staffords*, p. 11.

17. McFarlane, *Nobility*, p. 196.

18. Ibid.; Rawcliffe, *The Staffords*, p. 11; GEC, vol. XII (1), p. 179, n. i.

19. GEC, vol. XII (1), p. 179, n. i; Rosenthal, *Nobles*, p. 84.

20. Rawcliffe, *The Staffords*, p. 11; McFarlane, *Nobility*, p. 203.

21. Hugh's feoffees, who administered the property for the better part of eighteen years, acquired the Basset inheritance for the Stafford family after a costly legal battle. Rawcliffe, *The Staffords*, p. 12. The estates are listed on p. 192. For a discussion of the institution of wardship, see Chapter 2, including n. 13.

22. *CPR, Richard II* (London, 1895–1901), vol. IV, *1388–1392*, p. 160.

23. GEC, vol. XII (1), p. 180.

24. McFarlane, *Nobility*, p. 204.

25. *CPR, Richard II*, vol. V, *1391–1396*, p. 574.

26. Ibid., vol. VI, *1396–1399*, p. 376.

27. Ibid., p. 500; see genealogy, Appendix D.

28. GEC, vol. XII (1), p. 181.

29. See Rawcliffe, *The Staffords*, pp. 12–18, on the Bohun inheritance and Countess Anne's efforts to make good her claims to half of it. The Bohun and Woodstock estates acquired by the Staffords through Anne are listed on pp. 192–93.

30. McFarlane, *Nobility*, p. 205.

31. Ibid., p. 203.

32. William C. Waller, "An Old Church Chest. Being notes of that at Theydon-Garnon, Essex," *Essex Archaeological Society Transactions*, New Series, 5 (1894–95), 7.

33. McFarlane, *Nobility*, pp. 181, 186.

34. Ibid., pp. 59, 184–85. G. A. Holmes makes the same point about the fourteenth-century nobility in *The Estates of the Higher Nobility in Fourteenth Century England* (Cambridge, Eng., 1957), ch. 1.

35. McFarlane, *Nobility*, pp. 179–81, 186.

36. T. B. Pugh, ed., *The Marcher Lordships of South Wales, 1415–1536, Select Documents* (Cardiff, 1963), pp. 176–77.

37. Rawcliffe, *The Staffords*, p. 117.

38. Ibid., pp. 118–19. All the magnates except the favorites of the court party had increasing difficulty in collecting the money the king owed them, whether as fees, annuities, or payment for specific services. Individual peers responded to this situation differently in the crises that punctuated the years from 1450 to 1461. In Buckingham's case, the crown's indebtedness to him certainly did not shake his loyalty to Henry VI.

40. J. R. Lander emphasizes the importance of the lord's personal involvement in managing his property. *Conflict and Stability in Fifteenth-Century England* (London, 1969), p. 30.

41. Pugh, *Marcher Lordships*, pp. 179–80.

42. Rawcliffe, *The Staffords*, pp. 49–50, 54.

43. Ibid., p. 54.

44. Ibid., pp. 45–54, 109–15.

45. McFarlane, *Nobility*, pp. 47–53, 138–41, 230–31.

46. See A. R. Bridbury, *Economic Growth: England in the Later Middle Ages* (Hassocks, Eng., 1975), pp. xxi–xxiii, and R. L. Storey, *The End of the House of Lancaster* (New York, 1967), pp. 18–20, for similar views on this issue.

47. Rawcliffe, *The Staffords*, pp. 111–17. R. R. Davies accepts the picture of the Stafford estates as beset by recurring arrears. He considers the collection of arrears one of the few ways to measure the efficiency of baronial administration. "Baronial Accounts, Incomes, and Arrears in the Later Middle Ages," *Economic History Review*, Second Series, 21,

no. 2 (Aug. 1968), 219, 229. See also A. C. Reeves, *Newport Lordship 1317–1536* (Ann Arbor, 1979), pp. 84–86. A valor was a statement of the potential or estimated receipts from an estate or group of estates in a particular year. Throughout the text, I have rounded monetary figures to the nearest shilling, except where the specific account or item involved makes this an invalid procedure.

48. Rawcliffe, *The Staffords*, p. 115.

49. Pugh, *Marcher Lordships*, p. 240, n. 3.

50. Theophilus Jones, *A History of the County of Brecknock* (Brecknock, Wales, 1805–9, 1898), vol. I, p. 104.

51. Ibid., p. 105.

52. See Pugh, *Marcher Lordships*, pp. 40–42, for a discussion of the practice of redeeming the Great Sessions.

53. Ibid., p. 20, n. 2.

54. Ibid., p. 20.

55. McFarlane, *Nobility*, p. 49.

56. Rawcliffe, *The Staffords*, p. 113.

57. McFarlane, *Nobility*, p. 58. The issue, which McFarlane does not make clear, was not agricultural profits per se so much as their distribution between the landowning and tenant classes.

58. Bridbury, *Economic Growth*, p. xxiii. Developments on the Percy estates fit the theory of declining income from land better than they do McFarlane's revisionist thesis. J. M. W. Bean presents a picture of declining income in the first six decades of the fifteenth century. "Had the number of manors in the possession of the Earls not increased, the Percy estates would by 1461 have lost about a quarter of their value in 1416." *The Estates of the Percy Family, 1416–1537* (Oxford, 1958), p. 41; for a detailed discussion of income on the Percy estates in this period, see pp. 12–42. I of course believe that developments on the Stafford estates point in the same direction. M. M. Postan agrees that the agricultural income of the baronage was declining in the fifteenth century. *The Medieval Economy and Society* (Baltimore, 1975), p. 196. He also doubts that most peers could have compensated for the decline by other sources of income. Ibid., pp. 198–201, and M. M. Postan, "The Fifteenth Century," in *Essays on Medieval Agriculture and General Problems of the Medieval Economy* (Cambridge, Eng., 1973), p. 48. R. R. Davies expresses doubts about the amount of income the nobility could expect from its land in the conditions of the late Middle Ages, but he is more sanguine about their compensating for losses in this area from other sources. "Baronial Accounts," p. 228. Rosenthal estimates that fifteenth-century revenues were 10–20 percent below their fourteenth-century peak, before the Black Death, but that the financial pressure on the nobility

came more from their tendency to spend than from the problem of declining income. He recognizes that some lords had trouble in collecting arrears, squeezing both their tenants and their officials, and sometimes in finding tenants. Rosenthal, *Nobles*, pp. 70–71. The first duke of Buckingham's difficulties stemmed from both the income and the expenditure sides of the equation. See also A. J. Pollard, "Estate Management in the Later Middle Ages: The Talbots and Whitchurch, 1383–1525," *Economic History Review*, Second Series, 25, no. 4 (Nov. 1972), 553–66.

59. For example, the Percies acquired the territories that catapulted them into the first rank of the English nobility in the fourteenth century. Their acquisitions stemmed from their service on the border during the Scottish wars, purchases, a marriage that brought them the huge Lucy inheritance, and various other personal relationships. Bean, *Estates*, pp. 1–11. The Howards rose from the gentry into the first ranks of the nobility by the marriage of Sir Robert Howard, who died before 1437, to Margaret Mowbray, daughter of Thomas Mowbray, duke of Norfolk. Gerald Brenan and Edward Phillips Statham, *The House of Howard* (New York, 1908), pp. 14–18. The Zouche estates grew by the steady accumulation of land brought into the family by their wives. Rosenthal, *Nobles*, pp. 59–62. See also Rawcliffe, *The Staffords*, pp. 8–9, 12–19; R. I. Jack, ed., "The Grey of Ruthin Valor, 1467–1468," *Bedfordshire Historical Record Society Publications*, 46 (1965), 4, 57.

60. Postan, *Medieval Economy*, pp. 197–201.

61. McFarlane, *Nobility*, p. 205.

62. William Dugdale, *The Baronage of England* (London, 1675), vol. I, p. 165.

63. Ibid.; GEC, vol. II, pp. 388–89.

64. Rawcliffe, *The Staffords*, pp. 118–19.

65. Ibid., pp. 20–21.

66. Buckingham was married to Anne, daughter of Ralph Neville, first earl of Westmorland, and his second wife Joan Beaufort. He married his son and heir to Margaret Beaufort, daughter of Edmund Beaufort, duke of Somerset. GEC, vol. II, pp. 388–89.

67. Rawcliffe, *The Staffords*, p. 20. *Six Town Chronicles*, ed. Ralph Flenley (Oxford, 1911), p. 114.

68. Rawcliffe, *The Staffords*, p. 20; Sir James Ramsay, *Lancaster and York* (Oxford, 1892), vol. II, p. 33.

69. A. H. Thomas and I. D. Thornley, eds., *The Great Chronicle of London* (London, 1938), p. 179; Rawcliffe, *The Staffords*, p. 21. Rawcliffe suggests that Duke Humphrey may even have been responsible for Gloucester's death. According to *The Great Chronicle*, Buckingham was *not* constable of England at the time.

70. Rawcliffe, *The Staffords*, p. 21.

71. In the interpretation of the 1450's in this and the next paragraph, I have drawn heavily on the following works: Charles Ross, *Edward IV* (Berkeley, Calif., 1974); Storey, *House of Lancaster*; D. M. Loades, *Politics and the Nation, 1450–1660: Obedience, Resistance and Public Order* (Brighton, Eng., 1974); S. B. Chrimes, C. D. Ross, and R. A. Griffiths, eds., *Fifteenth-Century England, 1399–1509* (New York, 1972), especially the essays by Storey and Griffiths; Ralph A. Griffiths, ed., *Patronage, the Crown and the Provinces in Later Medieval England* (Atlantic Highlands, N.J., 1981), especially the essays by Ailsa Herbert and Martin Cherry; and Robin Jeffs, "The Poynings-Percy Dispute: An Example of the Interplay of Open Strife and Legal Action in the Fifteenth Century," *Bulletin of the Institute of Historical Research*, 34, no. 90 (Nov. 1961), 148–64. For the details of the quarrel over the Berkeley inheritance, see John Smyth of Nibley, *The Berkeley Manuscripts: Lives of the Berkeleys*, ed. Sir John Maclean (Gloucester, 1883), vol. II, pp. 57–76, 102–17. On Derbyshire, see Storey, *House of Lancaster*, ch. 11.

72. K. B. McFarlane has stated incorrectly that "the war was fought because the nobility was unable to rescue the kingdom from the consequences of Henry VI's inanity by any other means." "The Wars of the Roses," Raleigh Lecture on History, *Proceedings of the British Academy* (London, 1964), p. 97. This analysis implies that the nobility had a common goal in the 1450's and were capable of working together. Had this been so, the wars need not have been fought. The problem was not so much Henry's inanity (or even insanity); had he not functioned at all, the magnates might well have devised a workable government, as they had during the long minority. The crux of the problem was that Henry VI had intervened decidedly in the government—and almost always for the worse. In the middle ages such a king could not easily be controlled, nor could government be carried on against his will.

73. Loades, *Politics*, p. 61.

74. Storey, *House of Lancaster*, p. 184. On Duke Humphrey's position in the tortuous politics of the 1450's see ibid., pp. 183–84; Rawcliffe, *The Staffords*, pp. 24–27; T. B. Pugh, "The Magnates, Knights and Gentry," in *Fifteenth-Century England 1399–1509: Studies in Politics and Society*, ed. S. B. Chrimes, C. D. Ross, and R. A. Griffiths (New York, 1972), pp. 106–7.

75. Rawcliffe, *The Staffords*, pp. 25–26; Ross, *Edward IV*, p. 27.

76. Rawcliffe, *The Staffords*, pp. 73–76; Pugh gives a figure of £452 for annuities to retainers, councillors, and household servants in 1447–48. "Magnates," p. 105.

77. Pugh, "Magnates," p. 105.

78. Rawcliffe, *The Staffords*, p. 115; Pugh, *Marcher Lordships*, pp. 176–78. A valor of Duke Humphrey's land in 1460 set the income from his land at £3,904 5s. SRO, 3723/2.

79. Rawcliffe, *The Staffords*, p. 76. Bean, *Estates*, pp. 91, 93–96. Although Bean agrees that the Percies did profit from the wardenship of the East March, he shows that during the Wars of the Roses, they faced a growing burden of debt. Bean concludes that "the struggle for political power and local influence was responsible for the growth of debt." Ibid., pp. 98–108; see especially the quote on p. 107.

80. Rawcliffe, *The Staffords*, pp. 72–77.

81. Ibid., p. 25.

82. McFarlane, "Wars of Roses," p. 91.

83. *Six Town Chronicles*, p. 129.

84. On this element in medieval English political ideology, see Rosenthal, *Nobles*, pp. 44–45.

85. Thomas and Thornley, *Great Chronicle*, pp. 182–83; *Six Town Chronicles*, pp. 129–30.

86. Thomas and Thornley, *Great Chronicle*, p. 183; *Six Town Chronicles*, pp. 130ff.

87. Thomas and Thornley, *Great Chronicle*, p. 188; *Six Town Chronicles*, p. 143.

88. Thomas and Thornley, *Great Chronicle*, p. 188.

89. *Six Town Chronicles*, p. 142.

90. Ramsay, *Lancaster and York*, vol. II, pp. 199ff; Rawcliffe, *The Staffords*, p. 25; K. B. McFarlane, "England: The Lancastrian Kings, 1399–1461," *Cambridge Medieval History*, vol. VIII, *The Close of the Middle Ages* (Cambridge, Eng., 1936), p. 414.

91. Robert Fabyan, *The New Chronicles of England and France*, ed. Henry Ellis (London, 1811), p. 636.

92. Rawcliffe, *The Staffords*, p. 27.

93. Ibid., p. 27; C. A. J. Armstrong, "Politics and the Battle of St. Albans, 1455," *Bulletin of the Institute of Historical Research*, 33 (1960), 67, 69, n. 5. See genealogy, Appendix D.

94. He was born Sept. 4, 1455. GEC, vol. II, p. 389.

95. Ross, *Edward IV*, pp. 65, 390; Loades, *Politics*, p. 68.

96. Rawcliffe, *The Staffords*, p. 28; Pugh, "Magnates," pp. 118–19, n. 13.

97. Rawcliffe, *The Staffords*, p. 121. The duchess's jointure was valued at £884 6s 3d. SRO, 3723/2. A dowry was the land or money that a father gave with his daughter to her husband or father-in-law. This was sometimes spoken of as the girl's portion, since it represented her share of her father's estate. The jointure was the amount of money promised to a woman by her father-in-law or husband in the event she became a

widow. Usually it took the form of income from land specifically set aside for that purpose at the time of the wedding. The amount of the dowry and jointure, and all the arrangements connected to them were normally spelled out in formal legal contracts.

98. *CPR, Edward IV, Edward V, and Richard III, A.D. 1461–1485* (London, 1897–1901), vol. I, pp. 324, 463–64. The wardship of the boys was taken from the duchess of Exeter and given to Elizabeth Woodville between Mar. 21, 1464, and Aug. 26, 1465.

99. GEC, vol. II, p. 390.

100. C. A. J. Armstrong, *The Usurpation of Richard the Third. Dominicus Mancinus ad Angelum Catonem de Occupatione Regni Anglie per Ricardum Tercium Libellus* (Oxford, 1969), p. 75; Rawcliffe, *The Staffords*, p. 28. Pugh does not think there was much objection to marriages between aristocratic families of different social origins. "Magnates," p. 87. On Warwick's reaction to the marriages of the Woodville sisters, see J. R. Lander, "Marriage and Politics in the Fifteenth-Century: The Nevilles and Wydevilles," in *Crown and Nobility*, pp. 94–126; also see ibid., p. 23; C. D. Ross, "Reign of Edward IV," in Chrimes et al., *Fifteenth-Century England*, pp. 50–51; Pugh, "Magnates," p. 88.

101. Rawcliffe, *The Staffords*, p. 28. Duchess Anne survived until 1480, so that the second duke did not enjoy the income from her dower lands until then. They included most of his English estates; their net worth was £1,245. Ibid., pp. 123, 125; Pugh, *Marcher Lordships*, p. 239, n. 5. Duke Henry received a license to enter the lands held by his deceased grandmother on Oct. 1, 1480. *CPR, Edward IV, Edward V, Richard III,* vol. I, p. 217.

102. See Rawcliffe, *The Staffords*, pp. 121–24, for more detailed information.

103. Figure for 1460 from SRO, 3723/2; 1473 figure from Rawcliffe, *The Staffords*, p. 123.

104. Pugh also emphasizes the significance of Herbert's personal supervision in raising the profits from Newport. *Marcher Lordships*, pp. 179–80.

105. Ross, *Edward IV*, pp. 72–83, 329ff.; Pugh, "Magnates," pp. 90–94. Humphrey Stafford, earl of Devon, was not related to the Stafford dukes of Buckingham.

106. It is worth remembering in this connection that the majority of the nobility continued to support the Lancastrian cause even after Edward IV's first accession to the throne. Ross, *Edward IV*, pp. 34, 83. Most of the peers remained relatively indifferent to Edward IV's fate. J. R. Lander, "Crown and Aristocracy," p. 213; Pugh, "Magnates," pp. 108–12.

107. Rawcliffe, *The Staffords*, p. 28.

108. Ross, *Edward IV*, pp. 334–35.

109. Rawcliffe, *The Staffords*, pp. 125–26.

110. Ibid., pp. 12–18.

111. Pugh, "Magnates," p. 111; Rawcliffe, *The Staffords*, pp. 30–31.

112. Howell T. Evans, *Wales and the Wars of the Roses* (Cambridge, Eng., 1915), p. 79, n. 1.

113. *CSP, Milan*, vol. I (London, 1912), p. 194.

114. David MacGibbon, *Elizabeth Woodville* (London, 1938), pp. 125–26.

115. *CPR, Edward IV, Edward V, Richard III*, vol. III, p. 63. James Gairdner, *History of the Life and Reign of Richard the Third*, rev. ed. (New York, 1968; orig. ed. 1898), p. 32.

116. *CPR, Edward IV, Edward V, Richard III*, vol. III, p. 69. Significantly, the income from this property was negligible. Rawcliffe, *The Staffords*, pp. 12–17, 125.

117. Charles D. Ross, *Richard III* (Berkeley, Calif., 1981), pp. 38–39, 77. Contemporary and near-contemporary historians disagree about when Gloucester revealed his full intention of usurping the throne to Buckingham. Polydore Vergil believed that he disclosed his plan to the duke when they met at Northampton shortly after Edward IV's death. Sir Henry Ellis, ed., *Three Books of Polydore Vergil's English History, Comprising the Reigns of Henry VI, Edward IV, and Richard III*, Camden Society, vol. XXIX, 1844 (New York, 1968), p. 174. This interpretation is also implied in the account in the Croyland chronicle. Ingulf, Abbot of Croyland, *Chronicle of the Abbey of Croyland, with the Continuations by Peter of Blois and Anonymous Writers*, trans. Henry T. Riley (London, 1854), pp. 486–87.

According to More, however, Gloucester did not reveal his full intention to Buckingham until after he had secured possession of the duke of York from sanctuary. At that time he employed "suttell folkes" to play on Buckingham's fears that the king, Edward V, would eventually take revenge on him for his part in helping Gloucester to seize power from the Woodvilles. Interestingly, More treated another point in Buckingham's life in a similar way: he ended his *History* with Bishop Morton manipulating Buckingham into rebelling against Richard. If this is an accurate rendition of what More learned from people who had known the duke, it provides an interesting insight into Buckingham's character. In addition to the other promises Richard made to Buckingham to gain his support, More mentioned a projected marriage between Richard's son and the duke's daughter. As far as I know, More's history is the only one to do so. *The History of King Richard III*, ed. by Richard S. Sylvester, *The Complete Works of St. Thomas More*, vol. II (New Haven, Conn., 1963), pp. 42–44.

Historians have long debated the value of More's work as a historical source. The most recent scholarly treatments of the subject are by Sylvester and by Alison Hanham, who reach very different conclusions. Ibid., pp. lxv–civ, and *Richard III and His Early Historians, 1485–1535* (Oxford, 1975), pp. 152–90. Hanham considers it "the least authentic of the early accounts of Richard" (p. 189) and virtually dismisses it as a "satirical drama." Sylvester recognizes that More deliberately created a compelling piece of literature out of his material, but also thinks his work has positive value as a historical source. Despite More's occasional slips about names, places, and dates, Sylvester considers the substance of his work an accurate reworking of the oral and written tradition hostile to Richard III, a tradition that originated in that king's time, not the Tudors'. Sylvester also notes how often Dominicus Mancini's chronicle supported More's account. I find Sylvester's analysis and conclusions more convincing than Hanham's and have used More accordingly in this book. See Ross, *Richard III*, pp. xxii–xxxi, on this issue.

118. Samuel Bentley, ed., *Excerpta Historica* (London, 1833), pp. 12–13; Ingulph, *Chronicle of Croyland*, p. 486. All references to the Croyland chronicle are from the second continuation, which historians consider a valuable independent source for the fifteenth century. Hanham, *Richard III*, pp. 1, 74–97; Vergil, *English History*, pp. 174–75; Armstrong, *Richard III*, pp. 75–77.

119. Ingulf, *Chronicle of Croyland*, p. 487.

120. *CPR, Edward IV, Edward V, Richard III*, vol. III, pp. 349–50, 356, 363.

121. Robert Davies, ed., *Extracts from the Municipal Records of the City of York During the Reigns of Edward IV, Edward V, and Richard III* (London, 1843), p. 149.

122. More, *History*, p. 53. I am following Charles Ross on the date of Hastings's execution. *Richard III*, pp. 83–84.

123. Ingulph, *Chronicle of Croyland*, p. 489.

124. Charles L. Kingsford, ed., *The Stonor Letters and Papers, 1290–1483*, Camden Society, Third Series, vol. XXX (London, 1919), p. 161.

125. Ibid., p. 161.

126. Armstrong, *Richard III*, p. 99.

127. Vergil, *English History*, p. 187.

128. Fabyan, *New Chronicles*, p. 669.

129. Vergil, *English History*, pp. 177–78; More, *History*, pp. 27–33.

130. Ingulf *Chronicle of Croyland*, p. 488. Armstrong, *Richard III*, p. 89; Ross, *Richard III*, p. 86.

131. More, *History*, pp. 69–74; Vergil, *English History*, pp. 185–86; Armstrong, *Richard III*, p. 97.

132. More, *History*, p. 78; Fabyan, *New Chronicles*, p. 669.

133. *Rolls of Parliament*, vol. VI, p. 241; Buckingham's speech on this occasion was written into the act settling the crown on Richard III and his heirs.

134. Dugdale, *Baronage*, vol. I, p. 168.

135. Ibid.; Bentley, *Excerpta*, p. 380.

136. See above, p. 21, for an explanation of why this was such a sensitive issue.

137. Printed in Dugdale, *Baronage*, vol. I, pp. 168–69.

138. Gairdner, *Richard III*, p. 106.

139. J. D. Mackie takes this view. *The Earlier Tudors, 1485–1558* (Oxford, 1952), p. 18. Among the early historians, Polydore Vergil shared this opinion. *English History*, pp. 192–94. Thomas More was rather noncommittal on this issue, which he discussed at some length. *History of King Richard III*, pp. 89–90; see also Ross, *Richard III*, p. 114.

140. Mackie, *Earlier Tudors*, p. 18.

141. More, *History*, p. 90.

142. Vergil, *English History*, p. 195.

143. Gairdner, *Richard III*, p. 107. Paul Kendall claims that whatever the technicalities, "most people of the fifteenth century took it for granted that the legitimating patent barred the Beauforts from the throne." *Richard the Third* (New York, 1956), p. 185.

144. *L&P, Henry VIII*, vol. III (1), 1284 (p. 492).

145. Fabyan, *New Chronicles*, p. 670; Thomas and Thornley, *Great Chronicle*, p. 234; Edward Hall, *Union of the Two Noble and Illustrious Families of Lancaster and York* (London, 1809), p. 387.

146. Thomas and Thornley, *Great Chronicle*, p. 234; Armstrong, *Richard III*, pp. 61, 93–95; Ingulf, *Chronicle of Croyland*, p. 491. More gave a much fuller account of the murder, *History*, pp. 83–86. It should not be taken literally, but as a dramatic elaboration of the anti-Richard tradition on which his work was based. For a fuller discussion of this point see n. 117 above. Vergil presented a more straightforward rendition of the facts contained in More's account. *English History*, pp. 187–89. Historians differ on the relationship between these two works. Hanham states that Vergil supplied the factual basis of More's works, while in his edition of *The History of Richard III* Sylvester denies that More depended on any one source and minimizes the influence that More and Vergil exerted on each other. Hanham, *Richard III*, pp. 146, 159; More, *History*, pp. lxxvi–lxxvii.

147. Kendall, *Richard III*, p. 495; Ross, *Richard III*, ch. 5.

148. Kendall, *Richard III*, pp. 487–95.

149. Vergil strongly suggested that Buckingham knew of the murders when he revealed "his just cause of hatred" and "unfoldyd all

thynges" to Bishop Morton. *English History*, pp. 194–95. His account of the conspiracy between Elizabeth Woodville and Margaret, countess of Richmond, indicates that the murders were common knowledge even earlier.

150. More, *History*, pp. 90–93. Rawcliffe thinks that More exaggerated Morton's role in Buckingham's about-face. *The Staffords*, p. 32.

151. Vergil, *English History*, pp. 194–95. Vergil's account certainly supports Rawcliffe's judgment on this point.

152. Ibid., pp. 195–96.

153. Ingulph, *Chronicle of Croyland*, pp. 490–91.

154. Ibid., p. 491.

155. Ibid., pp. 491–92; Vergil, *English History*, pp. 198–99.

156. Henry Ellis, *Original Letters Illustrative of English History*, Second Series (London, 1827), vol. I, p. 160. This is also the impression given by the act of attainder subsequently passed, which refers to Buckingham as "now late daies stondyng and beinge in as greate favour, tender trust, and affection with the kyng oure Sovereigne Lorde, as ever eny subgeits was with his Prynce and Leige Lorde, as was notarily and opynly knowen by all this Reams." *Rolls of Parliament*, vol. VI, p. 245.

157. Ingulf, *Chronicle of Croyland*, p. 491.

158. Ellis, *Letters*, vol. I, p. 160.

159. A letter from the duke of Norfolk to John Paston dated Oct. 10 indicates that the rising in Kent had begun by that date. *The Paston Letters, 1422–1509*, ed. James Gairdner (Westminster, 1900), vol. III, p. 308. Two letters from Richard III, one dated Oct. 11 to the Corporation of York and the other dated Oct. 13 to the Mayor of Southampton, refer to Buckingham's conspiracy but do not make clear whether he had yet taken the field. HMC, Eleventh Report, Appendix III, *Manuscripts of the Corporations of Southampton and King's Lynn* (London, 1887), p. 103; H. Owen and J. B. Blakeway, *A History of Shrewsbury* (London, 1825), vol. I, p. 235, n. 2.

160. The act that subsequently attainted Buckingham gave the 18th as the date of his rising. *Rolls of Parliament*, vol. VI, p. 245.

161. For example, both Dugdale (*Baronage*, vol. I, pp. 169–70) and Gairdner (*Richard III*, p. 138) repeat this story.

162. Ingulf, *Chronicle of Croyland*, pp. 491–92.

163. Vergil, *English History*, p. 199. The disaster attending Buckingham's rebellion showed that he was not nearly as strong in Wales and the marches as he seemed. His monopoly of offices under the crown antagonized the gentry; on the other hand, he suffered all the disadvantages of an absentee landlord. Rawcliffe, *The Staffords*, pp. 32–35; Pugh, *Marcher Lordships*, pp. 240–41; Gairdner, *Richard III*, pp. 133–34, 219.

164. Vergil, *English History*, p. 199.

165. Fabyan, *New Chronicles*, pp. 670–71. Thomas and Thornley (*Great Chronicle*, pp. 234–35) and Vergil (*English History*, pp. 199–201) both question whether Bannaster betrayed Buckingham for money or out of fear. The similarity in their accounts cannot be taken as two pieces of independent evidence since Fabyan was one of Vergil's main sources. Denis Hay, *Polydore Vergil: Renaissance Historian and Man of Letters* (Oxford, 1952), p. 87. The question of the whole tradition of Bannaster's treason has been raised because the earliest account, Ingulf's *Chronicle of Croyland*, p. 492, says the reason the duke was discovered at his house was that so much food was being brought there. The story of betrayal goes back to Fabyan. Richard III granted Bannaster the manor of Yalding in Kent from Buckingham's forfeited estates as a reward for "taking and bringing of our said rebell unto our hands," which supports the tradition that he deliberately betrayed the duke. Ellis, *Letters*, Third Series, vol. I (1846), p. 101. There is some uncertainty about Bannaster's first name. The *Croyland Chronicle* and Vergil call him Humphrey; Richard's grant, Ralph. Bannaster's action inspired a number of ballads on the general theme of a great lord betrayed by those he trusted. Rawcliffe, *The Staffords*, p. 35 and n. 23; Charles Kingsford, *English Historical Literature in the Fifteenth Century* (New York, 1962), p. 249. A recent work on the subject asserts definitely that Bannaster's first name was Ralph. Ralph A. Griffiths and Roger S. Thomas, *The Making of the Tudor Dynasty* (London, 1985), p. 99.

166. Ingulf, *Chronicle of Croyland*, p. 492.

## Chapter Two

1. SRO, D1721/1/1, f. 222.

2. SRO, D1721/1/11, f. 241–43. This document is the basis of the next five paragraphs unless otherwise indicated. It is reprinted in H. Owen and J. B. Blakeway, *A History of Shrewsbury* (London, 1825), vol. I, pp. 241–42.

3. Ingulf, Abbot of Croyland, *Ingulph's Chronicle of the Abbey of Croyland, with the Continuations by Peter of Blois and Anonymous Writers*, trans. Henry T. Riley (London, 1854), p. 492. Sir Walter Devereux was a consistent Yorkist and died fighting for Richard III at Bosworth. His connection with the Staffords is unclear. During the minority of Henry, second duke of Buckingham, he had served as steward of the lordships of Brecon, Hay, and Huntingdon, and constable of their castles. GEC, vol. V, pp. 321–25. Josiah Wedgewood, *History of Parliament: Biographies of Members of the Commons House, 1439–1509* (London, 1936), pp. 272–73.

4. On the Delabeares see Carole Rawcliffe, *The Staffords, Earls of*

*Stafford and Dukes of Buckingham, 1394–1521* (Cambridge, Eng., 1978), pp. 223, 232, 236, and Wedgewood, *Biographies*, pp. 266–67.

5. Joan, daughter of the first duke of Buckingham, married Sir William Knevet (1440–1515) as her second husband. Sir William Knevet was therefore uncle to the second duke and great-uncle to the third. GEC, vol. II, p. 63. Knevet, who was an important landowner in Norfolk and served as knight of the shire, was later attainted for his part in the second duke's rebellion but managed to escape execution. He subsequently served as the third duke's councillor and chamberlain. Rawcliffe, *The Staffords*, p. 227; Wedgewood, *Biographies*, pp. 520–21; *Rolls of Parliament*, vol. VI, p. 245.

6. For other examples of this phenomenon in the Stafford family, see below, Chapter 3.

7. Dame Elizabeth was Richard Delabeare's servant at the time of the second duke of Buckingham's rebellion. Her name was Elizabeth Mors. She married Sir Richard subsequently. The source that tells the story was written for the second duke's son, the subject of this book, some twenty years later from information supplied by Elizabeth. By that time Elizabeth had married Sir Richard and she is referred to by the name of Delabeare throughout the source. Ralph A. Griffiths and Roger S. Thomas, *The Making of the Tudor Dynasty* (London, 1985), pp. 99–100.

8. The quaint detail that Dame Elizabeth shaved Edward's head when she dressed him as a girl refers to the fact that in this period the fashion was to shave women's foreheads and temples. C. Willett Cunnington and Phillis Cunnington, *Handbook of English Medieval Costume* (London, 1952), p. 131.

9. *CPR, Edward IV, Edward V, and Richard III, A.D. 1476–85* (London, 1897–1901), vol. III, p. 436.

10. The marriage took place before Nov. 7, 1485; that is, within the very first months of Henry VII's reign. GEC, vol. II, p. 73.

11. William Campbell, *Materials for the Reign of Henry VII* (London, 1877), vol. II, p. 19; Walter C. B. Metcalfe, *A Book of Knights Banneret, Knights of the Bath and Knights Bachelor Made Between Four Henry VI and the Restoration of King Charles II* (London, 1885), p. 11.

12. *Rolls of Parliament*, vol. VI, p. 285.

13. H. E. Bell, *An Introduction to the History and Records of the Court of Wards and Liveries* (Cambridge, Eng., 1953), p. 2, n. 2. In the case of a girl, the situation was somewhat complicated. She escaped wardship entirely if she was over fourteen when her father died but not if she was under fourteen. However, when a female ward reached fourteen, she remained in wardship for two more years. If she refused a husband offered to her by her guardian during that time, her guardian could

hold her land until she was 21 and longer if necessary to extract the value of the marriage from her estates. If she had been pre-contracted in childhood, she could choose between the person named in that pre-contract and the selection of her guardian made between the ages of fourteen and sixteen. Joel Hurstfield, *The Queen's Wards: Wardship and Marriage Under Elizabeth I* (London, 1973), pp. 137–38.

14. For a description of general livery see Hurstfield, *Queen's Wards*, pp. 170–72.

15. Ibid., pp. 172–73.

16. *CPR, Henry VII*, vol. I (London, 1914), p. 113.

17. Ibid.; *Statutes of the Realm*, vol. II, p. 603; *Rolls of Parliament*, vol. VI, pp. 299, 498.

18. Paul V. B. Jones, *The Household of a Tudor Nobleman* (New York, 1970; orig. pub. 1917), pp. 31, 42–43; Sue Sheridan Walker, "Widow and Ward: The Feudal Law of Child Custody in Medieval England," *Feminist Studies*, 3, no. 3/4 (Spring–Summer 1976), 109–10.

19. Gerald Brenan and Edward Phillips Statham, *The House of Howard* (New York, 1908), pp. 19, 61, 120.

20. Norman Davis, ed., *Paston Letters and Papers of the Fifteenth Century* (Oxford, 1971), vol. I, pp. lix, 399, 401.

21. *A Relation, or Rather a True Account of the Island of England . . . About the Year 1500*, ed. Charlotte A. Sneyd, Camden Society, Old Series, vol. XXXVII, 1847 (New York, 1968), pp. 24–26; Lawrence Stone, *The Crisis of the Aristocracy, 1558–1641* (Oxford, 1965), pp. 589–93; Lawrence Stone, *The Family, Sex and Marriage in England, 1500–1800* (London, 1977), pp. 105–14.

22. Quoted in Violet A. Wilson, *Society Women of Shakespeare's Time* (Port Washington, N.Y., 1970), p. 66.

23. *CSP, Spanish* (London, 1862–83), vol. I, 204 (p. 163), 205, 210 (p. 178).

24. M. A. E. Wood Green, *Letters of Royal and Illustrious Ladies of Great Britain*, vol. I (London, 1846), p. 118; Sir Henry Ellis, *Original Letters Illustrative of English History*, First Series (London, 1824), vol. I, p. 18; Campbell, *Henry VII*, vol. I, pp. 429–30.

25. Charles Henry Cooper, *Memoir of Margaret, Countess of Richmond and Derby*, ed. John E. M. Mayor (Cambridge, Eng., 1874), p. 11. Lady Margaret was also related to the Staffords many times through the Beauforts. Her first cousin, also named Margaret Beaufort, married Humphrey, the eldest brother of the countess's second husband, Henry Stafford. Humphrey was father of the second duke of Buckingham and grandfather of the countess's two wards. Her mother-in-law, Anne, wife of the first duke of Buckingham, was the daughter of Ralph Neville,

first earl of Westmorland, and Joan Beaufort. Joan was Lady Margaret's great-aunt.

26. SRO, D641/1/2/181–82.

27. Cooper, *Memoir*, pp. 11, 14; GEC, vol. X, p. 826. Sir Henry died before Oct. 7, 1471. *CPR, Edward IV and Henry VI, 1467–1477* (London, 1900), p. 298; J. P. Cooper, "Patterns of Inheritance and Settlement by Great Landowners from the Fifteenth to the Eighteenth Centuries," *Family and Inheritance: Rural Society in Western Europe, 1200–1800*, ed. Jack Goody, Joan Thirsk, and E. P. Thompson (Cambridge, Eng., 1976), p. 315. Sir Henry also held the family manor of Norton, Staffordshire. BL, Add'l Mss., 36,542, f. 47.

28. The most revealing contemporary estimate of Lady Margaret was John Fisher's sermon at her "moneth minde" in 1509. John Fisher, *A Mornynge Remembraunce, had at the moneth minde of her noble prynces Margarete, Countess of Richmonde and Darbye . . .* (London, 1906). Fisher mentioned specifically that Margaret had not been taught Latin, an interesting insight into the education of the most privileged women in the mid-fifteenth century. Fifty years later the best-educated women (Sir Thomas More's and Henry VIII's daughters, for example) were routinely taught Latin. See also Polydore, *The Anglica Historia*, ed. and trans. Denys Hay, Camden Society, Third Series, vol. LXXIV (London, 1950), pp. 145–57.

29. A. B. Emden, *A Biographical Register of the University of Oxford to A.D. 1500* (Oxford, 1959), vol. III, p. 2020.

30. J. J. Scarisbrick, *Henry VIII* (Berkeley, Calif., 1968), p. 6 and n. 1.

31. These daughters were Anne, 1475–1510, married in 1495 to Thomas, earl of Surrey; Catherine, 1479–1527, married in 1495 to William, earl of Devon; and Bridget, who became a nun. *DNB*, vol. XVIII, p. 546. Catherine took a vow of perpetual chastity after the death of her husband in 1511 (GEC, vol. IV, p. 330). A few years earlier, Lady Margaret had taken such a vow following the death of her third husband, Thomas Stanley, earl of Derby. The countess of Richmond's action may well have influenced her former charge. Charles Henry Cooper, "Vow of Widowhood of Margaret, Countess of Richmond and Derby . . . with Notices of Similar Vows in the 14th, 15th and 16th Centuries," *Cambridge Antiquarian Society, Proceedings*, 1 (1859), 71–79.

32. One, Alan Percy, later became master of St. John's, Margaret's foundation at Cambridge. J. B. Mullinger, *St. John's College: College Histories* (Cambridge, Eng., 1901), p. 19. I have not been able to find out which one of Northumberland's other children lived in Lady Margaret's household. It may have been Alianore, who was Henry VII's ward after her father's murder in 1489.

33. This was Ralph, earl of Westmorland, who died in 1498. West-morland's father had been a supporter of Richard III. When Henry VII came to the throne, his father gave the king bonds of £400 and 400 marks, as well as the keeping, rule, and marriage of his eldest son, the earl who was raised in Lady Margaret's household. GEC, vol. XII (2), p. 551; John Heneague Jesse, *Memoirs of the Court of England: King Richard the Third and Some of His Contemporaries* (Boston, 1862), pp. 34–35.

34. Clifford was reared with Henry VIII and may therefore have lived with him during the years when Margaret Beaufort was in charge of him. A. G. Dickens, *Clifford Letters of the Sixteenth Century*, Surtees Society, vol. CLXXII (London, 1962), p. 140.

35. Scarisbrick, *Henry VIII*, p. 6, n. 1. Margaret's mother's first husband was Sir Oliver St. John (d. 1438), by whom she had a number of children. The Sir John St. John raised in Margaret's household was apparently the son of one of the countess's half-brothers. He eventually became Lady Margaret's chamberlain and was remembered in her will. Cambridge University, St. John's College, *Collegium Divi Johannis Evangelistae, 1511–1911* (Cambridge, 1911), pp. 122–23; *Select Cases Before the King's Council in the Star Chamber, 1509–1544*, ed. I. S. Leadam, Selden Society, vol. XXV (London, 1911), p. 25, n. 3.

36. Leonard E. Elliott-Binns, *England and the New Learning* (London, 1937), pp. 64–65; *DNB*, vol. XIV, pp. 999–1000, and vol. XVIII, p. 546; Ralph Churton, *The Lives of William Smyth, Bishop of Lincoln and Sir Richard Sutton, Knight* (Oxford, 1800), pp. 12–13.

37. Mervyn E. James, "The First Earl of Cumberland (1493–1542) and the Decline of Northern Feudalism," *Northern History*, 1 (1966), 45.

38. See Chapter 1, notes 96–98 for documentation on the childhood of Henry, the second duke of Buckingham.

39. Preface to *L&P, Henry VIII*, vol. I, p. xciv, n. 1.

40. The letters are W'min Abbey, 16053 and 16062. The other manuscripts are BL, Royal and King Collection, 7f XIV, 1–19, 14B XXXVA, 1–5, 7–12, XXXVB, XXXVC, XXXVD, XXXVE, XXXVF. The manuscripts in the Royal and King Collection are calendared in *L&P, Henry VIII*, vol. III (1), 1285 (pp. 495–99, 501–4).

41. K. B. McFarlane, *The Nobility of Later Medieval England* (Oxford, 1973), p. 239.

42. Charles Henry Cooper, *Athenae Cantabrigienses* (Cambridge, 1858), vol. I, p. 24. Many donors never attended the universities or colleges to which they made gifts. Buckingham's former guardian, Margaret Beaufort, is another example of someone who supported educational institutions she had not attended.

43. Cooper, *Memoir*, p. 250.

44. *VCH, Huntingdonshire*, vol. III (London, 1936), p. 223.

45. BL, Add'l Mss., 36,542, f. 98.

46. *L&P, Henry VIII*, vol. III (1), p. 500; PRO, E36/220, m. 20.

47. Rawcliffe, *The Staffords*, p. 95. I question Rawcliffe's assumption that the duke purchased the 74 books printed before his death that were catalogued at Stafford Castle in 1556. There is no evidence on the point. SRO, D641/1/3/7; BL, Add'l Mss., 40,859B; SRO, D1721/1/10.

48. Chevalier au Cynge, *The History of Helyas, Knight of the Swan*, trans. by Robert Copland from the French version published in Paris in 1504, reprint of version published by Wynkin de Worde in London 1512 (New York, 1901).

49. PRO, SP1/22, f. 183.

50. Rawcliffe, *The Staffords*, p. 103.

51. Cooper, *Memoir*, p. 250.

52. K. B. McFarlane, "The Education of the Nobility in Later Medieval England," in *Nobility*, pp. 228–47. Early in the twentieth century, Gairdner evaluated the state of education and literacy in the century before the Reformation positively on the basis of his work on the Paston letters. *Paston Letters*, vol. IV, pp. ccclxiii–ccclxiv. See also Joel T. Rosenthal, "Aristocratic Cultural Patronage and Book Bequests, 1350–1500," *Bulletin of the John Ryland University Library of Manchester*, 64, no. 2 (Spring 1982), 522–48; and Susan Groag Bell, "Medieval Women Book Owners: Arbiters of Lay Piety and Ambassadors of Culture," *Signs*, 7, no. 4 (Spring 1982), 742–68.

53. Melvin J. Tucker, *The Life of Thomas Howard, Earl of Surrey and Second Duke of Norfolk, 1443–1524* (The Hague, 1964), pp. 22–23; *Household Books of John Duke of Norfolk and Thomas Earl of Surrey, 1481–1490*, ed. J. Payne Collier, Roxburghe Club (London, 1844), p. xxvii.

54. *Clifford Letters*, pp. 18–20, 135.

55. Edward Barrington De Fonblanque, *Annals of the House of Percy* (London, 1877), vol. I, pp. 331–32.

56. *Clifford Letters*, p. 17. See letters 23–43. Northumberland's letters are nos. 31, 33, and 34; Anne Clifford's, no. 23; and Katherine Scrope's, no. 35.

57. *Paston Letters*, vol. III, no. 737, p. 108.

58. J. H. Hexter, "The Education of the Aristocracy in the Renaissance," in *Reappraisals in History: New Views on History and Society in Early Modern Europe* (New York, 1961), pp. 45–70; Stone, *Crisis*, pp. 672–83; Charles D. Ross, *Edward IV* (Berkeley, 1974), pp. 8, 268; Lawrence Stone, "The Educational Revolution in England, 1560–1640," *Past and*

*Present*, no. 28 (July 1964), 41–80; Joan Simon, *Education and Society in Tudor England* (Cambridge, Eng., 1966); and Kenneth Charlton, *Education in Renaissance England* (London, 1965).

59. J. M. W. Bean notes that "the so-called 'incidents' of tenure were at least as important as military service in the creation of feudal tenure. . . . English feudalism was in its origins as much a fiscal as a military institution." *The Decline of English Feudalism, 1215–1540* (New York, 1968), p. 5. He also observed (p. 256) that the "inroads which uses had made into its feudal revenue . . . forced the crown to resort to the unscrupulous rapacity which is associated with the names of Empson and Dudley."

60. *CPR, Henry VII* (London, 1914–16), vol. I, p. 113. Relief was a payment made to the feudal overlord by the heir of a feudal tenant on taking up possession of the vacant estate.

61. Rawcliffe, *The Staffords*, pp. 128–29.

62. There is no valor for Buckingham's estates in 1485. The £5,000 figure is an estimate, based on a number of sources. The estates were also valued at £5,000 during the lifetime of the first duke of Buckingham. T. B. Pugh, ed., *The Marcher Lordships of South Wales, 1415–1536: Select Documents* (Cardiff, 1963), pp. 176–77. Three copies of the valor made by Thomas Magnus and William Walwyn in 1521 survive: PRO, E36/150 and E36/181, and BL, Add'l Mss., 25,294. I have compared the income for each property listed in them. In almost every case, the figures in two of the three (though not necessarily the same two each time) were identical, and in many cases they were the same in all three. Thus, I eliminated careless errors in the documents. These documents yield a figure of £5,061 18s per annum. Finally, a portion of a valor drawn up in 1498–99 survives (SRO, D641/1/2/27). Enough discrepancies crop up in the figures for individual manors to indicate that the 1521 valor was not a copy of this one. Yet the total for the Stafford, Kent, Surrey, and York receiverships was £1,453 in the valor of 1498–99 and £1,452 10s in that of 1521. Apparently the expected income from the Stafford estates was quite stable during the period 1450–1521.

63. SRO, D641/1/2/192–99.

64. SRO, D641/1/2/193–96.

65. SRO, D641/1/2/197, mm. 13–13b.

66. SRO, D641/1/2/198, m. 9; D641/1/2/199, m. 10.

67. SRO, D641/1/2/79, m. 9d.

68. SRO, D641/1/2/76–78, m. 8d, in all three rolls.

69. Pugh, *Marcher Lordships*, p. 242, n. 2.

70. BL, Egerton Rolls, 2192, f. 2d.

71. Ibid., f. 3d; John Lloyd, *The Great Forest of Brecon* (London, 1905), p. 8.

72. BL, Egerton Rolls, 2192; PRO, SC6/Henry 7/1651.

73. The estate accounts ran from Michaelmas to Michaelmas. I shall refer here to the fiscal year by the year in which it terminated. Thus, by 1489 I mean the year that ran from Michaelmas 1488 to Michaelmas 1489. Income is the money actually turned over by the receiver to whoever was holding the land. BL, Egerton Rolls, 2192 (1486); PRO, SC6/Henry 7/1651, mm. 5d–6 (1489); PRO, SC6/Henry 7/1652, m. 6d (1494); BL, Egerton Rolls, 2193 (1496).

74. Pugh, *Marcher Lordships*, p. 242.

75. Ibid., p. 183.

76. Ibid., p. 181.

77. BL, Egerton Rolls, 2198, mm. 1, 2d–3.

78. Westminster Abbey, Account of Richard Harpus, 32,349.

79. Westminster Abbey, Account of William Bedell, 32,348.

80. Pugh, *Marcher Lordships*, pp. 176–77. See above, Chapter 1.

81. Pugh, *Marcher Lordships*, p. 181.

82. The estates assigned as jointure to Katherine, duchess of Bedford, are listed in *Rolls of Parliament*, vol. VI, p. 284. I have used the valors of 1521, listed in note 62 of this chapter, to establish their value.

83. If the total income of the Stafford estates was £5,000 (according to contemporary valors) and the duchess of Bedford held lands worth £1,500, then Margaret Beaufort's estates should have been worth £3,500.

84. Margaret was left some property by her father, John, duke of Somerset. Cooper, *Memoir*, p. 3. She also collected a great deal of land as jointure through her three marriages to Edmund Tudor, Sir Henry Stafford, and Thomas Stanley, earl of Derby. Finally, her son granted her an enormous amount of property after his accession to the throne as Henry VII. *CPR, Henry VII*, vol. I, p. 154. When Lady Margaret died, she left money, plate, jewels, and goods worth £17,664 4s, an extraordinary sum in that period. *L&P, Henry VIII*, vol. II (2), 4183.

85. *CSP, Spanish*, vol. I, 25, 29.

86. Campbell, *Henry VII*, vol. II, pp. 554–55. The excerpt in Campbell is misdated 1490. J. M. W. Bean, *The Estates of the Percy Family, 1416–1537* (Oxford, 1958), p. 134, n. 5. According to Bean, the purchase price of Alianore's marriage was 4,000 marks, not £4,000. Bean, *Decline of English Feudalism*, p. 246, n. 2. Her father had left her 3,000 marks in his will. Cooper, "Inheritance," pp. 308, n. d, and 315–16.

87. Cooper, "Inheritance," pp. 306–12, especially Table 1, p. 307. Helen J. Miller said "£1,000 seems to have been roughly speaking the

normal sum with which to endow the daughter of a considerable noble-man." "The Early Tudor Peerage, 1485–1527" (London University masters thesis, 1950), p. 60.

88. *Statutes of the Realm*, vol. III, p. 267. Compare this with the 500 marks, £60 that Buckingham promised his eldest daughter, wife of the duke of Norfolk. *The Works of Henry Howard, Earl of Surrey and of Sir Thomas Wyatt the Elder*, ed. George Frederick Nott (London, 1815), Appendix, pp. lxviii and lxxii.

89. *L&P, Richard III and Henry VII*, ed. James Gairdner, Rolls Series (London, 1861), vol. I, p. 393; Ralph Flenley, *Six Town Chronicles* (Oxford, 1911), pp. 164–66.

90. *CPR, Henry VII*, vol. II, pp. 29–30, 33.

91. Ibid., p. 72; *CSP, Venice* (London, 1864–71), vol. I, p. 263; A. F. Pollard, *The Reign of Henry VII from Contemporary Sources* (London, 1913), vol. I, p. 162; *CSP, Venice*, vol. I, p. 263.

92. Edward Hall, *Union of the Two Noble and Illustrious Families of Lancaster and York* (London, 1809), p. 484.

93. In strict feudal theory, a woman could not hold land by knight service since she could not perform the requisite military functions. By the twelfth century, however, the right of inheritance by daughters, in the absence of a male heir, was recognized. Furthermore, a woman could hold a portion of her deceased husband's lands as her jointure. In these cases, since the woman could not perform the knight service, her husband did it for her. Before she married or remarried she had to secure the permission of her feudal lord so that he could assure himself that her mate was fit to do military service. Henry VII was the feudal overlord of Edward's mother. Of course, by that time feudal armies were outmoded and the right of approving a marriage was exploited purely as another source of money. Had Katherine asked the king for permission to marry Wingfield, he probably would have consented in return for a substantial consideration. See Pugh, *Marcher Lordships*, p. 241, n. 5, for the date of Katherine's marriage; SRO, D1721/1/1, f. 378d, for the fine.

94. SRO, D1721/1/1/, f. 378d.

95. *CPR, Henry VII*, vol. II, p. 131.

96. Edward Owen, *Catalogue of Manuscripts Relating to Wales in the British Museum*, Cymmrodorion Record Series (London, 1900–1922), vol. III, p. 109. The actual date on the duke's birth certificate, expressed in terms of the pre-Reformation calendar, is Feb. 3, 1477; I use modern dates in the text.

97. *CPR, Henry VII*, vol. II, p. 131.

98. SRO, D1721/1/1, f. 378d.

99. Robert Keilway, *Reports d'Ascuns Cases* (London, 1638), pp. 176b–177.

100. SRO, D1721/1/1, f. 378d.

101. Ibid.

102. *CCR, Henry VII* (London, 1955, 1963), vol. II, p. 816; *CPR, Henry VII*, vol. II, p. 626. BL, Lansdowne Mss., 127, f. 47d.

103. SRO, D1721/1/1, f. 378d.

104. Ibid., f. 379.

105. BL, Lansdowne Mss., 160, f. 311.

106. *CCR, Henry VII*, vol. II, 955 (p. 356).

*Chapter Three*

1. *L&P, Henry VIII*, vol. III (1), 1285, pp. 499–500; PRO, E32/220, m. 9.

2. PRO, SP1/22, ff. 70d–80.

3. Calendared in *L&P, Henry VIII*, vol. III (1), 1070. Printed in full in Henry Ellis, *Original Letters Illustrative of English History*, Third Series (London, 1846), vol. I, p. 224.

4. SRO, D641/1/3/5.

5. SRO, D641/1/2/235.

6. PRO, E101/518/5, pt. 1; SRO, D641/1/3/9.

7. SRO, D641/1/3/9.

8. *L&P, Henry VIII*, vol. III (1), 1285 (p. 498).

9. PRO, E36/220, f. 25.

10. Ibid., f. 22.

11. *L&P, Henry VIII*, vol. III (1), 1070, p. 392; 1285 (p. 505).

12. HMC, Fourth Report (London, 1874), Appendix, p. 326. A contemporary example of this open provision for illegitimate children occurred in the will of Sir Edward Howard, lord admiral of England and a younger son of the second duke of Norfolk. He asked the king to take one of his two bastard sons, "beseeching his grace to be good lord to them, and that when he cometh of age he may be his servant." The other he left to the king's favorite, Charles Brandon, the future duke of Suffolk, "praying him to be good master to him." Howard left a boat and £50 to stock it with to the son chosen by the king and 100 marks to the other. Gerald Brenan and Edward Phillips Statham, *The House of Howard* (New York, 1908), pp. 93–94.

13. HMC, Fourth Report, Appendix, p. 328.

14. Letter of Elizabeth to Thomas Cromwell, Oct. 24, 1537. Calendared in *L&P, Henry VIII*, vol. XII (2), 976. Printed in full in *The Works of Henry Howard, Earl of Surrey and of Sir Thomas Wyatt the Elder*, ed. George Frederick Nott (London, 1815), Appendix, letter 29, p. lxxiii; original is BL, Cotton Mss., Titus B.1, f. 383c.

15. SRO, D1721/1/1, f.390. Printed in full in *A Relation, or Rather a True Account of the Island of England . . . About the Year 1500*, ed. Charlotte August Sneyd, Camden Society, Old Series, vol. XXXVII, 1847 (New York, 1968), n. 38, pp. 75–76.

16. PRO, E101/518/5, pt. 1.

17. SRO, D1721/1/1, f. 390.

18. Ibid.

19. *L&P, Henry VIII*, vol. II (1), 1893.

20. SRO, D1721/1/5. Printed in *Archaeologia*, 25 (1834). PRO, SP1/29, f. 66.

21. *L&P, Henry VIII*, vol. III (1), 1285, p. 499.

22. The duchess's poem, a prayer to the Virgin, is found in BL, Arundel Mss., 318, f. 152. Elizabeth wrote a series of letters to Thomas Cromwell when her marriage broke down in the 1530's. She signed them all, added a paragraph to one in her own hand, and added a postscript in her own hand to another. The letter with the postscript is calendared in *L&P, Henry VIII*, vol. XII (2), 1332 (p. 478), and printed in full in M. A. E. Wood Green, *Letters of Royal and Illustrious Ladies of Great Britain* (London, 1846), vol. III, pp. 190–91. The original is BL, Cotton Mss., Titus B.1, f. 162. The letter containing a whole paragraph in the duchess's hand is printed in full in Green, *Letters*, vol. II, pp. 220–21; the original is BL, Cotton Mss., Vespasian, F.13, f. 151. It is calendared in *L&P, Henry VIII*, vol. VII, 1534. His daughter Catherine's autograph is reproduced in Edmund Lodge, *Illustrations of British History, Biography and Manners in the Reigns of Henry VIII, Edward VI, Mary, Elizabeth and James I* (London, 1837), pl. 19, sig. 3. I have not found any evidence on the duke's third daughter Mary, but she was probably educated in much the same way as her sisters.

23. Nott, *Works of Howard and Wyatt*, vol. I, p. xx.

24. Carole Rawcliffe, *The Staffords, Earls of Stafford and Dukes of Buckingham, 1394–1521* (Cambridge, Eng., 1978), p. 95.

25. GEC, vol. XII (1), p. 183; Anthony Wood, *Athenae Oxonienses* (London, 1813), vol. I, col. 266; Charles Henry Cooper, *Athenae Cantabrigienses* (Cambridge, Eng., 1858), vol. I, p. 216.

26. GEC, vol. XII (1), p. 184, n. f; Wood, *Athenae Oxonienses*, vol. I, col. 266.

27. Wood, *Athenae Oxonienses*, vol. I, col. 266; Cooper, *Athenae Cantabrigienses*, vol. I, p. 216.

28. Cooper, *Athenae Cantabrigienses*, vol. I, p. 216.

29. Ibid.

30. According to Lawrence Stone, "the brother-sister relationship was often the closest in the family." *The Family, Sex and Marriage in En-*

*gland, 1500–1800* (London, 1977), p. 115. On the other hand, an "embittered sense of envy" often poisoned the relationship between a peer and his younger brothers.

31. SRO, D641/1/1/6/4, f. 848, n. c.

32. GEC, vol. 12 (2), p. 848, n. c.

33. Rawcliffe, *The Staffords*, pp. 173–74; SRO, D641/1/1/6/4.

34. SRO, D641/1/1/6/4.

35. PRO, SP1/22, ff. 70d, 73, 82d, 83d, 86d; household book, printed in *Archaeologia*, 25 (1834), 319, 321, 329.

36. *CPR, Henry VII, 1485–1509* (London, 1916), vol. II, p. 601. Sir Walter's father, William Herbert, earl of Pembroke, was succeeded by his legitimate son William Herbert, earl of Pembroke and then earl of Huntingdon. The younger William's legal heir was a daughter, Elizabeth, who should have succeeded to Raglan Castle.

37. GEC, vol. VI, p. 655.

38. Rawcliffe, *The Staffords*, p. 40; HMC, *Hastings Manuscripts* (London, 1928), vol. I, p. 307.

39. HMC, *Hastings Manuscripts*, vol. II, pp. 1–2.

40. William Dugdale, *The Baronage of England* (London, 1675), vol. I, p. 587. One of their daughters, Dorothy, married the son and heir of Walter Devereux, Lord Ferrers, in July 1536. Her dowry was £8,000. HMC, *Hastings Manuscripts*, vol. I, pp. 313–14.

41. GEC, vol. XII (1), p. 519.

42. J. R. Lander, *Crown and Nobility, 1450–1509* (London, 1976), pp. 274–75.

43. Dugdale, *Baronage*, vol. II, p. 286.

44. PRO, SP1/22, f. 83d.

45. *CSP, Spanish* (London, 1862–83), supplement to vols. I and II, 8, 39–40.

46. *L&P, Henry VIII*, vol. III (1), 1070.

47. PRO, E36/220, m. 13 (pencil no. 15).

48. Household book, *Archaeologia*, 25 (1834), 335.

49. *L&P, Henry VIII*, vol. II (1), 1893.

50. Ibid., vol. III (1), 1285 (p. 498).

51. Gerald Brenan, *A History of the Family of Percy* (London, 1902), p. 133.

52. T. B. Pugh, ed., *The Marcher Lordships of South Wales: Select Documents* (Cardiff, 1963), p. 262.

53. PRO, SC6/Henry 7/1075, f. 8.

54. BL, Egerton Rolls, 2203; SRO, D641/1/4U/1, f. 1.

55. PRO, E36/150, ff. 25, 112; Rawcliffe, *The Staffords*, pp. 207–8, 230.

56. Rawcliffe, *The Staffords*, p. 215.

57. PRO, SP1/29, f. 174, 176.

58. *CCR, Henry VII* (London, 1955, 1963), vol. II, pp. 165–66, 224; GEC, vol. XII (2), p. 738; Dugdale, *Baronage*, vol. I, p. 720. Cicely, marchioness of Dorset, had 15 children, seven sons and eight daughters by her first husband. Of these, three died young. Henry Stafford was born c. 1479, Cicely c. 1460. She was thus about 44 or 45 when she married Henry Stafford in 1504 or 1505.

59. *CCR, Henry VII*, vol. II, p. 184.

60. Ibid., pp. 414, 435.

61. *L&P, Henry VIII*, vol. III (1), 1153.

62. Green, *Letters*, vol. II, pp. 1–2. Evidently, only half of Lady Cicely's eight daughters survived her.

63. BL, Lansdowne Mss., 127, ff. 37, 55; Rawcliffe, *The Staffords*, p. 162.

64. PRO, SP1/22, f. 72d; *Court of Requests, Select Cases, 1497–1569*, ed. I. S. Leadam, Selden Society, vol. XII (London, 1898), p. 45, n. 1; PRO, SP1/29, f. 183.

65. PRO, E101/518/5, pt. 1; SRO, D641/1/3/9.

66. The legal documents executed in connection with the marriage of Buckingham's children were carefully stored in chests in the muniments room at Thornbury Castle. The room was located in the top story of the tower at the southwest corner of the inner court. BL, Add'l Mss., 36,542, ff. 97–98; SRO, D1721/1/10, at the end of Stafford's Letter Book (no pagination).

67. BL, Cotton Mss., Titus B.1, f. 383c.

68. Letter of Elizabeth, duchess of Norfolk, to Thomas Cromwell, June 26, 1537. Calendared in *L&P, Henry VIII*, vol. XII (2), 143. Printed in full in *Works of Howard and Wyatt*, Appendix, letter 28, p. lxviii. The original is BL, Cotton Mss., Titus B.1, f. 383a. The average dowry for the daughter of a peer in the early Tudor period was probably about £1,000. Helen J. Miller, "The Early Tudor Peerage, 1485–1547" (London University master's thesis, 1950), p. 60; J. P. Cooper gave the slightly higher figure of £1,150 in "Patterns of Inheritance and Settlement by Great Landowners from the Fifteenth to the Eighteenth Centuries," in *Family and Inheritance: Rural Society in Western Europe, 1200–1800*, ed. Jack Goody, Joan Thirsk, and E. P. Thompson (Cambridge, Eng., 1976), pp. 306–12. Occasionally a peer gave his daughter a much larger sum. Sometime before 1503, Edward, Lord Hastings, gave his daughter 4,000 marks on her marriage to Thomas Stanley, second earl of Derby. Miller, "Early Tudor Peerage," p. 58. The earl of Oxford's daughter received a dowry of 4,000 marks on her marriage to Henry, earl of Surrey, in 1532. E. R. Casady, *Henry Howard, Earl of Surrey*, Modern Language Associa-

tion Revolving Fund VIII (New York, 1938), p. 36. As we have seen, Ursula Pole's dowry when she married Henry Stafford was 3,000 marks.

69. BL, Cotton Mss., Titus B.1, f. 383c.

70. Ibid.

71. Ibid.; also f. 383a.

72. T. H. Hollingsworth, "A Demographic Study of British Ducal Families," in D. V. Glass and D. E. C. Everseley, eds., *Population in History* (Chicago, 1965), p. 365. Between 1330 and 1479 the mean age of female marriage in this class was 17.1 years; between 1480 and 1679, Elizabeth's cohort, it rose to 19.5.

73. BL, Cotton Mss., Titus B.1, f. 383c.

74. SRO, D641/1/3/9. This wardrobe account for the period Apr. 1, 1516–Mar. 31, 1917, contains a number of references to Lord and Lady Westmorland.

75. GEC, vol. XII (2), p. 554.

76. *L&P, Henry VIII*, vol. II (1), 1893.

77. Ibid., 1970.

78. Ibid., 1893.

79. HMC, Seventh Report (London, 1879), Appendix, p. 584.

80. Dugdale, *Baronage*, vol. I, p. 170.

81. HMC, Seventh Report, Appendix, p. 584.

82. *L&P, Henry VIII*, vol. III (1), 1285, p. 498.

83. Hollingsworth, "Ducal Families," p. 365.

84. Ellis, *Letters*, Third Series, vol. I, p. 223. Thomas Leukenor was a landowner in Kent. He received a pension of £5 from Buckingham by 1502. Rawcliffe, *The Staffords*, p. 242.

85. GEC, vol. I, p. 33.

86. Ibid. Bergavenny was born in 1479, her father in 1477. Mary's birth date is unknown. She could have been born between Elizabeth (b. 1497) and Henry (b. 1501) or after Henry. The earliest possible birth date is therefore 1498, which would have made her 21 in 1519. Chances are she was younger than that.

87. *L&P, Henry VIII*, vol. III (1), 1285, p. 502. Why a dispensation was necessary is unknown.

88. Elizabeth's 2,000 marks equaled £1,333 6s 8d.

89. *L&P, Henry VIII*, vol. IV (3), 6123.

90. GEC, vol. XII (1), p. 184, n. d; *L&P, Henry VIII*, vol. XII (I), 608, 638.

91. *L&P, Henry VIII*, vol. III (1), 1285, pp. 499, 501; PRO, E36/220, ff. 7, 23 (pencil nos. 9, 25).

92. BL, Add'l Mss., 36,542, f. 119; SRO, D1721/1/1, f. 399d.

93. GEC, vol. XII (1), pp. 184–85.

94. Letter from Elizabeth, duchess of Norfolk, to her brother Lord Henry Stafford, undated, but before 1547. Printed in Green, *Letters*, vol. III, p. 190; calendared in *L&P, Henry VIII*, vol. XII (2), 1332; the original is BL, Cotton Mss., Titus B.1, f. 162. SRO, D1721/1/10, pp. 2, 248, 258.

95. Green, *Letters*, vol. III, p. 182.

96. Ibid., p. 183; *L&P, Henry VIII*, vol. XII (1), 345. Numbers 148, 919, 1087 (p. 495), and 1088 (2) contain further evidence of her vigorous activity during this crisis.

97. *L&P, Henry VIII*, vol. III (1), 1070.

98. Dugdale, *Baronage*, vol. I, p. 311.

99. On the Howards, the earls of Westmorland, and Lord Bergavenny, see J. R. Lander, *Crown and Nobility*, pp. 275, n. 41, 283, 289–90. For further details on Westmorland, see John Heneague Jesse, *Memoirs of the Court of England: King Richard the Third and Some of His Contemporaries* (Boston, 1862), pp. 34–35. The Poles were in a precarious position because of their Yorkist blood. Their mother, Margaret, countess of Salisbury, was the daughter of George, duke of Clarence, Edward IV's brother. She married Sir Richard Pole, by whom she had four children. Henry VII executed her brother Edward, earl of Warick, in 1499. On the Percies, see Mervyn E. James, *A Tudor Magnate and the Tudor State: Henry, Fifth Earl of Northumberland*, Borthwick Papers, no. 30 (York, 1966), pp. 22–26, and Lander, *Crown and Nobility*, pp. 285–86. On the Radcliffes, see above p. 51; on the Greys, Lander, *Crown and Nobility*, pp. 286–88; on Hastings, *DNB*, vol. IX, p. 123, and *L&P, Henry VIII*, vol. II (1), 1959, 2018.

100. *DNB*, vol. XIX, p. 313.

101. *L&P, Henry VIII*, vol. III (2), 3695 (p. 1531); PRO, SP1/29, f. 177.

102. *L&P, Henry VIII*, 2d ed., vol. I (1), 157.

103. *L&P, Henry VIII*, vol. III (1), 1.

104. Polydore Vergil, *Anglica Historia*, ed. Denys Hay, Camden Society, Third Series, vol. LXXIV (London, 1950), p. 265.

105. *L&P, Henry VIII*, vol. XXI (2), 554, p. 283.

106. For this description of Thomas Howard, see Melvin J. Tucker, *The Life of Thomas Howard, Earl of Surrey and Second Duke of Norfolk, 1443–1524* (The Hague, 1964), p. 102; Chapter 6 below substantiates this description of Buckingham.

107. According to his wife, Howard was 35 when they married in 1512. See n. 71 in this chapter. Stafford was born in 1477 and was therefore also 35 in that year. See chapter 2, n. 1.

108. *L&P, Henry VIII*, 2d ed., vol. I (1), 157.

109. Tucker, *Howard*, p. 123.

110. *L&P, Henry VIII*, vol. II (1), 1959.

111. Ibid., vol. III (1), 1.

112. Ibid., 1070. This letter is printed in full in Ellis, *Letters*, Series III, vol. I, p. 221.

113. Edward Hall, *Union of the Two Noble and Illustrious Families of Lancaster and York* (London, 1809), pp. 623–24; BL, Harleian Mss., 540, art. 13, f. 50d; Harleian Mss., 2194, ff. 11/12d–15/16d. (Harleian Ms. 2194 has two systems of pagination; the reference is to the page bearing both the numbers indicated.)

114. *L&P, Henry VIII*, vol. II (1), 1959.

115. Ibid., vol. III (1), 1284 (p. 492).

116. PRO, SP1/29, ff. 182–83.

117. *L&P, Henry VIII*, vol. III (1), 1284 (p. 494).

118. Ibid., 1285, p. 499.

119. *CSP, Venice* (London, 1964–71), vol. III, 204.

120. The material on Elizabeth Stafford's marriage appeared initially in an article entitled "Marriage Sixteenth-Century Style: Elizabeth Stafford and the Third Duke of Norfolk," *The Journal of Social History*, 15, no. 3 (Spring 1982), 373–82.

121. BL, Cotton Mss., Titus B.1, f. 383a.

122. Ibid.                              123. Ibid., f. 383c.

124. Ibid., f. 383a.                    125. See p. 51 in this chapter.

126. BL, Cotton Mss., Titus B.1, f. 383a, f. 383d.

127. Brenan and Statham, *House of Howard*, p. 158.

128. BL, Cotton Mss., Titus B.1, f. 383a.

129. GEC, vol. IX, p. 620, n. b.

130. *The Crisis of the Aristocracy, 1558–1641* (Oxford, 1965), pp. 612, 662–63.

131. "The Double Standard," *The Journal of the History of Ideas*, 20 (Apr. 1959), 209–16.

132. Baldassare Castiglione, *The Book of the Courtier*, trans. Charles S. Singleton (Garden City, N.Y., 1959), p. 241.

133. See pp. 46–47 in this chapter.

134. The letters from Norfolk and Cromwell to Henry Stafford have not survived. Stafford's replies are calendared in *L&P, Henry VIII*, vol. VI, 474 and 475, under the date May 15, 1533. They are printed in full in Green, *Letters*, vol. II, pp. 218–19 (the reply to Cromwell), and vol. III, pp. 96–97 (the reply to Norfolk). The originals are in PRO, SP1/76, ff. 38–39.

135. PRO, SP1/76, f. 38.

136. Ibid., f. 39.

137. "The Weightiest Business: Marriage in an Upper-Gentry Family in Seventeenth-Century England," *Past and Present*, no. 72 (1976), p. 32.

138. PRO, SP1/76, f. 39.          139. Ibid., f. 38.

140. *L&P, Henry VIII*, vol. V, 70.      141. Ibid., p. 238.

142. Ibid., vol. VI, 585.            143. Ibid., 923.

144. BL, Cotton Mss., Titus B.1, f. 383c.

145. *Works of Howard and Wyatt*, Appendix, letter 32, p. lxxvi (letter of the duke of Norfolk to Thomas Cromwell, undated).

146. BL, Cotton Mss., Titus B.1, ff. 383a, 383c, 383d.

147. Ibid., f. 383c.            148. Ibid., f. 383a.

149. Ibid., f. 383d.            150. Ibid., f. 386.

151. PRO, SP1/115, f. 80d.

152. BL, Cotton Mss., Titus B.1, ff. 383b, 383c, 383d.

153. Ibid., f. 383c.

154. Brenan and Statham, *House of Howard*, p. 174.

155. BL, Cotton Mss., Titus B.1, f. 383a.

156. Ibid., f. 383b.

157. Ibid., f. 383d.

158. PRO, SP1/158, f. 249.

159. BL, Cotton Mss., Titus B.1, ff. 383b, 383d, 384.

160. Ibid., f. 383a.            161. Ibid., f. 383c.

162. Ibid., ff. 383a, 384.       163. Ibid., f. 383d.

164. Ibid., f. 383a.            165. Ibid., f. 384.

166. Ibid., ff. 383a, 383c, 384.

167. BL, Cotton Mss., Vespasian, F.13, art. 101, f. 151.

168. BL, Cotton Mss., Titus B.1, f. 384.

169. Ibid., f. 383d.

170. PRO, SP1/144, ff. 16–17; BL, Cotton Mss., Titus B.1, f. 383d.

171. PRO, SP1/115, f. 80d.

172. PRO, SP1/144, ff. 16–17.

173. Divorce in the twentieth-century sense—i.e., the end of a marriage and the right of each party to remarry—did not exist in Tudor England. The term referred to the separation of a couple, "of bed and board," in the contemporary phrase. The separation left the husband free to do virtually anything but remarry. The wife received an allowance for her support. It is not clear why the duke of Norfolk was willing to pay his wife so much for a divorce of this type since they were, in fact, living in this situation de facto. He may have wanted a legal separation to clarify and limit Duchess Elizabeth's financial claims on him. There is an outside chance he sought an annulment of the type Henry

VIII secured against Catherine of Aragon, but this is unlikely since it would have illegitimated his children.

174. BL, Cotton Mss., Titus B.1, f. 383b.

175. PRO, SP1/158, f. 249. The Dorothy mentioned in this letter may well have been her brother Henry's daughter rather than Westmorland's. That Dorothy seems to have been a great favorite of the duchess of Norfolk's. See below, p. 73. Furthermore, Dorothy seems to have lived away from home, either with or in close proximity to Westmorland and her Aunt Hastings. SRO, D1721/1/10, f. 258.

176. BL, Cotton Mss., Titus B.1, f. 162.

177. Stone, *Family*, pp. 174–76. In an analysis of diaries and autobiographies, Linda Pollock did not find a single Puritan diary concerned with breaking a child's will. *Forgotten Children: Parent-Child Relations from 1500 to 1900* (Cambridge, Eng., 1983), p. 116. Cotton Mather explicitly disapproved of physical punishment (ibid., p. 155). One of Pollock's main points is that in any period and in any social class, there are many kinds of parents, whose styles of childrearing reflect their personalities more than any other single factor (pp. 65, 149, 155), and certainly more than the advice found in prescriptive literature (pp. 22–23, 43–46, 64–66, 173). My own work on the period 1450–1550 supports Pollock on this point.

178. The financial arrangements for children living in homes other than their parents' varied greatly, but usually parents supplied their offsprings' clothing and pocket money, even if they were "at the finding" of the people with whom they lived (i.e., their guardians assumed the cost of their room and board). See, for example, the cases of Anne and Mary Basset, two stepdaughters of Arthur, Viscount Lisle, during the same period; *The Lisle Letters*, ed. Muriel St. Clare Byrne (Chicago, 1981), vol. III, p. 135.

179. SRO, D1721/1/10, f. 266.

180. The duchess's husband and her eldest son, Henry, had both been arrested and accused of high treason. Henry was executed on Jan. 19, 1547; her husband was saved by Henry VIII's death on Jan. 27, but he remained imprisoned until after Mary's accession to the throne in 1553.

181. *Wills from Doctors' Commons: A Selection from the Wills of Eminent Persons, 1495–1695*, ed. John Gough Nichols and John Bruce, Camden Society, Old Series (London, 1863), vol. LXXXIII, pp. 54–55.

182. Green, *Letters*, vol. III, p. 189.

183. PRO, SP1/76, f. 39.

184. Professor Lawrence Stone first called my attention to this point

at the spring 1979 meeting of the Middle Atlantic Conference of British Studies, where I read a paper on Elizabeth Stafford's marriage.

### Chapter Four

1. "The Age of the Household: Politics, Society and the Arts c.1350–c.1550," in *The Context of English Literature: The Later Middle Ages*, ed. Stephen Medcalf (London, 1981), pp. 225–89. Felicity Heal underscores the centrality of the household in the lives and careers of bishops in this period. *Of Prelates and Princes: A Study of the Economic and Social Position of the Tudor Episcopate* (Cambridge, Eng., 1980), pp. 39, 74–79.

2. Richard Goldthwaite, *The Building of Renaissance Florence: An Economic and Social History* (Baltimore, 1980), p. 83.

3. K. B. McFarlane, *The Nobility of Later Medieval England* (Oxford, 1973), p. 96.

4. See the description of the regulations governing the service of meals in the household of Henry Percy, fifth earl of Northumberland (Buckingham's brother-in-law), in Paul V. B. Jones, *The Household of a Tudor Nobleman* (New York, 1970; originally pub. 1917), pp. 151–73.

5. SRO, D641/1/3/8.

6. SRO, D1721/1/5. Part of this household book is printed in *Archaeologia*, 25 (1834), 318–41.

7. McFarlane, *Nobility*, pp. 110–11.

8. SRO, D1721/1/5.

9. SRO, D641/1/3/9.

10. PRO, E101/518/5, pt. 1.

11. Edward Barrington De Fonblanque, *Annals of the House of Percy* (London, 1887), vol. I, p. 324.

12. Jones, *Household*, pp. 9–11; according to Heal (*Prelates*, p. 75), the households of the early Tudor bishops were as large as or larger than those of the lay lords.

13. PRO, E101/631/20, m.19.

14. SRO, D641/1/3/9.

15. SRO, D1721/1/5, f. 6. The date is Nov. 13, 1507.

16. Ibid., ff. 46, 58.

17. Ibid., ff. 58–59.

18. *A Relation, or Rather a True Account of the Island of England . . . About the Year 1500*, ed. Charlotte Augusta Sneyd, Camden Society, Old Series, vol. XXXVII, 1847 (New York, 1968), pp. 21–22.

19. SRO, D641/1/3/7a.

20. SRO, D641/1/3/9.

21. SRO, D641/1/3/10. The inventory of the goods of John de Vere, thirteenth earl of Oxford (d. 1513), reveals a similar level of opulence

and conspicuous consumption. The total value of his goods was £4,773. In addition, he had £2,100 in cash on hand and £1,333 6s 8d owed to him. See Sir William H. St. John Hope, "The Last Testament and Inventory of John de Veer, Thirteenth Earl of Oxford," *Archaeologia*, 66, (1915), 288. To appreciate the magnitude of these expenditures, compare them with the income of the average peer, about £1,000 a year; of the average knight, about £204 a year; and of the typical laborer. In this period craftsmen and laborers in the building trade earned about 6d and 4d a day, respectively. If they worked 180 days during the year (the highest number in W. G. Hoskins's estimate), their annual incomes were £4 and £3. See E. H. Phelps Brown and Sheila V. Hopkins, "Seven Centuries of Building Wages," in *Essays in Economic History*, ed. E. M. Carus-Wilson (London, 1962), vol. II, p. 174; W. G. Hoskins, *The Age of Plunder: The England of Henry VIII, 1500–1547* (New York, 1976), pp. 54, 111; Heal, *Prelates*, p. 72; Helen J. Miller, "The Early Tudor Peerage, 1485–1547" (London University master's thesis, 1950), p. 127.

22. *Chronicle of Calais*, ed. John Gough Nichols, Camden Society, vol. XXXV (London, 1846), pp. 50–51.

23. A. H. Thomas and I. D. Thornley, eds., *The Great London Chronicle* (London, 1938), p. 311.

24. Ibid., p. 339.

25. Richard Grafton, *Chronicle or History of England* (London, 1809), vol. II, p. 260.

26. Jones, *Household*, ch. 7.

27. SRO, D1721/1/5, or see excerpts of household book in *Archaeologia*, 25 (1834), 318–41. The duke also had a private dining room, but there is no evidence indicating when he ate there instead of in the great chamber.

28. That was the practice in the household of Buckingham's brother-in-law, the fifth earl of Northumberland. Jones, *Household*, p. 153. The duke was not likely to insult knights and members of the gentry by relegating them to the hall with his servants. They would have been treated almost like social equals.

29. SRO, D1721/1/5, or see excerpts of household book in *Archaeologia*, 25 (1834), 318–41.

30. Jones, *Household*, p. 152.

31. PRO, SP1/22, ff. 66–88.

32. SRO, D1721/1/5, ff. 58–59.

33. PRO, E36/220/4 and 12 (pencil nos. 6 and 14).

34. SRO, D641/1/3/5.

35. The two years were 1511 and 1517. In 1510 Buckingham had a furious quarrel with the king and may have stayed away or been forbid-

den from attending the court in 1511 on that account. See Chapter 3. The reasons for his absence in 1517 are unknown.

36. SRO, D641/1/3/7a; D641/1/3/8.

37. PRO, SP1/22, ff. 70d–86d; SRO, D1721/1/5, ff. 81–103.

38. L&P, Henry VIII, vol. III (1), 370, 412.

39. Ibid., 1284 (p. 492), 1285 (p. 502).

40. Ibid., 1284 (p. 492); SRO, D1721/1/4A/27, f. 9.

41. L&P, Henry VIII, vol. III (1), 1284 (p. 492); CSP, Venice (London, 1862–1910), vol. III, 50 (pp. 15–20).

42. CSP, Venice, vol. III, 50 (p. 20).

43. Ibid., 106.

44. PRO, E36/220, mm. 21–22 (pencil nos. 23–24).

45. PRO, SP1/22, ff. 74, 78d; E36/220, m. 21 (pencil no. 23).

46. T. B. Pugh, ed., The Marcher Lordships of South Wales, 1415–1536: Select Documents (Cardiff, 1963), p. 284. The instructions of 1504 are printed in toto on pp. 281–86. The original is SRO, D641/1/5/4.

47. PRO, E36/150.

48. Pugh, Marcher Lordships, p. 284.

49. Book of Information, f. 6, bound in SRO, D1721/1/6.

50. Ibid., ff. 9d–10d.

51. I. S. Leadam, "The Inquisition of 1517: Inclosures and Evictions," Transactions of the Royal Historical Society, New Series, 6 (1892), 187–88. Eric Kerridge has pointed out that the inquisitions contained allegations that had to be proved in a subsequent trial. However, there is independent evidence for Buckingham's enclosures in Gloucestershire. See sources listed in this chapter, nn. 54, 56–58; for a discussion of copyholding, see Chapter 5, n. 59.

52. L&P, Henry VIII, vol. I, 1157; vol. II (2), 3022.

53. Leadam, "Inquisition," pp. 187–88.

54. PRO, E36/150, ff. 19–20.

55. John Daunce was a leading civil servant and one of the outer circle of Henry VIII's councillors. He was appointed general surveyor in 1517. Since escheated lands were administered by the court of general survey, it is logical that the tenants petitioned him in this matter. G. R. Elton, The Tudor Revolution in Government (Cambridge, Eng., 1960), pp. 46 (n. 1), 51, 336.

56. PRO, SP1/22, f. 97.

57. VCH, Huntingdonshire, vol. II (London, 1932), p. 85.

58. VCH, Stafford, vol. V (London, 1959), p. 94.

59. Leadam, "Inquisition," p. 177.

60. W'min Abbey, 5470, f. 15b.

61. L&P, Henry VIII, vol. I, 1157. There are expenses for building at Thornbury in the accounts for 1508. PRO, SP1/22.

62. W. D. Simpson, "'Bastard Feudalism' and Later Castles," *Antiquaries Journal*, 26 (1946), p. 165.

63. Lawrence Stone, *The Crisis of the Aristocracy, 1558–1641* (Oxford, 1965), p. 217. Since the new castle incorporated the hall and chapel of the manor that had stood on the site, Thornbury was not, strictly speaking, built from scratch.

64. McFarlane, *Nobility*, p. 209.

65. Letter to Barbara J. Harris from A. D. K. Hawkyard, dated Jan. 11, 1968.

66. Letter to Barbara J. Harris from A. D. K. Hawkyard, dated Jan. 26, 1969.

67. *L&P, Henry VIII*, vol. V, 80 (36) for Basing; vol. XVII, 137 (54) for Titchfield Abbey; vol. VI, 105 (25) for Cowdray Park.

68. Stone, *Crisis*, p. 220.

69. Carole Rawcliffe, *The Staffords, Earls of Stafford and Dukes of Buckingham, 1394–1521* (Cambridge, Eng., 1978), p. 86; Stone, *Crisis*, p. 217.

70. The description of Thornbury that follows is based on PRO, E36/150, f. 19; Simpson, "Later Castles," pp. 165–70; and A. Pugin and A. W. Pugin, *Examples of Gothic Architecture* (London, 1836), vol. II, pp. 30–38.

71. *The Itinerary of John Leland, 1535–1543*, ed. Lucy Toulmin Smith (London, 1964), vol. V, pts. 9–11, p. 100.

72. Simpson, "Later Castles," p. 167.

73. Ibid., p. 168.

74. Lawrence Stone, *The Family, Sex and Marriage in England, 1500–1800* (London, 1977), pp. 253–54.

75. Simpson, "Later Castles," pp. 168–69.

76. Thomas Garner and Arthur Stratton, *The Domestic Architecture of England During the Tudor Period*, 2d ed. (London, 1929), pp. 1–2; H. Avray Tipping, *English Homes, Period I and II: Medieval and Early Tudor, 1066–1558* (London, 1937), pt. 2, p. xv.

77. Tipping, *English Homes*, pp. xxxix, xliv; Garner and Stratton, *Domestic Architecture*, pp. 12–15.

78. Tipping, *English Homes*, pp. xlii–xliii.

79. Garner and Stratton, *Domestic Architecture*, pp. 45–46.

80. Simpson, "Later Castles," p. 168.

81. PRO, SP1/22, ff. 66–88.

82. Rawcliffe, *The Staffords*, p. 137.

83. PRO, E36/220, m. 25 (pencil no. 27).

84. PRO, E36/150, f. 22.

85. Rawcliffe, *The Staffords*, p. 137.

86. PRO, SP1/22, ff. 70d–71.

87. PRO, E36/220, mm. 21–22 (pencil nos. 23–24).

88. Ibid., m. 28 (pencil no. 30).

89. *L&P, Henry VIII*, vol. III (2), 1284 (p. 495).

90. PRO, SP1/22, ff. 70d, 73, 78d; E36/220, mm. 6, 18, 24 (pencil nos. 8, 20, 26).

91. *Philanthropy in England 1480–1660* (New York, 1959), p. 343; Jones, *Household*, pp. 188–90.

92. SRO, D1721/1/5, ff. 46, 58.

93. *L&P, Henry VIII*, vol. III (1), 1277; see J. S. Brewer, *The Reign of Henry VIII from His Accession to the Death of Wolsey*, ed. James Gairdner (London, 1884), vol. I, p. 386, n. 2, for full text of letter from Hopkins to Buckingham.

94. *L&P, Henry VIII*, vol. III (1), 1285 (pp. 502–3).

95. Brewer, *Reign of Henry VIII*, p. 386, n. 2.

96. Jordan, *Philanthropy*, p. 343.

97. PRO, SP1/22, f. 82.

98. *L&P, Henry VIII*, vol. I, 5289, 5293.

99. R. Bigland, *Historical Collections Relating to the County of Gloucester* (London, 1791–92), vol. I, p. 537.

100. Edward Purnell, *Magdalene College* (London, 1904), pp. 5–6.

101. Starkey, "Age of the Household," p. 255.

102. Household book in *Archaeologia*, 25 (1834), 321–23. For Anthony and Robert Poyntz, see *DNB*, vol. XVI, p. 277; for Sir William Kingston, see *DNB*, vol. XI, pp. 186–87; for Maurice Berkeley, see GEC, vol. II, p. 135; for James Berkeley, see John Smyth of Nibley, *The Berkeley Manuscripts: Lives of the Berkeleys*, ed. Sir John Maclean (Gloucester, 1883), vol. II, p. 177; for Richard Berkeley, see ibid., vol. II, pp. 180–81, 200, 203.

103. For Boughey, see Walter Chetwynd, "Collections for a History of Pirehall Hundred," *Collections for a History of Staffordshire*, William Salt Society, New Series, vol. XII (London, 1909), p. 197, notes; for Partesoil, see Rawcliffe, *The Staffords*, p. 203, CCR, *Henry VIII* (London, 1955, 1963), vol. II, 882, and *L&P, Henry VIII*, vol. I, 835; for Kemys, see Pugh, *Marcher Lordships*, pp. 291–93.

104. SRO, D641/1/2/198 (Poyntz); D641/1/2/82–94, and D641/1/2/6 (Boughey); PRO, SC6/Henry 7/1665 (Kemys).

105. Julian Cornwall has given a figure of 1 percent. "The Early Tudor Gentry," *Economic History Review*, Second Series, 17, no. 3 (April 1965), 457. Hoskins has given one of 2–3 percent. *Age of Plunder*, p. 56. J. P. Cooper has estimated that in all of England there were about 250 knights between 1509 and 1514, and 200 between 1519 and 1526. "The Social Distribution of Land and Men in England, 1436–1700," *Economic History Review*, Second Series, 20, no. 3 (1967), 422–23.

106. PRO, E101/518/5, pt. 1.

107. See above, Chapter 3.

108. PRO, SP1/29, ff. 182–83.

109. SRO, D641/1/3/9; PRO, E101/631/20, m. 19. The men were William Bedell, Sebastian Boughey, John Corbet, Thomas Denton, Thomas Leweth, Hugh Marvyn, John ap Morgan, Thomas ap Morgan, James Newell, Edward Osborne, Walter Vaughan, and William Wodegate.

110. The exception was Boughey, but his uncle Hugh held an estate office in Staffordshire (see n. 104 above). See Appendixes A and B for further information on these men.

111. BL, Add'l Mss., 40,859B; SRO, D641/1/3/8.

112. Ibid. The households of other late medieval magnates were organized in much the same way as Buckingham's. Jones, *Household*; F. R. H. DuBoulay, *An Age of Ambition* (New York, 1970), pp. 109–11.

113. J. R. Lander, *Conflict and Stability in Fifteenth-Century England* (London, 1969), p. 30.

114. See Appendix A. In an appendix entitled "Duke Edward's Councillors," Rawcliffe has included a list of 15 lawyers and administrators of justice (*The Staffords*, pp. 227–31); her list of administrative staff includes 2 lawyers. I have omitted 5 of these men from my list of lawyers who served as Buckingham's councillors or household servants: John Estrange, Humphrey Henry, Richard Littleton, Sir Walter Luke, and Thomas Stephens. I have seen no evidence indicating that Henry was a lawyer. Luke held a position as an estate official; I have seen no evidence that he was a councillor or a member of the household. The three other men, Estrange, Littleton, and Stephens, served Buckingham as itinerant justices in Wales. The evidence does not support the assumption that all men who worked for him in that capacity were part of his permanent council or staff. Finally, I have found evidence that William Walwyn was a lawyer and therefore have included him in my list.

115. Rawcliffe, *The Staffords*, pp. 91–92.

116. Brewer, *Reign of Henry VIII*, p. 386, n. 2.

117. See Appendix A.

118. Ibid.

119. Rawcliffe, *The Staffords*, p. 161.

120. See Appendix B.           121. *The Staffords*, p. 92.

122. See Appendix A.           123. *The Staffords*, p. 161.

124. Lander, *Conflict and Stability*, p. 169; McFarlane, *Nobility*, p. 115; Robin Jeffs, "The Poynings-Percy Dispute: An Example of the Interplay of Open Strife and Legal Action in the Fifteenth Century," *Bulletin of the Institute of Historical Research*, 34, no. 90 (Nov. 1961), 163.

125. Stone, *Crisis*, pp. 240–42.

126. Rawcliffe, *The Staffords*, pp. 164–65.

127. "The Common Lawyers in Pre-Reformation England," *Transactions of the Royal Historical Society*, Fifth Series, 18 (1968), 148–49; Eric Ives, "The Reputation of the Common Lawyers in English Society, 1450–1550," *University of Birmingham Historical Journal*, 7 (1959–60), 159–60; on this subject, also see Carole Rawcliffe, "Baronial Councils in the Later Middle Ages," in *Patronage, Pedigree and Power in Later Medieval England*, ed. Charles Ross (Totowa, N. J., 1979), pp. 90–91. The bishops were as likely to employ lawyers as were the secular peers (Heal, p. 81).

128. Rawcliffe, *The Staffords*, p. 168.

129. Ibid., p. 248.

130. PRO, Sta Cha 2/26/386.

131. Pugh, *Marcher Lordships*, p. 296.

132. PRO, Sta Cha 2/23/111.

133. Buckingham probably exaggerated Russell's low social origins. Russell had already owned land worth £30 or £40 per annum before he inherited his father's lands in 1516. His family belonged to the minor gentry. PRO, Sta Cha 2/23/111, 2/26/386; Pugh, *Marcher Lordships*, p. 296.

134. PRO, Sta Cha 2/26/386.

135. BL, Add'l Mss., 40,859B. In this document Buckingham acknowledged receiving £281 11s 11½d from Russell.

136. SRO, D641/1/3/6.

137. Book of Information, f. 18, bound in SRO, D1721/1/6.

138. Ibid., f. 18.

139. Ibid., f. 6d; SRO, D1721/1/6.

140. Rawcliffe, *The Staffords*, p. 167.

141. PRO, SP1/22, f. 104.

142. Henry Ellis, *Original Letters Illustrative of English History*, Third Series (London, 1846), vol. I, pp. 223–24. This is a reprint of BL, Cotton Mss., Titus, B.1, f. 171. It is calendared in *L&P, Henry VIII*, vol. III (1), 1070.

143. Ellis, *Letters*, vol. I, p. 224.

144. The cofferer received the entire net income from the duke's estates in the first instance and disbursed it as necessary to other household officials, particularly the treasurer of the household and the master of the wardrobe. His account recorded these transfers of funds within the household, as well as actual outlays.

145. Buckingham's household accounts ran from Apr. 1 to Mar. 31 until 1517 and from Oct. 1 to Sept. 30 after that. In this book I will refer to a fiscal year by the year in which it terminates. Thus 1504 means the fiscal year that ran from Apr. 1, 1503, to Mar. 31, 1504. For 1517, the year

the accounting system changed, there are accounts for the transitional period Apr. 1 to Sept. 30.

The table summarizes the amounts spent in household and wardrobe in 1504 and in 1517–20, and estimates the duke's total expenditures in 1504, in the last six months of 1517, in 1518, in 1519, and in 1520. It also includes a household account for the full year ending Sept. 1517 and a wardrobe account for the full year ending Mar. 1517 to give a further idea of the annual expenses in those two departments. These have not been added to form a composite figure, since they are from different accounting periods. Rawcliffe gives slightly higher figures for the expenses of the household in 1518–19 (*The Staffords*, p. 134). She has included payments to the duke's creditors, which were listed after total expenses. The differences are relatively small (£101 in 1518, £61 in 1519, and £109 in 1520) and do not affect the conclusions I have drawn from these accounts.

146. PRO, SP1/22, ff. 66–88.

147. PRO, E36/220.

148. Since the expenses listed in the cofferer's accounts are only a small fraction of the total annual expenditure and do not change nearly so much as those of the household and the wardrobe, I do not think too much distortion is involved in adding the figure of 1508 to the household and wardrobe expenses of 1504 to approximate the total for 1504, or in adding that of 1521 to the household and wardrobe expenses of 1517–20. For 1517 I have halved the estimate of the cofferer's annual expense for 1521 to £599 17s since we are dealing there with only six months. No claim of exactitude is made for this method, but it allows the closest approach to an estimate of Buckingham's annual expenditure.

149. Doubling the figure for Buckingham's expenses for the last six months of 1517 suggests an annual expenditure of £3,879 10s; the figure of £6,247 15s is about 60 percent larger. The annual estimate for 1517 is very much in the range of both estimates for 1504.

150. SRO, D641/1/3/8; BL, Add'l Mss., 40,859B (1504); Royal and King Collection Mss., 14B. XXVB (1518). The household book of the fifth earl of Northumberland allocated £144 17s 8d in 1512, considerably less than the expenditure of his brother-in-law, the third duke of Buckingham. Whether he actually kept his expenses to that amount is unknown. *The Earl of Northumberland's Household Book* began in 1512 (London, 1770); see p. 157.

151. SRO, D641/1/3/7a (1504); D641/1/3/9 (1517).

152. BL, Royal and King Collection Mss., 14B. XXXVC.

153. Ibid.

154. Ibid. and Royal and King Collection Mss., 14B. XXXVB.

155. Ibid.

156. HMC, *Seventh Report* (London, 1879), Appendix, p. 584.

157. *L&P, Henry VIII*, vol. III (1), 1285 (p. 499). Most noblemen paid their daughters' dowries in installments since they rarely had much cash at their disposal. As we have seen, Buckingham agreed to pay his daughter Elizabeth 2,000 marks in 1512. *L&P, Henry VIII*, vol. XII (2), 976. In May 1518 he still owed her husband £333 6s 8d, or one-fourth of the sum. A memorandum of Mar. 1520 states that Buckingham owed Bergavenny £666 13s 4d for Mary's marriage, but a memo of Nov. 1520 says he owed him £1,666 13s 4d. *L&P, Henry VIII*, vol. III (1), 1285, pp. 504–5. Since the earl of Westmorland was Buckingham's ward, the duke did not have to pay a dowry for Catherine's marriage to him.

158. *L&P, Henry VIII*, vol. III (1), 412.

159. *Rutland Papers*, ed. William Jerdan, Camden Society, vol. XXI (London, 1842), p. 29.

*Chapter Five*

1. This chapter contains material from my article "Landlords and Tenants in the Later Middle Ages: The Buckingham Estates," which first appeared in *Past and Present*, no. 43 (May 1969), 146–50.

2. PRO, E36/150 and E36/181; BL, Add'l Mss., 25,294. These are all copies of the survey of Buckingham's lands made by Magnus and Walwyn in 1521. E36/150 is the most descriptive and E36/181 the most detailed in terms of analyzing the income of each property.

3. I have arrived at this figure by comparing the income for each property listed in the three extant copies of the valor of 1521. This figure does not include the judicial revenues from the Welsh marches, which were not part of the regular annual income. (See Chapter 2, n. 64).

4. Barry Coward, *The Stanleys, Lords Stanley and Earls of Derby, 1385–1672: The Origins, Wealth, and Power of a Landowning Family*, Chetham Society, Third Series, vol. XXX (Manchester, 1983), p. 186.

5. J. M. W. Bean, *The Estates of the Percy Family, 1416–1537* (Oxford, 1958), p. 140.

6. For example, the lands of Henry Courtenay, Marquess of Exeter, were worth a minimum of £3,000; those of Thomas Manners, first earl of Rutland, £2,600; those of Thomas Howard, second duke of Norfolk, £2,241 net; those of George Talbot, earl of Shrewsbury, £1,735; and those of George Neville, Lord Bergavenny, £1,622. See H. J. Miller, "The Early Tudor Peerage, 1485–1547" (London University master's thesis, 1950), p. 134, and *L&P, Henry VIII*, vol. XIII (2), 454, for Courtenay; Lawrence Stone, *Family and Fortune: Studies in Aristocratic Finance in the Sixteenth and Seventeenth Centuries* (Oxford, 1973), p. 167, for Manners; R. Virgoe,

"The Recovery of the Howards in East Anglia, 1485–1529," in *Wealth and Power in Tudor England: Essays Presented to S. T. Bindoff*, ed. E. W. Ives, R. J. Knecht, and J. J. Scarisbrick (London, 1978), p. 18, for Howard; G. W. Bernard, *The Power of the Early Tudor Nobility: A Study of the Fourth and Fifth Earls of Shrewsbury* (Totowa, N.J., 1985), p. 143, for Talbot; and *L&P, Henry VIII*, vol. III (1), 1291, for Neville.

    7. See Chapter 2, pp. 38–41.

    8. See Chapter 1.

    9. T. B. Pugh, ed., *The Marcher Lordships of South Wales, Select Documents* (Cardiff, 1963), pp. 239, n. 6, and 239–42.

    10. Ibid., p. 242, n. 2.

    11. See Chapter 2, pp. 42–43.

    12. The administrative structure on Buckingham's estates was much like that of other great estates, lay and ecclesiastical, in the later middle ages. See, for example, Joel T. Rosenthal, "The Estates and Finances of Richard, Duke of York (1411–1460)," in *Studies in Medieval and Renaissance History*, ed. William M. Bowsky (Lincoln, Nebr., 1965), pp. 122, 161–72; John Hatcher, *Rural Economy and Society in the Duchy of Cornwall, 1300–1500* (Cambridge, Eng., 1970), ch. 2; and Lawrence Stone, *The Crisis of the Aristocracy* (Oxford, 1965), p. 286.

    13. PRO, SP1/29, ff. 173–83.

    14. For other examples of this attitude, see Rosenthal, "Estates," p. 171; Hatcher, *Rural Economy*, pp. 47–48; Christopher Dyer, *Lords and Peasants in a Changing Society: The Estates of the Bishop of Worcester, 680–1540* (Cambridge, Eng., 1980), pp. 156–59; and K. B. McFarlane, *The Nobility of Later Medieval England* (Oxford, 1973), p. 107.

    15. These figures are compiled from PRO, E36/150 and E36/181, and *L&P, Henry VIII*, vol. III (2), 3695.

    16. *Herbage and pannage* refers to the natural pasture of land as a form of property distinct from the land itself; *agistment* refers to the right to the herbage of a forest.

    17. Book of Information, f. 5d bound in SRO, D1721/1/6.

    18. W'min Abbey, 5470, f. 45.

    19. A large number of the rolls of these courts are on deposit at the Stafford Record Office; see D641/1/4A/22–26; D641/1/4C/11A; D641/1/4K/4; D641/1/4L/1–2; D641/1/4P/2–3; D641/4Q/1; D641/1/4U/1; D641/1/4U/3–6; D641/1/4W/4–5; D641/1/4X/22–23; and D641/1/4X/28–29. Each roll contains the record of a number of sessions of a particular manorial court.

    20. Book of Information, f. 5d, in SRO, D1721/1/6.

    21. Ibid., f. 11d.        22. Ibid., f. 1.

    23. W'min Abbey, 5470, f. 4.      24. Ibid., f. 15d.

25. PRO, E36/181, mm. 15, 56.

26. PRO, SC6/Henry 7/1076.

27. The income in 1504 was £18 (PRO, SC6/Henry 8/1476, m. 3d); in 1521 it was £22 16s (PRO, SC6/Henry 8/5808, m. 2d).

28. PRO, SC6/Henry 7/454; PRO, SC6/Henry 8/2756, m. 6.

29. Pugh, *Marcher Lordships*, pp. 264–65; PRO, SC6/Henry 7/1665, m. 10.

30. Pugh, *Marcher Lordships*, p. 285.

31. SRO, D641/1/2/259, m. 3 (1499); PRO, SC6/Henry 8/863, m. 1d (1521).

32. Pugh, *Marcher Lordships*, p. 282.

33. Petition and answer printed ibid., pp. 286–87 (quote, p. 287).

34. The *primo recognito* for the individual lordships: Brecon lordship and town, £506 13s 4d; Hay, English and Welsh, £20; Cantref Selyf, £66 13s 4d; Penkelly, English and Welsh, £33 6s 8d; Kington and Huntingdon, £40; Newport, £171 13s. PRO, E36/150, f. 25, 55, 58–62; Pugh, *Marcher Lordships*, p. 147.

35. *Archaeologia*, 25 (1834), 321.

36. PRO, E36/220.

37. Pugh, *Marcher Lordships*, p. 262.

38. PRO, SC6/Henry 7/1075, m. 8.

39. BL, Egerton Rolls, 2203; SRO, D641/1/4U/1, m. 1.

40. PRO, E36/150, mm. 25, 112.

41. These documents are printed in Pugh, *Marcher Lordships*, pp. 262–75, 281–86. Footnotes are to his edition. The originals, which I have examined, are SRO, D641/1/5/3, and SRO, D641/1/5/4.

42. SRO, D1721/1/6, is the book compiled in 1515–16; W'min Abbey, 5470, that compiled in 1518–19.

43. Pugh, *Marcher Lordships*, p. 271.

44. Ibid., pp. 266, 270, 285.

45. Ibid., p. 283.

46. Ibid., p. 283.

47. Ibid., pp. 265, 271, 285.

48. Ibid., p. 266.

49. Ibid., p. 282.

50. Ibid., pp. 262, 268.

51. Ibid., pp. 268, 272, 282.

52. Ibid., p. 285.

53. Ibid., p. 283.

54. For further information on Buckingham's efforts to store and catalogue his records, see Carole Rawcliffe, "A Tudor Nobleman as Archivist: The Papers of Edward, Third Duke of Buckingham," *Journal of Society of Archivists*, 5, no. 5 (1976), 294–300.

55. PRO, SC6/Henry 7/1075, m. 7d.

56. Book of Information, f. 8, in SRO, D1721/1/6.

57. Ibid., f. 5.

58. W'min Abbey, 5470, f. 16d.

59. Copyhold is a form of land tenure that evolved in the fourteenth and fifteenth centuries from land held in villeinage. The custom by which the tenant held the land and his obligations in return for tenure were recorded in the manorial court roll. The tenant received a copy, which filled many of the functions of a deed for freehold; hence the term "copyhold."

60. Pugh, *Marcher Lordships*, pp. 273, 285.

61. Walter Parker paid £40 for his manumission. Buckingham returned the money to him in 1519. *L&P, Henry VIII*, vol. III (1), 1285 (p. 498).

62. See, for example, Frances G. Davenport, *The Economic Development of a Norfolk Manor, 1086–1565* (New York, 1967; first published 1906), pp. 70–73, 88–97; Dyer, *Lords and Peasants*, pp. 120, 141–42, 269–75; and Barbara Harvey, *Westminster Abbey and Its Estates in the Middle Ages* (Oxford, 1977), ch. 10.

63. Pugh, *Marcher Lordships*, p. 268.

64. Ibid., p. 275.

65. Book of Information, f. 17, SRO, D1721/1/6.

66. W'min Abbey, 5470, ff. 3d–4.

67. Ibid., f. 46d.

68. *Ballads from Manuscripts*, ed. Frederick J. Furnivale (London, 1868–72), vol. I, p. 12.

69. Ibid., p. 12.

70. PRO, E36/150.

71. Pugh, *Marcher Lordships*, p. 275. The feodary was an official who collected dues, such as relief, owed by tenants who held their land by knight service.

72. Ibid., p. 269.

73. Ibid., p. 274. *Ringild* was a Welsh term for a manorial official comparable to the English bailiff.

74. Ibid., p. 267.

75. Ibid., p. 284.

76. Ibid., p. 285.

77. Ibid., p. 285.

78. Ibid., p. 283.

79. W'min Abbey, 5470, f. 32.

80. Pugh, *Marcher Lordships*, p. 282.

81. Ibid., pp. 263, 274.

82. PRO, E36/150, f. 25.

83. The accounts of Buckingham's estate officials were not designed to show true profit and loss but to calculate what the official concerned owed his master. This type of account is known as "charge-discharge" account. The charge side (i.e., what the official is charged with) included money due from previous years, "arrears," as well as money

that should have been collected during the year of the account. It was not, therefore, in any sense a statement of actual receipts or current annual profit. The discharge side showed all the officer's expenses, any salaries he paid, and the money he had given to the duke's receivers or cofferer. If the discharge side did not equal the charge side, there would be a list explaining who still owed the officer money. In Wales, the accounts included revenues from the Great Sessions in years when they were held. The charge side showed the fine for redeeming the sessions and/or fines levied on those who had failed to attend the court; the discharge side would show the sums that had not actually been collected. See, for example, PRO, SC6/Henry 8/4775.

There are two types of accounts: the reeve's or bailiff's and the receiver's. The former shows the accounts of an individual manor, the latter those of the entire receivership. From the point of view of determining the actual income of an estate or receivership, the most significant item is the *liberacio denariorum* or the amount of cash actually turned over to the receiver by the bailiff or by the receiver to the duke's cofferer. The total *liberacio denariorum* in the receiver's account is the closest one can come to determining the actual cash income of a receivership in a given year. It is a much more accurate indication of the money available to the lord for his household and other expenses than the totals derived by adding up cash liveries indicated on the bailiffs' and reeves' accounts, since the receiver spent a substantial portion of the money he collected from individual manors on wages, annuities, and repairs. However, the total of the receivers' *liberacio denariorum* does not indicate the annual profit of the estates. First, the money turned over to the lord might well include payments of arrears from previous years. Second, the cost of annuities would have to be added to the cash liveries, since annuities cannot reasonably be regarded as administrative overhead or estate charges. R. R. Davies, "Baronial Accounts, Income and Arrears in the Later Middle Ages," *Economic History Review*, Second Series, 21, no. 2 (Aug. 1968), 217.

84. On arrears, see A. J. Pollard, "Estate Management in the Later Middle Ages: The Talbots and Whitchurch, 1383–1525," *Economic History Review*, Second Series, 25, no. 4 (Nov. 1972), 563–65; Davies, "Baronial Accounts," pp. 220–29.

85. McFarlane, *Nobility*, p. 178.

86. Pugh, *Marcher Lordships*, pp. 281–82.

87. PRO, LR12/9/275, m. 1.

88. BL, Egerton Rolls, 2193, m. 4 (1496).

89. PRO, SC6/Henry 7/1665, m. 10.

90. SRO, D641/1/2/294, m. 1.

91. PRO, SC6/Henry 7/1076, m. 14.

92. PRO, SC6/Henry 8/4224.    93. SRO, D641/1/2/88.

94. BL, Egerton Rolls, 2207.    95. SRO, D641/1/2/248.

96. BL, Egerton Rolls, 2200.

97. PRO, SC6/Henry 8/4775, m. 9.

98. PRO, SC6/Henry 8/5853, m. 5.

99. SRO, D641/1/2/79, m. 9.    100. SRO, D641/1/2/88.

101. SRO, D641/1/2/96, m. 1.    102. PRO, SC6/Henry 8/5804.

103. Eric Kerridge, "Movement of Rent, 1540–1640," *Economic History Review*, Second Series, 6 (1953–54), 19.

104. Coward, *The Stanleys*, p. 22.

105. Pugh, *Marcher Lordships*, pp. 265, 270, 285.

106. Ibid., p. 264.

107. Ibid., pp. 264–70.

108. For a discussion of copyhold tenures, see Mildred Campbell, *The English Yeoman* (New Haven, 1942), pp. 120ff.

109. W'min Abbey, 5470, f. 44.

110. Ibid., f. 48.

111. Pugh, *Marcher Lordships*, p. 265.

112. Ibid., p. 270.

113. PRO, SC6/Henry 8/4775, f. 1d.

114. Pugh, *Marcher Lordships*, p. 272.

115. Ibid., pp. 274–75.    116. Ibid., p. 270.

117. Ibid., p. 274.    118. Ibid., p. 273.

119. For Tillington, see SRO, D641/1/2/80, m. 6 (1499); PRO, SC6/Henry 8/5804, m. 9 (1521). For Bayhall, Dacherst, and the mills of Tonbridge, see SRO, D641/1/2/27, mm. 10d–11 (1499); PRO, SC6/Henry 8/5795, mm. 1–2. For Edenbridge, see SRO, D641/1/2/27, m. 11d (1499); PRO, SC6/Henry 7/1076, m. 12d (1506).

120. W'min Abbey, 5470, f. 54d; PRO, SC6/Henry 7/462, mm. 1d–2.

121. SRO, D641/1/4A/27, m. 9.

122. W'min Abbey, 5470, f. 17d; PRO, SC6/Henry 8/863, m. 4d.

123. Pugh, *Marcher Lordships*, p. 275; PRO, SC6/Henry 7/1075, m. 6d.

124. W'min Abbey, 5470, f. 3d.    125. PRO, E36/181.

126. PRO, E36/150, f. 15.    127. PRO, E36/150, f. 53.

128. *L&P, Henry VIII*, grants listed in vols. IV–XXI.

129. Pugh, *Marcher Lordships*, pp. 264, 270.

130. Ibid., p. 264.    131. Ibid., p. 274.

132. Ibid., p. 273.    133. Ibid., p. 282.

134. W'min Abbey 5470, ff. 56b–57.

135. Ibid., f. 56.

136. SRO, D641/1/2/76, m. 5; D641/1/2/77, m. 5; D641/1/2/78, m. 4d; D641/1/2/79, m. 4d; D641/1/2/80, m. 5.

137. SRO, D641/1/2/192, m. 7d; D641/1/2/193, m. 5d; D641/1/2/194, m. 6d; D641/1/2/195, m. 5; D641/1/2/196, m. 5d; D641/1/2/197, m. 7d; D641/1/2/198, m. 5; D641/1/2/199, m. 4.

138. SRO, D641/1/2/199, m. 3d; D641/1/2/200, m. 5.

139. SRO, D641/1/2/192, m. 6d; D641/1/2/193, m. 7d; D641/1/2/194, m. 8d; D641/1/2/195, m. 7; D641/1/2/196, m. 7d; D641/1/2/197, m. 10d; D641/1/2/198, m. 6d; D641/1/2/199, m. 6; D641/1/2/201, m. 7d.

140. SRO, D641/1/2/192, m. 3d; D641/1/2/193, m. 3d; D641/1/2/194, m. 4; D641/1/2/195, m. 3; D641/1/2/196, m. 3; D641/1/2/197, m. 4d; D641/1/2/198, m. 3d; D641/1/2/199, m. 2d; D641/1/2/200, m. 3d.

141. Pollard suggests that the personal element in management had only a marginal effect on increases and decreases in revenues. "Estate Management," p. 563.

142. Peter H. Ramsey, *The Price Revolution in Sixteenth-Century England* (London, 1971), p. 4; R. B. Outhwaite, *Inflation in Tudor and Early Stuart England* (London, 1969), pp. 9–15.

143. Kerridge, "Movement of Rent," pp. 24–25, 28.

144. Ian Blanchard, "Population Change, Enclosure, and the Early Tudor Economy," *Economic History Review*, Second Series, 23, no. 3 (Dec. 1970), 434–41.

145. Pollard, "Estate Management," pp. 563, 565, n. 2; Bean, *Estates*, pp. 48, 67–68; Dyer, *Lords and Peasants*, ch. 13; Bernard, *Power*, p. 144.

146. Mervyn James, "The First Earl of Cumberland (1493–1542) and the Decline of Northern Feudalism," *Northern History*, 1 (1966), 53–57.

147. Ramsey, *Price Revolution*, p. 79; Outhwaite, *Inflation*, pp. 10–13.

148. Blanchard, "Population Change," pp. 435–41.

149. Pugh, *Marcher Lordships*, pp. 266, 270, 274–75, 284–85.

150. Ibid., pp. 273–74, 283.

151. Ibid., p. 266.

152. Book of Information, f. 7d, in SRO, D1721/1/6.

153. Ibid., f. 11.

154. PRO, SC6/Henry 7/1077, m. 10 (1507); SRO, D641/1/2/89, m. 11; D641/1/90, m. 8d.

155. Book of evidence collected by William Popley, ff. 22–24, bound in SRO, D1721/1/6; D641/1/2/205, m. 9d.

156. PRO, E36/220, m. 26; PRO, E36/150, ff. 26, 59, 112, 115.

157. PRO, E36/150, f. 59.

158. Ibid.

159. The figure of £66 9s 7d is based on the estimates for individual

manors appearing in PRO, E36/181, and that of £50 on examining all the rents for these rights in all the extant reeves' and bailiffs' accounts. The number of woods, forests, and parks is taken from PRO, E36/150.

160. Pugh, *Marcher Lordships*, p. 266.

161. Ibid., p. 266.

162. Ibid., p. 271.

163. Ibid., pp. 272–73.

164. Book of Information, f. 19, in SRO, D1721/1/6.

165. PRO, E36/150, f. 67.

166. The surveyors of 1521 listed recent woodsales in their reports, partly because in many cases the wood had not been cut down and the king could abrogate the bargain if he desired. It is not specific about dates. PRO, E36/150.

167. Ibid., f. 111.

168. Ibid., f. 67.

169. W'min Abbey, 5470, f. 4.

170. Pugh, *Marcher Lordships*, p. 268.

171. Ibid., p. 273.

172. Ibid., pp. 268, 271–72, 273.

173. Ibid., pp. 254–56.

174. BL, Egerton Rolls, 2203; SRO, 641/1/4U/1, m. 1.

175. See Chapter 1.

176. Brecon Lordship, £1,333 6s; Brecon Villa, £72 15s; Newport, £500; Hay Burgus, £13 7s; Hay Welsh, £83 12s; Cantref Selyf, £66 13s; Penkelly, £33 7s. PRO, E36/181, mm. 55–61.

177. SRO, D1721/1/1, 378–79.

178. BL, Lansdowne Mss., 127, f. 29d.

179. Figure compiled from PRO, SC6/Henry 8/5841 (general circuit), SC6/Henry 8/5804 (Stafford receivership), SC6/Henry 8/5795 (Kent and Surrey), SC6/Henry 8/5819 (Gloucester receivership).

180. For York and Wales, I have added the figure closest to 1521: PRO, SC6/Henry 7/1029 (York, 1508); SC6/Henry 8/4776 (Brecon, Hay, Huntingdon, 1519); BL, Egerton Rolls, 2207 (Newport, 1513); Egerton Rolls, 2195 (Cantrecelly, Penkelly, Alexanderstone, 1517), Egerton Rolls, 2200 (Caus, 1517).

181. See table in Chapter 4 for Buckingham's expenses.

182. PRO, SC6/Henry 7/1476, m. 3; PRO, SC/Henry 8/863.

183. PRO, E36/181.

184. SRO, D641/3/5, dorsal side.

185. Pugh, *Marcher Lordships*, p. 247.

186. PRO, SC6/Henry 8/5841; PRO, E36/220, m. 5. The valor of 1521 estimated £42 10s routine repairs in the general circuit. PRO, E36/181.

187. PRO, E36/150, f. 55.

188. Pugh, *Marcher Lordships*, pp. 283–84.

189. PRO, E36/150, f. 24.   190. Ibid., f. 58.

191. Ibid., ff. 59, 62.   192. Ibid., f. 111.

193. Ibid., f. 38.   194. Ibid., f. 138.

195. Ibid., f. 65.   196. Ibid., f. 115.

197. Ibid., f. 127.

198. Book of Information, f. 5d, in SRO, 1721/1/6.

199. PRO, E36/150, f. 31.   200. Ibid., f. 71.

201. W'min Abbey, 5470, f. 44.   202. PRO, E36/150, f. 68.

203. Ibid., f. 133.

204. Book of Information, 11d, in SRO, 1721/1/6.

205. PRO, E36/150, f. 48.

206. SRO, D641/3/7.

207. SRO, D641/3/9.

208. SRO, D641/3/5 (1500); BL, Add'l Mss., 40,859B (1504). The recently published Lisle letters, edited so magnificently by Muriel St. Clare Byrne, show that this method of stretching resources was a common one among early Tudor nobles.

209. PRO, SP1/22, f. 77; BL, Royal and King Collection, 14B. XXXVE, ff. 3–5, are bonds of the duke's servants to Robert Amadas, citizen of London, and Thomas Dowcra, prior of St. John's of Jerusalem.

210. *L&P, Henry VIII*, vol. III (1), 1285 (p. 505).

211. Ibid., vol. V, 1715.

212. Ibid., vol. III (1), 1285 (pp. 501, 502, 505).

213. Ibid., vol. V, 1715.

214. This figure was compiled from documents calendared *L&P, Henry VIII*, vol. III (1), 1285 (pp. 501, 505).

215. Ibid., 1285 (pp. 498–99, 501–2, 504–5).

216. Ibid., 1285 (pp. 504–5). The memorandum for March has no date on it, but Buckingham was at Bletchingley in March 1520. Ibid., 1285 (p. 492); SRO, D641/1/4A/27, m. 9.

217. *L&P, Henry VIII*, vol. III (1), 1285 (p. 502).

218. *Statutes of the Realm*, vol. III (London, 1817), pp. 276–78.

219. According to the valor of 1521, the annual value of the manor was £23 4s 2d. Normally, the sale value was figured at twenty times the annual value, and on this basis Sacheverell should have paid £464 3s 4d. See Stone, *Crisis*, p. 148, on the relation of annual value to sale value.

220. *L&P, Henry VIII*, vol. III (1), 1285 (p. 503); PRO, E36/150, ff. 115, 130.

221. *Statutes*, vol. III, pp. 273–76; PRO, E36/150, ff. 114, 118.

222. See Chapter 4.

*Chapter Six*

1. J. R. Lander, *Crown and Nobility, 1450–1509* (London, 1976), pp. 32–33.

2. See Chapter 5.

3. SRO, D641/1/3/5, D641/1/3/8, D641/1/3/9; K. B. McFarlane, *The Nobility of Later Medieval England* (Oxford, 1973), pp. 110–11; PRO, E101/631/20.

4. PRO, SP1/29, f. 183; E101/518/5, pt. 1; SRO, D641/1/6/4; William Dugdale, *The Baronage of England* (London, 1675), vol. I, p. 720. Also see Chapter 4 above.

5. These figures are compiled from PRO, E36/150 and E36/181, and from *L&P, Henry VIII*, vol. III (2), 3695.

6. *L&P, Henry VIII*, vol. III (2), 3695; SRO, D641/1/2/83; PRO, SC6/Henry 8/5853, m. 5; Carole Rawcliffe, *The Staffords, Earls of Stafford and Dukes of Buckingham* (Cambridge, Eng., 1978), pp. 207, 211. See Appendix B for the knights and gentlemen in this group.

7. For a perspective on the number of knights in Buckingham's affinity as a proportion of the total number of knights in England, see Chapter 4, n. 105.

8. See Appendix C.

9. Rawcliffe gives a list of Buckingham's annuitants. *The Staffords*, pp. 240–42. The only additional persons in this category I have discovered are Elizabeth Percy, who received £5 per annum (*L&P, Henry VIII*, vol. III (1), pp. 498, 504); Sir William Herbert, who received £10 (PRO, E36/220, f. 28); and William Tracy, treasurer of the duke's household in 1521, who received £2 (PRO, E36/220, f. 27).

10. PRO, SP1/29, ff. 180, 183.

11. Ibid., f. 183.

12. Ibid., f. 183; PRO, E36/220, f. 28. Although it is difficult to identify positively anyone with the common name of William Herbert, the recipient of Buckingham's pension was probably the William Herbert who became first earl of Pembroke of the second creation under Edward VI in 1551. Buckingham's accounts distinguish carefully between this William Herbert and Sir William Herbert of Troy (e.g., SRO, D641/1/3/9).

13. *Rolls of Parliament*, vol. VI, p. 245; *DNB*, vol. XIV, p. 566.

14. *DNB*, vol. XXI, p. 1063.

15. See Appendixes A, B, and C.

16. They were Sir Humphrey Coningsby, Sir Thomas Frowyck, and Willam Greville.

17. PRO, E101/631/120, ff. 19–20; SRO, D641/1/3/9.

18. Rawcliffe, *The Staffords*, p. 227.

19. On hospitality at Thornbury, see Chapter 4.

20. SRO, D641/1/3/9.

21. On Wriothesley, see Stanley Thomas Bindoff, *The House of Commons, 1509–1558* (London, 1982), vol. III, p. 664; on Dennis, Appendix B.

22. On Wadham, see PRO, *Lists and Indexes*, vol. IX, List of Sheriffs (London, 1898), pp. 51, 124, and *L&P, Henry VIII*, vol. I, 1159; on Walsh, see ibid., vol. IX, p. 51, and Samuel Rudder, *A New History of Gloucestershire* (Cirencester, 1779), p. 677.

23. PRO, SP1/22, f. 83.

24. Ibid., f. 66; on the Hungerfords, see Bindoff, *The Commons*, vol. II, pp. 409–12.

25. PRO, E36/220, m. 19.

26. *L&P, Henry VIII*, vol. III (2), p. 498; on the Guildfords, see Bindoff, *The Commons*, vol. II, pp. 262–65.

27. PRO, E36/220, m. 24.

28. Ibid., m. 10.

29. Ibid., m. 4; on Darrell, see Bindoff, *The Commons*, vol. II, pp. 18–19.

30. Lawrence Stone, *The Crisis of the Aristocracy, 1558–1641* (Oxford, 1965), pp. 204–5.

31. W'min Abbey, 5470, f. 39.

32. I have compiled the number of his servants from PRO, E36/150, E36/181, and SP1/29, ff. 173–82; and SRO, D641/1/3/8. The manred is taken from PRO, E36/150.

33. Stone, *Crisis*, p. 203.

34. For example, Buckingham had to call on Henry VII for help in collecting the fine for redeeming the sessions in Brecon. BL, Lansdowne Mss., 127, f. 29d. He had to obtain privy seals from the king when he wanted to punish the murderers of a burgess of Brecon. *L&P, Henry VIII*, vol. III (1), 1288 (3).

35. PRO, Sta Cha 2/19/223.

36. *L&P, Henry VIII*, vol. III (1), 1070.

37. Ibid., 1070.

38. PRO, E36/150, f. 64. Also see Chapter 3.

39. *CSP, Spanish* (London, 1862–83), supplement to vols. I and II, 8 (pp. 39–40).

40. Rawcliffe, *The Staffords*, pp. 244–51.

41. John Smyth of Nibley, *The Berkeley Manuscripts: Lives of the Berkeleys*, ed. Sir John Maclean (Gloucester, 1883), vol. II, pp. 206–7, 215. For Buckingham's visit to Berkeley, see *L&P, Henry VIII*, vol. III (1), 1285 (p. 499).

42. *Calendar of Inquisitions Post Mortem, Henry VII*, vol. II (London, 1915), 883, 931; vol. III (London, 1955), 34, 117.

43. Sir Bernard Burke, *Extinct Peerage*, new ed. (London, 1883), p. 32.

44. SRO, D1721/1/1, f. 378d.

45. Bedminster was part of the Gloucester receivership, and there are numerous accounts from this area during the minority and the early years of Buckingham's majority. Yet Bedminster does not appear in any of them. SRO, D641/1/2/192–202, 294; PRO, SC6/Henry 7/1075; the latest of these accounts is D641/1/2/204, for 1504.

46. *Rolls of Parliament*, vol. VI, p. 454.

47. *CPR, Henry VII* (London, 1914, 1916), vol. II, 626.

48. PRO, SP1/22, f. 94.

49. BL, Add'l Mss., 25,294, f. 1d; PRO, E36/150, f. 14.

50. *L&P, Henry VIII*, vol. III (1), 1070.

51. *VCH, Stafford*, vol. IV (London, 1958), p. 138, for Haughton; Dugdale, *Baronage*, vol. II, p. 132, for Send.

52. See genealogy, Appendix D, for a clarification of this relationship.

53. *L&P, Henry VIII*, vol. III (2), 2218.

54. In 1528 Upper Clatford was granted to Berners. Ibid., vol. IV (2), 3991 (15).

55. SRO, D641/1/6/4.

56. SRO, D1721/1/1, f. 428 or pfo. 222d (there are two systems of pagination in the first half of the manuscript). *DNB*, vol. XV, pp. 525–26.

57. SRO, D1721/1/1, ff. 363–67.

58. Bindoff, *The Commons*, vol. II, p. 553.

59. SRO, D641/1/2/199.

60. SRO, D1721/11, ff. 363–64.

61. John Bruce, "A Second Letter on the Court of Star Chamber," *Archaeologia*, 25 (1834), 374.

62. Ibid.

## Chapter Seven

1. For a discussion of the early Tudors' attitude and policy toward the nobility, see M. M. Condon, "Ruling Elites in the Reign of Henry VII," in *Patronage, Pedigree and Power in Later Medieval England*, ed. Charles Ross (Totowa, N.J., 1979), pp. 109–42; J. P. Cooper, "Retainers in Tudor England," in *Land, Men and Beliefs: Studies in Early-Modern History*, ed. G. E. Aylmer and J. S. Morrill (Ronceverte, W. Va., 1983), pp. 78–96; G. R. Elton, *Reform and Reformation: England, 1509–1558* (Cambridge, Mass., 1977); Mervyn E. James, *A Tudor Magnate and the Tudor State: Henry, Fifth Earl of Northumberland*, Borthwick Papers, no. 30 (York, 1966); J. R. Lander, *Conflict and Stability in Fifteenth-Century England* (London, 1969); Lander, *Crown and Nobility, 1450–1509* (London, 1976); D. M. Loades, *Politics and the Nation 1450–1660: Obedience, Resistance and Public Order* (Brighton, Eng., 1974); A. J. Slavin, *The Precarious Balance:*

*English Government and Society* (New York, 1973); Penry Williams, *The Tudor Regime* (Oxford, 1979).

2. Slavin, *Precarious Balance*, p. 94.

3. James, *Tudor Magnate*, pp. 17, 22–23.

4. For a discussion of the material in this and the following paragraph, see Condon, "Ruling Elites," pp. 109–42.

5. Ibid., p. 130.

6. Ibid., p. 115; Melvin J. Tucker, *The Life of Thomas Howard, Earl of Surrey and Second Duke of Norfolk, 1443–1524* (The Hague, 1964), p. 70.

7. On the statutes against retaining, see Cooper, "Retainers," pp. 81–82; William Huse Dunham, Jr., *Lord Hastings' Indentured Retainers 1461–83: The Lawfulness of Livery and Retaining Under the Yorkists and Tudors* (Hampden, Conn., 1970; originally pub. 1955), pp. 70–106; Lander, *Conflict and Stability*, pp. 182–83; Lander, *Crown and Nobility*, pp. 32–34; Loades, *Politics*, p. 123; James, *Tudor Magnate*, p. 5; R. L. Storey, *The Reign of Henry VII* (New York, 1968), pp. 151–56; Charles Ross, *Edward IV* (Berkeley, Calif., 1974), pp. 412–13.

8. 13 Richard II, stat. 3, c. 1; *Rolls of Parliament*, vol. III, p. 365.

9. 8 Edward IV, c. 2.

10. Storey (*Henry VII*, p. 154), Ross (*Edward IV*, p. 412), and Lander (*Crown and Nobility*, p. 34) express this view.

11. A. Cameron, "The Giving of Livery and Retaining in Henry VII's Reign," *Renaissance and Modern Studies*, 18 (1974), 22–23; *L&P, Henry VIII*, 2d ed., vol. I (2), 2053 (1).

12. Dunham, *Indentured Retainers*, pp. 92–99.

13. 19 Henry VII, c. 14.

14. Dunham, *Indentured Retainers*, pp. 92–99; Loades, *Politics*, p. 123; Lander, *Crown and Nobility*, p. 34; Condon, "Ruling Elites," p. 115.

15. Cameron, "Livery and Retaining," p. 34.

16. Bergavenny was punished for violating the statute of 1390. See Lander, *Crown and Nobility*, pp. 289–90, and Cameron, "Livery and Retaining," pp. 31–34, for a full account of the case. S. B. Chrimes, *Henry VII* (London, 1972), pp. 190–91, and Barry Coward, *The Stanleys, Lords Stanley and Earls of Derby 1385–1672: The Origins, Wealth, and Power of a Landowning Family*, Chetham Society, Third Series, vol. XXX (Manchester, 1983), p. 146, assert that the only prosecution of a peer for retaining was the case of Lord Bergavenny. However, Cameron notes indictments against Edward Grey, Lord Lisle; Henry, Lord Grey of Codnor; John Lord Grey of Wilton; Henry Percy, fifth earl of Northumberland; Edward Stafford, third duke of Buckingham; Lady Margaret Beaufort; John de Vere, thirteenth earl of Oxford; Thomas Stanley, second earl of Derby; George Talbot, fourth earl of Shrewsbury; and Henry Bourchier,

second earl of Essex. "Livery and Retaining," pp. 26–27. Cameron gives no indication of the outcome of these indictments except in the case of the earl of Northumberland, which was dismissed for lack of evidence. I have found no evidence that Buckingham was convicted or fined for illegal retaining during Henry VII's reign. Edward Courtenay, earl of Devon, was also fined for illegal retaining. BL, Lansdowne Mss., 160, f. 311.

17. R. Virgoe, "The Recovery of the Howards in East Anglia, 1485–1529," in *Wealth and Power in Tudor England: Essays Presented to S. T. Bindoff*, ed. E. W. Ives, R. J. Knecht, and J. J. Scarisbrick (London, 1978), p. 10 and n. 4.

18. On the subject of bonds and recognizances, see Lander, "Bonds, Coercion and Fear: Henry VII and the Peerage," in *Crown and Nobility*, pp. 267–300, and K. B. McFarlane, "Calendar of Close Rolls, Henry VII, 1500–1509," *English Historical Review*, 81 (Jan. 1966), 153–54. See also BL, Lansdowne Ms. 160, f. 311; C. J. Harrison, "The Petition of Edmund Dudley," *English Historical Review*, 87 (Jan. 1972), 82–99; B. Coward, "A 'Crisis of the Aristocracy' in the Sixteenth and Early Seventeenth Centuries? The Case of the Stanleys, Earls of Derby, 1504–1642," *Northern History*, 18 (1982), 63–64; and M. E. James, "The First Earl of Cumberland (1493–1542) and the Decline of Northern Feudalism," *Northern History*, 1 (1966), 51–52. On the use of bonds under Richard III, see Charles Ross, *Richard III* (Berkeley, Calif., 1981), pp. 180–81, and Lander, "Bonds," pp. 280–81. I find unconvincing G. W. Bernard's thesis that the bonds and recognizances Henry VII extracted from Richard, third earl of Kent, are "best seen as an attempt . . . to preserve rather than to destroy, Kent's patrimony." "The Fortunes of the Greys, Earls of Kent, in the Early Sixteenth Century," *Historical Journal*, 25, no. 3 (1982), 671–85 (quote from p. 676). M. M. Condon, "Ruling Elites," p. 112, and Felicity Heal, *Of Prelates and Princes: A Study of the Economic and Social Position of the Tudor Episcopate* (Cambridge, Eng., 1980), p. 94, point out that Henry was as ruthless in extracting fines, bonds, and recognizances from bishops as from nobles. In 1506 James Stanley, bishop of Ely and uncle of Thomas, second earl of Derby, was fined £245,680 for illegal retaining. Significantly, his nephew was forced to sign obligations and bonds to pay more than £2,000 toward his fine. Coward, *The Stanleys*, p. 147.

19. Lander, *Crown and Nobility*, p. 292.

20. *Politics*, p. 12.

21. Lander, *Crown and Nobility*, p. 275; Virgoe, "Recovery of the Howards," pp. 1–20; Tucker, *Howard*, ch. 3 to end.

22. James, *Tudor Magnate*; Condon, "Ruling Elites," pp. 116–19.

23. *Letters and Papers of Richard III and Henry VII*, ed. James Gairdner, Rolls Series, vol. XXIV (London, 1861), vol. I, 26 (p. 233).

24. For details, see Chapter 2.

25. Edward Hall, *Union of the Two Noble and Illustrious Families of Lancaster and York* (London, 1809), pp. 484–85.

26. *Six Town Chronicles*, ed. Ralph Flenley (Oxford, 1911), p. 166; A. H. Thomas and I. D. Thornley, *The Great Chronicle of London* (London, 1938), p. 318; "Calendar of Baga de Secretis," *Third Report of the Deputy Keeper of Public Records* (London, 1840), Appendix II, p. 218.

27. *England Under the Tudors* (New York, 1954), p. 43.

28. David Starkey, "From Feud to Faction: English Politics circa 1450–1550," *History Today*, 32 (Nov. 1982), 17.

29. On Percy in this connection, see James, *Tudor Magnate*, pp. 22–23.

30. William Campbell, *Materials for the Reign of Henry VII* (London, 1877), vol. II, p. 19; Walter C. Metcalfe, *A Book of Knights Banneret, Knights of the Bath and Knights Bachelor Made Between Four Henry VI and the Restoration of King Charles II* (London, 1885), p. 11.

31. *L&P, Richard III and Henry VII*, vol. I, Appendix A, 6 (p. 393).

32. Sydney Anglo, *Spectacle, Pageantry, and Early Tudor Policy* (Oxford, 1969), p. 53.

33. *CSP, Venice* (London, 1864–71), vol. I, 754.

34. *CSP, Milan* (London, 1912), vol. I, 614; *CSP, Venice*, vol. I, 794.

35. See description in *Chronicle of Calais*, ed. John Gough Nichols, Camden Society, vol. XXXV (London, 1846), pp. 50–51. See also p. 79, above.

36. Thomas and Thornley, *Great Chronicle*, p. 311.

37. Anglo, *Spectacle*, p. 98.

38. Thomas and Thornley, *Great Chronicle*, p. 311.

39. Ibid., p. 314.

40. Hall, *Two Families*, p. 313.

41. Charles Henry Cooper, *Athenae Cantabrigienses* (Cambridge, Eng., 1858), vol. I, p. 24.

42. Richard Grafton, *Chronicle or History of England* (London, 1809), vol. II, p. 229.

43. Thomas and Thornley, *Great Chronicle*, pp. 328–29.

44. Sir Henry Ellis, *Original Letters Illustrative of English History*, Third Series (London, 1846), vol. I, p. 218.

45. John Leland, *Antiquarii de Rebus Britannicis Collectanea* (Oxford, 1770), vol. VI, pp. 16–24. The yearbook reporter who recorded the duke's trial referred to him in that way. *Yearbooks, Henry VIII* (London, 1591), year 13, p. 12.

46. PRO, E36/150, f. 43.

47. Ibid., f. 38.

48. *CPR, Henry VII, 1485–1509* (London, 1914, 1916), vol. II, 463.

49. J. D. Mackie, *The Earlier Tudors, 1485–1558* (Oxford, 1952), p. 192.

50. For explanation, see above, pp. 12–13, 128–29.

51. T. B. Pugh, "'The Indenture for the Marches,' Between Henry VII and Edward Stafford (1477–1521), Duke of Buckingham," *English Historical Review*, 71 (July 1956), 437–38.

52. BL, Add'l Mss., 36,542, f. 191, printed in Pugh, "Indenture" pp. 440–41.

53. See below, pp. 172–75.

54. J. J. Scarisbrick, *Henry VIII* (Berkeley, Calif., 1968), p. 19.

55. Ibid., pp. 17–20; Starkey, "Feud to Faction," pp. 18–19; Tucker, *Howard*, pp. 92–93.

56. Starkey, "Feud to Faction," pp. 18–19.

57. Elton, *Reform and Reformation*, pp. 6–7; Harrison, "Petition"; Lander, *Crown and Nobility*, pp. 54–55, 297–300; Loades, *Politics*, p. 125; Tucker, *Howard*, pp. 95–96.

58. *L&P, Henry VIII*, vol. I, 765.

59. Ibid., 835. See Appendix A on Bannaster, Gilbert, and Walwyn; Appendix C on Bedell. Robert Partesoil was a Bedfordshire gentleman who had served the duke's mother as steward of Kimbolton, Huntingdonshire. *CCR, Henry VII* (London, 1955, 1963), vol. II, 822; Carole Rawcliffe, *The Staffords, Earls of Stafford and Dukes of Buckingham, 1394–1521* (Cambridge, Eng., 1978), p. 203. He was at Thornbury for the Epiphany feast in 1508. Sir John Guise of Holte, Worcestershire, held land from Buckingham of the honor of Hereford for half a knight's fee and the rent of a clove (Sir John Maclean, "Elmore and the Family of Guyse," *Bristol and Gloucestershire Archaeological Society, Transactions*, 3 (1878–79), 58–59, 69).

60. BL, Harleian Mss., 4900, f. 9d. The grant of the earldom to Buckingham's younger brother was all the more surprising because he had been sent to the Tower on suspicion of treason the day after Henry VIII ascended the throne. Although nothing was proved against him, he remained in prison until early 1510. Whatever the meaning of this obscure and mysterious incident, Henry Stafford appears to have been in the king's favor from the time of his release. Hall, *Two Families*, pp. 505, 512.

61. Robert Keilway, *Reports d'Ascuns Cases* (London, 1638), p. 177.

62. *L&P, Henry VIII*, I, 1156; III (1), 497.

63. Ibid., II (2), 4075.

64. Ibid., III (1), 412. No account of the visit has survived.

65. Quoted in Tucker, *Howard*, p. 96.

66. Quoted in William Huse Dunham, Jr., "Wolsey's Rule of the King's Whole Council," *American Historical Review*, 49 (Oct. 1943–July 1944), 655.

67. *Reform and Reformation*, p. 49.

68. Ibid., p. 25; G. R. Elton, "Tudor Government: The Points of Contact, III. The Court," Presidential Address, *Transactions of the Royal Historical Society*, Fifth Series, 26 (1976), 211–18, esp. 212–16; G. W. Bernard, "The Rise of Sir William Compton, Early Tudor Courtier," *English Historical Review*, 96 (1981), 754–77; Eric Ives, "Patronage at the Court of Henry VIII: The Case of Sir Ralph Egerton of Ridley," *Bulletin of John Ryland University Library of Manchester*, 52 (1970), 346–74.

69. "English Politics and the Concept of Honour, 1485–1642," *Past and Present*, Supplement no. 3 (1978), 15–18.

70. Tucker, *Howard*, chs. 4, 6.

71. *L&P, Henry VIII*, vol. I (1), 157.

72. Ibid., vol. II (2), 4124.

73. Ibid., vol. III (1), 1.

74. Ibid., vol. XII (1), 1118.

75. James, "First Earl of Cumberland," pp. 43–69.

76. James, *Tudor Magnate*, pp. 21–22, 25–26; Condon, "Ruling Elites," p. 119.

77. J. M. W. Bean, *The Estates of the Percy Family 1416–1537* (Oxford, 1958), pt. 3, ch. 3.

78. Elton, *Reform and Reformation*, pp. 7–8; Coward, *The Stanleys*, pp. 147–48.

79. Coward, *The Stanleys*, pp. 21, 147–48.

80. Lander, *Crown and Nobility*, pp. 290–91; Bernard, "Greys, Earls of Kent," pp. 674–79.

81. Keilway, *Reports*, p. 177.

82. For details, see Chapter 2.

83. *L&P, Henry VIII*, vol. II (1), 1836, 1861.

84. Ibid., vol. II (1), 1959, 2018; Edmund Lodge, *Illustrations of British History, Biography, and Manners in the Reigns of Henry VIII, Edward VI, Mary, Elizabeth, and James I* (London, 1828), vol. I, pp. 23, 27–28.

85. Coward, *The Stanleys*, p. 148.

86. G. W. Bernard, *The Power of the Early Tudor Nobility: A Study of the Fourth and Fifth Earls of Shrewsbury* (Totowa, N.J., 1985), pp. 20–23.

87. Ibid., pp. 16–21 (quote p. 21); *L&P, Henry VIII*, vol. II (1), 1959, 2018; Lodge, *Illustrations*, vol. I, pp. 19, 23.

88. Lodge, *Illustrations*, vol. I, p. 23; *L&P, Henry VIII*, vol. II (1), 1893, 1959.

89. Hall, *Two Families*, pp. 599–600; Polydore Vergil, *Anglica Historia*,

ed. and trans. Denys Hay, Camden Society, Third Series, vol. LXXIV (London, 1950), p. 263; quotations from Hall. Vergil tells the story with less detail and greater emphasis on Wolsey's role in exploiting the incident to ruin Buckingham.

90. Ellis, *Letters*, Third Series, vol. I, p. 223.

91. Unsigned letter to Wolsey quoted in J. S. Brewer, *The Reign of Henry VIII from His Accession to the Death of Wolsey*, ed. James Gairdner (London, 1884), vol. I, p. 379; calendared in *L&P, Henry VIII*, vol. III (1), 1283 (p. 490).

92. *L&P, Henry VIII*, vol. III (1), 1245.

93. Ibid., vol. I, 697; *CSP, Spanish* (London, 1862–83), vol. II, 72 (p. 78).

94. *Journals of the House of Lords*, vol. 1 (1509–77), pp. 4, 10, 18.

95. *L&P, Henry VIII*, 2d ed., vol. I (1), 342.

96. Lawrence Stone, *The Crisis of the Aristocracy, 1558–1641* (Oxford, 1965), p. 203.

97. Grafton, *Chronicle*, vol. II, p. 262.

98. Thomas and Thornley, *Great Chronicle*, p. 341.

99. Ibid., p. 339.

100. Grafton, *Chronicle*, vol. II, p. 260.

101. *L&P, Henry VIII*, vol. I, 5322.

102. *CSP, Venice*, vol. II, 505 (p. 200).

103. Sebastian Giustinian, *Four Years at the Court of Henry VIII* (London, 1854), vol. II, pp. 226–27.

104. *L&P, Henry VIII*, vol. II (2), p. 1373.

105. Leland, *Antiquarii*, vol. VI, pp. 33–34.

106. John Stow, *Annales* (London, 1631), p. 507.

107. *Rutland Papers*, ed. William Jerdan, Camden Society, vol. XXI (London, 1842), p. 29.

108. Anglo, *Spectacle*, p. 144.

109. *CSP, Venice*, vol. III, p. 20.

110. Hall, *Two Families*, pp. 615, 620.

111. *Chronicle of Calais*, p. 89.

112. *L&P, Henry VIII*, vol. III (1), 906 (p. 326); Brewer, *Reign of Henry VIII*, vol. I, p. 376.

113. William Hudson, "A Treatise of the Court of Star Chamber," in *Collectanea Juridica*, ed. Francis Hargrave (London, 1792), vol. II, pp. 138–39; SRO, D1721/1/11, ff. 133–36; GEC, vol. II, p. 390, n. b. For Buckingham's claim to be de Bohun's heir, see above, pp. 21, 24–25.

114. Starkey, "Feud to Faction," p. 19.

115. Brewer, *Reign of Henry VIII*, vol. I, p. 391.

116. Ibid.; for the antifeudal thrust of Wolsey's policies, see Cooper,

"Retainers," p. 83; A. F. Pollard, *Henry VIII* (New York, 1966; originally pub. 1905), p. 95; Dunham, "Wolsey's Rule," p. 644; Elton, *Reform and Reformation*, pp. 63–64; A. F. Pollard, *Wolsey*, ed. A. G. Dickens (New York, 1966; originally pub. 1929), p. 80; and J. A. Guy, "Wolsey, the Council and the Council Courts," *English Historical Review*, 91 (July 1976), 482, 486.

117. Vergil, *Anglica Historia*, p. 263.

118. *CSP, Spanish*, vol. II, 44 (p. 43).

119. *CSP, Venice*, vol. II, 117 (p. 49).

120. Giustinian, *Court of Henry VIII*, vol. II, p. 287.

121. Vergil, *Anglica Historia*, p. 263.

122. Ibid.

123. *L&P, Henry VIII*, vol. III (1), 728 (p. 255).

124. For the duke's rising expenses, see Chapter 4, especially table; for a discussion of property sales, see p. 134.

125. Bean, *Estates*, p. 141.

126. BL, Egerton Rolls, 2195.

127. This is deduced from the prohibition of these practices in PRO, Sta Cha 2/35/21, printed in T. B. Pugh, ed., *The Marcher Lordships of South Wales, 1415–1536: Select Documents* (Cardiff, 1963), pp. 135–38.

128. PRO, SC6/Henry 8/4775, m. 9d.

129. Ibid., m. 1.

130. BL, Add'l Mss., 32,091, f. 107, printed in C. A. J. Skeel, *Council in the Marches of Wales* (London, 1904), pp. 35–36.

131. Pugh, *Marcher Lordships*, p. 133.

132. The tenants' answer is PRO, Sta Cha 2/26/247, and is printed in Pugh, *Marcher Lordships*, pp. 133–34.

133. PRO, Sta Cha 2/35/21, printed in Pugh, *Marcher Lordships*, pp. 135–38.

134. *L&P, Henry VIII*, vol. III (1), 1065; PRO, Sta Cha 2/19/223.

135. PRO, Sta Cha 2/21/115.

136. Ellis, *Letters*, vol. 1, p. 226.

137. *Faction in Tudor England* (London, 1979), p. 16.

138. Starkey, "Feud to Faction," p. 19.

139. *L&P, Henry VIII*, vol. III (1), 1284, no. 3, item 7 (p. 494).

140. Ibid., 1070, nos. 12, 20; 1284, no. 4 (p. 495).

141. See above, Chapter 3.

142. *L&P, Henry VIII*, vol. I (1), 157.

143. See above, pp. 165–66.

144. *L&P, Henry VIII*, vol. III (1), 1.

145. Ibid., vol. XXI (2), 554, p. 283.

146. Ibid., vol. I (1), 157.

147. Ives, *Faction in Tudor England*, p. 12.

148. See above, pp. 165–66.

149. *L&P, Henry VIII*, vol. III (1), 1.

150. PRO, SP1/22, f. 161.

151. *L&P, Henry VIII*, vol. III (1), 1049.

152. PRO, SP1/29, ff. 177, 180.

153. Ellis, *Letters*, vol. I, p. 221.

154. *L&P, Henry VIII*, vol. II (1), 1893.

155. Ibid., 1970.

156. Bernard, *Power*, p. 11.

### Chapter Eight

1. *L&P, Henry VIII*, vol. III (1), 1284 (p. 495).

2. See above, pp. 167–68.

3. Henry Ellis, *Original Letters Illustrative of English History*, Third Series (London, 1846), vol. I, p. 221; calendared in *L&P, Henry VIII*, vol. III (1), 1070.

4. Ellis, *Letters*, vol. I, p. 224.

5. *L&P, Henry VIII*, vol. III (2), 3695 (p. 1532); also see Appendix B.

6. Ellis, *Letters*, vol. I, p. 224.

7. Ibid., p. 226.

8. See *L&P, Henry VIII*, vol. III (1), 1220, 1232, 1233, for evidence that Henry was at Greenwich.

9. Ibid., 1285 (p. 501).

10. Narrative based on Edward Hall, *Union of the Two Illustrious Families of Lancaster and York* (London, 1809), pp. 622–23.

11. The indictment was based on examinations of Buckingham's servants by Thomas Ruthal, bishop of Durham; presumably they had overheard these conversations. *L&P, Henry VIII*, vol. III (1), 1233 (p. 468).

12. The indictment is printed in full in *L&P, Henry VIII*, vol. III (1), 1284.

13. *CSP, Venice* (London, 1864–71), vol. III, 213 (p. 124).

14. Hall, *Two Families*, p. 623; BL, Harleian Mss., 540, art. 13, f. 50d; Harleian Mss., 2194, art. 4, f. 11/12d. (Harleian Ms. 2194 has two systems of pagination; the reference is to the page bearing both the numbers indicated.) As has been stated earlier, Norfolk was the father of Buckingham's son-in-law, Thomas Howard, the earl of Surrey and future third duke.

15. The narrative of the trial and execution is based on Hall, *Two Families*, pp. 623–24; John Stow, *Annales* (London, 1631), pp. 512ff; and Harleian Mss., 2194, art. 4, 11/12d–15/16d, except as otherwise indicated. Direct quotes are from Hall.

16. J. S. Brewer, *The Reign of Henry VIII from His Accession to the Death of Wolsey*, ed. James Gairdner (London, 1884), vol. I, pp. 391–92.

17. *Yearbooks, Henry VIII* (London, 1591), anno 13, p. 12.

18. *CSP, Venice*, vol. III, 213 (p. 124).

19. Mervyn E. James, "English Politics and the Concept of Honour, 1485–1642," *Past and Present*, suppl. 3 (1978), pp. 54–55.

20. "Let it alone; my state now will but mock me. When I came hither, I was Lord High Constable and Duke of Buckingham; now, poor Edward Bohun." William Shakespeare, *Henry the Eighth*, II.i.102–4.

21. *CSP, Venice*, vol. III, 213 (p. 125).

22. Garrett Mattingly, *Catherine of Aragon* (London, 1963; originally pub. 1942), p. 161.

23. *CSP, Venice*, vol. III, 213 (p. 125).

24. BL, Egerton Rolls, 2642, f. 16. This account appears to be John Stow's. See Stow, *Annales*, p. 513, for an identical account.

25. The act of attainder is 14 and 15 Henry VIII, c. 20.

26. PRO, SP11/1, f. 37d.; Polydore Vergil, *Anglica Historia*, ed. and trans. Denys Hay, Camden Society, Third Series, vol. LXXIV (London, 1950), p. 279. Joan, daughter of the first duke of Buckingham, married as her second husband Sir William Knevet, a Norfolk gentleman. William Dugdale, *The Baronage of England* (London, 1675), vol. I, p. 167; Josiah Wedgewood, *History of Parliament: Biographies of Members of Commons House, 1439–1509* (London, 1936), pp. 520–21. Sir William was therefore the third duke's great-uncle (see genealogy, Appendix D, for clarification). He risked his life to save the third duke from Richard III (see above, Chapter 2). Sir William was a Norfolk gentleman. I have not been able to find Charles Knevet in the genealogies of the Knevet family. Since he was the third duke's receiver in Norfolk in 1508–15, it is likely that he was related to Sir William Knevet in some way. PRO, SC6/Henry 7/427, m. 4d; SC6/Henry 7/428, m. 4d. Edward Hall specifically said Knevet was the duke's cousin. *Two Families*, p. 623. Charles was still in Buckingham's service in May 1520, a fact that supports the chroniclers' story that he was discharged just before Buckingham departed for the Field of Cloth of Gold.

27. PRO, SP11/1, f. 37d.; Vergil, *Anglica Historia*, p. 279.

28. Vergil, *Anglica Historia*, p. 279; Richard Fiddes, *The Life of Cardinal Wolsey* (London, 1726), p. 258.

29. PRO, SP11/1, f. 37d.

30. Brewer, *Reign of Henry VIII*, vol. I, p. 379; calendared in *L&P, Henry VIII*, vol. III (1), 1283 (p. 490). Mr. Lark was Thomas Lark, a priest and the brother of Wolsey's mistress. Lark became Wolsey's confessor and servant. A. F. Pollard, *Wolsey*, ed. A. G. Dickens (New York, 1966; originally pub. 1929), pp. 306–7.

31. *L&P, Henry VIII*, vol. III (1), 1283 (p. 490); quoted in full in Brewer, *Reign of Henry VIII*, vol. I, pp. 379–80.

32. Brewer, *Reign of Henry VIII*, vol. I, pp. 379–81.

33. PRO, SP11/1, f. 37d; Vergil, *Anglica Historia*, p. 279; Hall, *Two Families*, p. 623.

34. *L&P, Henry VIII*, vol. III (1), p. cxv (Brewer's introduction); Brewer, *Reign of Henry VIII*, pp. 381, 386.

35. See indictment in *L&P, Henry VIII*, 1284 (pp. 490–92).

36. BL, Lansdowne Mss., 979, f. 10.

37. SRO, D641/1/2/235.

38. *L&P, Henry VIII*, vol. III (1), 1070.

39. Brewer, *Reign of Henry VIII*, vol. I, p. 380.

40. *L&P, Henry VIII*, vol. III (1), 1070.

41. Ibid.                             42. Ibid.

43. PRO, E36/220, mm. 15, 25.        44. PRO, E36/150, f. 22.

45. PRO, SP1/22, f. 77; A. B. Emden, *A Biographical Register of the University of Oxford to A.D. 1500* (Oxford, 1957), vol. II, p. 767; *VCH, Buckinghamshire*, vol. IV (London, 1927), pp. 423, 425; Carole Rawcliffe, *The Staffords, Earls of Stafford and Dukes of Buckingham, 1394–1521* (Cambridge, Eng., 1976).

46. Brewer, *Reign of Henry VIII*, vol. I, p. 379.

47. Hall, *Two Families*, p. 623.

48. Emden, *Oxford*, vol. II, p. 767.

49. Brewer, *Reign of Henry VIII*, vol. I, p. 379.

50. BL, Lansdowne Mss., 979, f. 10; *L&P, Henry VIII*, vol. III (1), 1284 (pp. 490–92).

51. Hall, *Two Families*, p. 622.

52. Brewer, *Reign of Henry VIII*, vol. I, pp. 379–80.

53. *L&P, Henry VIII*, vol. III (1), 1284 (p. 495); Rawcliffe, *The Staffords*, p. 229.

54. Brewer, *Reign of Henry VIII*, vol. I, p. 379.

55. This analysis of Buckingham's trial appeared initially as an article entitled "The Trial of the Third Duke of Buckingham—A Revisionist View," *Amer. Jour. Legal History*, 20, no. 1 (Jan. 1976), pp. 15–26.

56. *Henry VIII* (New York, 1966; originally pub. 1905), p. 146.

57. Brewer, *Reign of Henry VIII*, vol. I, pp. 392–94; Fisher, *The History of England from the Accession of Henry VII to the Death of Henry VIII* (London, 1919), pp. 238–39; Mattingly, *Catherine of Aragon*, pp. 160–61; Pickthorne, *Early Tudor Government, Henry VIII* (Cambridge, Eng., 1951), pp. 46–48; Levine, "The Fall of Edward, Duke of Buckingham," in *Tudor Men and Institutions*, ed. Arthur J. Slavin (Baton Rouge, 1972).

58. L. W. Vernon Harcourt, *His Grace the Steward and Trial of Peers* (London, 1907), p. 442.

59. Levine, "Fall of Edward," p. 35; Elton, *Policy and Police* (Cambridge, Eng., 1972), p. 264.

60. Elton, *Policy and Police*, pp. 378–79, 425, 429; *Rolls of Parliament*, vol. V, 31, and 32 Henry VI, p. 249; T. B. Howell, *State Trials* (London, 1816), vol. I, pp. 407–8; J. G. Bellamy, *The Tudor Law of Treason* (Toronto, 1979), p. 171.

61. Bellamy, *The Law of Treason in England in the Later Middle Ages* (Cambridge, Eng., 1970), pp. 175–76.

62. Members of the jury were Thomas Howard, duke of Norfolk; Charles Brandon, duke of Suffolk; Thomas Grey, marquess of Dorset; George Talbot, earl of Shrewsbury; Richard Grey, earl of Kent; Thomas Stanley, earl of Derby; Henry Courtenay, earl of Devonshire; Charles Somerset, earl of Worcester; John de Vere, earl of Oxford; Henry Bourchier, earl of Essex; Thomas Manners, Lord de Roos; William Willoughby, Lord Willoughby; Thomas West, Lord de la Warr; Henry Parker, Lord Morley; Thomas Fiennes, Lord Dacre of the South; Walter Devereux, Lord Ferrers; Thomas Broke, Lord Cobham; John Bourchier, Lord Fitzwarin; William Blount, Lord Mountjoy; and Thomas Dowcra, prior of St. John's of Jerusalem. This list is based on PRO, KB8, Bundle V, 30 (*Baga de Secretis*), and Hall, *Two Families*, p. 623. Lord de Roos, Lord Dacre of the South, Lord Ferrers, and Lord Mountjoy are listed only in the *Baga de Secretis*.

63. Norfolk was appointed Lord High Steward specifically for Buckingham's trial. This was not a hereditary office attached to the dukedom of Norfolk or to the Howard family. *L&P, Henry VIII*, vol. III (1), 1284 (1).

64. See Chapter 6.

65. Helen J. Miller, "The Early Tudor Peerage, 1485–1547" (London University master's thesis, 1950), Appendix B.

66. Bellamy, *Tudor Law*, pp. 171–72.

67. John H. Langbein, "The Origins of Public Prosecution at Common Law," *American Journal of Legal History*, 17 (1973), 316.

68. Bellamy, *Law of Treason*, p. 166; Bellamy, *Tudor Law*, pp. 140–41.

69. Brewer, *Reign of Henry VIII*, pp. 392–94.

70. *Yearbooks, Henry VIII*, years 13, ff. 11d–12; Sir William Stanford, *Les Plees del Coron* (London, 1607), p. 152; Sir Edward Coke, *The Third Part of the Institutes of the Lawes of England*, 4th ed. (London, 1669), pp. 28–30. The preceding paragraph was based on these sources.

71. Elton, *Policy and Police*, pp. 293–94; Bellamy, *Law of Treason*, p. 166; Bellamy, *Tudor Law*, pp. 141–43.

72. Langbein, "Common Law," p. 316.

73. Bellamy, *Law of Treason*, p. 166; Bellamy, *Tudor Law*, p. 178.

74. Langbein, *Prosecuting Crime in the Renaissance: England, Germany, France* (Cambridge, Mass., 1974), pp. 1–125, esp. p. 39.

75. Bellamy, *Law of Treason*, p. 138; Bellamy, *Tudor Law*, p. 128.

76. Most authorities accept this interpretation of the act of 1352. See, for example, Isobel D. Thornley, "The Treason Legislation of Henry VIII," *Transactions of the Royal Historical Society*, Third Series, 11 (1917), 106–7; and Elton, *Policy and Police*, pp. 263–64. Bellamy denied the requirement of an overt act in the case of imagining or compassing the king's death (*Law of Treason*, p. 122). He stated that fifteenth-century treason by words depended on judicial construction (ibid., p. 116). I agree with Elton that Samuel Reznick's interpretation of the statute, which defines words as the overt act, is "at best a quibble." Elton, *Policy and Police*, p. 288.

77. Thornley, "Treason Legislation," p. 107; Elton, *Policy and Police*, p. 263. If the statute of 1352 did not require an overt act to convict for compassing the death or deposition of the king, the statute of 1397 seems to have been superfluous.

78. *Yearbooks, Henry VIII*, year 13, p. 12. See above, p. 185, for Fyneux's ruling.

79. Isobel D. Thornley, "Treason by Words in the Fifteenth Century," *English Historical Review*, 32 (1917), 556–58.

80. Sir George Croke, *Reports* (London, 1657), p. 118.

81. "Calendar of *Baga de Secretis*," *Third Report of the Deputy Keeper of Public Records* (London, 1840), Appendix II, pp. 213–14.

82. Sir Matthew Hale, *The History of the Pleas of the Crown* (London, 1736), vol. I, p. 115.

83. Howell, *State Trials*, p. 282.

84. A number of other cases are cited in Bellamy, *Law of Treason*, pp. 118–19, and in Elton, *Policy and Police*, p. 288.

85. Elton, *Policy and Police*, p. 265 and n. 1.

86. Bellamy, *Law of Treason*, pp. 116–20; *Tudor Law*, pp. 10–11.

87. Reznick, "Constructive Treason by Words in the Fifteenth Century," *American Historical Review*, 33, no. 3 (Apr. 1928), 545–46; also see n. 76 above. Although he disputed the existence of a common-law treason of words, Reznick did refer to a common law of treason in other connections. See, for example, "The Early History of the Parliamentary Declaration of Treason," *English Historical Review*, 42, no. 168 (Oct. 1927), 508; and "The Trial of Treason in Tudor England," in *Essays in History and Political Theory in Honor of Charles Howard McIlwain* (Cambridge, Mass., 1936), pp. 273–74.

88. Elton, *Policy and Police*, p. 265; Bellamy, *Law of Treason*, p. 101.

89. Quoted in Bellamy, *Law of Treason*, p. 123.

90. Thornley, "Treason by Words," pp. 537–38; "Treason Legislation," pp. 109–10; Elton, *Policy and Police*, pp. 274–75.

## Conclusion

1. PRO, SP1/1, ff. 37–37d; Polydore Vergil, *Anglica Historia*, ed. and trans. Denys Hay, Camden Society, Third Series, vol. LXXIV (London, 1950), p. 263; William Roy, "Rede me and be nott wrothe," 1st ed. (n.p., 1528), p. cv (there is a copy of the first edition at Houghton Library, Harvard University); "An Impeachment of Wolsey," *Ballads from Manuscripts*, ed. Frederick J. Furnivale (London, 1868–72), vol. I, p. 355.

2. Raphael Holinshed, *Chronicles of England, Scotland, and Ireland* (London, 1808), vol. III, pp. 657–58; Edward Lord Herbert of Cherbury, *The Life and Reign of King Henry the Eighth* (London, 1672), p. 98; Francis Godwin, *Rerum Anglicarum Henrico VIII, Edwardo VI et Maria . . . regnantibus annales* (London, 1676), pp. 65–66; William Shakespeare, "Henry the Eighth," I.i and ii, II.i; William Dugdale, *The Baronage of England* (London, 1675), vol. I, p. 170; David Lloyd, *State Worthies* (London, 1766), vol. I, p. 172; Theodore Maynard, *Henry the Eighth* (Milwaukee, 1949), p. 104; Garrett Mattingly, *Catherine of Aragon* (London, 1963; originally pub. 1942), pp. 160–61.

3. Mattingly, *Catherine of Aragon*, esp. pp. 167–82.

4. J. S. Brewer, *The Reign of Henry VIII from His Accession to the Death of Wolsey*, ed. James Gairdner (London, 1884), vol. I, pp. 381 and 382n.

5. William Roy, "Rede me"; Sir Henry Ellis, *Original Letters Illustrative of English History*, First Series (London, 1827), vol. I, pp. 176–77. The swan was a heraldic device of the Bohuns taken over by the Staffords as a symbol of their claim to be the rightful Bohun heirs.

6. Edward Hall, *Union of the Two Noble and Illustrious Families of Lancaster and York* (London, 1809), pp. 623–24.

7. "Lament of the Duke of Buckingham," *Ballads from Manuscripts*, ed. W. R. Morfill (Hartford, Conn., 1973), vol. II (2), p. 63.

8. *L&P, Henry VIII*, vol. III (1), 1283 (p. 490); quoted in full in Brewer, *Reign of Henry VIII*, vol. I, pp. 379–80. See above, Chapter 8.

9. *L&P, Henry VIII*, vol. III (1), pp. cxiv–cxvi (Brewer's introduction).

10. Ibid., vol. II (1), 1893; vol. II (2), 2987; vol. III (1), 1070, 1288.

11. Vergil, *Anglica Historia*, p. 263.

12. *L&P, Henry VIII*, vol. III (1), pp. cviii–cix (Brewer's introduction); *Chronicle of Calais*, ed. John Gough Nichols, Camden Society, vol. XXXV (London, 1846), p. 89.

13. *L&P, Henry VIII*, vol. II (2), 3973. This report raises intriguing questions: Why would France be anxious to remove Wolsey at the very time he was working for an Anglo-French alliance? If the francophobic duke was included in the "party" mentioned, how did he come to be cooperating with the French?

14. *L&P, Henry VIII*, vol. III (1), 1.

15. *CSP, Venice* (London, 1864–71), vol. III, 209 (p. 122).

16. See above, pp. 188–89.

17. *L&P, Henry VIII*, vol. III (1), 1233 (p. 468).

18. Ibid., 1204.

19. Stone, *The Crisis of the Aristocracy, 1558–1641* (Oxford, 1965), pp. 217, 253–54.

20. This idea did not originate with me. See A. F. Pollard, *Henry VIII* (New York, 1966; originally pub. 1905), p. 146; Kenneth Pickthorne, *Early Tudor Government: Henry VIII* (Cambridge, Eng., 1951), p. 47; and G. R. Elton, *England Under the Tudors* (London, 1963), pp. 99–100.

21. J. J. Scarisbrick, *Henry VIII* (Berkeley, Calif., 1963), p. 150.

22. J. D. Mackie, *The Earlier Tudors, 1485–1558* (Oxford, 1952), pp. 167–71.

23. *L&P, Richard III and Henry VII*, ed. James Gairdner, Rolls Series, vol. XXIV (London, 1861), vol. I, 26 (p. 233).

24. The de la Poles were sons of Edward IV's sister Elizabeth and John de la Pole, earl of Suffolk. The eldest, John, earl of Lincoln, died fighting for Lambert Simnel at Stoke in 1487. The second, Edmund, led a checkered career that ended in his flight to the continent in 1501. In 1506 the duke of Burgundy handed him over to Henry VII, who imprisoned him in the Tower; Henry VIII executed him in 1513. The third son, Richard, lived in exile on the continent and was not a serious threat to the Tudors. He died fighting on the French side at the Battle of Pavia in 1525.

25. Mackie, *Earlier Tudors*, p. 169.

26. Edward Hall, *Two Families*, pp. 505, 512.

27. Ibid.

28. *L&P, Henry VIII*, 2d. ed. vol. 1 (1), p. 157; for greater detail on the subject, see Chapter 7 above.

29. See above, Chapter 7, for a full discussion of this point.

30. *L&P, Henry VIII*, vol. II (2), 3973.

31. *CSP, Venice*, vol. III, 209 (p. 122).

32. *L&P, Henry VIII*, vol. III (1), 282.

33. *CSP, Venice*, vol. II, 1287 (p. 561).

34. *L&P, Henry VIII*, vol. III (1), 1.

35. Hall, *Two Families*, pp. 599–600; Vergil, *Anglica Historia*, p. 263.

36. Brewer, *Reign of Henry VIII*, p. 379.

37. *L&P, Henry VIII*, vol. III (1), 1284.

38. Ellis, *Letters*, vol. I, p. 226; calendared in *L&P, Henry VIII*, vol. III (1), 1070.

39. *L&P, Henry VIII*, vol. III (1), 1284.

40. Hall, *Two Families*, p. 624.

41. *L&P, Henry VIII*, vol. III (1), 1204; J. E. Paul, *Catherine of Aragon and Her Friends* (London, 1966), p. 54.

42. *L&P, Henry VIII*, vol. III (1), 1204, 1293; *CSP, Venice*, vol. III, 204 (p. 120).

43. The chief representative of the Yorkist line in this period was Edward IV's niece, Margaret Pole, countess of Salisbury. She had four sons, Henry, Geoffrey, Arthur, and Reginald. Henry VIII eventually executed the countess and her two elder sons, Henry and Geoffrey, for treason when they opposed the break with Rome. Reginald became a famous cardinal.

44. PRO, SP1/29, f. 161; *L&P, Henry VIII*, vol. III (1), 1290; vol. III (2), 2049.

45. *L&P, Henry VIII*, vol. VI, 1164 (p. 487). Chapuys, the imperial ambassador to Henry VIII's court, used this phrase in a letter to Charles V, dated Sept. 27, 1533, in which he discussed members of the English nobility who opposed Henry VIII's marriage to Anne Boleyn. He included Lord Bergavenny in that group and was trying to explain Bergavenny's hostility to the king.

46. See Hall, *Two Families*, p. 623, for a discussion of Edward Neville.

47. *L&P, Henry VIII*, 1293.

48. S. T. Bindoff, *Tudor England*, the Pelican History of England, vol. V (Baltimore, Md., 1959), pp. 58–60; quotations from p. 60.

49. S. B. Chrimes, *Lancastrians, Yorkists, and Henry VII* (London, 1964); J. R. Lander, *Conflict and Stability in Fifteenth Century England* (London, 1969), ch. 7; J. R. Lander, *Crown and Nobility, 1450–1509* (London, 1976); A. J. Slavin, *The Precarious Balance: English Government and Society* (New York, 1973), pp. 49, 81, 85–6, 91; and B. P. Wolffe, *The Crown Lands, 1461–1536* (New York, 1970).

50. K. B. McFarlane, *The Nobility of Later Medieval England* (Oxford, 1973), p. 283.

51. Charles D. Ross, *Edward IV* (Berkeley, Calif., 1974), pp. 331–41.

52. J. M. W. Bean, *The Estates of the Percy Family, 1416–1537* (Oxford, 1958); Mervyn E. James, "The First Earl of Cumberland (1493–1542) and the Decline of Northern Feudalism," *Northern History*, 1 (1966), 43–69; Mervyn E. James, *A Tudor Magnate and the Tudor State: Henry, Fifth Earl of Northumberland*, Borthwick Papers, 30 (York, 1966); on Bergavenny see above, Chapter 7, and Lander, *Crown and Nobility*, pp. 289–90.

# Bibliography

## Primary Sources

*Manuscripts*

**BRITISH LIBRARY**

Additional Charters. 19,868. Certificate of birth of Edward, duke of Buckingham.

———. 26,873 and 26,874. Account of estates of Edward, third duke of Buckingham, in the counties of Southampton and Wiltshire, 1498–99 and 1511–12.

Additional Mss. 25,294. Survey of the lands of Edward Stafford, duke of Buckingham, by Thomas Magnus and William Walwyn, 1521.

———. 32,091, f. 107. Letter of Henry VIII to Edward, third duke of Buckingham, for the peace of the marches (copy).

———. 36,542. Register of evidences and documents concerning the family of Stafford.

———. 40,859B. Household account, Edward, third duke of Buckingham, 1503–4.

Cotton Mss. Titus B.1. Includes letters of Elizabeth, duchess of Norfolk.

Egerton Rolls. 2181–2210. Stafford Manuscripts. Described in an article by B. Schofield in *The British Museum Quarterly*, 11 (1936–37), 125–27.

———. 2642, f. 16. Degradation of Edward, duke of Buckingham, as Knight of the Garter, 1521.

Harleian Mss. 283, ff. 70, 72. Depositions against Edward Stafford, duke of Buckingham.

———. 540, art. 13, f. 50d. Trial and execution of Edward Stafford, duke of Buckingham, 1521.

———. 2194, art. 4, ff. 11/12d–15/16d. Trial and execution of Edward Stafford, duke of Buckingham, 1521.

———. 4900, art. 7, f. 9d. Patent creating Henry Stafford earl of Wiltshire.

Lansdowne Mss. 1, art. 16, f. 195–96. Arraignment and sentence of Edward, duke of Buckingham.

————. 61, art. 31. Schedule of lands and revenues of Edward, duke of Buckingham, in the county of Brecon.

————. 111, f. 17. Valor of the duke of Buckingham's land in Brecon.

————. 127, f. 29d. Edmund Dudley's Declaration of Sums He Had Received to Use of Henry 7, Sept. 9, 1504.

————. 979, art. 6. Trial, conviction, and execution of Edward, third duke of Buckingham.

Royal and King Collection. 14B. XXXVA, 1–5, 7–12; -B, -C, -D, -E, -F; 7F. XIV, 1–19. Private accounts, 1517–22, 1518–19.

————. 14B. XL. Valor of the lordship of Holderness, belonging to Edward, third duke of Buckingham.

PUBLIC RECORD OFFICE

Exchequer Accounts, Miscellaneous (Treasury of Receipt). E36/150 and E36/181. Both manuscripts are copies of the posthumous survey of the duke's lands made for the king by Thomas Magnus and William Walwyn.

————. E36/220. William Cholmeley's account as cofferer to the duke of Buckingham from Oct. 1520 to Apr. 1521.

Exchequer (King's Remembrancer Accounts). E101/518/5, E101/518/6, and E101/631/20. Accounts from the third duke's household and wardrobe.

Exchequer (Land Revenue) Receiver's Accounts. LR12/9/275 is an account for the third duke's Welsh lordships in 1500–1501.

Ministers' Accounts. SC6/Henry VII and SC6/Henry VIII contain 48 manorial accounts from the duke of Buckingham's lifetime. The documents are listed in PRO, *Lists and Indexes*, vol. XXXIV (2), pp. 1–234 (by county), 254–59.

Star Chamber Records. Sta Cha 2/19/223, Walter Vaughan et al. v. Buckingham; Sta Cha 2/21/115, tenants of Penkelly v. Buckingham; Sta Cha 2/23/111 and 2/26/386, John Russell v. Buckingham; Sta Cha 2/26/247, Buckingham v. Richard ap Hoell et al.; and Sta Cha 2/35/21, decree to settle all outstanding disputes between Buckingham and his Welsh tenants in 1518.

State Papers, Henry VIII. SP1.

State Papers, Mary. SP11/1, f. 37–37b. Petition from Henry Lord Stafford, Oct. 23, 1553, giving his version of his father's trial and execution.

STAFFORD COUNTY RECORD OFFICE

Bagot Collection. D1721/1. Extensive and diversified collection that includes copies of plea rolls; petitions to the crown; copies of statutes, deeds, court rolls, rentals, and surveys; a book of information compiled from reports of the duke's tenants and estate officials in 1515–18; the famous household book of 1508; and genealogies.

Stafford Papers. D641/1. Extensive collection of estate and household accounts that includes 47 estate accounts and 23 court rolls; an incomplete valor made in 1498–99; an account of the treasurer of the household, 1503–4; a cofferer's account, 1503–4; a wardrobe account for 1516–17; an incomplete survey of the duke's estates from 1500; and directions issued to the duke's estate officers in 1504.

WESTMINSTER ABBEY MUNIMENT ROOM

Accounts of Richard Harpur, receiver general of the duke of Buckingham's lands in the possession of the countess of Richmond, 1485–88 and 1495–96. Nos. 32,348 and 32,349.

Book of Information, compiled by John Pickering, receiver general, in 1517–18. No. 5470.

## Printed Sources

Armstrong, C. A. J. *The Usurpation of Richard the Third. Dominicus Mancinus ad Angelum Catonem de Occupatione Regni Anglie per Ricardum Tercium Libellus.* Oxford, 1969.

Bacon, Francis. *The History of the Reign of Henry the Seventh,* ed. Roger Lockyer, 1st ed., 1622. London, 1971.

"Calendar of *Baga de Secretis,*" *Third Report of the Deputy Keeper of Public Records,* Appendix II. London, 1840, pp. 213–14, 230–34.

*Calendar of Close Rolls, Edward IV, Edward V, Richard III, A.D. 1476–1485.* London, 1954.

*Calendar of Close Rolls, Henry VII, 1485–1509,* vols. I and II. London, 1955, 1963.

*Calendar of the Inner Temple Records,* ed. F. A. Inderwick, vol. I. London, 1896.

*Calendar of Inquisitions Post Mortem, Henry VII,* vols. I–III. London, 1898, 1915, 1955.

*Calendar of the Patent Rolls: Edward IV, Edward V, and Richard III, A.D. 1476–1485,* 3 vols. London, 1897–1901.

*Calendar of Patent Rolls: Henry VII, 1485–1509,* vols. I and II. London, 1914, 1916.

*Calendar of State Papers of Henry VIII,* vols. I–V. London, 1836–52.

*Calendar of State Papers, Milan,* vol. I. London, 1912.

*Calendar of State Papers, Spanish,* vols. I–II and supplements to vols. I–II. London, 1862–83.

*Calendar of State Papers, Venice,* vols. I–IV. London, 1864–71.

Campbell, William. *Materials for the Reign of Henry VII,* vols. I–II. London, 1873, 1877.

Chevalier au Cynge. *The History of Helyas, Knight of the Swan*. Trans. Robert Copland from the French version published in Paris in 1504. Reprint of version published by Wynken de Worde in London in 1512. New York, 1901.

*Chronicle of Calais*, ed. John Gough Nichols, Camden Society, vol. XXXV. London, 1846.

*Clifford Letters of the Sixteenth Century*, ed. A. G. Dickens, Surtees Society, vol. CLXXII, 1957. London, 1962.

Coke, Sir Edward. *The Second Part of the Institutes of the Lawes of England*. London, 1642.

———. *The Third Part of the Institutes of the Lawes of England*, 4th ed. London, 1669.

*Court of Requests, Select Cases, 1497–1569*, ed. I. S. Leadam, Selden Society, vol. XII. London, 1898.

Croke, Sir George. *Reports*. London, 1657.

Crompton, R. *Star Chamber Cases*. London, 1641.

Davies, Robert, ed. *Extracts from the Municipal Records of the City of York During the Reigns of Edward IV, Edward V, and Richard III*. London, 1843.

*The Earl of Northumberland's Household Book*. London, 1770.

Ellis, Sir Henry. *Original Letters Illustrative of English History*, Series 1, 2, 3. 11 vols. London, 1824, 1827, 1846.

Ellis, Sir Henry, ed. *Three Books of Polydore Vergil's English History, Comprising the Reigns of Henry VI, Edward IV, and Richard III*, Camden Society, vol. XXIX, 1844. New York, 1968.

*Excerpta Historica*, ed. Samuel Bentley. London, 1833.

Fabyan, Robert. *The New Chronicles of England and France*, ed. Henry Ellis. London, 1811.

Giustinian, Sebastian. *Four Years at the Court of Henry VIII*. London, 1854.

Godwin, Francis. *Rerum Anglicarum Henrico VIII, Edwardo VI et Maria . . . Regnantibus Annales*. London, 1676.

Grafton, Richard. *Chronicle or History of England*, vol. II. London, 1809.

Green, M. A. E. Wood. *Letters of Royal and Illustrious Ladies of Great Britain*, 3 vols. London, 1846.

Hall, Edward. *Union of the Two Noble and Illustrious Families of Lancaster and York*. London, 1809.

Holbourne, Sir Robert. *Learned Readings Upon the Statute of 25 Edward III Statute 5, cap. 2, being the Statute of Treasons, at Lincoln's Inn, Feb. 28, 1641*. London, 1681.

Holinshed, Raphael. *Chronicles of England, Scotlande, and Ireland*, 6 vols. London, 1808.

Holles, Gervase. *Memorials of the Holles Family*, Camden Society, Third Series, vol. LV. London, 1937.

Hope, William H. St. John. "The Last Testament and Inventory of John de Veer, Thirteenth Earl of Oxford," *Archaeologia*, 66 (1915), 275–345.

"Household Book of Edward Stafford, Duke of Buckingham," with letter from John Gage, esquire, to Sir Henry Ellis, *Archaeologia*, 25 (1834), 311–41.

*Household Books of John Duke of Norfolk and Thomas Earl of Surrey, 1481–1490*, ed. J. Payne Collier, Roxburghe Club. London, 1844.

Howell, T. B. *State Trials*, vol. I. London, 1816.

Hudson, William. "A Treatise of the Court of Star Chamber," in *Collectanea Juridica*, ed. Francis Hargrave, vol. II. London, 1792.

Ingulf, Abbot of Croyland. *Ingulph's Chronicle of the Abbey of Croyland, with the Continuations by Peter of Blois and Anonymous Writers*, trans. Henry T. Riley. London, 1854.

Keilway, Robert. *Reports d'Ascuns Cases*. London, 1688.

Leland, John. *Antiquarii de Rebus Britannicis Collectanea*, vol. VI. London, 1770.

*Letters and Papers of Henry VIII*, vols. I–IV, ed. J. S. Brewer; vols. V–IX, ed. James Gairdner; vols. XIV–XXI, ed. James Gairdner and R. H. Brodie. London, 1862–1910. Vol. 1, 2d. ed., ed. R. H. Brodie. London, 1920.

*Letters and Papers of Richard III and Henry VII*, 2 vols., ed. James Gairdner, Rolls Series. London, 1861–63.

*The Lisle Letters*, ed. Muriel St. Clare Byrne, 6 vols. Chicago, 1981.

Lodge, Edmund. *Illustrations of British History, Biography, and Manners in the Reigns of Henry VIII, Edward VI, Mary, Elizabeth, and James I*, vol. I. London, 1791 and 1828.

MacGeagh, Sir Henry F., and H. A. C. Sturgess. *Register of Admissions to the Honourable Society of the Middle Temple*. London, 1949.

More, Thomas. *The History of King Richard III*, ed. Richard S. Sylvester, *The Complete Works of St. Thomas More*, vol. II. New Haven, Conn., 1963.

Owen, Edward. *Catalogue of Manuscripts Relating to Wales in the British Museum*, Cymmrodorion Record Series, no. 4. London, 1900–1922.

*The Paston Letters, 1422–1509*, ed. James Gairdner. Westminster, 1900.

*Plumpton Correspondence*, ed. Thomas Stapleton, Camden Society, vol. IV. London, 1839.

Pollard, A. F. *The Reign of Henry VII from Contemporary Sources*, 3 vols. London, 1913, 1914.

Pugh, T. B., ed. *The Marcher Lordships of South Wales, 1415–1536: Select Documents*. Cardiff, 1963.

Raine, James, ed. *Wills and Inventories of the Northern Counties of England from the Eleventh Century Downwards*, pt. I, Surtees Society Publications, no. 2. London, 1835.

*The Records of the Honourable Society of Lincoln's Inn*, vol. I, *Admissions from 1420–1799*. London, 1896.

*A Relation, or Rather a True Account of the Island of England . . . About the year 1500*, ed. Charlotte Augusta Sneyd, Camden Society, Old Series, vol. XXXVII, 1847. New York, 1968.

*Rolls of Parliament*, vols. V and VI.

Roy, William. *Rede me and be nott wrothe*, 1st ed. N.p., 1528.

*Rutland Papers*, ed. William Jerdan, Camden Society, vol. XXI. London, 1842.

*Select Cases Before the King's Council*, ed. I. S. Leadam, Selden Society, vol. XXXV. London, 1918.

*Select Cases Before the King's Council in the Star Chamber*, ed. I. S. Leadam, vols. I and II, Selden Society, vols. XVI and XXV. London, 1903, 1911.

*Select Cases in the Council of Henry VII*, ed. C. G. Bayne and W. H. Dunham, Selden Society, vol. LXXV. London, 1958.

*Six Town Chronicles*, ed. Ralph Flenley. Oxford, 1911.

Smyth, John, of Nibley. *The Berkeley Manuscripts: Lives of the Berkeleys*, ed. Sir John Maclean, 2 vols. Gloucester, 1883.

Stanford, Sir William. *Les Plees del Corone*. London, 1607.

*Statutes of the Realm*, vols. I and III. London, 1810, 1817.

*The Stonor Letters and Papers, 1290–1483*, ed. Charles L. Kingsford, Camden Society, Third Series, vol. XXX. London, 1919.

Stow, John. *Annales*. London, 1631.

———. *Survey of London*, ed. Charles L. Kingsford, 2 vols. Oxford, 1908.

Thomas, A. H., and I. D. Thornley, eds. *The Great Chronicle of London*. London, 1938.

*Two Italian Accounts of Tudor England*, ed. and trans. C. V. Malfatti. Barcelona, 1953.

Vergil, Polydore. *Anglica Historia*, ed. and trans. Denys Hay, Camden Society, Third Series, vol. LXXIV. London, 1950.

Williamson, J. Bruce. *The Middle Temple Bench Book, A Register of Benchers of the Middle Temple*, 2d ed. London, 1937.

*Wills from Doctors' Commons: A Selection from the Wills of Eminent Persons, 1495–1695*, ed. John Gough Nichols and John Bruce, Camden Society, Old Series, vol. LXXXIII. London, 1863.

*The Works of Henry Howard, Earl of Surrey, and of Sir Thomas Wyatt the Elder*, ed. George Frederick Nott. London, 1815.

*Yearbooks, Henry VIII*, (years 12–14, 18, 17, 19, 26, 27). London, 1591.

## Secondary Sources

### Reference Works

Bindoff, Stanley Thomas. *The House of Commons, 1509–1558*, 3 vols. London, 1982.

Cokayne, George E. *Complete Peerage of England, Scotland, Ireland*, ed. Vicary Gibbs, H. A. Doubleday, G. H. White, and R. S. Lea, rev. ed., 12 vols. London, 1910–59.

Cooper, Charles Henry. *Athenae Cantabrigienses*, vol. I. Cambridge, Eng., 1858.

*Dictionary of National Biography*, ed. Sir Leslie Stephens and Sir Sidney Lee, 63 vols. New York, 1908–9.

Dugdale, William. *The Baronage of England*. London, 1675.

Emden, A. B. *A Biographical Register of the University of Cambridge to A.D. 1500*. Cambridge, Eng., 1963.

Emden, A. B. *A Biographical Register of the University of Oxford to A.D. 1500*. Oxford, 1957.

Foss, Edward. *Judges of England*, 9 vols. London, 1848–64.

Foster, Joseph. *Alumni Oxonienses, 1500–1714*, 4 vols. Oxford, 1891–92.

Lloyd, David. *State Worthies*, vol. I. London, 1766.

Public Record Office. *Lists and Indexes*, vol. IX, *List of Sheriffs*. London, 1898.

———. *Lists and Indexes*, vol. XXV, *Rentals and Surveys*. New York, 1963.

———. *Lists and Indexes*, vol. XXIX, *Index of Inquisitions, Henry VIII to Philip and Mary*. London, 1907.

———. *Lists and Indexes*, vol. XXXIV, *List of Original Ministers' Accounts*, pt. 2. London, 1910.

Venn, John, and J. A. Venn. *Alumni Cantabrigienses*, pt. 1, vol. IV, Cambridge, Eng., 1927.

Wedgewood, Josiah C. *History of Parliament: Biographies of Members of the Commons House, 1439–1509*. London, 1936.

### Books and Periodicals

Anderson, Andrew H. "Henry Lord Stafford (1501–63) in Local and Central Government," *English Historical Review*, 78 (1963), 225–42.

Bagot, William. *Memorials of the Bagot Family*. Blithfield, Eng., 1824.

Bean, J. M. W. *The Decline of English Feudalism, 1215–1540*. New York, 1968.

———. *The Estates of the Percy Family, 1416–1537*. Oxford, 1958.

Bell, H. E. *An Introduction to the History and Records of the Court of Wards and Liveries*. Cambridge, Eng., 1953.

Bell, Susan Groag. "Medieval Women Book Owners: Arbiters of Lay Piety and Ambassadors of Culture," *Signs*, 7, no. 4 (Spring 1972), 742–68.

Bellamy, J. G. *The Law of Treason in England in the Later Middle Ages.* Cambridge, Eng., 1970.

———. *The Tudor Law of Treason.* Toronto, 1979.

Bernard, G. W. "The Fortunes of the Greys, Earls of Kent, in the Early Sixteenth Century," *Historical Journal*, 25, no. 3 (Sept. 1982), 671–85.

———. *The Power of the Early Tudor Nobility: A Study of the Fourth and Fifth Earls of Shrewsbury.* Totowa, N.J., 1985.

———. "The Rise of Sir William Compton, Early Tudor Courtier," *English Historical Review*, 96 (Oct. 1981), 754–77.

Bindoff, Stanley Thomas. *Tudor England*, The Pelican History of England, vol. V. Baltimore, Md., 1959.

Blanchard, Ian. "Population Change, Enclosure, and the Early Tudor Economy," *Economic History Review*, Second Series, 23, no. 3 (Dec. 1970), 434–41.

Bolton, J. L. *The Medieval English Economy, 1150–1500.* Totowa, N.J., 1980.

Brenan, Gerald. *A History of the House of Percy.* London, 1902.

Brenan, Gerald, and Edward Phillips Statham. *The House of Howard.* New York, 1908.

Brewer, J. S. *The Reign of Henry VIII from His Accession to the Death of Wolsey*, ed. James Gairdner. London, 1884.

Bridbury, A. R. *Economic Growth: England in the Later Middle Ages.* Hassocks, Eng., 1975.

Brown, E. H. Phelps, and Sheila V. Hopkins. "Seven Centuries of Building Wages," in *Essays in Economic History*, ed. E. M. Carus-Wilson, vol. II, pp. 168–78. Originally pub. 1955. London, 1962.

Bruce, John. "A Second Letter on the Court of Star Chamber," *Archaeologia*, 25 (1834), 361–93.

Bush, M. L. "The Tudors and the Royal Race," *History*, New Series, 55 (1970), 37–48.

Cameron, A. "The Giving of Livery and Retaining in Henry VII's Reign," *Renaissance and Modern Studies*, 18 (1974), 17–35.

Carpenter, Christine. "The Beauchamp Affinity: A Study of Bastard Feudalism at Work," *English Historical Review*, 75 (July 1980), 514–32.

Cavendish, George. *Wolsey.* London, 1973.

Charlton, Kenneth. *Education in Renaissance England.* London, 1965.

Chrimes, S. B. *Henry VII.* London, 1972.

———. *Lancastrians, Yorkists, and Henry VII.* London, 1964.

Chrimes, S. B., C. D. Ross, and R. A. Griffiths, eds. *Fifteenth-Century England, 1399–1509.* New York, 1972.

Churton, Ralph. *The Lives of William Smyth, Bishop of Lincoln, and Sir Richard Sutton, Knight.* Oxford, 1800.

Colvin, H. M. "Castles and Government in Early Tudor Government," *English Historical Review,* 83 (Apr. 1968), 225–34.

Condon, M. M. "Ruling Elites in the Reign of Henry VII," in *Patronage, Pedigree and Power in Later Medieval England,* ed. Charles Ross, pp. 108–42. Totowa, N.J., 1979.

Cooper, Charles Henry. *Memoir of Margaret, Countess of Richmond and Derby,* ed. John E. M. Mayor. Cambridge, Eng., 1874.

Cooper, J. P. *Land, Men and Beliefs: Studies in Early-Modern History,* ed. G. E. Aylmer and J. S. Morrill. Ronceverte, W. Va., 1983.

———. "Patterns of Inheritance and Settlement by Great Landowners from the Fifteenth to the Eighteenth Centuries," in *Family and Inheritance: Rural Society in Western Europe, 1200–1800,* ed. Jack Goody, Joan Thirsk, and E. P. Thompson, pp. 192–327. Cambridge, Eng., 1976.

———. "The Social Distribution of Land and Men in England, 1436–1700," *Economic History Review,* Second Series, 20, no. 3 (Dec. 1967), 419–40.

Cornwall, Julian. "The Early Tudor Gentry," *Economic History Review,* Second Series, 17, no. 3 (Apr. 1965), 465–71.

Coward, Barry. "A 'Crisis of the Aristocracy' in the Sixteenth and Early Seventeenth Centuries? The Case of the Stanleys, Earls of Derby, 1504–1642," *Northern History,* 18, (1982), 54–77.

———. *The Stanleys, Lords Stanley and Earls of Derby, 1385–1672: The Origins, Wealth, and Power of a Landowning Family,* Chetham Society, Third Series, vol. XXX. Manchester, 1983.

Davenport, Frances G. *The Economic Development of a Norfolk Manor, 1086–1565,* originally pub. 1906. New York, 1967.

Davies, C. S. L. "Pre-Industrial England," *History,* 62 (Oct. 1977), 433–38.

Davies, R. R. "Baronial Accounts, Incomes, and Arrears in the Later Middle Ages," *Economic History Review,* Second Series, 21, no. 2 (Aug. 1968), 211–29.

De Fonblanque, Edward Barrington. *Annals of the House of Percy,* 2 vols. London, 1887.

DuBoulay, F. R. H. *An Age of Ambition.* New York, 1970.

———. "Who Were Farming the English Demesnes at the End of the Middle Ages?" *Economic History Review,* Second Series, 17, no. 3 (Apr. 1965), 443–55.

Dunham, William Huse, Jr. *Lord Hastings' Indentured Retainers 1461–83: The Lawfulness of Livery and Retaining Under the Yorkists and Tudors,* originally pub. 1955. Hampden, Conn., 1970.

————. "The Members of Henry VIII's Whole Council, 1509–1527," *English Historical Review*, 59 (May 1944), 187–210.

————. "Wolsey's Rule of the King's Whole Council," *American Historical Review*, 49 (Oct. 1943–July 1944), 644–62.

Dyer, Christopher. *Lords and Peasants in a Changing Society: The Estates of the Bishop of Worcester, 680–1540*. Cambridge, Eng., 1980.

Elton, G. R. *England Under the Tudors*. London, 1963.

————. *Policy and Police*. Cambridge, Eng., 1972.

————. *Reform and Reformation: England, 1509–1558*. Cambridge, Mass., 1977.

————. "Rule of Law in Sixteenth Century England," in *Studies in Tudor and Stuart Politics and Government*, vol. I, pp. 260–84. Cambridge, Eng., 1974.

————. "Tudor Government: The Points of Contact, III. The Court," Presidential Address, *Transactions of the Royal Historical Society*, Fifth Series, 26 (1976), 211–28.

Evans, Howell T. *Wales and the Wars of the Roses*. Cambridge, Eng., 1915.

Ferguson, Charles. *Naked to Mine Enemies: The Life of Cardinal Wolsey*. Boston, 1958.

Fiddes, Richard. *The Life of Cardinal Wolsey*. London, 1726.

Fisher, H. A. L. *The History of England from the Accession of Henry VII to the Death of Henry VIII*. London, 1919.

Gairdner, James. *Henry the Seventh*. London, 1889.

————. *History of the Life and Reign of Richard the Third*, rev. ed., originally published in Cambridge, Eng., in 1898. New York, 1968.

Gay, E. F. "Inclosures in England in the Sixteenth Century," *Quarterly Journal of Economics*, 17 (Aug. 1903), 576–97.

Gray, Charles. *Copyhold, Equity and the Common Law*. Cambridge, Mass., 1963.

Griffiths, Ralph A. "Local Rivalries and National Politics: The Percies, the Nevilles, and the Duke of Exeter, 1452–1455," *Speculum*, 43 (Oct. 1968), 589–632.

————, ed. *Patronage, the Crown and the Provinces in Later Medieval England*. Atlantic Highlands, N.J., 1981.

————. "Public and Private Bureaucracy in the Fifteenth Century," *Transactions of the Royal Historical Society*, Fifth Series, 30 (1980), 109–30.

Griffiths, Ralph A., and Roger S. Thomas, *The Making of the Tudor Dynasty*. Gloucester, 1985.

Guth, Delloyd J. "Fifteenth Century England: Recent Scholarship and Future Directions," *The British Studies Monitor*, 7, no. 2 (Spring 1977), 3–50.

Guy, J. A. "Wolsey, The Council and the Council Courts," *English Historical Review*, 91 (July 1976), 482–503.

————. "Wolsey's Star Chamber: A Study in Archival Reconstruction," *Journal of Society of Archivists*, 5 (Apr. 1975), 169–80.

Halsted, Caroline. *Richard III*. London, 1844.

Hanham, Allison. *Richard III and His Early Historians, 1485–1535*. Oxford, 1975.

Harcourt, L. W. Vernon. *His Grace the Steward and Trial of Peers*. London, 1907.

Harrison, C. J. "The Petition of Edmund Dudley," *English Historical Review*, 87 (Jan., 1972), 82–99.

Harvey, Barbara. *Westminster Abbey and Its Estates in the Middle Ages*. Oxford, 1977.

Hatcher, John. *Rural Economy and Society in the Duchy of Cornwall, 1300–1500*. Cambridge, Eng., 1970.

Hay, Denys. *Polydore Vergil: Renaissance Historian and Man of Letters*. Oxford, 1952.

Heal, Felicity. *Of Prelates and Princes: A Study of the Economic and Social Position of the Tudor Episcopate*. Cambridge, Eng., 1980.

Hexter, J. H. "The Education of the Aristocracy in the Renaissance," in *Reappraisals in History: New Views on History and Society in Early Modern Europe*, pp. 45–70. New York, 1961.

Hicks, M. A. "Dynastic Change and Northern Society: The Career of the Fourth Earl of Northumberland, 1470–89," *Northern History*, 14 (1978), 78–107.

Hilton, R. H. *The Development of Some Leicestershire Estates in the Fourteenth and Fifteenth Centuries*. London, 1947.

————. *The English Peasantry in the Later Middle Ages*. Oxford, 1975.

Holdsworth, William. "The Legal Profession in the Fourteenth and Fifteenth Centuries," *Law Quarterly Review*, 23 (Oct. 1907), 148–60, and 24 (Apr. 1908), 172–83.

Hollingsworth, T. H. "A Demographic Study of British Ducal Families," in D. V. Glass and D. E. C. Everseley, eds., *Population in History*, pp. 354–78. Chicago, 1965.

Holmes, George. *The Later Middle Ages*. Edinburgh, 1962.

Hoskins, W. G. *The Age of Plunder: The England of Henry VIII, 1500–1547*. New York, 1976.

Hurstfield, Joel. *The Queen's Wards: Wardship and Marriage Under Elizabeth I*. London, 1973.

Ives, Eric W. "The Common Lawyers in Pre-Reformation England," *Transactions of the Royal Historical Society*, Fifth Series, 18 (1968), 145–73.

————. *Faction in Tudor England*. London, 1979.

———. "Patronage at the Court of Henry VIII: The Case of Sir Ralph Egerton of Ridley," *Bulletin of the John Ryland University Library of Manchester*, 52 (Spring 1970), 346–74.

———. "Promotion in the Legal Profession of Yorkist and Early Tudor England," *Law Quarterly Review*, 75 (July 1959), 348–63.

———. "The Reputation of the Common Lawyers in English Society, 1450–1550," *University of Birmingham Historical Journal*, 7 (1959–60), 130–61.

James, Mervyn E. "English Politics and the Concept of Honour, 1485–1642," *Past and Present*, Supplement, no. 3 (1978).

———. *Family, Lineage and Civil Society*. Oxford, 1974.

———. "The First Earl of Cumberland (1493–1542) and the Decline of Northern Feudalism," *Northern History*, 1 (1966), 43–69.

———. *A Tudor Magnate and the Tudor State: Henry, Fifth Earl of Northumberland*, Borthwick Papers, no. 30. York, 1966.

Jeffs, Robin. "The Poynings-Percy Dispute: An Example of the Interplay of Open Strife and Legal Action in the Fifteenth Century," *Bulletin of the Institute of Historical Research*, 34, no. 90 (Nov. 1961), 148–64.

Jesse, John Heneague. *Memoirs of the Court of England: King Richard the Third and Some of His Contemporaries*. Boston, 1862.

Jones, Paul V. B. *The Household of a Tudor Nobleman*. Originally pub. 1917. New York, 1970.

Kendall, Paul. *Richard the Third* (New York, 1956).

Kerridge, Eric. *Agrarian Problems in the Sixteenth Century and After*. New York, 1969.

———. "Movement of Rent, 1540–1640," *Economic History Review*, Second Series, 6 (1953–54), 16–34.

———. "The Returns of the Inquisitions of Depopulation," *English Historical Review*, 70 (Apr. 1955), 212–28.

Kingsford, Charles L. *English Historical Literature in the Fifteenth Century*. Originally published in 1913. New York, 1962.

———. *Prejudice and Promise in Fifteenth Century England*. London, 1962.

Lander, J. R. *Conflict and Stability in Fifteenth-Century England*. London, 1969.

———. "The Crown and the Aristocracy in England, 1450–1509," *Albion*, 8, no. 3 (Fall 1976), 203–18.

———. *Crown and Nobility, 1450–1509*. London, 1976.

———. "Edward IV: The Modern Legend and a Revision," *History*, 41 (Feb.–Oct. 1956), 38–52.

Langbein, John H. "The Origins of Public Prosecution at Common Law," *American Journal of Legal History*, 17 (Oct. 1973), 313–35.

———. *Prosecuting Crime in the Renaissance: England, Germany, France*. Cambridge, Mass., 1974.

Leadam, I. S. "The Inquisition of 1517: Inclosures and Eviction, Edited from Lansdowne Manuscript I. 153," *Transactions of the Royal Historical Society*, New Series, 6 (1892), 167–314; 7 (1893), 127–292; 8 (1894), 251–331.

———. "The Last Days of Bondage in England," *Law Quarterly Review*, 9 (Oct. 1893), 348–65.

Lehmberg, Stanford. "Star Chamber, 1485–1509," *Huntingdon Library Quarterly*, 24, no. 2 (May 1961), 189–214.

Levett, A. E. *Studies in Manorial History*. New York, 1963.

Levine, Mortimer. "The Fall of Edward, Duke of Buckingham," in *Tudor Men and Institutions*, ed. Arthur J. Slavin. Baton Rouge, 1972.

———. "Richard III—Usurper or Lawful King?," *Speculum*, 34 (July 1959), 391–401.

Lloyd, John. *The Great Forest of Brecon*. London, 1905.

Loades, D. M. *Politics and the Nation, 1450–1660: Obedience, Resistance and Public Order*. Brighton, Eng., 1974.

McFarlane, K. B. "'Bastard Feudalism,'" *Bulletin of the Institute of Historical Research*, 20, no. 61 (May–Nov. 1945), 161–80.

———. *The Nobility of Later Medieval England*. Oxford, 1973.

———. "Parliament and 'Bastard Feudalism,'" in *Essays in Medieval History*, ed. R. W. Southern, pp. 240–63. New York, 1968.

———. "The Wars of the Roses," Raleigh Lecture on History, *Proceedings of the British Academy*, vol. L. London, 1964.

Mackie, J. D. *The Earlier Tudors, 1485–1558*. Oxford, 1952.

Markland, James H. "Some Remarks on the Rent Roll of Humphrey, Duke of Buckingham, 26 & 27 Henry VI, 1447–1448," *Archaeological Journal*, 8 (1851), 259–81.

Mattingly, Garrett. *Catherine of Aragon*. Originally pub. 1942. London, 1963.

Meyers, A. R. "Richard III and Historical Tradition," *History*, 53, no. 178 (June 1968), 181–202.

Miller, Helen J. *The Early Tudor Peerage, 1485–1547*. London University master's thesis, 1950.

Outhwaite, R. B. *Inflation in Tudor and Stuart England*. London, 1969.

Owen, H., and J. B. Blakeway. *A History of Shrewsbury*. London, 1825.

Pickthorne, Kenneth. *Early Tudor Government: Henry VIII*. Cambridge, Eng., 1951.

Pollard, A. F. *Henry VIII*. Originally pub. 1905. New York, 1966.

———. *Wolsey*, ed. A. G. Dickens. Originally pub. 1929. New York, 1966.

Pollard, A. J. "Estate Management in the Later Middle Ages: The Talbots and Whitchurch, 1383–1525," *Economic History Review*, Second Series, 25, no. 4 (Nov. 1972), 553–66.

Pollock, Linda. *Forgotten Children: Parent-Child Relations from 1500 to 1900*. Cambridge, Eng., 1983.

Postan, M. M. *Essays on Medieval Agriculture and General Problems of the Medieval Economy*. Cambridge, Eng., 1973.

———. "The Fifteenth Century," *Economic History Review*, 9 (May 1939), 160–67.

———. *The Medieval Economy and Society*. Baltimore, 1975.

———. "Some Social Consequences of the Hundred Years' War," *Economic History Review*, 12 (1942), 1–12.

Pugh, T. B. "'The Indenture for the Marches,' Between Henry VII and Edward Stafford (1477–1521), Duke of Buckingham," *English Historical Review*, 71 (July 1956), 436–41.

Pugh, T. B. "The Magnates, Knights and Gentry," in *Fifteenth-Century England 1399–1509: Studies in Politics and Society*. New York, 1972.

Ramsay, Sir James. *Lancaster and York*, 2 vols. Oxford, 1892.

Ramsey, Peter H. *The Price Revolution in Sixteenth-Century England*. London, 1971.

Rawcliffe, Carole. "Baronial Councils in the Later Middle Ages," in *Patronage, Pedigree and Power in Later Medieval England*, ed. Charles Ross, pp. 87–108. Totowa, N.J., 1979.

———. *The Staffords, Earls of Stafford and Dukes of Buckingham, 1394–1521*. Cambridge, Eng., 1978.

———. "A Tudor Nobleman as Archivist: The Papers of Edward, Third Duke of Buckingham," *Journal of Society of Archivists*, 5, no. 5 (Apr. 1976), 294–300.

Reeves, A. C. *Newport Lordship, 1317–1536*. Ann Arbor, Mich., 1979.

Rezneck, Samuel. "Constructive Treason By Words in the Fifteenth Century," *American Historical Review*, 33, no. 3 (Apr. 1928), 544–52.

———. "The Early History of the Parliamentary Declaration of Treason," *English Historical Review*, 42 (Oct. 1927), 497–513.

———. "The Trial of Treason in Tudor England," in *Essays in History and Political Theory in Honor of Charles Howard McIlwain*, pp. 258–88. Cambridge, Mass., 1936.

Richmond, Colin. "After McFarlane," *History*, 68 (Feb. 1983), 46–60.

Rogers, W. H. Hamilton. *The Strife of the Roses and Days of the Tudors in the West*. Exeter, 1890.

Rosenthal, Joel T. "Aristocratic Cultural Patronage and Book Bequests, 1350–1500," *Bulletin of the John Ryland University Library of Manchester*, 64, no. 2 (Spring 1982), 522–48.

———. "The Estates and Finances of Richard, Duke of York (1411–1460)," in *Studies in Medieval and Renaissance History*, ed. William M. Bowsky, pp. 117–204. Lincoln, Nebr., 1965.

———. *Nobles and the Noble Life, 1295–1500*. New York, 1976.

Ross, Charles D. *Edward IV*. Berkeley, Calif., 1974.

———. "The Estates and Finances of Richard Beauchamp, Earl of Warwick," *Dugdale Society Occasional Papers*, no. 13. Oxford, 1956.

———, ed. *Patronage, Pedigree and Power in Later Medieval England*. Totowa, N.J., 1979.

———. "Review of Joel T. Rosenthal on the Estates and Finances of Richard, Duke of York," *Welsh History Review*, 3 (1966–67), 299–302.

———. *Richard III*. Berkeley, Calif., 1981.

Ross, Charles D., and T. B. Pugh. "Materials for the Study of Baronial Incomes in Fifteenth Century England," *Economic History Review*, Second Series, 6 (1953), 185–94.

Russell, Joycelyne. *The Field of Cloth of Gold*. New York, 1969.

Savine, Alexander. "English Customary Tenure in the Tudor Period," *Quarterly Journal of Economics*, 19 (Nov. 1904– 5), 33–80.

Scarisbrick, J. J. *Henry VIII*. Berkeley, Calif., 1968.

Simon, Joan. *Education and Society in Tudor England*. Cambridge, Eng., 1966.

Simpson, W. D. "'Bastard Feudalism' and Later Castles," *Antiquaries Journal*, 26 (July–Oct. 1946), 145–71.

Skeel, C. A. J. *Council in the Marches of Wales*. London, 1904.

Slater, Miriam. "The Weightiest Business: Marriage in an Upper-Gentry Family in Seventeenth-Century England," *Past and Present*, no. 72 (1976), 25–54.

Slavin, A. J. *Politics and Profit: A Study of Sir Ralph Sadler, 1507–1547*. Cambridge, Eng., 1966.

———. *The Precarious Balance: English Government and Society*. New York, 1973.

Smith, Lacey Baldwin. "English Treason Trials and Confessions in the Sixteenth Century," *The Journal of the History of Ideas*, 15, no. 1 (Jan. 1954), 471–98.

———. *Henry VIII: The Mask of Royalty*. Boston, 1971.

Somerville, R. "Henry VII's 'Council Learned in the Law,'" *English Historical Review*, 54 (July 1939), 427–42.

Starkey, David. "The Age of the Household: Politics, Society and the Arts c. 1350–c. 1550," in *The Context of English Literature: The Later Middle Ages*, ed. Stephen Medcalf, pp. 226–89. London, 1981.

———. "From Feud to Faction: English Politics circa 1450–1550," *History Today*, 32 (Nov. 1982), 16–22.

———. "Representation Through Intimacy," *Symbols and Sentiment. Cross Cultural Studies in Symbolism*, ed. Ioan Lewis, pp. 187–224. New York, 1977.

Stone, Lawrence. *The Crisis of the Aristocracy, 1558–1641.* Oxford, 1965.

————. "The Educational Revolution in England, 1560–1640," *Past and Present*, no. 28 (July 1964), 41–80.

————. *Family and Fortune: Studies in Aristocratic Finance in the Sixteenth and Seventeenth Centuries.* Oxford, 1973.

————. *The Family, Sex and Marriage in England, 1500–1800.* London, 1977.

————. "Marriage Among the English Nobility in the Sixteenth and Seventeenth Centuries," *Comparative Studies in Society and History*, 3 (Oct. 1960–July 1961), 182–206.

Storey, R. L. *The End of the House of Lancaster.* New York, 1967.

————. "Lincolnshire and the Wars of the Roses," *Nottingham Medieval Studies*, 14 (1970), 64–83.

————. *The Reign of Henry VII.* New York, 1968.

Thomas, Keith. "The Double Standard," *The Journal of the History of Ideas*, 20 (Apr. 1959), 209–16.

Thornley, Isobel D. "Treason by Words in the Fifteenth Century," *English Historical Review*, 32 (Oct. 1917), 556–61.

————. "The Treason Legislation of Henry VIII," *Transactions of the Royal Historical Society*, Third Series, 11 (1917), 87–214.

Tucker, Melvin J. *The Life of Thomas Howard, Earl of Surrey and Second Duke of Norfolk, 1443–1524.* The Hague, 1964.

Virgoe, R. "The Recovery of the Howards in East Anglia, 1485–1529," in *Wealth and Power in Tudor England: Essays Presented to S. T. Bindoff*, ed. E. W. Ives, R. J. Knecht, and J. J. Scarisbrick, pp. 1–20. London, 1978.

Weiss, Michael. "A Power in the North? The Percies in the Fifteenth Century," *Historical Journal*, 19 (Sept. 1976), 501–9.

William, C. H. "The So-Called Star Chamber Act," *History*, New Series, 15 (Apr. 1930–Jan. 1931), 129–35.

Williams, Neville. *Henry VIII and His Court.* London, 1971.

Williams, Perry. *The Tudor Regime.* Oxford, 1979.

Wolffe, B. P. *The Crown Lands, 1461–1536.* New York, 1970.

# Index

Library of Congress Cataloging-in-Publication Data

Harris, Barbara J. (Barbara Jean), 1942–
    Edward Stafford, third duke of Buckingham, 1478–1521.

    Bibliography: p.
    Includes index.
    1. Buckingham, Edward Stafford, Duke of, 1478–1521.
2. Great Britain—Nobility—Biography.    3. Great
Britain—Politics and government—1485–1603.    4. Tudor,
House of.    5. England—Social life and customs—
16th century.    I. Title.
DA317.8.B83H37    1986        941.04'092'4 [B]        86-5742
ISBN 0-8047-1316-2 (alk. paper)